Guangdong in
the Twenty-first Century:
Stagnation
or Second Take-off?

Guangdong in the Twenty-first Century: Stagnation or Second Take-off?

Edited by
Joseph Y. S. CHENG

City University of Hong Kong Press

First published 2000
Printed in Hong Kong

ISBN 962-937-066-2

Published by
City University of Hong Kong Press
Tat Chee Avenue, Kowloon, Hong Kong

Internet: http://www.cityu.edu.hk/upress/
E-mail: upress@cityu.edu.hk

Contents

Detailed Chapter Contents

Preface

The research team on developments in Guangdong is proud to present its fourth volume on the subject. The Contemporary China Research Centre, upon its establishment in1992, considered the study of Guangdong a major focus of its activities. The importance of Guangdong in Hong Kong's future development no longer requires any explanation; the huge number of Hong Kong people visiting Shenzhen every weekend is perhaps the best illustration of the growing integration between Hong Kong and the Pearl River Delta. From an academic point of view, the research team believes that its solid field work in the province will give it an edge over its local and overseas competitors. Every team member has now established an excellent network of ties in support of his or her research.

In the first volume of the project, the research team concentrated on the factors contributing to the spectacular economic growth of Guangdong. The second volume then focused on the different models of development within the province, emphasizing Guangdong's role as a laboratory for experiments in economic reforms in China. By the mid-1990s, Guangdong's leaders realized that the province had to face a new set of challenges; and the acquisition of expertise as well as the formulation of strategies with a new vision were demanded for the new stage of development. This was exactly the theme of our third book.

In this fourth volume, the research team members, while working on their individual topics, also attempt to study the impact of Zhu Rongji's reform and the Asia-Pacific region's economic crises on the development of the province; examine competition from other regions in China, especially the Yangtze Delta region; analyze the strengths and weaknesses of Guangdong's economy and of its development strategy so far; and consider the options open for Guangdong at this stage. The team attempts to cover a broad range of policy areas which it believes have a significant bearing on Guangdong's long-term development.

The research team is most grateful for the co-operation and support given by Mr. Patrick Kwong and Dr. Paul Kwong of the City University of Hong Kong Press in the publication of this book. The editor would also like to thank the authors for their hard work and patience; and to thank Mr. Ian Storey for his indispensable editorial assistance. Naturally the editor and the authors have to be responsible for whatever errors and omissions.

Joseph Y. S. CHENG
August 2000

List of Illustrations

Figures

Tables

Acronyms and Abbreviations

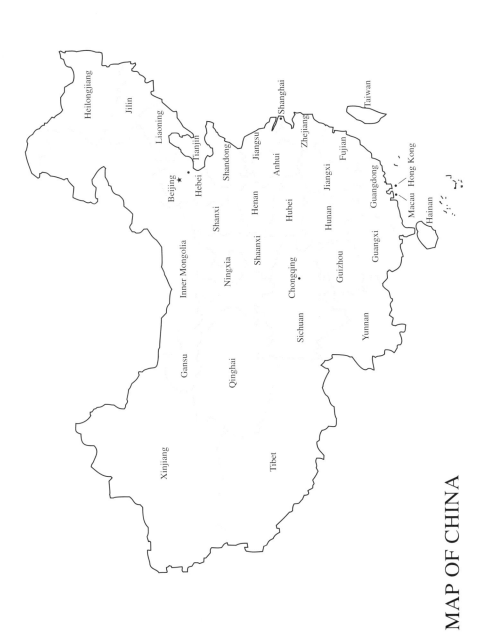

MAP OF CHINA

Administrative Division of the Pearl River Economic Region

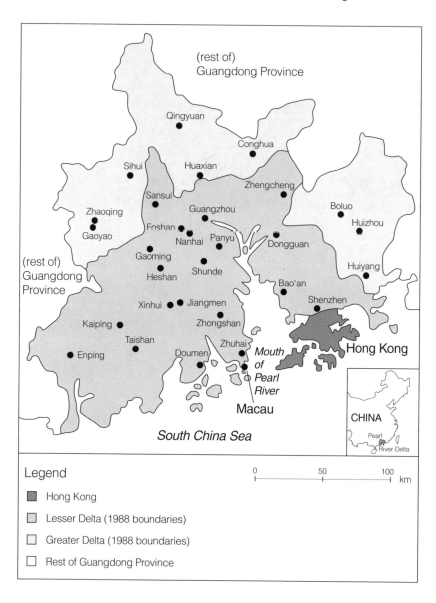

Guangdong in the Twenty-first Century:
Stagnation or Second Take-off?

CHAPTER 1

Introduction

Joseph Y. S. CHENG

Economic development in Guangdong in the era of reforms and opening up to the outside world has been outstanding by national and international standards. Before 1978, the growth rates of the province's major economic indicators were slightly below the national averages. Between 1978 and 1998, Guangdong's gross domestic product rose from 18.585 billion yuan to 791.912 billion yuan, showing an average annual real growth rate of 14%. In the same period, Guangdong's per capita gross domestic product grew from 369 yuan to 11,143 yuan, indicating an average annual real growth rate of 12%.[1] Guangdong has also claimed a number of national "firsts": for 12 years it has been first in terms of gross light industrial output value among the provincial units, accounting for 15% of the national total in 1998; for 13 years it has been first in terms of foreign trade among the provincial units, accounting for 41.21% of China's exports and 40.13% of China's imports in 1998; for seven years it has been first in terms of delivery of industrial and commercial taxes, accounting for one-seventh of the national total; and in 1998, Guangdong also became first in terms of per capita urban family income, amounting to 8,840 yuan.[2]

This spectacular economic growth, however, appears to be losing momentum, and people in Guangdong, from the top provincial leaders to the unemployed, are obviously worried. In the first three

1

quarters of 1999, the province's economy grew by only 9.2%. It has been suffering from deflation too; by August 1999, its consumer price index had been in decline for 18 consecutive months, and its retail price index had been in negative territory for 25 consecutive months. The rise in prices in September 1999, though largely interpreted as an indicator of Guangdong overcoming sluggish demand since 1997, was undeniably partly the result of a typhoon which raised vegetable prices by 29.7%. The province's state-owned enterprises (SOEs) continued to face difficulties: 1,852 firms (58.8% of the province's total) lost money in the first eight months of 1999, 7.2% higher than the previous year. In the same period, actually realized foreign direct investment (FDI) amounted to US$8.3 billion, showing a decline of 13.9% on a year-on-year basis.[3]

Guangdong's previous success was perhaps best demonstrated by the following statement: "Shenzhen learns from Hong Kong, Guangdong learns from Shenzhen, and the whole country learns from Guangdong". Today, Shanghai and Beijing turn to the United States for models to emulate, and they no longer consider the Guangdong experiences relevant. Guangdong's past innovations too reflected a reluctance to observe the central government's policy line, as described by the following saying: "Go quickly when the green light is on; proceed immediately when the (red) light turns yellow; and find a bypass route to proceed when the red light is on". Such attitude naturally arouses suspicion from the central leadership.

In recent years, this suspicion has been exacerbated by rampant corruption, major smuggling cases and financial scandals. The bankruptcy of Guangdong's leading window company, the Guangdong International Trust and Investment Corporation (GITIC), and the exposure of the smuggling racket in Zhanjiang (a seaport in southwest Guangdong) leading to the arrest of more than 60 top-ranking cadres, considerably compromised the position of Guangdong leaders in their negotiations with the central leadership. The departure of Xie Fei, the former secretary of the provincial Party committee and Politburo member, and his replacement by Li Changchun, a native of northeast Liaoning province, heralded serious crackdowns in the province. Xie's death in late 1999 probably strengthened the feelings of indignation among local cadres against Beijing's heavy handedness.[4]

Local cadres are conscious of their inadequacies in formal educational qualifications, especially in comparison with their counterparts in Shanghai and Beijing. In contrast to the latter, there are not many in the middle or upper-middle ranks with postgraduate degrees from the leading universities in the West and working experience with the leading multinational corporations. These weaknesses are perhaps most vividly reflected in Guangdong's lack of success in attracting FDI from major Western firms. Despite their pragmatism, senior cadres and leading entrepreneurs in the province have often been criticized for lack of vision.

The International Consultative Conference held in mid-November 1999 in Guangzhou was symbolic of the above shortcomings and an attempt by the provincial leadership to overcome them. The conference brought together provincial officials and 20 international industrialists, academics and scientists to discuss the future development of Guangdong's economy. At the end of the conference, Lu Ruihua, the provincial governor, stated that; "the promotion and expansion of the information-technology industry in Guangdong will be a new and major breakthrough for our economy". Lu also indicated that Guangdong would seek to work further with Hong Kong to create synergies and mutual advantages, particularly in the development of information-technology industries.[5]

The following chapters study the development of Guangdong in the next century, and attempt to answer the question whether it will achieve a second take-off or see its competitive edge gradually eroded. The chapters are divided into four sections, concentrating respectively on political trends, economic reforms, legal innovations and developments in social services.

Organizational streamlining and economic restructuring have been the priorities of Chinese leaders in recent years, and the process will continue in the early years of the twenty-first century. The Guangdong leadership appreciates that organizational streamlining ultimately depends on separating the government from enterprises, which in turn has to rely on the establishment of new state assets management systems. The latter have allowed the local governments in Guangdong to give up their authorities of administering their state enterprises to the asset management companies; and this in turn facilitates the local governments to streamline their organizations.

As argued by the editor's chapter, re-defining government functions is both a prerequisite and a logical consequence of state enterprise reform. The objective is to promote "small government, big society". Guangdong's success in economic restructuring has enabled it to make satisfactory progress in organizational streamlining. However, the regionalized character of economic restructuring and administrative reforms has also complicated central-provincial relations. A wealthy province like Guangdong has attracted special attention because it is expected to contribute more to the central government's fiscal revenue, and it has the potential of deviating from the policy line of the central government.

Corruption has provided an added incentive for the central authorities to exert pressure on Guangdong because corruption implicitly poses a challenge to Party leadership. When local governments become thoroughly corrupt, it means that the central government has lost control. The paradox is that while Guangdong has been relatively successful in organizational streamlining and economic restructuring, and has thus become a model for the country, serious corruption has attracted central interference and has tarnished its reputation and that of its leaders. The complex relationships among organizational streamlining, economic restructuring and anti-corruption, as well as their associated problems, raise the fundamental question of the limitations of the reforms in the absence of democratic reforms.

The chapter by Wang Tong and K. K. Leung examines the issue of interest articulation between the government and private enterprises, using the Shenzhen Special Economic Zone as a case study. In socialist China, the nature of private enterprise organizations is semi-governmental. Their major roles are to implement the Party line and the laws and regulations of the state, as well as to reflect entrepreneurs' opinions and demands to the government. Apparently, their function is to mediate the interests of the government and entrepreneurs, as well as to resolve their conflicts. Yet according to the *Regulations on the Registration and Management of Social Groups*, they have to secure the endorsement of a government department willing to assume responsibility for their work before they can apply for registration with the civil administration department of the local government concerned.

Wang and Leung study the work of the Shenzhen Folk Entrepreneurs' Chamber of Commerce and the Shenzhen Municipal Private Enterprises Association. The former comes under the United Front Department of the Shenzhen municipal Party committee; and the latter is led by both the Shenzhen municipal Party committee and the Shenzhen municipal government. They observe that these private enterprise organizations also perform certain economic and social functions such as the provision of market information and legal services, liaison with domestic and international enterprises, etc.

The authors go on to make a bold prediction. They believe that the networking of private enterprises will help to raise the status of the middle class, and the latter's rise represents the beginning of a civil society. More significantly still, the Party representing different interests may differentiate into factions engaging in checks-and-balances among each other.

As observed by Lau Pui-king, the domination of the industrial (50.4% of the economy in 1998) and tertiary sectors (36.9% of the economy in 1998) in the economy indicates that the province has already been transformed into a modern economy through industrialization and urbanization. Among its ten major manufacturing industries, at the top are new industries such as electronics and telecommunications, electrical power and hot water supply, electrical equipment and machinery. Next on the list are traditional industries such as garments, chemical products, textiles, mineral products, transport equipment and metal products which seem to maintain their vitality. Petroleum and natural gas extraction are also on the list. These industries are heavily concentrated in the Pearl River Delta region, while the Northeast region and the Western region have failed to improve their attraction.

Though the growth rate of township and village enterprises (TVEs) has slowed in recent years, many TVEs in Guangdong have grown in scale. They have developed nation-wide market networks as well as have entered international markets. Lau especially praises the local officials in the Pearl River Delta region: they have been ambitious and have learnt management skills from their Hong Kong partners. The local authorities often establish their own trading companies in Hong Kong, and they can then by-pass administrative controls and seek financing from banks in Hong Kong via their subsidiaries. Inadequate investment in education and scientific research and development, as well as inefficiencies in the capital market, are perceived as significant weaknesses to be overcome.

In the 1990s, Foreign Direct Investment (FDI) assumed a more and more important role in support of China's economic growth; but in recent years, even before the Asian financial crises of 1997–98, the growth rate of FDI in China had been in decline. Since 1979, Guangdong and Fujian have been designated experimental provinces to adopt "special policies and flexible measures" to attract foreign investment; and Guangdong has been successful in exploiting this advantage, as it has occupied the first position in utilizing FDI among all provincial units since the mid-1980s.

In the 1990s, however, Guangdong's actually utilized FDI as a proportion of China's total had been in decline. It dropped from 41.75% in 1991 to 25.87% in 1997. According to Zeng Kaisheng, the following factors were behind this decline; the completion of the transfer of Hong Kong's manufacturing industries to the province; rising production costs; the relatively low quality labour force compared with other provinces; the over-supply situation in the provincial consumer markets; and the improved transportation networks in many other provinces.

In response to Guangdong's declining attractiveness, the provincial government has been introducing new strategies. In recent years, the focus of attracting FDI has shifted to infrastructure construction, advanced technology and agriculture. The provincial Foreign Economic Co-operation and Trade Commission too tries to attract major multinationals from North America and Western

Europe to upgrade the technology of important enterprises in the province. At the same time, provincial leaders are more concerned with the adverse impact of foreign investment, especially environmental pollution and the encroachment on cultivated land. They are also acutely aware that the province has to be prepared for keener and keener competition from other provincial units, notably the municipalities of Shanghai, Beijing and Tianjin.

Zhang Xiaohe's chapter compares the environments for FDI in Guangdong and Beijing. Zhang attempts to identify the motivations, objectives, locations and partner selection criteria of FDI in China by surveying 106 foreign enterprises in Guangdong and Beijing. The results indicate that the main motivations are China's huge potential market size, low labour costs and the government's preferential tax treatment. The major determinants of geographical locations are locations of the Chinese partners, familiarity with the Chinese partners and preferential fiscal policy. The significant factors affecting partner selection are; mutual trust among the parties concerned, capability to deal with local authorities and the Chinese partners' good credit standing. Regarding long-term objectives, the respondents indicated that entry into the China market, economy of scale, expansion of another foreign market other than China and transfer of production to a low-cost location are important considerations.

Zhang's survey further reflects that the respondents in Beijing attached more weight to familiarity with the Chinese partners, while the respondents in Guangdong emphasized the geographical locations of the Chinese partners. It also appears that the respondents in Beijing were more dependent on preferential policies offered by the government, while their counterparts in Guangdong were more attracted by good infrastructure. The fact that the respondents in the two localities expressed the same level of satisfaction is a severe warning to Guangdong because the edge it enjoys over its competitors is fast eroding. It is surprising that the respondents in Guangdong still complained a lot about the time-consuming procedures in getting projects approved, and naturally they were very concerned with the local charges.

The development of the market economy and the labour market has led to more tense labour relations and more frequent labour disputes. By the mid-1990s, the Chinese authorities realized that administrative measures would be inadequate in handling labour relations, and they introduced a system of collective contracts which was supposed to start in non-SOEs. The All-China Federation of Trade Unions (ACFTU) has been keen to promote the system because it is premised on the basis of equal consultation; the federation also sees collective bargaining as a tool to protect workers' interests, as well as a means to legitimize its existence.

According to Ngok King-lun and Grace O. M. Lee, Guangdong has been a leader in implementing the collective contract system. The *Regulations on Collective Contracts in the Enterprises of Guangdong Province* was promulgated by the provincial people's congress in June 1996; and the province managed to secure close co-operation among trade unions, local Party organizations, local governments and their labour bureaux at all levels.

Obviously there are still many shortcomings in the implementation of the system which cannot be compared with the Western collective bargaining tradition. Its adoption was largely the result of a "top down" initiative, usually in the form of targets being set for subsidiary trade unions, and the whole process resembled a campaign. In practice, the provisions of most collective contracts were simply copied from the "model" contract designed by the government, and few of them were the results of bargaining. Success in consultation and its resultant collective contract often depends on the goodwill of the enterprise concerned, especially in the case of non-SOEs. In sum, a good beginning has been made, but much greater efforts are still required.

Sun Wen-bin notes that the Open Door Policy and the reform of SOEs set in motion fundamental changes in labour relations in China. Their character has changed from mainly state job assignment to contractual terms between labour and enterprises. As a result, the total number of arbitration cases of labour disputes has been growing year by year. Her study examines the causes, patterns and settlements of labour disputes in Shenzhen since the 1980s, illustrating the radical changes of the interest relations between workers and enterprises.

Sun considers that the conflicts examined are not simply responses to the economic reforms, they in fact often shape future reform policies at both central and local levels and they often lead to positive institutional arrangements. She believes that the role of the trade unions needs to be re-defined. Workers have lost confidence in them because they seldom address real labour issues or represent workers' interests. Similarly, the government has not given the issue of labour protection priority, and it is therefore difficult to develop a long-term strategy to protect workers. The Chinese government still perceives industrial action as a threat to social stability and economic development.

In the era of economic reforms and opening up to the outside world, Guangdong has been given wider powers to promulgate rules and regulations. Naturally Guangdong has benefited much from Hong Kong's experience, and many of Guangdong's regulations have become pioneers for national legislation. Zhang Xianchu's chapter observes that local economic legislation has been playing a crucial role in facilitating rapid economic development in the province, and that local legislation has contributed much to the transition from traditional government domination in a socialist regime to a governance model guided by the rule of law.

Regarding legal problems faced by Guangdong in the next century, Zhang believes that local governments within the province have been assuming excessive roles in local economic development to pursue their own interests and goals; as a result, the provincial market has been irrationally divided up and a provincial development strategy cannot be successfully enforced. Moreover, the tension between the central government and the provincial government over the exact extent of provincial autonomy has to be resolved eventually. In the past two decades, the tension has been resolved largely by local circumvention. Guangdong has earned a reputation for getting things done through devising strategies to bypass central policy. This is certainly not satisfactory. Rampant corruption and the deteriorating law and order situation pose obvious threats to the integrity and dignity of the legal system too. Meanwhile, the economic integration of Guangdong and Hong Kong has offered opportunities and challenges for the legal reforms of the province.

As the legal consciousness among the people and the development of the legal institutional framework remain backward, the notion of law in Guangdong cannot be regarded as institutionalized social relations, and it has to be recognized that legislation does not necessarily lead to the rule of law. Hand in hand with economic development, the demand for political pluralism, widespread corruption, poor law enforcement, the emergence of organized crime, exploitation of labour, environmental pollution and illegal migration have well demonstrated the inadequacies of the legal system and the pressing demand for its improvements.

Gu Minkang praises Guangdong as "the leading province that has promulgated a comprehensive set of legislation". Since the 1980s, Guangdong has adopted ways of seeking public opinion in the legislation process. It was the first province to introduce legislation on the management of prices; and in September 1999, the Guangdong provincial people's congress established a public hearing system. However, recent financial scandals in the province have certainly exposed the problems in its financial institutions, as well as the weaknesses of the legal framework regulating them.

Gu believes that strengthening financial legislation is an important task for Guangdong in the years ahead. Commercial banks must protect their legal interests by taking secured interests, and the courts must try to protect the legal interests of commercial banks, including the enforcement of verdicts on repaying loans to banks by debtors. Legislation is essential too in defining the rules of competition between domestic financial institutions and foreign-funded financial institutions. Gu is disappointed to note that even though the Guangdong government plans to promulgate 35 sets of rules and regulations from 1998 to 2002, none of them is directly related to financial management and supervision. Combating smuggling activities and corruption is another important concern of Gu, and legal measures certainly constitute an important part of the mechanisms for their resolution.

Both Zhang and Gu emphasize legal education; and Gu considers that legal education should not only extend to ordinary people, but also to law enforcement personnel. The spread of legal education and legal consciousness among ordinary people is an important prerequisite to realize the objective of establishing the rule of law in China.

In line with the development of the market economy, education in Guangdong has gone through important changes in recent years with the aim of better equipping the province to face future challenges. The central government's policy line of decentralization applies to the higher education sector as well. As Nixon K. H. Mok's study indicates, the state's role as the provider of a public good has been diminishing, but its functions as a regulator and overall service co-ordinator has been strengthening; and Mok describes this change as the shift from "state control" to "governance".

Under the policy of decentralization, the sources of educational financing have been diversified; and tertiary institutions in Guangdong now depend on surcharges in both urban and rural areas, tuition and miscellaneous fees, enterprises run by tertiary institutions themselves, donations from businesses and individuals, etc. At the same time, the provincial government of Guangdong and the Ministry of Education (formerly the State Education Commission) have decided to pool their resources to improve the standards of the tertiary institutions in the province. Following the example of their counterparts outside the state sector which are run by a new management system of "presidential responsibility" under the supervision of boards of directors, some public universities have formed boards of trustees to cultivate close links with the business community and other sectors of society. These reforms, however, may still be inadequate to equip tertiary institutions in Guangdong to compete with the small number of universities selected for "strategic development" by the Ministry of Education.

The aging of the population will be one of the most serious problems encountered by China in the coming century. Its elderly population aged 60 years and above will increase to 130 million in 2000, about 10% of the population, when Chinese society will be considered an aged society. By 2020, the proportion will rise to 15.6%; and in 2050, it will further expand to about 25%. According to the *Law of Protecting the Rights and Interests of the Aged*, the Chinese government pledges to implement policies to ensure that the elderly will have appropriate material and financial support, medical care, educational opportunities, channels to achieve a sense of accomplishment as well as entertainment and leisure activities.

Alex Y. H. Kwan's chapter discusses the strategies at various levels of government to meet the challenge of providing for the elderly. In May 1997, the Guangdong provincial government promulgated the *Regulations of Managing Non-governmental Organizations in Guangdong Province*, and one of its major objectives was to promote, regulate and support elderly welfare service development. It appears that the gaps in the quality of life of the elderly between well-off areas and backward areas in the province have been narrowing, and traditional values related to respect for old people still prevail. However, medical care and the social security system are far from well established; social care for the aged is limited, and the daily life of the elderly remains monotonous. Scholars are concerned with the impact of the one-child policy on the caring of the elderly; and they believe that, in the best of circumstances, the traditional family support system and the formal system of institutional care can work together.

Crime is another social problem in Guangdong, and will likely remain so in the early part of the twenty-first century. Criminologists in China tend to regard the unequal distribution of wealth, rising unemployment, migration and the Open Door Policy as important causes of crime. Che Wai-kin's study attempts to analyze the rising crime rate in Guangdong, especially cross border crime between the province and Hong Kong. Guangzhou, the provincial capital which has had the highest crime rate in the province, has also been selected by Che for more detailed examination. Since the mid-1990s, the number of criminal offences has risen considerably. New types of criminal offences have also emerged, including the trafficking, peddling and manufacturing of illicit drugs, organized crime, illegal activities of triad-related criminal gangs, etc. Criminals come from many sources outside the province, and they have better chances of escaping to other places.

The provincial authorities, understandably, feel the pressure, especially when smuggling activities have attracted the attention of the central leadership and the international media, and when foreign investors begin to worry about the crime scene. The public security apparatus has been strengthened by recruiting more policemen and acquiring more advanced equipment. Provincial leaders have also encouraged local governments to organize security patrol teams at the grassroots level to help maintain law and order. In recent years, the provincial leadership has become more concerned with the issue of the rehabilitation of offenders. Obviously it has been unsuccessful as in some prosperous cities, about a half to two-thirds of the criminals arrested were ex-offenders. Meanwhile, crime prevention is still handicapped by the shortage of funds.

At the turn of the century, China is acutely aware of its problem of environmental pollution, and it is willing to spend more resources to resolve the problem. The rapid industrialization of Guangdong since 1978 has resulted in much pollution, especially in the Pearl River Delta. According to Lin Feng, however, the Pearl River Delta region has now developed a well-structured legal framework for the control of water pollution and the protection of the water environment, especially the quality of its drinking water sources. Special water quality standards have been set for various water sources, and various mechanisms have been incorporated into both national and local legislation for meeting those standards. In order to protect the quality of water resources, some legal mechanisms are mandatory, regardless of the costs to the polluters.

Yet it is important to note that in the Pearl River Delta region, certain legislative provisions are regarded as objectives to be achieved in the near future. Various authorities, including those which promulgate the legislation, do not treat them as strictly enforceable. Such attitudes sometimes lead to lack of strict enforcement of relevant water pollution control and water sources protection legislation. Moreover, some other factors such as lack of enforcement officers, inadequate legal penalties for violation of relevant legislation, possible abuse of discretionary power in granting special approval for emitting water pollutants and so on, may all affect the quality of the implementation of relevant water pollution control and water sources protection legislation. All these will eventually affect the sustainability of the water environment in the Pearl River Delta region. Lin Feng's chapter also examines the potential impact of the 1999 policy speech of Tung Chee-hwa, Chief Executive of the Hong Kong Special Administrative Region, on the prevention and control of water pollution both in the Pearl River Delta region and in Hong Kong.

The study of Carlos W. H. Lo and Chung Shan-shan on solid waste management in Guangzhou offers a good example of the seriousness of environmental pollution in Guangdong as well as efforts made in pursuit of sustainable development. Like most developing cities, Guangzhou's environmental infrastructure is underdeveloped and its pollution control capacity is inadequate. Yet, on a per capita basis, municipal waste generation in Guangzhou is already higher than that in southern Thailand, Delhi, Hong Kong and South Korea. According to Lo and Chung, Guangzhou does not have an effective system to collect, transport and dispose of solid waste, and it lacks safe procedures and proper facilities to dispose of clinical waste, industrial hazardous material and radioactive waste. At the same time, the cost effectiveness of solid waste management is far from satisfactory in Guangzhou. The relative costs for landfilling, domestic waste collection and capital investment for landfills in Guangzhou are higher than those in Hong Kong.

Lo and Chung are not optimistic regarding quick improvements in the Guangzhou system. The obstacles are many, and they include the relatively low policy priority accorded to solid waste management which means that financial commitment from the city government is limited, the absence of economic incentives for the regulators to implement vigorous control under the current funding arrangements, and the lack of incentives for those to be regulated to co-operate with the authorities under the existing system of charges. Furthermore, Guangzhou citizens do not have a high level of environmental awareness, and government officials concerned are not knowledgeable of the policy area. Established channels for Guangzhou citizens to take part in the solid waste management system are inadequate, which in turn reduce the system's accountability. It seems that they are common problems in many Chinese cities.

On the whole, the contributors to this volume share a consensus. Their studies all indicate that leaders at various levels of government in Guangdong are aware of the challenges ahead, and they are concerned with the increasing domestic and international competition. However, overcoming the structural problems takes time, and meanwhile Guangdong's competitive edge continues to be eroded. As usual in China, people expect the provincial leadership to solve their problems, but corruption and distrust by the central government for the local leaders have become severe handicaps.

Notes

1. Chen Minjin, "Gaige Kaifang Ershinian Chengjiu Huigu (Reflections on the Achievements of Twenty Years of Reforms and Opening to the Outside World)", Guangdong Yearbook Editorial Board (ed.), *Guangdong Nianjian 1999* (Guangdong Yearbook 1999) (Guangzhou: Guangdong Nianjianshe, August 1999), p. 122.

2. Ding Xiaolun and Tang Guobin, "*Guangdong Zhi Zui* [Disiji] (The Best of Guangdong [The Fourth Series])", Guangdong Yearbook Editorial Board (ed.), *op.cit.*, p. 142.

3. *South China Morning Post*, 20 October 1999.

4. *Ibid.*, 12 November 1999.

5. *Ibid.*, 15 November 1999.

CHAPTER 2

Guangdong's Challenges:
Organizational Streamlining, Economic
Restructuring and Anti-Corruption

Joseph Y. S. CHENG

Introduction

In his report delivered at the Fifteenth National Congress of the Chinese Communist Party (CCP) on 12 September 1997, President Jiang Zemin severely criticized the over-expansion of the administrative bureaucracy in China. Jiang stated: "Unwieldy organization, over-staffing, failure to separate the functions of the government from those of enterprises and serious bureaucratism directly hamper the deepening of reforms and economic development and impair the relationship between the Party and the masses."[1] The Chinese leadership therefore intends to alter the functions of the government and separate them from those of enterprises so that they will be given genuine powers regarding production, operation and management. Jiang put forward the principles of simplification, uniformity and efficiency; and demanded that departments in charge of comprehensive economic management should shift their functions to macro-economic control, while specialized economic departments should be re-organized or reduced.[2]

This organizational streamlining would start at the central government level and would then be extended to the local level. Local government reform would follow the design of the State

Council. It was scheduled that the central government would complete its restructuring by the end of 1998, and provincial government reform would begin in 1999. It was reported that leaders of the industrial provinces in the northeast requested that the reforms be postponed; but the governor of Guangdong, Lu Ruihua, claimed that Guangdong had enough jobs to relocate government cadres. Lu believed that as many provincial officials had been selected from enterprises, it was natural to let them return to these companies.[3]

In the process of economic reform, many transitional economies choose one or more provinces/regions as pioneers. This is particularly true for China because it is a huge and diverse country. Identifying a number of testing grounds has been a standard practice for the Chinese authorities in introducing new policy programmes. Since 1979, Guangdong has been looked upon as a laboratory for testing various reform policies and their political limits. Guangdong's proximity to Hong Kong and its strong overseas Chinese connections led the Chinese leadership to identify it and Fujian as the two provinces which would take the lead in opening up to the outside world. Conservatives within the Chinese leadership often expressed their reservations regarding the reforms in the Special Economic Zones (SEZs) and Guangdong. There were many stories in the 1980s about old revolutionaries bursting into tears during their visits to the SEZs and Guangdong because they thought their revolutionary goals had all been forgotten. At the same time, other provincial units were jealous of Guangdong's special policy privileges as a pioneer in economic reforms and opening up to the outside world.

The decentralization of economic power since 1979 has been highly successful because local governments (as well as the enterprises they manage), individual workers and farmers can clearly see the connection between remuneration and performance. The impressive success of the responsibility system in the rural sector facilitated Deng Xiaoping and his supporters to persist in their economic reforms and extend them to the urban sector. The same success also generated much enthusiasm on the part of local governments to initiate reforms and innovations. Gradually local governments became bold enough to engage often in the following practice: *shang you zhengce, xia you duice* (in response to policies from higher levels of government, there are all sorts of counter-measures from the lower levels of government). By the second half of the 1980s, a majority of local governments were keeping two sets of accounts; one for the central government and one for their respective senior officials. Increasingly, regionalism has emerged in China as local governments jealously guard against central interference in policy areas where they believe they should have a decisive say. They will certainly seek to gradually expand the scope of such policy areas and their autonomy in general.[4]

This regionalism has not only generated tension between the central government and Guangdong, it has similarly generated tension, though to a lesser extent, between Guangdong and its lower levels of government. The province's 1994 development strategy emphasized a regional approach because the provincial leaders wanted to break away from the economic pattern defined by the administrative boundaries of cities and counties.[5] Such a pattern created the following problems: similar production structures in cities and counties, irrational regional planning and division of labour, lack of benefits of economies of scale, wasteful repetition in construction projects, unnecessary competition, etc.[6]

The regionalism issue has been compounded by corruption. While the central leaders maintain Party leadership and set limits on regionalism, they have been encouraging initiatives from local governments and shifting financial burdens, including those of social security, onto them.[7] At the same time, corruption has been draining state revenues, especially central government revenues, and eroding support for the Chinese leadership. In the fuel-oil sector, for example, the influx of cheap, illegal imports led to the closure of 3,700 Chinese wells in 1997 and losses of more than US$330 million in the first quarter of 1998.[8] This meant higher unemployment and another serious obstacle to realizing Premier Zhu Rongji's economic growth targets. When smuggling is organized by strategically-located units of the Party, the People's Liberation Army (PLA) and the government, the Chinese leadership feels threatened because this may well be the first signal of the decline of the communist regime.

Organizational streamlining, economic restructuring and anti-corruption are related issues in China today. In Maoist China, major reorganizations and streamlining of the administrative structure and the bureaucracy were closely connected with political conflicts and ideological controversies.[9] Administrative efficiency was mentioned from time to time, but it was often regarded as a secondary consideration. In the post-Mao era, the retreat of politics and the emphasis on pragmatism have reflected as well as contributed to the strategic shift from continuing revolutions to economic modernization. Progress of economic reforms and restructuring as well as their logic have either rendered many old functions of the Party and state machinery redundant, or demanded the Party and state bureaucracies to abandon these obsolete functions which are perceived as obstacles to economic reform.[10]

In the 1990s, the most significant aspect of China's economic reform has been transforming state enterprises into independent legal entities responsible for their own profits and losses.[11] Re-defining government functions have been viewed both as a prerequisite and as a logical consequence of such reforms of state enterprises. The thrust of economic restructuring has thus been separating government from enterprises, and the promotion of "small government, big society". The latter implies that governments at all levels should limit their functions, and allow the people to acquire the goods and services they want from the market.

In the reform era, corruption undeniably has been increasing;[12] and in Guangdong the situation is particularly serious. With regulatory power heavily concentrated in the hands of cadres who are poorly paid, reliance on campaigns to combat corruption cannot be very successful. Economic restructuring aims to reduce the regulatory functions of government agencies, and allows the market to function guided by a well-defined legal framework. Organizational streamlining reduces the size of the bureaucracy and facilitates improvements in remuneration for civil servants. Only when the number of government employees has been reduced by two-thirds, and their salaries increased twofold, will the Chinese authorities be in a position to seriously combat corruption and severely sanction cadres for receiving illegal incomes. As long as government agencies have to operate enterprises in order to give bonuses to civil servants so that they can make ends meet, and as long as they solicit "kickbacks" and impose fines to be distributed among cadres, efforts to curb corruption can only produce a limited deterrence effect by propagating corrupt cases involving notable senior officials.

This chapter examines the complex relationships among organizational streamlining, economic restructuring and anti-corruption in China, using Guangdong as an important case study. Economic reforms and administrative reforms in China have increasingly taken on a regionalized character.[13] Guangdong has been a pioneer in economic restructuring in the reform era, and its success has enabled it to make progress in organizational streamlining with relative ease. However, corruption has been rampant in Guangdong, and this has weakened the position of the provincial leadership. Economic development and prosperity have reduced the extortionary type of corruption in the province; but the temptation of wealth appears irresistible among cadres at all levels, and very senior cadres have been involved in smuggling and commercial fraud.

Previous Organizational Reform Efforts since 1949

The recent round of governmental organizational reforms is sometimes called "the seventh revolution" because there have been six previous rounds.[14] The first attempt was made in 1952–53 when central government ministries and agencies were increased from 35 to 42. The objective then was to strengthen centralization of power in preparation for the launch of the First Five-Year Plan, and local governments were considered to be deficient in organizational and management skills. The second round of organizational reforms took place in 1958–59, and central ministries and agencies were reduced from 81 to 60, while economic management ministries and agencies dropped from 50 to 36. In 1956, Mao Zedong in his famous article "On the Ten Major Relationships" argued that China should steer clear of imitating the Soviet Union by concentrating everything on the central government, as local governments in China had been placed under close scrutiny and had lost all initiatives.[15] In response to the problems of over-centralization, over-staffing and low efficiency, the central government transferred the enterprises and institutions it managed to local governments; at the same time, the State Council also streamlined its organization.

Soon afterwards, the central government's loss of control during the Great Leap Forward campaign prompted it to re-emphasize centralization and unified leadership in 1960. Some of the ministries which had been abolished were re-established and new ones were formed; by the end of 1965, there were 79 ministries and agencies at the central government level, while economic ministries and agencies rose from 36 to 50. There were, however, two attempts to reduce the personnel establishment of the State Council, one in 1960–61 and another in 1962–64. Altogether central ministries and agencies lost over 26,000 cadres, and most of them were sent to grassroots units or the first line of production.

The fourth round of reforming the administrative management system took place in the era of economic reform. The basic objectives were to streamline organizations and reduce their establishments. Reforms at the central government level were scheduled to be completed by 1982, followed by the provincial and prefectural governments by September 1983, and the county governments and below by the winter of 1984. The emphasis at this stage was to establish a "revolutionary, young, educated and professional" leadership, and to abolish life employment for those holding leadership positions. Economic structural reforms had not been taken into consideration in the governmental organizational reforms of the early 1980s.

In April 1988, the first session of the Seventh National People's Congress (NPC) endorsed Premier Li Peng's State Council organizational reform proposals. The latter were aimed at promoting the alteration of government functions. Government ministries and agencies responsible for economic management would have to change from direct management to indirect management; they would have to strengthen their macro-management functions, and drastically reduce their micro-management functions. The objectives of separating the Party from the government and separating the government from enterprises were clearly spelled out. Despite the significant goals, the reforms did not make much progress because of the 1989 Tiananmen Incident and the subsequent economic retrenchment programme.

In October 1992, the Fourteenth National Congress of the CCP indicated its determination to proceed with reforms of the administrative management system and government organizations. By then, ministries and agencies in the State Council numbered 86, and, on average, provincial governments each had over 70 bureaux and departments. Again the emphasis of the reforms was changing government functions through the separation of the government from enterprises, but the reforms this time were designed to promote the development of the socialist market economy.[16] The State Economic and Trade Commission was formed, and some specialized economic ministries became economic entities or trade associations. The Chinese leadership, however, was still unclear then as to what type of government organizations would be in line with the needs of a market economy, and there was inadequate political will to streamline the over-staffed bureaucracies.

The political will was prominently displayed in "the seventh revolution". At the end of 1997 and the beginning of 1998, Zhu Rongji, who was deputy premier and expected to become premier soon, held two rounds of discussions with heads of central ministries and commissions.[17] In March 1998, the Ninth NPC was presented with an ambitious plan to reduce the 40 ministries and commissions in the State Council to 29.[18] In the following June, Zhu Rongji announced that in the State Council agencies at the bureau level had been reduced by a quarter, i.e., over 200; and the personnel establishment had dropped by 47.5%. Taking into consideration that the State Commission of Science, Technology and Industry for

National Defence and another four bureaux had been newly created, the streamlining process was able to achieve the original target of cutting the number of cadres by half.[19]

Zhu Rongji's determination had been facilitated by two other favourable factors. The reform of state-owned enterprises (SOEs) had gradually won the support of the people, and it was generally expected that the state sector, including the state bureaucracies, had to be streamlined and its efficiency improved. Further, a considerable segment of senior officials had reached retirement age, and their resistance to retrenchment was thus considerably weakened.

Another important theme of the Fifteenth National Congress of the CCP was further reform of SOEs. Jiang Zemin appealed to cadres to strive to find practical and diverse forms of public ownership which could stimulate a rise in productivity; and all operational methods, and organizational forms reflecting the laws of socialized production were encouraged. The fundamental criteria for assessing the ownership structure are the three standards put forward by Deng Xiaoping in 1992: "Whether it promotes the growth of productive forces in a socialist society, increases the overall strength of the socialist state and raises living standards." The shareholding system is exactly considered a form of public ownership which can facilitate the development of productive forces.[20]

The introduction of the shareholding system among SOEs was nothing new. Shunde city in Guangdong, for example, began to reform the ownership structure of enterprises owned by its towns and higher-levels of administrative units in 1992 and completed the process in just over three years. All these enterprises eventually adopted a shareholding or shareholding co-operative system.[21] Shunde city, together with Zhucheng county in Shandong and other places, had already become models to be emulated by the mid-1990s. The CCP's endorsement, however, was essential in providing the ideological foundation and therefore the legitimacy for this line of reform. Deng Xiaoping had earlier defined socialism as the domination of public ownership and the avoidance of the polarization between the rich and poor. Jiang Zemin, as General Secretary of the CCP, had to demonstrate therefore that the shareholding system was not equivalent to privatization and its introduction to SOEs would not erode the dominant position of public ownership. Hence the introduction of the shareholding system would not be against "the cause of building socialism with Chinese characteristics".

Jiang Zemin was also naturally eager to offer his ideological contributions as the core of the third-generation leadership. In this report to the Fifteenth National Congress of the CCP, he stated:

> "The public sector includes not only the state- and collectively-owned sectors, but also the state- and collectively-owned elements in the sector of mixed owner- ship. The dominant position of public ownership should manifest itself mainly as follows: Public assets dominate in the total assets in society and the state-owned sector controls the life-blood of the national economy and plays a leading role in economic development."[22]

This means that state ownership is not necessary in sectors which are not considered the life-blood of the economy. Domination of public assets at this stage may well mean over 50% ownership of the total assets in society. At a later stage, domination may imply 35% of ownership, as is the norm among companies listed on the stock exchanges of developed countries. The public sector is no longer equivalent to the state sector; it includes the collectively-owned sector, as well as the state- and collectively-owned elements in the sector of mixed ownership. Hence for a major steel mill originally owned by the state, as long as 51% of the shares are owned by the central government, various local governments, and various pension-funds, medical-insurance funds owned by enterprises and local governments, it can offer 49% of its shares to private individuals and enterprises. For enterprises in the non-strategic sectors, they can certainly be sold to individuals, enterprises and even foreign firms.

In the Maoist era, the central government exercised strong con- trol over the various administrative reform campaigns. Guangdong did not manage to catch the limelight in these campaigns nor offer models for national emulation. It obviously had to toe the central government's line and dared not deviate from the demands of the central authorities. In the reform era, Guangdong has probably gone further than any other province in administrative/organizational reforms. It is significant that more progress has been made at the prefectural city and county-level city/county[23] levels than at the provincial level. While the cities have been given the green light, the provincial government is still accountable to the central government which has been reluctant to give Guangdong too many privileges. The key objectives of the administrative reforms launched in the late 1980s have been to separate the government from enterprises and to adjust the Party and government offices to meet the challenges of a market economy. Guangdong cadres' support for a market economy helped to reduce much resistance to the changes, and a new political culture began to take root at least in the more prosperous parts of Guangdong.

Foreign investment — mostly from Hong Kong — promoted economic growth and created joint ventures with the local governments which attracted cadres eager to change their careers. These companies also generated openings and absorbed officials made redundant when the bureaucracy was slashed. Furthermore, economic development offered sources of revenue for the local governments to provide social security benefits for the entire population. In sum, Guangdong has demonstrated that economic development has provided a good foundation for administrative/organizational reforms.

Important Issues in Organizational Streamlining and Economic Restructuring

The previous rounds of organizational streamlining did not achieve satisfactory results because they were implemented by administrative fiat. The Chinese leadership now appreciates that it has to be based on changing government functions and separating government functions from enterprise management. Obviously, this is easier said than done.

Government organs are usually reluctant to see their establishments and powers reduced. When they transfer powers to enterprises, they view that this is their prerogative to do so, implying that the exercise of such powers by enterprises is at their discretion. They seldom see the transfer of power to enterprises as the proper thing to do, and in doing so they are just following the policies of the Chinese leadership. Ministries concerned often retain the mentality that they are the authorities supervising the enterprises under them. In many cases, local governments at various levels tend to usurp powers of higher levels of government and recoup powers supposedly already decentralized to lower levels of local government or enterprises. Regarding the latter, government organs often possess certain powers of intervention as they retain powers of monitoring the work of enterprises, endorsing enterprises' major decisions, etc. Above all, when SOEs are not entirely separated from the government, they should not be completely independent either. Hence the foundation of separating enterprise from government and changing government functions lies in ending the direct asset relationship between government and enterprise. For example, a local government may set up asset management companies to manage its assets, and the latter will act as owners/shareholders of SOEs which will act as independent legal entities.

Organizational streamlining is very much related to changing government functions. In a planned economy, the government is engaged in all aspects of administration and management; and this naturally generates a huge bureaucracy with many specialized economic departments. With the termination of the direct asset relationship between the government and enterprise, the size of the state sector is reduced, and organizational streamlining can be achieved more easily. In practice, however, the problem of making arrangements for cadres stepping down from their posts is not to be under-estimated. This means that Zhu Rongji is under a great deal of pressure, and he has antagonized a substantial number of cadres.

Senior cadres who have lost their positions have many complaints, because although they may retain their ranks and nominal remuneration, they have lost their power and influence, and their lifestyles have become considerably different. They probably will be relocated to enterprises, and they normally cannot expect to be welcomed. Enterprises themselves are under pressure to streamline, and they generally hope to create openings for the promotion of their own staff members rather than to accommodate senior cadres stepping down from their posts. The latter may be transferred to lower levels of local government, but this really amounts to pushing the problem down the government hierarchy. This explains why organizational streamlining is easier at the central government level.

The associated question is how to ensure that cadres perform well in enterprises. Cadres have to be aware that they are no longer sent to enterprises as government officials to administer enterprises. They are to work as members of enterprises and to contribute to the functioning of enterprises according to the demands of the market economy. Admittedly cadres sent to work in enterprises have certain advantages. They normally have good educational qualifications, administrative and even leadership experience, and good connections with the relevant Party and government organs. Their major difficulty is that decades of working as cadres has cultivated a certain "cadre mentality", i.e., a mode of operation as well as a way of thinking and doing things which may not be appropriate for enterprises giving top priority to profit-making. Moreover, some cadres, especially senior cadres, are reluctant to accept retraining programmes to improve their skills for the new challenges of working in enterprises. Concern for the above problems usually make enterprises even more reluctant to accept cadres into their staff establishments.

However, at least two sets of factors help to reduce the resistance to organizational streamlining. In the first place, there is an awareness that streamlining is instrumental in improving cadre remuneration in the long term. Reducing the size of the bureaucracy also allows competent cadres to better demonstrate their performance. Meanwhile, the gradual development of the market economy exerts pressure on cadres; they understand that their incomes have been in decline relative to those in the private sector. They also realize that there is less work for them in the bureaucracy, and that the major challenges in China have increasingly been shifted away from the government bureaucracy. There is therefore a temptation for some cadres to leave the government bureaucracy. Where the two sets of factors are strongest, as in the case of Guangdong, organizational streamlining encounters the least obstacles.

The Chinese leadership has avoided raising the issue of separating the Party from the government in the recent organizational streamlining campaign. While it advocates "small government, big society", it makes no attempt to reduce the control of the Party. Hence, in most cases, Party committees at the lower levels of local government and at the grassroots level still make decisions on many minor issues. Leadership of the Party remains the most important of the Four Cardinal Principles,[24] and the Party has no intention of giving up its monopoly of power. Today the exercise of Party leadership is mainly realized through its decisions on appointments at all levels. In view of the government's changing functions and the reduction of the size of the state sector, the scope of such Party appointments should be correspondingly reduced. However, at this stage there is yet no concrete evidence that the Party accepts the gradual reduction of its power of making appointments. Herein lies the contradiction. After the adoption of the shareholding system and the termination of the direct asset relationship between government and enterprise, the Party should allow the board of directors concerned to appoint the manager of the enterprise. Organizational streamlining and economic restructuring ultimately demand the Party to restrict its appointment powers to the key positions in the government bureaucracy, and the Chinese leadership may not consider this compatible with the leadership of the Party.

According to the new Shenzhen model, for example, the asset management companies under the state assets management committee of the city government have been given the power to manage the leading cadres of the enterprises whose assets are wholly or partly owned by the asset management companies. It has also been stipulated that the boards of directors of the enterprises have the power to appoint and remove their managers. At the same time, however, Shenzhen leaders called for the strengthening of the building of the Party committees of Shenzhen enterprises and asset management companies, and such Party committees were expected to assume the function of "Party managing cadres". Shenzhen leaders believed that their model would better implement the principle of "Party managing cadres" in the context of a market economy and fulfilling the requirements of the country's Company Law.[25]

Another significant problem in organizational streamlining is the fact that the establishment of the government bureaucracy has not been separated from those of the Party and the mass organizations. There are now over 30 million cadres in China, and a significant proportion of them work for the Party and the mass organizations such as the trade unions, women's federations, etc. However, they draw their salaries as employees of the government bureaucracy. Avoiding the issues of separating the Party and the government, as well as separating the Party and enterprises, will not solve the problem.

Gradually, various mass organizations in China will be hard pressed by their memberships to articulate their interests and seek greater autonomy from Party control. There is no intention to confront the Party and state authorities concerned; the approach is usually low-key, patient and pragmatic. The Party and state authorities are persuaded that their vital interests are not threatened, that they will retain ultimate control, but in order to improve Party-mass relations, it will be better for the Party to reduce its presence and interference in the daily affairs of the mass organizations.

The trade unions offer a very interesting example. The Party wants to strengthen its influence among workers. There is a serious concern that with market reforms, separation of state from enterprises, emphasis on profits, etc., the Party faces a considerable erosion of its previous role among workers. Since the early 1990s, the Party has openly demanded for the establishment of Party organs and official trade union branches in foreign-owned enterprises and joint ventures. Yet as Kevin Jiang has observed, under pressure from the workers and for its own self-interest, the All-China Federation of Trade Unions (ACFTU) "has sought to represent workers' interests and to attain organizational autonomy by confronting a paternalistic, authoritarian political structure". The ACFTU has been moving cautiously given the current political constraints, and Jiang believes that it should not be seen as "conservative" but "pragmatic".[26]

The ultimate test for China's mass organizations will be financial self-sufficiency. In the foreseeable future, they will have to continue to rely on subsidies from the state, including their staff members drawing their salaries from the state bureaucracy. However, increasingly they will have to find means of expanding their incomes through charging fees for their services and establishing enterprises of their own. State subsidies will be reduced and they will probably come as lump sums, while mass organizations will have to pay the salaries of their staff members from their own budgets. Under such circumstances, mass organizations will have to streamline their organizations.

Elections at the grassroots level will enhance cadres' sense of accountability and of being "servants of the people". At this stage, only village heads are directly elected, and the Chinese leadership is still reluctant to extend direct elections to the level of town and township heads. However, accountability among cadres at higher levels has been strengthened in another way. In China today, a satisfactory performance record has become increasingly important for cadres' career advancement. Zhu Rongji is an outstanding example. Cadres at the middle-level and above now feel considerable pressure to perform; and, if their performance fails to satisfy their superiors, colleagues, subordinates and clients, they will find it difficult to remain in their positions. This is especially true in SOEs. SOEs which lose money will have to lay off workers, reduce or stop bonuses, and may even have to close. This certainly involves the livelihood of the workers concerned and they therefore expect the management to deliver.

The Reform of SOEs and Organizational Streamlining in Guangdong

The Guangdong leadership appreciates that organizational streamlining ultimately depends on separating the government from enterprises, which in turn has to rely on the establishment of new state assets management systems. In the second half of the 1990s, the province experimented with various schemes of decentralizing state assets management authority. The nine cities of Shenzhen, Guangzhou, Zhuhai, Foshan, Huizhou, Jiangmen, Zhaoqing, Shantou and Yunfu all established their respective state assets management committees; and on this basis, they explored ways of establishing organs responsible for asset management.[27]

Guangzhou combined this exercise with government organizational reforms, and transformed its enterprise administrative bureau (*qiye zhuguanju*) into an asset management company, while economic committees and offices were retained as organs administering various trades. Foshan and Huizhou formed state assets investment general companies under their respective state assets management committees, and placed the state capital of the original state enterprises now adopting a shareholding system as assets to be managed by these companies. Jiangmen and Zhaoqing too used the economic organs of their respective city governments as the foundations to establish asset management companies.[28]

Shenzhen has been at the forefront of Guangdong and China in economic reforms. As early as 1987, the Shenzhen city government had already formed a Shenzhen City Investment Management Company to manage the city's state assets. By the end of 1996, Shenzhen had further refined and improved its three-tier state assets management system: city state assets management committee — city asset management companies — enterprises.[29] The city state assets management committee was given the responsibility to formulate policies and draw up development plans, but the actual investment decisions would be made by the city asset management companies which were expected to act as holding companies with the principal goal of making a profit. The Shenzhen government claimed such a system separated the socio-economic management functions of the government and its functions as the owner of state assets at the top level; separated the administrative functions relating to state assets from their management functions at the intermediate level; and separated the ultimate ownership of the state and the property rights of enterprises as legal entities at the basic level. The fundamental objective was to ensure the concrete existence of organs responsible for state assets. It was argued that asset management companies were the key link in the system. As organs authorized by the state to invest, they exercised the rights of ownership on behalf of the state and were responsible for protecting and enhancing the value of the state assets entrusted to them.

At the end of 1996, after a re-organization process, three asset management companies were created: the city investment management company, the city construction investment holding company and the city commerce and trade investment holding company. They specialized in high-tech industries; construction and real estate development; and commerce, trade and tourism respectively. It was hoped that these three asset management companies would establish a new mode of operation to be emulated. The relationship between these companies and their enterprises would not be one between leaders and the led; instead it should be one between investors (owners of state assets) and enterprises as legal entities. On the basis of the ownership relationship, an asset management company would appoint representatives to the boards of directors of its enterprises, help the enterprises to shape their major investment decisions, and closely monitor its enterprises' loans, distribution of profits as well as distribution of wages and bonuses. An asset management company should not interfere in the production and management activities of its enterprises, and it should not violate the property rights of its enterprises as legal entities.

Through the establishment of the above system, the city government gave up its authority of administering its state enterprises to the asset management companies. The new arrangement was designed to facilitate the change of the city government's direct administration of its enterprises to indirect administration, and its micro-management of them to macro-management. This would obviously allow the city government to streamline its organization, and concentrate more on the development of the market economy and legal system. At the same time, the city government and the asset management companies wanted to shorten their chain of command. Enterprises under them had been graded according to their sizes; in 1996, attempts were made to eliminate the grade 4 and 5 enterprises, as well as to re-organize the grade 2 and 3 enterprises which were too small to achieve economies of scale. This was in line with the central government's policy of relaxing control over small SOEs by way of re-organization, association, merger, leasing, contract operation, joint stock partnership or sell-off. On the other hand, the city state assets management committee needed to strengthen its monitoring of the asset management companies. It had to establish a system of incentives and sanctions, a system of reporting and auditing, as well as to stipulate issues which would require the formal approval of the committee.

Like Shenzhen, Shunde has been another significant pioneer in China's reforms. In response to Deng Xiaoping's famous southern tour in 1992, Shunde in the three years thereafter concentrated on the introduction of a shareholding or shareholding co-operative system[30] in its enterprises. In the words of its mayor, Feng Runsheng, the objective was to eliminate the situation whereby "the mayor was head of enterprises, and heads of enterprises were mayors" (meaning that enterprises had to be responsible for the social services for their employees and families).[31] In the autumn of 1997, the leaders of Shunde claimed that the adoption of the shareholding or shareholding co-operative system was able to meet the requirements of "clearly established ownership, well defined power and responsibility, separation of enterprise from administration, and scientific management", as stated in Jiang Zemin's report to the Fifteenth Party Congress.[32]

The leaders of Shunde believed that the mentality of the heads of the city's SOEs had changed. Previously they had been bold enough to borrow as much money as possible. However, now they would carefully analyse the business risks involved. In 1995–97, the scale of fixed-asset investment of the city continued to decline. Apparently, the problems associated with "hunger for investment" and "soft budget constraints" commonly found in SOEs in socialist countries had been cured.[33] Shunde's reforms stimulated economic growth and enhanced revenues for the city government. The latter was able to improve its social services for the people and considerably eroded resistance to SOE reform. The gradual establishment of a city-wide social security system certainly reduced workers' fears and concerns. By 1997, the amount of taxes and revenue received by the Shunde authorities had been ahead of any county-level city in China for six consecutive years.[34] In 1996, the city's exports surpassed the US$1 billion level for the first time.[35]

When Deng Xiaoping visited Shunde in 1992, the Shunde leadership was acutely aware that further bold reforms were required to push the city into the next stage of economic development. Shunde had been leading the country by five years when in 1987 it attempted to decentralize power and profits to enterprises. By the early 1990s such reforms had reached their limits and the problems of unclear ownership, confusion in power and responsibility, merging of government and enterprises, as well as poor management were troubling Shunde's SOEs. The loss of state assets was a serious problem, and the situation was described as "enterprises were responsible for profits, banks for lending and government for debts". At that time, the city government was seriously worried about its debt burden.

By the autumn of 1997, Shunde had basically completed the reform of its SOEs. Among the 1,001 city-level and town-level enterprises, over 160 were either wholly owned by local governments, or local governments had controlling shares, or local governments participated as shareholders. The rest adopted a shareholding co-operative system. Public ownership of assets amounted to 62% of total assets of the enterprises. *Nanfang Ribao* offered a vivid example of the impact of the change in the form of ownership. Before the change, more than ten managers of a printing factory occupied a 1000 sq. m. new office building and still complained that the building lacked style. After the reform, the managers took the initiative and sold the building to repay the factory's debts; the managers occupied a part of the staff canteen as their office and accepted the deterioration in their working environment without any complaints.[36]

The examples of Shenzhen and Shunde spread to various parts of Guangdong, with modifications and local innovations. In 1996, in terms of number of enterprises, job positions and operating revenues, public ownership constituted a share of over 60% in Guangdong. Public ownership capital made up of 53.77% of enterprises which were legal entities, and this proportion included capital from state and collective enterprises invested in those of other forms of ownership.[37] At the end of 1996, public ownership capital in enterprises which were legal entities amounted to 561.77 billion yuan in Guangdong, with 96.82 billion yuan (17.23%) invested in enterprises which were legal entities of various kinds of mixed ownership. Public ownership capital invested in Hong Kong, Macau and Taiwan enterprises constituted 5.87%, 4.96% in shareholding enterprises, 3.98% in foreign enterprises, 2.1% in joint partnerships, 0.14% in private enterprises, and 0.18% in enterprises of other forms of ownership. These figures demonstrate that public ownership and other forms of ownership had been infiltrating each other in Guangdong.[38]

Since the reform era began in 1978, government organizational reforms in Guangdong have made more significant advances at the prefectural city and county-level city/county levels than at the provincial level.[39] Many cadres saw the transfer of management from Party and government agencies to economic entities as an opportunity to enhance their own economic well-being. Many of those interviewed by the author believed that they could prove their talents after the transfer. They were most likely influenced by the Hong Kong media (especially television) and various contacts with the territory's entrepreneurs who were much admired.

From the late 1980s, most senior Guangdong cadres were promoted from the lower levels of local government. Many of these cadres had considerable working experience in small enterprises,[40] and they fully appreciated that the revenues of local governments and their own incomes had been highly dependent on revenues from the enterprises they had operated and economic growth in the areas under their jurisdiction. Similarly, people in the counties, towns and townships closely monitored the economic performance of their local governments too, as this would significantly affect their direct incomes and the social services available. Their evaluation of the local cadres had an important bearing on the latter's reputation and chances of promotion. Cadres among local governments in Guangdong shared a strong sense of competition, and they normally wanted to do better than their neighbours. Moreover, most cadres at various levels of governments in Guangdong were natives of the province. They were very concerned with their reputation in the place where they worked; and unlike senior cadres in Shanghai, they were not too keen on seeking promotion elsewhere.

Town and township enterprises in Guangdong are officially classified as operating under "collective ownership", as opposed to state ownership. However, in fact they are run and financed by the town and township governments. Since the second half of the 1980s, most town and township governments have been managing their enterprises through their respective economic development general companies.[41] Such companies often had another signboard: town (township) enterprises office or industry and transport office. Depending on their jurisdiction and powers, they might be divided into three categories. The first type of general economic development company was comprehensive and it covered all the enterprises run by the town or township in the industrial, commercial, construction and agricultural sectors including various types of joint ventures. The second type concentrated on industrial enterprises only, and commercial, construction as well as agricultural enterprises which were accountable to other agencies. The third type was no more than a general office, while the specialized companies under it actually managed the enterprises in their respective sectors.[42]

The experiences of the town and township governments a decade ago provided valuable lessons for the separation of government from enterprises and the associated organizational streamlining in the prefectural-level cities in the second half of the 1990s. In such a way, one may even argue that there has been a considerable bottom-up approach in the organizational streamlining exercises in recent years; and obviously this has been another important factor reducing resistance and opposition.

The liquidation of the Guangdong International Trust and Investment Corporation (GITIC) in January 1999 provided further evidence of the separation of government from enterprises in Guangdong. When foreign banks met the liquidation committee of GITIC on 10 January, they were told that the provincial government would not provide additional funds to pay the creditors; instead, they would have to fight for their money in the bankruptcy court. The implications were obvious: Chinese SOEs which had been solely or largely dependent on government support had to assume financial responsibility as a legal entity; and *guanxi* (network of ties, connections) would no longer be an important consideration in foreign financial institutions' lending to Chinese enterprises. At the liquidation committee meeting, foreign bankers were also informed that Chinese bankruptcy law does not give priority to foreign creditors, and does not guarantee that all legally registered loans will be paid in full. Though the foreign creditors affected cried foul, the international business community accepted that placing GITIC in bankruptcy demonstrated "China is moving towards a more rules-based system".[43]

While the provincial government's decision on GITIC was logical, the bankruptcy of GITIC itself raised many serious questions. In the absence of a well-defined legal framework, the internal financial and accounting systems of Chinese SOEs were highly irregular. In the GITIC case, hundreds of millions of dollars simply disappeared and could not be traced. The huge losses of state assets in the economic restructuring process is no secret.[44] While the economic restructuring process offered opportunities for corruption and fraud, organizational streamlining provided incentives for the cadres in responsible positions to enrich themselves, especially those who were about to retire or be moved to second-line positions.

Like their counterparts in Southeast Asia, GITIC was a casualty of the regional financial crisis of 1997–98. Before the crisis, foreign banks were only too willing to lend to Chinese SOEs on the assumption that their loans were guaranteed by the Chinese authorities. The managers of the SOEs frequently engaged in highly speculative projects; and they expected to claim the profits for themselves and attribute the losses to the SOEs' accounts. At a time of economic crisis, the huge losses could no longer be hidden and the creditors demanded their money back. The provincial leaders obviously had to assume responsibility for the international scandal, and the central leadership made use of the opportunity to strengthen its control over Guangdong.

In early 1999, the Guangdong provincial government formulated its organizational streamlining plan in line with the State Council's timetable. It aimed at reducing the bureaucracy of the provincial government by half, and the provincial Party committee establishment by a third. Remuneration for cadres would be increased from 20% to 30% after the streamlining exercise; this would be acceptable to the central government as long as the latter did not have to assume the financial burden. Guangdong leaders intended to consolidate the province's status as the testing ground for reforms, and they were therefore prepared to exceed the targets set by the State Council. Naturally the broad objective was to establish a civil service of high quality, highly competent and well adapted to the needs of a market economy.

According to the preliminary proposal to be decided in March 1999, the following measures would be introduced:

(a) Those who were under 35 years of age without university degrees would leave their posts for further studies, and would have to compete for positions upon graduation;

(b) Cadres with ranks below section (*chu*) heads and who were over 55 years of age for males and over 50 years for females would have to retire early while receiving existing salaries;

(c) Institutions (*shiye danwei*) such as schools, hospitals/clinics, publishing houses, etc. within government and Party establishments would be hived off, and their staff members would no longer be cadres; and

(d) After the reforms, there would be competition for positions regarding certain segments of the bureaucracy still having surplus staff members.[45]

Reforming the Party and Government and Fighting Corruption

In view of the reform of SOEs, the provincial Party committee spent considerable efforts to strengthen the Party organization and the leadership of Guangdong's SOEs in 1997. The Chinese leaders have no intention of giving up the Party's monopoly of power, and leadership of the Party increasingly depends on its authority to make appointments at all levels. Following the instructions from the top Party leadership, the Organization Department of the Guangdong provincial Party committee held a conference in January 1997 to arrange for the monitor and audit of Party construction as well as the leaderships of the SOEs in Guangdong. Within the year, 4,528 inspection and audit teams had visited 9,913 enterprises. Readjustments in the SOE's leaderships involved 3,048 people — among them 1,123 lost their positions or were demoted.[46] Attempts to improve the leaderships of the SOEs also involved efforts to strengthen Party control.

In June 1997, the provincial Party committee organized a study conference for Party secretaries at the county level (including county-level cities and districts in prefectural-level cities). The major objectives were to strengthen ideological and political work, and to enhance supervision of county-level leaders by their superiors as well as by the masses.[47] Earlier decentralization of authority and resources often led to unhealthy competition among cities, counties and towns within the province. Local governments often deliberately hold back information from the higher-level authorities and refuse support for other local governments at the same level. Provincial officials sometimes complain about the accuracy of the statistical data delivered to them by local governments. In the past decade or so, Guangdong has usually been reluctant to follow the central government's call for macro-adjustment and retrenchment. Gradually, local cadres consider it legitimate to reject directives from higher authorities to promote what they perceive as local interests. The provincial leaders in recent years have been eager to improve regional planning and co-ordination within Guangdong and to strengthen vertical and horizontal communications in the provincial hierarchy of authorities.

Under such circumstances, separation of the Party and the government has been conveniently forgotten. In fact, Chinese leaders at all levels now appreciate that the maintenance of Party leadership has to rely more and more on its control of government appointments and promotions as the socialist market economy develops. On the other hand, mass organizations' articulation of interests has probably advanced further in Guangdong than in other province. This interest articulation has been facilitated by the following factors:

(a) Foreign investors, including those from Hong Kong, are most eager to exploit the local chambers of commerce and trade unions to articulate their interests;

(b) The mass media in Guangdong enjoys more freedom, and interest articulation by interests groups and mass organizations have a better chance of securing favourable coverage;

(c) The provincial and local authorities are keen to maintain an attractive investment environment, and they therefore maintain good relations with, and respond favourably to, the interest articulation by various groups, especially those representing economic interests.

Elections at the grassroots level have been making some progress in Guangdong too. Since town and township enterprises are well developed in Guangdong, and their profits often constitute a considerable proportion of the local inhabitants' incomes as well as a significant contribution to the provision of social services at the local level, people are very concerned with the leaders of the local governments which own the enterprises and appoint managers to run them. Hence voter participation is usually quite enthusiastic. Further, as elected offices carry prestige, good connections and sometimes even substantial financial rewards, there is often competition and genuine choices for the electorate. Competition among candidates naturally contributes to political mobilization. However, the attraction of elected offices also generates "money politics", and some candidates attempt to bribe voters to secure electoral victories.

At the Fourteenth Party Congress held in 1992, the issue of civil service reforms was again raised. Attempts were made to improve civil servants' remuneration. However, the kind of salary increases that Chinese leaders had in mind were far from adequate to catch up with inflation, deter corruption, and encourage career dedication among civil servants. Undeniably, corruption was rampant in Guangdong where cadres had to use illegal means or exploit loopholes to make ends meet. Entrepreneurs, especially those at the sub-provincial level, were able to rig elections through their influence. More shocking still were rumours that important positions were for sale at the prefectural city government level and below. A corrupt official had to accumulate a fortune to acquire a lucrative strategic position, but he could expect to make an even larger fortune during his tenure.

Corruption is often a symptom of a rapidly modernizing society.[48] Bureaucrats in China have had considerable discretion to transform the economy without worrying too much about laws and regulations which are either inadequate or non-existent. At the same time, lowly-paid officials have been managing assets and making decisions involving hundreds of millions of yuan. The opportunities and incentives for corrupt practices are abundant, but the Guangdong authorities are aware that they have to curb corruption in order to continue attracting investors. They are also mindful that the Hong Kong media and business community monitor their performance with considerable interest, and that scandals would be reported internationally.

In April 1997, the Guangdong provincial Party committee decided to introduce a system of open recruitment for cadres at the deputy bureau head level. Candidates were to be recommended by organizations, the masses or by the candidates themselves. They then had to sit an examination and go through a review process. The posts open for the first round of recruitment were six: deputy head of the provincial Economic Commission, deputy head of the provincial Higher Education Bureau, deputy head of the provincial Education Bureau, deputy general manager of GITIC, deputy general manager of Guangdong Second Light Industrial Group Companies, and deputy general manager of Guangdong Textile Industrial General Company.[49] In early 1999, the provincial people's congress adopted an amendment to its Rules of Procedure allowing 30 or more deputies to collectively nominate top provincial officials, including the governor and deputy governors.[50] The last amendment to the Rules of Procedure was made a decade ago.

The Guangdong leadership was aware that while most cadres in the province had considerable grassroots work experience, many of them lacked formal tertiary qualifications. This was one aspect which compared rather unfavourably with their counterparts in other provincial units, especially Shanghai and Beijing. In 1996, the provincial authorities drew up a five-year plan (1996–2000) for the education and training of cadres in the province. It was stipulated that leading cadres in Party and government organs at the county level and above should at least spend three months in their respective terms of appointment on full-time study. Party schools at the provincial and prefectural-city levels were given the responsibility to train 5,000 young and middle-aged cadres in these five years. Other cadre schools also had to assume the annual duty of training specific numbers of young and middle-aged cadres, as well as enterprise management personnel, scientific and technical personnel, cadres from national minorities, women cadres, Communist Youth League cadres and non-Party-member cadres.[51] In early 1999, the provincial government decided to send 300 officials to be trained overseas (mainly in Western countries, excluding Hong Kong) in the following three years, to study international economics and finance as well as management. Local governments in Shenzhen, Zhuhai, etc. would start similar programmes of their own.[52] The recent regional financial crisis obviously made Guangdong leaders more acutely aware of their inadequacies.

At the same time, a five-year plan on administering the province according to the law was endorsed by the provincial Party committee in 1996. The objectives were to establish a system of local laws and regulations in line with Guangdong's developments by 2000; to establish a high-quality team of law-enforcement personnel, to strengthen law-enforcement responsibility mechanisms and law enforcement supervisory mechanisms; and to enhance the sense of law among cadres and people.[53] In the latter half of 1997, the provincial authorities launched an inspection and audit exercise on the establishment of law-enforcement responsibility systems in executive organs directly under the provincial government.[54]

Following the general trend of reforms as advocated by the Chinese leadership, various levels of governments in Guangdong made efforts to reduce meetings/conferences, documents and leaders' public activities. Shenzhen apparently took the lead in Guangdong and launched a media campaign to this effect in August 1998; leaders in Shenzhen wanted to use the media to play a supervisory role in monitoring the results of their decision.[55] It was hoped that the campaign would reduce government expenditure and allow local government leaders more time for important decisions.

The above efforts to improve Party and government work, however, were much over-shadowed by reports outside China in late 1998 on smuggling and corruption in Guangdong.[56] Subsequent to a national work conference on the combat of smuggling convened by the Party Central Committee and the State Council in July 1998, Premier Zhu Rongji visited Guangdong and Guangxi in the following October to assess the local authorities progress in combating smuggling activities in the two provincial units. Due to the high tariffs imposed by the Chinese authorities, the avoidance of tariffs through smuggling was very lucrative. Smuggling not only causes the loss of tariff revenue on the part of the central government, it also damages the domestic industries protected by the tariffs. The sources of smuggled goods are diverse, and they usually enter China along the coast and are then transported throughout the country. It is generally believed that smuggling activities are conducted by corrupt officials in the coastal cities, usually in co-operation with the customs authorities and the navy. On the basis of cases prosecuted, cadres at the level of prefectural cities have been involved.

The industries of edible oils, refined petroleum, automobiles, motorcycles, textile raw materials and chemical raw materials have been hardest hit by smuggling activities. The petrochemical industry, for example, incurred substantial losses in the first half of 1998; but serious efforts to combat smuggling beginning in July enabled the industry to become profitable again. In October 1998, it was reported that a case of smuggling automobiles into China involved the naval bases and the police in Shantou in Guangdong and Beihai in Guangxi. Zhu Rongji promised to improve the equipment of the Beihai customs authorities so that they could better combat the well-equipped smugglers. At the same time, the head and deputy head of the Zhanjiang customs authorities were said to be involved in the smuggling of steel, automobiles, etc. amounting to 10 billion yuan. Guangzhou too admitted that a record number of its officials were convicted of corruption in 1998.[57]

Another major objective of Zhu Rongji's southern trip was to deter all types of violations and fraud relating to China's foreign exchange controls. In view of the financial crisis in the Asia-Pacific region and Russia, and in view of the considerable gap between increases in China's foreign exchange reserves and its trade surpluses, Zhu believed that it was high time to tackle the loss of foreign exchange through illegal channels. Again Guangdong was an obvious target.[58] Zhu Rongji declared that the Chinese authorities would try their best to bring to justice the smugglers and those who had cheated the state of its foreign exchange, even if they had escaped overseas. Further, the computer networks of banks, customs authorities and the State Foreign Exchange Control Administration would be linked so as to better monitor the illegal flows of foreign exchange out of the country.

Under such circumstances, the Chinese leadership naturally wants to strengthen control over Guangdong. Li Changchun, member of the Party Political Bureau, was appointed secretary of the Guangdong provincial Party committee in February 1998. Li is generally considered a rising star among the next generation of leaders, and has been tipped for promotion to the central leadership. Hence he will toe the central leadership's line in Guangdong and ensure that all levels of local government in the province will place national interests above local interests. Earlier Wang Qishan was appointed deputy governor of Guangdong. Wang was head of the Construction Bank of China before coming to the province, and he is responsible for overseeing Guangdong's financial and banking systems to guarantee that they will follow guidelines from the central government. Political gossip emerged in late 1998 that Li Changchun and Wang Qishan had encountered resistance from other Guangdong leaders.[59] Li on the other hand, transferred senior officials into Guangdong from other provinces.[60] It was reported in January 1999 that Lin Yuanhe, deputy secretary general of the Anhui provincial government and head of its Economic and Trade Commission, was transferred to Guangzhou to serve as a standing committee member of its city Party committee and a deputy mayor. Similarly, Jiang Jin, mayor of Yangzhou in Jiangsu, moved to Jiangmen as deputy secretary of the city Party committee and acting mayor; another official from Xiamen in Fujian would also move to Guangdong. At the same time, at least three senior officials in Guangdong were moved to other provinces.[61]

Meanwhile, it was also reported that former leaders of Guangdong, including former governor Ye Xuanping, former secretary of provincial Party committee Xie Fei, former governor Zhu Shenlin, and the incumbent governor Lu Ruihua, had come under pressure from the central leadership regarding various land deals in the province during their tenures. From 1985 to 1996, land sales in Guangdong amounted to over 1,370 billion yuan, but the provincial government only reported revenues of about 953 billion yuan to the State Council. The central government wanted the loss of over 417 billion yuan to be accounted for.[62]

Conclusion

The complex interaction among organizational streamlining, economic restructuring and anti-corruption as well as their associated problems, raise the fundamental question of the limitations of the reforms in the absence of democratic reforms. The Chinese Communist Party has no intention of allowing any erosion of its monopoly of power. As the socialist market economy has developed, the Party's control over the economy and society has been in decline. Leadership of the Party is preserved at the expense of genuine checks and balances mechanisms. The Party alone controls government and public sector appointments at all levels, and it maintains control of the people's congress system, the media as well as mass organizations and interest groups.

The Chinese communist regime attempts to secure its legitimacy through the improvement of people's living standards, and upholding discipline within its ranks through internal rectification campaigns. While economic reforms have largely been successful in promoting economic growth since 1978, internal rectification campaigns have failed miserably in stamping out corruption. Economic restructuring is essential for generating new momentum for economic growth, and organizational streamlining has been designed to facilitate economic reforms. In the absence of well-established internal monitoring and accounting systems within the bureaucracy and the SOEs, both processes have often exacerbated the problem of corruption, which in turn erodes the legitimacy of the regime.

Economic restructuring may not be adequate in promoting economic development at this stage. As the extensive mode of economic growth gives way to the intensive mode and as the raising of efficiency and productivity becomes the key to development, the limitations of administrative reforms become obvious. The regionalized character of economic restructuring and administrative reforms has further complicated the picture by introducing the variable of central-provincial relations. The central government, for example, has been exploiting macro-economic adjustments and controls to increase government revenue and especially the central government's share of fiscal revenue. A wealthy province like Guangdong has attracted special attention because it is expected to contribute more to the central government's fiscal revenue, and it has the potential of deviating from the line of the central government which takes resources from the rich provinces to subsidize the poor ones.

Corruption has provided an added incentive for the central authorities to exert pressure on Guangdong because corruption poses an implicit challenge to Party leadership. When local governments become thoroughly corrupt, it means that the central government has lost control. The paradox is that while Guangdong has been relatively successful in organizational streamlining and economic restructuring and thus has become a model for the country, serious corruption has attracted central interference and has tarnished its reputation and that of its leaders.

Automobile, petrochemical and steel industries have been identified as the pillar industries in Guangdong's new stage of development, and multinationals are considered the essential source of technical inputs. It appears that while many multinationals are looking for sites and partners all over China, many are bypassing Guangdong. Local governments and entrepreneurs in Guangdong lack the information, expertise and experience to deal with multinationals. The latter have found Guangdong's counterparts in the Yangtze Delta considerably more attractive. Guangdong's recent smuggling and corruption scandals have further reduced its appeal.

The author's interviews with a number of Guangdong officials in 1996–98 revealed that the cadres detected a sense of complacency among enterprises in Guangdong. The managers, as well as the workers, were over eager to enjoy the fruits of previous achievements, and it was difficult to persuade them to defer gratification for future investment. The officials interviewed admitted that other coastal provinces performed better in the re-investment of profits. Corruption was probably related to this eagerness to enjoy life; and it is important to analyse why economic restructuring has not been able to stimulate investment.

While the achievements of organizational streamlining and economic restructuring have been satisfactory, Guangdong has not been a forerunner in political reforms. There were suggestions that direct elections of town and township heads might first be held in the economically developed areas in Guangdong, but in 1998 this was still not acceptable to the Chinese leadership. Political reforms will help to make various levels of local governments in Guangdong more accountable to the people, and the strengthening of accountability hopefully will provide the impetus for further political and economic reforms.

At the beginning of 1999, it was anticipated that a more cautious attitude would prevail in the coming sessions of the provincial people's congress and provincial people's political consultative conference. Social stability would be the major concern.[63] As Guangdong's economy has been highly dependent on exports, the economic difficulties in the Asia-Pacific region have had a severely adverse impact. In the first ten months of 1998, Guangdong's exports only increased 3.5% over the corresponding period in the previous year; and there was an actual decline in the August–October period.[64] The Guangdong provincial government forecast only 3% growth in exports and foreign direct investment in 1999 as it considered that the impact of the Asian economic crisis would continue to take its toll.[65] In line with this concern for social stability and the central leadership's tightening of the control over the mass media, Guangdong's outspoken publications encountered severe pressure in late 1998.[66]

On the whole, Guangdong has already formulated its new development strategy; a workable blueprint to guide its present stage of economic development.[67] Despite various difficulties, it still secured 10% growth in gross domestic product in 1998, and is expected to achieve 8.5% growth in 1999, while forecasts of export growth fell within the range of 0–3%.[68] Bold political reforms are not anticipated in the foreseeable future, but organizational streamlining has its limits, and the combat of corruption demands the clear establishment of political accountability to the people. Guangdong remains a litmus test to see if economic development will eventually lead to political reform in China.

Notes

This chapter first appeared as "Guangdong's Challenges: Organizational Streamlining, Economic Restructuring and Anti-Corruption", *Pacific Affairs*, Vol. 73, No. 1, Spring 2000, pp. 9–35.

1. For the text of Jiang Zemin's report entitled "Hold High the Great Banner of Deng Xiaoping Theory for an All-Round Advancement of the Cause of Building Socialism with Chinese Characteristics into the 21st Century", see *Beijing Review*, Vol. 40, No. 40, 6–12 October 1997, pp. 10–33, especially p. 25.

2. *Ibid.*

3. *Sunday Morning Post*, 15 March 1998.

4. Yu-ming Shaw (ed.), *Tendencies of Regionalism in Contemporary China* (Taipei: Institute of International Relations, National Chengchi University, 1997).

5. See *Nanfang Ribao*, 6 November 1994 and *Yuegang Xinxi Ribao* (*Guangdong–Hong Kong Information Daily*, a Guangzhou Chinese language newspaper), 27 November 1994. See also Xie Fei's speech at the third plenum of the Seventh Guangdong Provincial Party Committee on 8 October 1994, *Nanfang Ribao*, 3 November 1994.

6. See, for example, Zhang Gaoli, "Guihua 'Longtou', Tidu Tuijin, Zaizao Zhujiang Sanjiaozhou Jingjiqu Xinhuihuang (Planning the 'Dragon Head', Progress Along the Hierarchy, Remake New Brilliance for the Pearl River Delta Economic Zone)", *Ibid.*, 22 November 1994.

7. By the end of 1997, all 21 prefectural-level cities and 121 county-level administrative units had established social security management organs directly under the respective local governments. See Provincial Social Security Bureau, "Shehui Baoxian (Social Security)", in *Guangdong Nianjian* Editorial Committee (ed.), *Guangdong Nianjian 1998* (*Guangdong Yearbook 1998*) (Guangzhou: Guangdong Nianjianshe, August 1998), p. 475.

8. Dorinda Elliott, "Cleaning Up Corruption", *Newsweek*, Vol. CXXXII, No. 24, 14 December 1998, p. 15.

9. See Harry Harding, *Organizing China: The Problem of Bureaucracy, 1949–76* (Stanford: Stanford University Press, 1981).

10. See Lam Tao-chiu and Cheung Kai-chee, "The Rise and Challenge of Administrative Reform in China: Post-Mao and Beyond", in Joseph Y. S. Cheng (ed.), *China in the Post-Deng Era* (Hong Kong: The Chinese University Press, 1998), pp. 137–170.

11. See G. H. Jefferson and Thomas G. Rawski, "Enterprise Reform in Chinese Industry", *Journal of Economic Perspectives*, Vol. 8, No. 2, Spring 1994, pp. 47–70; Barry Naughton, *Growing Out of the Plan: Chinese Economic Reform, 1978–93* (New York: Cambridge University Press 1994); and Thomas G. Rawski, "Chinese Industrial Reform: Accomplishments, Prospects, and Implications", AEA Papers and Proceedings, *American Economic Review*, Vol. 84, No. 2, May 1994, pp. 271–275.

12. See T. Wing Lo, *Corruption and Politics in Hong Kong and China* (Buckingham, U.K.: Open University Press, 1993).

13. On the regionalized character of China's economic reforms, see Jia Hao and Lin Zhimin (eds.), *Changing Central-Local Relations in China: Reform and State Capacity* (Boulder, Colorado: Westview Press, 1994); and David Goodman and Gerald Segal (eds.), *China Deconstructs: Politics, Trade and Regionalism* (London: Routledge, 1994).

14. See Chapter 8 "1949–97 Nian Zhongguo Zhengfu Jigou Gaige Licheng (The Course of Chinese Government Organizational Reforms, 1949–97)", in Liu Zhifeng, *Diqici Geming — 1998 Zhongguo Zhengfu Jigou Gaige Beiwanglu* (*Memorandum on Chinese Government Organizational Reforms in 1998*) (Beijing: Jingji Ribao Chubanshe, 1998), pp. 289–314.

15. *Mao Zedong Xuanji* (*Selected Works of Mao Zedong*), Vol. 5 (Beijing: Renmin Chubanshe, 1977), pp. 267–288.

16. See the author and Ting Wang, "Administrative Reforms in China in 1992: Streamlining, Decentralization and Changing Government Functions", in the author and Maurice Brosseau (eds.), *China Review 1993* (Hong Kong: The Chinese University Press, 1993), pp. 4.1–4.20.

17. Chapter 3 "Zhu Rongji Zhiding Gaige Fangan Neiqing (The Inside Story of Zhu Rongji Formulating His Reform Plan)", in Liu Zhifeng, *Diqici Geming*, *op.cit.*, p. 67.

18. *South China Morning Post*, 7 March 1998.

19. *Ming Pao* (a Hong Kong Chinese language newspaper), 22 June 1998.

20. See, for example, Yuan Pingzhou, "15th CCP Congress: Succeeding and Developing Deng Xiaoping Theory", *Beijing Review*, Vol. 40, No. 40, 6–12 October 1997 p. 4. See also Jiang Zemin's report, *op. cit.*, pp. 18–19.

21. *Nanfang Ribao* (a Guangzhou Chinese language newspaper), 24 September 1997.

22. See Jiang Zemin's report, *op.cit.*, p. 19.

23. City (*shi*) is a very complicated concept in China. There are different administrative grades of cities depending on status and size. Beijing, Shanghai, Tianjin and Chongqing are known as municipalities and enjoy provincial status. Then there are over a dozen major cities with independent economic plans directly accountable to the State Council economically; Guangzhou and Shenzhen belong to this category. Sometimes they are said to enjoy sub-provincial status. Most cities in China are prefectural cities; i.e., they are below provinces and are above counties. They usually administer their urban areas (divided into districts) and the rural counties around the urban areas. Finally, some counties have become urbanized and they are given the status of county-level cities. They are still administered by prefectural cities. In this chapter, cities usually refer to prefectural cities.

24. The Four Cardinal Principles were set by Deng Xiaoping in March 1979. The other three are the road of socialism, people's democratic dictatorship, and Marxism-Leninism and Mao Zedong Thought.

25. Special Commentator's article, "Guoqi Gaige de Zhongda Tupo (Significant Breakthroughs in the Reform of State-owned Enterprises)", *Shenzhen Shangbao* (*Shenzhen Economic Daily*), 26 December 1996.

26. See Kevin Jiang, "Gonghui yu Dang-Guojia de Chongtu — Bashiniandai Yilai de Zhongguo Gonghui Gaige (The Conflicts Between Trade Unions and the Party-State — the Reform of Chinese Trade Unions Since the 1980s)", *Hong Kong Journal of Social Sciences*, No. 8, Autumn 1996, pp. 121–158, especially p. 121.

27. Qiu Yitong and Chen Chi, "Tizhi Gaige Gaikuang (General Situation of Structural Reforms)", in *Guangdong Nianjian* Editorial Committee (ed.), *Guangdong Nianjian 1998* (*Guangdong Yearbook 1998*), *op.cit.*, pp. 145–146.

28. *Ibid.*

29. Special Commentator's article, "Guoqi Gaige de Zhongda Tupo (Significant Breakthrough in Reforms of State-owned Enterprises)", *Shenzhen Shangbao*, 26 December 1996.

30. A shareholding co-operative system (*gufen hezuo zhi*) means that in introducing a joint stock/shareholding system to an enterprise, the shares are distributed and held mainly or solely among the managers and workers of the enterprise. The enterprise then is similar to a co-operative. This system usually applies to small enterprises or town and township enterprises.

31. *Nanfang Ribao*, 24 September 1997.

32. See Jiang Zemin's report to the Fifteenth Party Congress, *Beijing Review*, *op.cit.*, pp. 19–20.

33. See Janos Kornai, *Economics of Shortage* (Amsterdam: North-Holland Publishing Company, 1980).

34. *Nanfang Ribao*, 24 September 1997.

35. *Ibid.*, 2 October 1997.

36. *Ibid.*

37. Guangdong Provincial Statistical Bureau (ed.), *Statistical Yearbook of Guangdong 1998* (Beijing: China Statistical Publishing House, August 1998), p. 34.

38. *Ibid.*

39. See the author's "Organizational Reforms in Local Government in Guangdong", in the author and Stewart MacPherson (eds.), *Development in Southern China* (Hong Kong: Longman, 1995), pp. 38–43.

40. Ting Wang, *Li Changchun yu Guangdong Zhengtan — Guangdong Jiebanqun, Quyu Jingji he Zuqun Wenhua (Li Changchun and the Guangdong Political Scene: The Guangdong Successors, Regional Economics, and the Culture of the Ethnic Groups)* (Hong Kong: Celebrities Press, 1998), Chapters 5–8.

41. See the author's "Structures and Functions of Town and Township Governments in Guangdong", in Stewart MacPherson and the author (eds.), *Economic and Social Development in South China* (Cheltenham, U.K.: Edward Elgar, 1996), pp. 57–75.

42. Li Shi, "Shundexian Zhenban Qiye Guanli Jigou de Xianzhuang ji Weilai Quxiang de Tantao (An Examination of the Present State and Future Directions Concerning the Management Agencies of the Town Enterprises of Shunde County)", in Pearl River Delta Economic Development and Management Research Centre, Zhongshan University (ed.), *Zhujiang Sanjiaozhou Jingji Fazhan Huigu yu Qianzhan (Economic Development of the Pearl River Delta — A Retrospect and Prospects)* (Guangzhou: Zhongshan University Press, 1992), p. 235.

43. Trish Saywell, "Risky Business", *Far Eastern Economic Review*, Vol. 162, No. 3, 21 January 1999, p. 53.

44. Ho Qinglian, *Xiandaihua de Xianjing (The Traps of Modernization)* (Beijing: Jinri Zhongguo Chubanshe) 1998.

45. *Ming Pao*, 2 February 1999.

46. Yue Zuban, "Deng de Jianshe Gaikuang (General Situation of Party Construction)", in *Guangdong Nianjian* Editorial Committee (ed.), *op.cit.*, p. 154.

47. Zhang Guoyi, "Guangdongsheng Lingdao Jiguan (Leadership Organs of Guangdong)", in *Ibid.*, p.156.

48. See Paul Heywood (ed.), *Political Corruption* (Oxford, U.K.: Blackwell Publishers, 1997).

49. Zhang Guoyi, "Guangdongsheng Lingdao Jiguan ",*op.cit.*, pp. 156–157.

50. *South China Morning Post*, 3 February 1999.

51. Yue Zuban, "Guangdongsheng Lingdao Jiguan (Leadership Organs of Guangdong)", in *Guangdong Nianjian* Editorial Committee (ed.), *Guangdong Nianjian 1997* (*Guangdong Yearbook 1997*) (Guangzhou: *Guangdong Nianjianshe*, August 1997), pp. 156–157.

52. *Ming Pao*, 5 February 1999.

53. Huang Zhuo, "Guangdongsheng Lingdao Jiguan (Leadership Organs of Guangdong)", in *Guangdong Nianjian* Editorial Committee (ed.), *Guangdong Nianjian 1997* (*Guangdong Yearbook 1997*), *op.cit.*, p. 156.

54. Wu Xuetian, "Yifazhisheng Gongzuo (Work on Administering the Province According to the Law)", in Guangdong Nianjian Editorial Committee (ed.), *Guangdong Nianjian 1998* (*Guangdong Yearbook 1998*), *op.cit.*, p. 124.

55. *Shenzhen Tequbao* (*Shenzhen Special Zone Daily*), 13 September 1998.

56. Ye Tan, "Zhu Rongji Nanxia Dasi Jiemi (Revealing the Secrets of Zhu Rongji's Trip to Southern China to Combat Smuggling)", *The Mirror* (a pro-Beijing Hong Kong Chinese monthly), No. 257, December 1998, pp. 26–29; and Luo Bing, "Zhu Rongji Canjia Junwei Gongzuo (Zhu Rongji Participated in the Work of the Central Military Commission)", *Cheng Ming* (a Hong Kong Chinese monthly), No. 253, November 1998, pp. 6–7.

57. *South China Morning Post*, 8 February 1999.

58. Ye Tan, "Zhu Rongji Nanxia Dasi Jiemi", *op.cit.*

59. Luo Bing, "*Li Changchun Guangdong Zao Dizhi* (*Li Changchun Encountered Boycotts in Guangdong*)", *Cheng Ming*, No. 254, December 1998, pp. 6–8. See also Willy Wo-Lap Lam, "A power play shaking Guangdong", *South China Morning Post*, 3 February 1999.

60. *Ming Pao*, 20 January 1999.

61. *Ibid.*, 30 January 1999.

62. Luo Bing, "Guangdong Si Jutou Beizeling Jiancha (Four Top Leaders in Guangdong Demanded to Review Themselves)", *Cheng Ming*, No. 253, November 1998, pp. 8–10.

63. *Ming Pao*, 26 January 1999.

64. *Ibid.*, 19 November 1998.

65. *South China Morning Post*, 20 January 1999.

66. Xia Wensi, "Ding Guangen Fengsha Liangbao Yikan (Ding Guangen Struck at Two Newspapers and a Magazine)", *Open Magazine* (a Hong Kong Chinese monthly), No. 145, January 1999, pp. 14–15.

67. See the author's "Guangdong's New Development Strategy", Chapter 2 of his edited work, *The Guangdong Development Model and Its Challenges* (Hong Kong: City University of Hong Kong Press, 1998), pp. 13–42.

68. *South China Morning Post*, 5 January 1999.

CHAPTER 3

Interest Articulation between the Government and Private Enterprises:

A Case Study of the Shenzhen Special Economic Zone

WANG Tong and K. K. LEUNG

By the end of the 20th century, China had resumed sovereignty over Hong Kong and Macau, and returned to the international economic arena through membership of the World Trade Organization (WTO). Political and economic development in southern China, especially in Guangdong province and its fastest growing city Shenzhen, had become the most sensitive barometer of social change in China.

Shenzhen is one of China's original four Special Economic Zones (SEZs). Economic growth in the SEZ has been rapid since its establishment at the beginning of the reform era. Economic interests have gathered sufficient momentum for business sectors to come together to form groups to protect their own commonly established interests. Vertically, the Chinese Communist Party (CCP) has relinquished some of its power over the management of enterprises, and implemented a policy of separating enterprises from the state. Horizontally, the private enterprises, having benefited from the socialist market system, are networking themselves as interest groups to prevent the government from interfering in their autonomy in the market system.

When the Shenzhen SEZ was first established in 1980, there were only six self-employed entrepreneurs, with an annual business turnover of less than 30,000 yuan. By the end of 1989, the number of self-employed entrepreneurs had increased to 50,000, employing more than 100,000 workers with a registered capital of 200 million yuan.[1] Between 1991–97, the number of private enterprises in Shenzhen alone increased from 1,000 to 27,500 (out of a total of 120,300 in Guangdong province). During the same period, the number of employees increased from 21,300 to 272,600 (one sixth of the SEZ's population, 1,529,000 in Guangdong) and registered capital grew from 150 million yuan to 40,900 million yuan (107,650 million yuan in Guangdong), generating 5,741 million yuan of income tax (820 million per year on average) for the SEZ government. Shenzhen was the first place in Guangdong province where private enterprises flourished.[2] It was due to this rapid growth of enterprises that major organizations were established to safeguard their huge amount of labour and capital interests.

In this chapter, the authors first examine the development of enterprise privatization and the growing demand for establishing corresponding organizations for the enterprises in China. In the following section three popular conceptual perspectives are introduced to explain the changing relationship between the state and society; namely, corporatism, clientalism and civil society. As a case study, the roles and functions of private enterprises in Shenzhen are investigated in relation to the interests of local government. Finally, an open-ended scenario is suggested to see if the seeds of "civil society" can be planted in Guangdong first, and then in the whole of China, as Shenzhen-like development of private enterprise organizations burgeon without political checks from either the Party or the central government.

Development of Private Enterprises and Private Enterprise Organizations in China

After the establishment of the People's Republic of China (PRC) in 1949, the state monopolized all the important resources and activities of society through the socialist transformation movement. Factories, shops, banks and all other departments of the national economy were put under the control of the state's administrative plan. Economic and administrative units could only obtain resources from the state as no other channels could be accessed. The state also put individuals into an administrative framework through the "unit system" (*danwei zhidu*) and "residence system" (*hukou zhidu*). Thoughts and opinions of people were conditioned by the state through social education, political propaganda and political studies. Trade unions, youth leagues, women's associations and other social groups were all put under direct control of the state. They became the "transmission belt" of the Party and the government rather than organizations influencing and supervising the government.

One of the main objectives of the economic reforms in the Open Door Era was to limit the social functions of the state and enlarge the autonomous sphere of all kinds of socio-economic organizations. Great changes took place in China under the reform policy. The monopoly of social resources by the state was gradually released and the degree of state control over society was weakened.

Along with the development of the market system, the economic reforms awakened the self-consciousness of different classes and advanced the development of social interests. The opportunities provided by the market led to individuals and enterprises having divergent interests. The rapid economic development made people more driven by individual motives. The differentiation of interests strengthened people's group-consciousness. As a result, different social interests began to organize interest groups so as to pursue and defend their own interests. Different social groups sprang up like mushrooms during this period, such as the Self-employed Labourer's Association, the Customer's Association, the Cement Industry Association and the Economic Research Association. By the end of 1997, there were 180,000 associations at and above the county level, including 1,846 national associations and 21,406 provincial and municipal associations.[3] These new associations actively pursued their own interests and provided a systematic linkage between the government and society.

Under the economic reform policy, different kinds of economic units, such as self-employed labourers (*getihu*) and private enterprises (*siying qiye*) were established. After the Socialist Transformation Movement of 1956, 88,000 private industries and thousands of private businesses were transformed into socialist enterprises. As a result, the private economy disappeared in China. Almost all economic and financial resources, as well as human resources, were under the control of the state from then on. More than twenty years later, China's economic reform programme allowed private enterprises to reappear. Since 1978, private enterprises have developed gradually on the basis of self-employed entrepreneurs. A constitutional amendment on the private economy was adopted in 1987, in which the central government acknowledged the existence of private enterprises for the first time, and established the policy of "permitting existence, strengthening management, developing interests and getting rid of drawbacks, and guiding them gradually". In 1988, the State Council published the *Provisional Regulations on Private Enterprises in the People's Republic of China* which defined private enterprises as "economic organizations whose assets belong to individuals and which have more than eight employees". Under the encouragement of the central government, the private economy flourished quickly all over China.

Under the authoritarian system of the centrally planned economy, only state-owned and collective enterprises were allowed to exist. The state imposed strict management regulations on these enterprises. The policies and rules of the government could be transmitted from the top to the bottom through a set of integrated channels. The problems and difficulties of the enterprises could also be transmitted from the bottom to the top through the same channels. However, private enterprises are different from state enterprises. The state has no systematic control over private enterprises. Private entrepreneurs can design and develop their enterprises by themselves. Under these circumstances, the government deems that it is necessary to establish new channels to manage the new social sectors. Meanwhile, private enterprises cannot protect their own interests separately. They have to rely on the power of their organizations to protect their interests. Subsequently, private enterprise organizations were established in all provinces and cities under the encouragement of the government in the early 1990s.

The development of private enterprises and their organizations has attracted the interest of many scholars. How are private enterprises, as independent economic elements, managed by the state, and how do they express their interests and demands? How do private enterprise associations, as organizations for the interests of private entrepreneurs, act between the state and private entrepreneurs? These are questions which deserve further examination.

A Conceptual Interpretation: Corporatism, Clientalism and Civil Society

As far as the activities of private enterprise organizations are concerned, the concepts of corporatism, clientalism and civil society offer insights into understanding the relationship between the government and private enterprises in the reform era.

Philippe Schmitter defined corporatism as "a system of interest representation in which the constituent units are organized into a limited number of singular, compulsory, noncompetitive, hierarchically ordered and functionally differentiated categories, recognized or licensed (if not created) by the state and granted a deliberate representational monopoly within their respective categories in exchange for obtaining certain controls on their selection of leaders and articulation of demands and supports".[4] There are two kinds of corporatism. One is called "state corporatism", in which the state has ultimate control over associations. Under this system the state can even appoint and remove the leaders of associations. Another is "societal corporatism" or "neocorporatism", in which associations have more autonomy and the leaders of associations are mainly accountable to their members rather than to the state. In general, corporatism describes a corporate relationship between the state and particular interest groups. In a corporatist mechanism, the state and society acknowledge each other's legality and authority. The government recognizes one, and only one, national organization as the sole representative of each sector's interests, and the government conducts its relations with that sector through the association. The association sometimes even becomes involved in the government's policy-making processes, and sometimes helps implement state policy on the government's behalf, whereas to some extent, the state controls the leader's election and the interests of the association.[5] Corporatism is helpful in maintaining political and societal stability. Therefore countries which are at war or are pursuing rapid economic development are liable to adopt corporatist management methods.[6]

However, the changing relationship of the state and society in the reform era cannot be simply represented by only one concept of "corporatism". We cannot ignore the fact that the relations between the state and society can be explained in terms of personal networks. Although the state tries to provide a formal channel for private enterprises to express their interests through private enterprise organizations (which do serve this function), most private enterprises will not ask for the organization's help when they face difficulties and problems. They rely more on the informal relationship between themselves and government officials in seeking help or expressing their interests. This informal connection between the state and society is addressed as "clientalism". Andrew Walder and other scholars have discussed the clientalism networks of China in the Mao era.[7] David Wank, Ole Brunn and Liu Yaling focused on the analysis of the clientalism networks between private enterprises and officials after the introduction of economic reforms.[8] In Chinese, the word *guanxi* means clientalism. In Mao's era, workers' salaries, welfare, housing and promotion were all controlled by their unit (*danwei*), and unit leaders controlled the extensive allocation power of these resources. In a time of resource shortage and the absence of a free market, workers had to try and establish informal relationships with leaders so as to obtain advantages in housing or other welfare allocations.[9] Although the market has provided many opportunities and resources in the reform era, there are still many important resources controlled by the state. For example, the government controls the allocation of land, steel, iron, petroleum, electricity, water and many other resources. All these resources are important for an enterprise to develop its business. In order to obtain advantages in acquiring these resources, private enterprises try to establish informal relationships with government officials. Since the legal system and the management system are still not perfect, government officials can use their power either to help their relatives and friends or in exchange for money. As government officials still hold the power of allocation, informal clientalism still prevails in many fields of Chinese society.

As Nevitt said: "If economic reforms are generating a civil society in China, organized associations of private business would be the most obvious places to look for it".[10] The emergence of social organizations in China during the 1980s attracted the attention of many scholars.[11] They regarded it as evidence of a reform-generated civil society. The concept of "civil society" has a long and complicated pedigree in Western social and political thinking. Usually it is defined as the desire to curb the power of overweening states through a sphere of social organizations which are more or less autonomous from the state. Gordon White emphasizes civil society as an organic accompaniment to the spread of market relations and the consequent emergence of a new realm of social organizations based on voluntary participation.[12] Private enterprises are new strengths driven by economic reforms. They are sharply distinct from the Party-state and pursue their interests independent of the state. When scholars discuss whether the emergence of new social organizations represents the rebirth of civil society in China, they pay more attention to the organization of private enterprises.[13] Some scholars hold that business elites are the best hope of democratization in China. Business elites have obtained much economic freedom during the reform era. Consequently, they will try to acquire political freedom to protect their economic interests. Economic reform, it is argued, will eventually lead to democratization. However, opponents do not agree that economic reform will necessarily lead to democratization. They cite the example of Latin America to illustrate that the bourgeoisie are anti-democratic in a bureaucratic authoritarian system.[14]

A Political Analysis: The Politics of Interest Articulation in the Shenzhen SEZ

Interest articulation is "the process of forming and expressing demands by political interest groups and transmitting the demands to government authorities".[15] In China, interests are articulated in a limited way. On the one hand, there are few political interest groups in this socialist country. On the other hand, the groups are more prone to express rather than transmit their demands to the government. Moreover, the Chinese government is hesitant in receiving demands from the public. The government would like to shape the "demands" itself and convey them as support for public policies.

In response to calls at the 13th Party Congress in 1987 for the development of a socialist market economy, the theory of the primary stage of socialism, and the separation of the Party and the government, private enterprises were encouraged to develop in co-operation with the Party and the government. Two important "people's" organizations were set up in Shenzhen in the early 1990s; the Shenzhen Folk Entrepreneurs' Association in December 1991 (later renamed the Shenzhen Folk Entrepreneurs' Chamber of Commerce in April 1995), and the Shenzhen Municipal Private Enterprise Association in September 1993.

The nature of private enterprise organizations is semi-governmental, although the Shenzhen Folk Entrepreneurs' Chamber of Commerce (SFECC) under the leadership of the Municipal United Front Department is comparatively less "official" than the Shenzhen Municipal Private Enterprise Association (SMPEA) under the leadership of the Municipal Party Committee and Municipal Government.[16] This nature predetermines the roles of the two organizations. As two of their major roles are (a) to implement the

Party's lines, principles and policies and the state's laws and regulations, and (b) to reflect the opinions and demands of the entrepreneurs to the government concerned,[17] private enterprise organizations tend to be government oriented.

As a "bridge" and a "link" between the party-state and the enterprises, private enterprise organizations seem to perform the function of intermediating the interests and conflicts between the government and the entrepreneurs. However, the line of authority originates from the government. According to the *Regulations of the Management of Social Groups Registration*, social groups have to obtain the approval from the department responsible for their work (Article 9) before they can apply for registration in a civil administration department (Article 6). The department responsible for the work of the SMPEA is the Shenzhen Municipal Industrial and Commercial Management Bureau and that of the SFECC is the Shenzhen General Chamber of Commerce. The chairman of the SMPEA is concurrently the deputy head of the Shenzhen Municipal Industrial and Commercial Management Bureau and its honorary chairman is the head of the bureau. The board of directors of the SFECC, including one chairman and nine vice-chairmen, is appointed by the Municipal United Front. The interests of private entrepreneurs are represented by their organizations through the mouths of the government officials and delivered to the government departments concerned. Since the leaders of the associations are nominated by the government and elected by their members, they are accountable to both the government and their members. On the one hand, they help the government carry out policies. On the other hand, they articulate interests on behalf of their members through their close relationship with the government.

By definition, China's interest group system is in the category of "state corporatism". According to the *Regulations of the Management of Social Groups Registration*, all associations must be affiliated to an official or semi-official unit (*guakao danwei*), and must register with the Civil Administration Department or the Civil Administration Bureau. Each sector can only establish one association in each administrative area (Article 16). Usually the government nominates the leaders of the associations. Government officials even concurrently hold some posts in the associations. The government also provides funds to the associations, which enhances control over them. For example, the Municipal Private Enterprise Associations of Shenzhen, Hangzhou and Taiyuan are affiliated to their Municipal Industrial and Commercial Management Bureaux. One official of the Municipal Industrial and Commercial Management Bureau holds at least one leadership of each association. Other leaders are nominated, or at least approved by, the bureau. The staff in charge of finance of each association are also on the staff of the bureau, so they have control over the fiscal status of the association.[18]

Chinese political culture emphasizes collective interest rather than individual interest. Interest articulation was suppressed for thousands of years under authoritarian and paternalistic regimes. People relied on a good emperor to bring good luck to them, rather than pursuing their own interests. So it is relatively easy for state corporatism to be implemented in China, since people are used to co-operating with the government. The Chinese government also wants to make use of state corporatism to maintain societal stability by controlling the development of interest groups so that it can pre-empt the further control of other autonomous groups. Under state corporatism, corporatist associations provide a formal channel for interest articulation, through which dissatisfaction can be detected and addressed. Meanwhile, the government can use these associations to help it implement its related policies.

Apart from the political functions performed by the private enterprise organizations mentioned above, other economic and social functions include: (a) the study of the new development of private enterprises, (b) the provision of services including market, information and law, (c) the establishment of new enterprises and assistance to enterprises, (d) the provision of welfare services to entrepreneurs, and (e) co-operation with other enterprises at home and abroad.[19] As interest groups, the private enterprise organizations are well placed to secure their members' basic interests in the market system. However, when the organizations want to defend their own advanced interests in the name of pressure groups, they are assimilated as an executive arm of the government to implement, rather than to influence, the government's policies. In consideration of the limited functions of the SMPEA, Lan Zhenqiang[20] emphasized in a working report of the Association that;

> "as a bridging link to the government, the Association on the one hand acts as a good staff and assistance to the government, to implement state policy and government work on private enterprises and to help the government supervise and manage private enterprises. On the other hand, the Association has to press and assist the government to administer according to the law, protect the legal rights of private enterprises, safeguard the proper management of private enterprises, and prevent the interests of private enterprises from being infringed."[21]

During the reform era, accompanying the differentiation of social interests, there is a necessity for people to express their demands through effective channels. The expression of different interest demands can lead to dissatisfaction and even violent conflict if they are extensively suppressed. In order to maintain social stability, it is necessary for the government to organize these interests into manageable channels. State corporatism serves this purpose well. The management pattern of state corporatism enables the government to take advantage of social organizations to co-ordinate different interest groups in society, and enables state policies to be carried out trouble-free. In order to realize rapid economic development, the state has tried to establish corporatist organizations so as to block the rise of genuine independent organizations which might undermine the power of the state, and to provide a mechanism for airing their grievances through proper channels.

The difference between official and unofficial organizations rests on the dependency of a social group on the department responsible for its work. Academics and sports societies are purely unofficial, while those societies assisting the government are semi-official.[22]

The SMPEA and the SFECC belong to the latter social groups. The relationship between the Municipal Industrial and Commercial Management Bureau and the SMPEA is consultative,[23] while that between the Municipal United Front Department and the SFECC is supportive — in terms of providing offices and equipment, participating in the Chamber's activities, communicating with the media for the promotion of private enterprises, and co-ordinating with the Labour Bureau.[24] Through both consultative and supportive functions, the interests of the two social organizations are effectively articulated to the government.

The leadership of both organizations underscores the importance of good connections with the government. Several leaders and some members of SMPEA are deputies of the People's Congresses and Political Consultative Conference. Through the lobbying efforts of these deputies in the conferences of the People's Congresses and Political Consultative Conference, the SMPEA succeeded in obtaining housing benefits for its members. For a long time, only employees of state-owned enterprises could enjoy "cheap housing" (weili fang), which is provided by the government and is much cheaper than private housing. Because of this, it was hard for private enterprises to find good employees since people only wanted to enter state-owned enterprises so that they could take advantage of the cheap housing. Many private entrepreneurs complained about this to the SMPEA and demanded equal opportunities for the employees of private enterprises. Then the leaders of the SMPEA tried to express its members' interests during meetings in the People's Congresses and Political Consultative Conference. The SMPEA also tried to transmit their opinions to the Housing Bureau of Shenzhen, and invited some officials from the bureau to discuss this problem with its members together. They finally succeeded in persuading the People's Congress to pass a resolution that employees of private enterprises could also enjoy cheap housing.[25] Another obstacle to the development of private enterprises is the Chinese special residence system (hukou zhidu). The Personnel Bureau of the local government used quota restrictions to control population migration. State-owned enterprises exercised a good deal of control over personnel and could transfer workers and provide residence registration on their behalf. However, private enterprises had no quotas and could not provide residence registration for their employees. In China, food supply and children's entrance to schools were strictly controlled by residence registration. So high-qualified people who wanted to move to Shenzhen from other provinces flowed into the state-owned enterprises, since they could help them to obtain the Shenzhen residence registration. It was very disadvantageous for private enterprises to hire qualified personnel. The SMPEA complained about this to the Office of Policy Research of the municipal government. Finally, private enterprises were allowed the same control over personnel to that of the state-owned enterprises.

The SMPEA also succeeded in cancelling the private enterprise management fee, acquiring the authority of import and export trade and other benefits for private enterprises, through its relationship with the Municipal Industrial and Commercial Management Bureau. Before 1996, all private enterprises had to pay management fees to the Municipal Industrial and Commercial Management Bureau. Enterprises whose properties were valued above 10 million yuan had to pay a monthly management fee of 1,000 yuan. Enterprises whose properties were worth below 10 million yuan had to pay a monthly fee of 400 to 500 yuan. Private enterprises were very discontented with this additional charge. Their complaints were collected by the SMPEA. As the deputy head of the bureau was concurrently the chairman of the SMPEA, and the head of the bureau was concurrently the honorary chairman of the SMPEA, their demands were easily passed on to the bureau. The bureau realized the importance of reducing the burden of private enterprises and decided to cancel the management fee after 1996.[26] Before 1998, only state-owned enterprises could engage in import and export trade directly. To a great extent, this activity limited the development and expansion of private enterprises. The SMPEA tried to appeal to the bureau and express their demands to the central government through the bureau. In the end, private enterprises obtained what they wanted: manufacturing industries whose registration capital was above 2 million yuan, and commercial industries whose registration capital was above 5 million yuan, could independently engage in import and export trade.[27]

In addition, through the connection of the SFECC chairman as the ex-deputy head of the Shenzhen Security Bureau, the procedures for applying for visas to Hong Kong and other countries became easier. Many private enterprises of Shenzhen had commercial contacts with Hong Kong enterprises and had to travel to the territory frequently. But the procedures for applying for visas to Hong Kong were very complicated, and the examining and approving formalities of the Shenzhen Security Bureau, which is in charge of all passport and visa applications for Shenzhen citizens, were very strict and time-consuming. Luckily, the current chairman of the SFECC was the ex-deputy head of the Shenzhen Security Bureau. Through the help of the SFECC, members could acquire visas much easier than applying by themselves. Moreover, the SFECC promoted a new issuing system offered by the Security Bureau for its members: private enterprises whose tax payments exceeded 200,000 yuan could get a multiple entry-exit visa to Hong Kong and Macau.[28]

Members of the SFECC also faced the residence registration problem. Employees of their enterprises were very unstable since private enterprises could not provide residence registration for them. Leaders of the SFECC passed this on to the Municipal United Front Department. The Municipal United Front Department tried to negotiate with the Municipal Labour Bureau and the Municipal Personnel Bureau. Through the efforts of the Municipal United Front Department, members of the SFECC were finally given residence quotas in 1996. In March every year, the Municipal United Front Department held a labour-transferring meeting to give the members of the SFECC an opportunity to report their demands for residence registration. In 1997, the SFECC helped its members to get 23 quotas of residence registration. In 1998, it obtained 40 quotas for its members.[29] The Municipal United Front Department also helped the SFECC to negotiate with many other government agencies to resolve problems for private enterprises. For example, a contractor of one enterprise broke the contract unreasonably, resulting in a big loss to this enterprise. The Municipal United Front Department helped him to seek assistance from the district government of Futian (a district of Shenzhen) to get back his money.[30] Although the Municipal United Front Department is a government organization, members of the SFECC thought that the good relationship it had established with it was very helpful for their Chamber. Some members said that the better the SFECC's relations with the government were, the easier it was to solve problems and difficulties faced by its members. One said that the good relationship between the government and the SFECC could help private enterprises to have more opportunities to express their demands to officials.[31]

However, the cohesiveness and centripetal force of the two organizations is not high, as 30–40% of the SMPEA members did not pay membership dues,[32] and 70% of the SFECC members could not pay them on time.[33] However, both the SMPEA and the SFECC are disciplined in selecting membership. In 1996, 38 out of 60 SFECC members were disqualified for not paying membership dues for two consecutive years.[34] As private enterprises registered in the Municipal Industrial and Commercial Management Bureau are automatically members of the SMPEA, there should be about 30,000 members in the Association. However, as there is a rule that "no membership dues, no service",[35] there are only about 10,000 members in the Association.[36]

In interviews with the authors, the views of SMPEA members were not very positive. Two of the members did not attend any activities organized by the Association.[37] One member stated that the Association was established merely for the sake of accepting membership dues and gaining money, not serving its members.[38] Another member complained that the Association lacked transparency and management cohesiveness.[39] More critical comments against the Association came from entrepreneurs who did not join the SMPEA. One entrepreneur believed that the Association was not big enough, that its power would be greater if private enterprises played a bigger role in society, and that there was no proper channel to reflect opinions.[40] Another entrepreneur did not trust the Association because she thought that it was a government institution and its officers were not well-qualified. She thought that calling the Mayor of Shenzhen Municipal Government's hot line directly was more useful than expressing her interest through the Association.[41]

All those questioned, no matter whether they joined the Association or not, agreed that *guanxi* was important in solving their own problems. Whenever they met problems or had difficulties in their business, they tried to solve problems through networks rather than seeking help from the SMPEA.[42] One entrepreneur commented that Chinese society emphasizes human relationships rather than law and discipline; "It is not "rule by law" in China. Provided you have money and network, you can succeed".[43] One entrepreneur even said; "My impression is that many things can only be solved at the dinning table".[44] This is a typical reflection of Chinese business culture. This entrepreneur could not reach agreement with the local government when his enterprise wanted to rent a factory building in the suburbs of Shenzhen. He invited local officials, who were in charge of land, electricity and water, to lunch. At the dinning table, his generous entertainment successfully persuaded these officials to provide his enterprise with resources and protection.[45]

The views of SFECC members were more positive. One member made a comparison between the Association and the Chamber: "The Association was in form only and its members only paid membership dues and nothing else. In contrast, the Chamber organized many activities and gave much guidance and assistance to the enterprises".[46] Another member thought that the Association was organized by the government and was not very helpful. He said that participants in the Association were inferior to those in the Chamber. The Chamber was more cohesive and vigorous as all of its members were well established and more powerful than members of the Association. So he was more interested in taking part in activities held by the Chamber rather than the Association.[47] One member said that the Chamber was very cohesive, while the status of the Association was not high enough and not many entrepreneurs were concerned about it.[48] One member did not think that the Municipal

United Front Department was an obstacle to the Chamber but an asset for reflecting opinions and demands.[49] Four out the five interviewees revealed that they joined the Chamber to make friends, strengthen horizontal connections and communicate with one another.[50] Although the Chamber only had around 100 members, all members were from large enterprises. The capital of the Chamber's members was usually over 10 million yuan. It seems that private enterprises were proud of being a member of the Chamber, because it was a symbol that their enterprises were recognized as large-scale organizations. Meanwhile, as all members were large enterprises, entrepreneurs were very happy to join the Chamber since they had a good opportunity to learn from the experiences of other successful enterprises. So most of them said that their reason for joining the Chamber was to make friends and to broaden their outlook. Furthermore, since all enterprises were large and well developed, the members had more time to participate in social activities than those "infant" entrepreneurs. Also, they were more interested in strengthening horizontal connections with other large enterprises. That is why they were more active in taking part in the activities of the Chamber.

Jean Oi observed that: "In developing countries, where the formal channels for meaningful participation and interest articulation are weak, individuals regularly pursue their interests through the use of informal networks built upon personal ties".[51] Economic reforms create an economic market in which resources can be exchanged freely. But only part of the economic power is given to the market. Most resources are still controlled by the state. Besides, state officials can also decide which enterprises produce what kind of product and which enterprises can do what kind of business. The officials also control the allocation power of tax. Since the legal system is still far from perfect in China, the officials who hold the power have the arbitrary power of explanation, which leads to the creation of a black market. In this market, the managers of private enterprises establish extensive clientelism networks with officials using economic interests to exchange for the powers which are controlled by the officials.

Most private enterprises obtain more resources through these kinds of clientalism networks. They try to obtain permission for their application from the officials, or try to evade taxes. The effectiveness of clientalism networks with officials encourages private enterprises' dependence on *guanxi*, as this kind of *guanxi* can help them to resolve major difficulties and problems. However, if the *guanxi* is always aligned with the government, the network can also disintegrate the concerted power of the private enterprises and make them indifferent to forming collective action against the government even when their interests are infringed. Unless there is a common "enemy" and a common interest among the private enterprises, the "official" labelling effect continues to be attached to them. Therefore, the establishment of the legal relationship between the government and society at the expense of patron client relationship between the two is the only way to make the private enterprise organizations independent of the government as genuine "people's" autonomous groups.

An Open-ended Window for Guangdong: Private Enterprises in the Shenzhen SEZ as both Economic and Political Forces for Democratic Development in China

Strictly speaking, the SMPEA is para-governmental in nature, as one of its tasks is to provide grounds for government's policy making.[52] The SFECC is comparatively more liberal though it is closely watched by the Party through the Municipal United Front Department. One of its tasks is to promote the function of democratic supervision. However, another more important task is to assist the government in implementing its policies.[53] As one interviewee who did not join any social groups remarked; "The function of the government should be to supervise the management of private enterprises and not to manage them by itself, but the government insists on doing so, hence, the manpower market in

Shenzhen becomes dysfunctional".[54] From the viewpoint of policy makers, these two organizations are administratively absorbed by the government so as to mediate the tension between the socialist government and the emerging power of the newly born "bourgeoisie", or the so-called "red bourgeoisie".

Although only one third of private enterprises join the SMPEA and less than 100 are members of the SFECC, their activism and connections with the government[55] are good assets for their organizations. From the viewpoint of the private entrepreneurs, they are eager to break away from the monopoly of the state enterprises so that they can fairly compete with each other in the socialist market system. During the primary stage of socialism, they are making a narrow chance of going through the "parliamentary channel" to protect their own established interests. It can be expected that future elections in both the national and local people's congresses will be quite different from those in the past. In the past, candidates were chosen by the CCP. In the future, independent candidates supported by private enterprises will rise up to compete with Party members. The existing social groups will be transformed as pseudo-political groups which will perform the function of interest aggregation in addition to that of interest articulation. It is possible that fractionalization will be cultivated within the CCP. Different party factions backed up by different sectors of private enterprises will compete with one another to fight for their own vested interests.

By the end of 1997, there were 30 million private enterprises in China, employing 70 million workers with a registered capital of 900 billion yuan.[56] In March 1999, the National People's Congress formally gave protection to the private economy by amending the Constitution (Article 11). It is expected that by 2010, the proportion of the non-public economy will occupy one third of the total economy in China. As the reform process continues, the "monolithic structure" of the economy deteriorates. The monopoly of the state-owned enterprise is going to be undermined by the continuing policy of state-enterprise separation. The further separation between the ownership and the management stimulates the sudden rise of a gigantic social force — the "social intermediate stratum".[57]

We foresee fundamental change in the twenty-first century, especially now that China has become a member of the WTO. The Shenzhen SEZ and Guangdong as a whole will become a pivotal point for opening the huge economic market to the outside world. At the same time, there will be a tremendous political impact on the whole of Chinese society. The horizontal integration among the enterprises releases the liberty of the social groups and the individuals from the vertical control of the party and the government. The networking of the vested interests of private enterprises helps the elevation of the middle class, the culmination of which will eventually relieve the conflicts between the bourgeoisie and the proletariat. The rise of the middle class signifies the beginning of the "throes" of a civil society. The CCP will be challenged by a great force which is not from outside but from inside. The Party representing different interests will be potentially differentiate itself into different checks-and-balances factions. The forming of the huge middle class constituted by the emerging private entrepreneurs will then develop into a stable social vigor which in the long run will breed a civil society. Shenzhen SEZ is just an experimental unit to test the desirability and feasibility of breaking the democratic bottleneck by the private enterprises. With the concerted efforts made by the three tiers of development, i.e., Guangdong, Shenzhen and Hong Kong, in which the latter is a backup to the former and the former is being pushed by the latter, both economic and political take-offs can be expected in the near future.

Notes

1. Qiu Shuming, "Adapting the Needs of the Market Economy System and Opening Up the New Development of Private Economy in Shenzhen" (in Chinese), in the *Report on the First Meeting of Shenzhen Municipal Enterprises* (in Chinese), 1993, p. 8.

2. Shenzhen Municipal Private Enterprise Association (eds.), *China, Shenzhen, Private Enterprise* (in Chinese), 1998, p. 2; Wu Siqi, "Folk Entrepreneurs' Historical Responsibility" (in Chinese), unpublished report, April 1998, p. 1.

3. *Zhongguo Shehui Bao*, 28 April 1998.

4. Philippe Schmitter, "Still the Century of Corporatism?", in *The New Corporatism: Social-Political Structures in the Iberian World*, Fredrick B. Pike and Thomas Stritch (eds.) (Notre Dame: University of Notre Dame Press, 1974), pp. 93–94.

5. Zhang Jin, "The Core Problems of Corporatism" (in Chinese), *Shehuixue Yanjiu*, No. 5, 1996, pp. 39–44; Jonathan Unger, "'Bridges': Private Business, the Chinese Government and the Rise of New Associations", *The China Quarterly*, No. 147, 1996, pp. 795–796.

6. Jonathan Unger and Anita Chan, "Corporatism in China: A Developmental State in an East Asian Context", *The Australian Journal of Chinese Affairs*, No. 33, 1995, pp. 29–53.

7. Andrew G. Walder, *Communist Neo-Traditionalism: Work and Authority in Chinese Industry* (Berkeley: University of California Press, 1986).

8. David Wank, "Private Business, Bureaucracy, and Political Alliance in a Chinese City", *The Australian Journal of Chinese Affairs*, No. 33, January 1995, pp. 55–71; Ole Brunn, "Political Hierarchy and Private Entrepreneurship in a Chinese Neighbourhood", in *The Waning of the Communist State: Economic Origins of Political Change in China and Hungary*, Andrew G. Walder (ed.) (Berkeley: University of California Press, 1995), pp. 184–212; Liu Yaling, "Reform from Below: The Private Economy and Local Politics in the Rural Industrialization of Wenzhou", *The China Quarterly*, No. 130, June 1992, pp. 293–316.

9. Walder, *Communist Neo-Traditionalism*, *op.cit.*

10. Christopher Earle Nevitt, "Private Business Associations in China: Evidence of Civil Society or Local State Power?", *The China Journal*, No. 36, July 1996, p. 26.

11. For a discussion of this new phenomenon, see Gordon White, "Prospects for Civil Society in China: A Case Study of Xiaoshan City", *The Australian Journal of Chinese Affairs*, No. 29, January 1993, pp. 195–218; Wang Ying, Zhe Xiaoye and Sun Bingyao, *The Intermediary Level of Chinese Society: Reform and China's Associational Organizations* (in Chinese) (Beijing, Zhongguo Fazhan Chubanshe, 1993).

12. White, "Prospects for Civil Society", *op.cit.*, p. 197. White also investigated the social organizations of Xiaoshan City of Zhejiang province by using the concept of "civil society". His study shows that the socio-economic changes generated by economic reforms created a social space between the state and the economic agents. However, in the context of a semi-reformed economy, the state continued to retain a great deal of its power and tried to occupy this space. Although there were some impetuses for the formation of social organizations from below, the dominant impulse came from above. These organizations cannot be regarded as "independent" organizations, but they do exercise limited autonomy which reflects their intermediary roles. White thought that the space between the state and the enterprises could only be minimally bridged. These associations were

only taken as downward rung to connect the state and enterprises. Their influence on government and the state policies was limited. In sum, one can only detect embryonic elements of "civil society". *Ibid.*, pp. 195–218.

13. For related works see Nevitt, "Private Business Associations in China", *op. cit.*, pp. 25–43; Unger, "Corporatism in China", *op.cit.*, pp. 795–819. Margaret M. Pearson, *China's New Business Elite: The Political Consequences of Economic Reform* (Berkeley: University of California Press, 1997); Wank, "Private Business", *op. cit.*

14. Pearson, *China's New Business Elite*, *op.cit.*, pp. 3–23.

15. Austin Ranney, *Governing: An Introduction to Political Science* (Upper Saddle River, N. J.: Prentice-Hall, 1996), p. 32.

16. According to the *Regulations on the Management of Social Groups in the Shenzhen Special Economic Zone*, "social groups enjoy the rights of (1) participating in the management of social affairs, (2) submitting consultation opinions and suggestions to the state institutions, ..." (Article 24). Article 3 of the Rules of the Shenzhen Private Enterprise Association also reads: "Shenzhen Private Enterprise Association is under the leadership of the Municipal Party Committee and the Municipal Government, and under the guidance of the Municipal Industrial and Commercial Management Bureau and its Upper Level of Private Enterprise Association. It is the bridge and the link between the party-state and the enterprises." Article 1 of the Rules on Shenzhen Folk Entrepreneurs' Chamber of Commerce states that the Chamber is "under the leadership of the Shenzhen Municipal United Front and a direct group member of the Shenzhen General Chamber of Commerce".

17. Article 5 of the Rules of the Shenzhen Municipal Private Enterprise Association, hereafter SMPEA Rules, and Article 4 of the Rules of the Shenzhen Folk Entrepreneurs' Chamber of Commerce, hereafter SFECC Rules.

18. Interview with the Taiyuan Private Enterprise Association, 2 November 1998; interview with the Shenzhen Private Enterprise Association, 9 December 1998; interview with the Hangzhou Private Enterprise Association, 26 January 1999.

19. Article 5 of SMPEA Rules and Article 4 of SFECC Rules.

20. One of the Board of Directors of the Association.

21. Lan Zhenqiang, "To Establish a New Work for the Association under the Guidance of the Spirit of the 15th Party Congress" (in Chinese), unpublished report, 29 October 1998, p. 10.

22. Interview with Social Group Department of the Civil Administration Bureau, 22 July 1998 — hereafter 980722 Interview.

23. 980722 Interview.

24. Interview with SFECC, 12 August 1998 — hereafter 981208 Interview.

25. 980722 Interview. Interview with SMPEA, 9 January 1999 — hereafter 990109 Interview.

26. 980722 Interview.

27. *Ibid.*

28. 981208 Interview.

29. *Ibid.*

30. *Ibid.*

31. *Ibid.* Interview with Private Entrepreneurs, 28 January 1999 — hereafter 990128-2 Interview.

32. It is interesting to note that the members in remote areas like Bo On District and Long Gang District paid their separate dues to the District and not to the Association (980722 Interview).

33. 980722 and 981208 Interviews.

34. 981208 Interview.

35. Interview with SMPEA, 12 September 1998 — hereafter 981209 Interview.

36. Interview with SMPEA, 5 January 1999 — hereafter 990105 Interview.

37. Interview with Private Entrepreneurs, 10 December 1998 — hereafter 981210 Interview; Interview with private Entrepreneurs, 28 December 1998 — hereafter 981228 Interview.

38. 981210 Interview. According to 981209 Interview, every member of the SMPEA should pay annual membership fee of 480 yuan. This entrepreneur also complained that the SMPEA charged them money when it issued directories.

39. 981228 Interview.

40. Interview with Private Entrepreneurs, 29 December 1998 — hereafter 981229 Interview.

41. Interview with Private Entrepreneurs, 30 December 1998 — hereafter 981230.

42. 981210, 981228, 981229 and 981230 Interviews.

43. 981210 Interview.

44. 981229 Interview.

45. *Ibid.*

46. Interview with Private Entrepreneurs, 28 January 1999 — hereafter 990128-1 Interview.

47. Interview with Private Entrepreneurs, 28 January 1999 — hereafter 990128-3 Interview. The capital of the Chamber's members was usually over 10 million yuan and 11 members possessed capital over 100 million yuan (981208 Interview).

48. Interview with Private Entrepreneurs, 28 January 1999 — hereafter 990128-4 Interview.

49. Interview with Private Entrepreneurs, 28 January 1999 — hereafter 990128-2 Interview.

50. 990128-1,2,3,4 Interviews.

51. Quoted from Pearson, *China's New Business Elite*, *op.cit.*, p. 33.

52. Article 5 of SMPEA Rules.

53. Article 3 of SFECC Rules.

54. 981230 Interview.

55. For example, 17 out of 78 (21.8%) members of SFECC were deputies of the state by April 1998: one deputy of the National People's Congress (NPC), one deputy of the National Committee of the Chinese People's Political Consultative Conference (CPPCC), two deputies of the Local People's Congresses and 13 deputies of the Local Committee of the CPPCC; see Wu, "Folk Entrepreneurs", *op.cit.*, p. 1.

56. *Ming Pao*, 31 January 1999.

57. Wang, Zhe and Sun, *The Intermediary Level of Chinese Society*, *op.cit.*

CHAPTER 4

Industrial Structure and Industrial Policy in Guangdong Province

LAU Pui-king

Introduction

Guangdong is the most prosperous province in China in terms of GDP per capita, and industrial and commercial activities. In 1998, the GDP of Guangdong stood at 795.53 billion yuan, or 10% of China's total GDP.[1] Many questions have been asked about the development of Guangdong. What are the forces behind the changes? Will Guangdong be able to maintain its growth potential? Has the government played an active role in the transformation of its industrial structure? Can the economic environment and institutions sustain economic growth under the pressures of global technological change? Can the quality of the province's human resources support the ambitious modernization plans? The recent industrial development in the province may give us some ideas regarding the direction of development in southern China.

Industrialization of Guangdong

The industrial structure of Guangdong has been transformed drastically since 1978. The weighting of the primary sector has

Table 4.1

The Composition of Guangdong's GDP

(percentage)

Year	Primary	Secondary	Tertiary
1978	29.9	46.4	23.7
1980	33.8	41.1	25.1
1985	31.1	40.8	28.1
1990	26.1	39.9	34.0
1995	15.1	50.2	34.7
1996	14.4	50.2	35.4
1997	13.5	49.9	36.6
1998	12.7	50.4	36.9

Source: Guangdong Statistical Yearbook (*Guangdong Tongji Nianjian*) (Beijing: China Statistics Press, various issues 1978–98).

Table 4.2

Gross Output Value and Ownership of Industries in Guangdong

Year	Industry (%)		Ownership (%)				Gross Output Value (RMB 100 million)
	Light	Heavy	State	Collective	Private & Foreign	Others	
1978	57.3	42.7	67.8	26.1	–	6.1	199.65
1980	63.0	37.0	63.1	27.6	1.9	7.3	234.35
1985	67.5	32.5	52.5	30.5	4.6	12.4	505.08
1990	69.3	31.0	39.3	24.5	19.9	12.3	1,907.34
1995	62.4	37.6	19.1	21.7	50.9	6.7	7,770.46
1996	65.0	35.0	16.9	21.6	53.0	6.7	8,815.47
1997	61.6	38.4	15.6	20.0	55.5	6.7	10,461.52
1998	64.0	36.0	11.5	15.6	48.2	2.0	12,190.38

Source: *Guangdong Statistical Yearbook* (*Guangdong Tongji Nianjian*) (Beijing: China Statistics Press, various issues 1978–98).

Note: Gross output 1975–80 at 1970 constant prices; Gross output 1985–90 at 1980 constant prices; Gross output 1991–94 at 1990 constant prices.

dwindled from 30% in 1978 to about 13% in 1998 (See Table 4.1). During the same period, the secondary sector grew from 46% and remained at about 50%. The tertiary sector has expanded rapidly in recent years. Over 40% of the labour force is involved in the economic activities of the secondary and tertiary sectors. These manufacturing and servicing labourers are located in the major cities or the urbanized rural areas, especially in the Pearl River Delta

(PRD) region. The domination of industrial and tertiary sectors in the economy indicates that the province has already been transformed into a modern economy through industrialization and urbanization under the economic reform policies.

Before the economic reform process began, Guangdong had never been regarded as a major region for industrial development under the planned economy. It was not until the 1970s that investment in a few heavy industries began in major cities such as Guangzhou. After China's economic reforms were introduced, capital investment in the industrial sector by township and village enterprises (TVEs) was market oriented. Most of the TVEs were engaged in light industrial processing for export. Therefore, the proportion of light manufacturing industries in Guangdong is larger than that of the national economy. In 1998, the ratio of gross output value between light and heavy industries was 64:36, while the ratio of the national industrial sector was 49:51[2] (See Table 4.2).

Since Guangdong has emphasized investment in light industries by non-state enterprises, the proportion of gross output value by state-owned enterprises (SOEs) has been decreasing over the years. In 1998, the weighting of gross output value by SOEs dropped to 15.6%, and their influence on the overall performance of the Guangdong economy is not as significant as at the national level. In other words, industrial policy and orientation of capital investment by the provincial government has had little effect on the overall industrial structure of Guangdong province.

Changes in Industrial Structure

By the mid-1980s, the major industries in Guangdong were textiles and clothing, food processing, electronics and machine manufacturing. The economy had become export-led growth oriented by foreign investment under the Open Door Policy and the special policies accorded to Guangdong province granted by the central government. In 1990, electronics and telecommunications emerged as the fastest growing industries in the province. Today, they are the leading

Table 4.3

Value Added by Major Industries in Guangdong, 1997

Industry	Value-added (100 million yuan)	%
Provincial total	2,093.89	100.0
Electronic and telecommunications equipment	284.13	13.6
Electric power, steam and hot water supply	242.53	11.6
Electric equipment and machinery	158.37	7.6
Garments and other fiber products	99.42	4.7
Chemical materials and products	97.97	4.7
Textiles	92.28	4.4
Non-metal mineral products	83.65	4.0
Transport equipment manufacturing	78.58	3.8
Metal products	76.75	3.7
Petroleum and natural gas extraction	73.73	3.5

Source: *Guangdong Statistical Yearbook 1998* (Beijing: China Statistics Press, 1999).

Table 4.4

Guangdong's Location of Industry by Gross Output Value (GOV)
(RMB 100 million)

Region	1990 GOV	1990 %	1995 GOV	1995 %	1997 GOV	1997 %
PRD	1,218	74	4,373	78	5,931	79
NE	205	12	512	9	644	9
WR	231	14	695	12	898	12
Province	1,655	100	5,581	100	7,474	100

Source: *Guangdong Statistical Yearbook 1998* (Beijing: China Statistics Press, 1998), p. 313.

industries in Guangdong. By the end of the 1980s, the Guangdong provincial government placed more emphasis on capital investment in infrastructure, such as electricity supply, highway construction, etc. Investment in infrastructure constituted a significant share of gross industrial output in the economy during the first half of the decade. Electrical machinery also performed well. Textiles, clothing and leather works remained significant export commodities too. However, food processing lost its competitive edge and moved to the less developed regions, and eventually dropped out of the ten major industries in the province (see Table 4.3).

The electronic and electrical industries in Guangdong have won major market shares in China. Those products, which dominate the domestic market, include radios (91%), cassette recorders (87%), watches (83%), cameras (77%), electrical fans (67%), colour TV sets (30%) and household refrigerators (32%). Other major products include household washing machines (16%), household ceramics (23%), detergents (11%), cement (10%), paper and paper products (11%), bicycles (22%) and electricity (9%). Most of those popular commodities are major contributors to Guangdong's industrial output. In fact, the ten major manufacturing industries have contributed up to 61.6% in terms of value-added to the industrial output of Guangdong province. At the top are new industries such as electronics and telecommunications, electrical power and hot water supply, electrical equipment and machinery. Next comes traditional industries such as garments, chemical products, textiles, mineral products, transport equipment and metal products. Petroleum and natural gas extraction are also on the list.

These major industries have been developed since the introduction of the economic reform process. Traditional industries survived and became competitive because of the development of export market demand and the transfer of manufacturing processing from Hong Kong to the PRD region.

Location of Industry

Guangdong province can be divided into three areas according to economic development: the PRD Region, the Northeast Region (NE), and the Western Region (WR).[3] The economic reforms, Open Door Policy and preferential treatment accorded to the coastal areas and Special Economic Zones (SEZs) have strengthened the investment environment of the PRD. The proportion of industrial output among the three regions has shifted from 74:12:14 in 1990 to 79:9:12 in 1997 respectively (see Table 4.4). The three regions have different geographical environments as well as varying demographic backgrounds, which added to the differentiation of the pace of development. The PRD is densely populated and has the advantage of proximity to Hong Kong. When Shenzhen and Zhuhai became SEZs with more autonomy and preferential treatment to attract foreign investment, they became industrial processing zones for the manufacturing sector that had suffered from high production costs in Hong Kong. Neither the NE nor WR regions had advantages in terms of location, connection or infrastructure to attract foreign investment.

The institutional structure regarding the exploration and exploitation of natural resources also affects the capital accumulation of different localities. For example, Shaoguan, a city in the northern region of the province, is very rich in mineral resources. Under the planned economy, natural resources were state-owned and the income generated from that industry had to be remitted to the central government. Due to its location, which is far from the cities with more vibrant economies, and lacking a good communications network, Shaoguan had to rely on its own efforts to accumulate capital investment. When the central government took away the revenue and re-appropriated funds only for the operation of existing units, the economy failed to diversify into other economic activities. The narrowly based industrial structure limited people's opportunities to find employment, thus their incomes remained below the provincial level.

Another problem is that it was impossible for a city to share its prosperity with other locations under the planned economy. There was no free trade across different cities or regions. Guangzhou was prosperous, yet its northern neighbour Shaoguan was economically underdeveloped. After 20 years of reforms, Guangdong has become the richest province. The economic statistics indicate, however, that the disparities among the economies of the three regions have become more serious. The share of industrial output of the PRD has increased from 74% in 1990 to 79% in 1997, while the shares of NE and WR dropped from 12% and 14% to 9% and 12% respectively (see Table 4.4).

Cities in the PRD region have topped the list in the ranking of gross industrial output. Guangzhou, the capital, ranks first for two reasons. Firstly, it received most of the fiscal investment funding. Secondly, it includes four prosperous cities at the county level, i.e., Huadu, Zengcheng, Panyu and Zhonghua. The Shenzhen SEZ ranks second and has become the major centre for high-tech industries in Guangdong, such as electronics and telecommunications. Foshan, which ranks third, is small in terms of geographical area and population. The entrepreneurship embodied in their people and local government officials contributed to its success. Jiagmen is relatively large in area and has become the industrial base for traditional industries in Guangdong. Huizhou has become prosperous by developing industrial processing and real estate development and ranks fifth. Zhuhai is another SEZ that has enjoyed special treatment in the reform era. Its major economic activities are tourism. It has a few large Foreign Invested Enterprises (FIEs) to boost the gross industrial output of the city. Zhongshan has aimed at the development of high-tech industries and is more balanced in its development. Dongguan has one of the most active industrial processing sectors. The only two cities with better economic performances located outside the PRD are Shantou, which is one of the four SEZs in the province, and Zhaoqing, which is a large urban city in the WR region.

Ownership and Financing of Industrial Enterprises

Guangdong is the only province in China in which collective and Hong Kong, Macau and Taiwanese FIEs have contributed most to gross industrial output. At the national level, over half of the fixed capital in industry came from the state; yet it produced only a quarter of the total output value. While in Guangdong, over half of the fixed capital came from overseas, and it contributed to half of the total output value. Obviously, SOEs are less efficient as compared with the FIEs in terms of capital productivity. State-owned public utilities and light industries have performed better compared with SOEs in other industries because those public utilities are

Table 4.5

Fixed Capital Investment and Output Value of Industries, 1997

Ownership	National (%)		Guangdong (%)	
	Capital	Output	Capital	Output
State	51	26	23	13
Collective	16	38	13	33
Individual	8	18	7	12
Foreign	14	18	21	43
HK, Macau & Taiwan	10	–	35	–
Total	100	100	100	100

Source: *China Statistical Yearbook, 1998* (Beijing: China Statistics Press, 1999).

Table 4.6

Ownership by Gross Industrial Output Value (GOV) in Guangdong

(RMB Millionε)

Year	State-owned		Collective		Others					
							FIEs		HK, Macau & Taiwan	
	No. of Estab-lish-ments	GOV	No. of Esta-blish-ments	GOV	No. of Estab-lish-ments	GOV	No. of Estab-lish-ments	GOV	No. of Estab-lish-ments	GOV
1978	6,034	13,541	15,178	5,215	–	1,209	n.a.	n.a.	n.a.	n.a.
1980	5,654	14,792	16,720	6,479	–	2,164	n.a.	n.a.	n.a.	n.a.
1985	5,717	26,513	17,768	15,428	394	8,567	n.a.	n.a.	n.a.	n.a.
1990	6,886	50,125	20,641	38,044	2,877	54,911	563	11,186	180	2,254
1995[4]	6,873	106,706	23,556	121,383	12,251	330,085	2,154	90,930	8,776	193,212
1996	6,783	108,678	23,063	139,019	13,562	396,696	2,777	132,879	7,969	208,919
1997	4,757	99,196	4,395	140,538	11,705	519,732	1,448	162,748	6,061	281,604
1998[5]	3,683	104,047	4,338	141,761	9,959	660,564	1,336	173,829	6,508	348,113

Source: *Guangdong Statistical Yearbook* (Beijing: China Statistics Press, various issues).

Note: GOV: Gross Output Value, FIEs: Foreign Invested Enterprises

government controlled and operate a monopoly, while light industries compete in a market environment.

TVEs in Guangdong

In 1998, the 721,600 TVEs in Guangdong generated 737.4 billion yuan of gross output value. The TVEs employed 9,874,000 staff and workers, accounting for 26.1% of the total employment in Guangdong.[6] About half of the TVEs are located in the PRD region. In terms of gross output value, the most productive TVEs were located in Foshan, Guangzhou, Jiangmen, Jieyang and Shantou.

The development of TVEs in the PRD region in the 1980s stemmed from policy changes in Mainland China and the constraints that Hong Kong manufacturers encountered in their export manufacturing. At the same time as Hong Kong was facing higher labour costs in its manufacturing industries, Guangdong was granted flexible policies that gave the local authorities more autonomy in decision-making, especially towards foreign investment. The autonomy was extended to the lower levels of the administration, including cities and counties. Because local officials had to seek approval from higher authorities, cadres in the counties, townships and villages tended to adopt more liberal management policies. Because taxation is levied mainly at the municipal level, the local authorities had to rely on the revenue from their business activities, then the major source of extra-budgetary funding to finance local development and support administrative expansion. The enthusiasm of local officials in attracting foreign capital for industrial processing became the breakthrough point for the industrialization of rural areas in the PRD region. The local government, in partnership with joint ventures and recipients of processing fees, successfully accumulated experience and capital to set-up and operate their own TVE businesses.

The TVEs obtained funding from local authorities and their businesses were market oriented. However, the nature of the firms in terms of control and management were similar to SOEs. Thus, the problems which plagued the SOEs also affected the performance of the TVEs, i.e., property rights problems, and extravagance and corruption by local officials and management.

According to the First National Agricultural Census in 1996,[7] about 12,880 TVEs in Guangdong province were joint ventures with foreign investors, and about 9,904 of these involved investors from Hong Kong, Macau and Taiwan. Their exports to overseas markets amounted to US$15.4 billion, which accounted for 30.5% of the

total exports of Guangdong province. The industrial structure of
TVEs is similar to that of FIEs in Guangdong. Of the 138,000 TVEs,
79% are engaged in manufacturing, 12.3% in retailing and
restaurants, whilst the rest are involved in construction, social
services and transport. Their major export commodities are light
industrial products, textiles, clothing, and arts and crafts. In the same
year, foreign investment in TVEs reached US$3.64 billion, 26.2% of
total foreign investments in the province. However, the rate of
growth has slowed down in recent years.

In China, most of the TVEs are small and medium sized. Yet in
Guangdong, many TVEs are large enterprises, or enterprise groups.
They have developed nation-wide market networks as well as
entering international markets. These enterprises manufacture
electrical fans, rice cookers, air conditioners, soft drinks, porcelain
and ceramics, feeds, toys, medicine, cement, textiles and clothing,
footwear, etc. They are at the top national rating in terms of quantity
and output value. Over 100 of them are share-holding companies
and some are listed on the Hong Kong Stock Exchange.

In the PRD region, local officials have been ambitious and have
learnt management skills from their Hong Kong partners. They have
also had the benefit of investment funding from bank loans. They
borrowed from local banks to finance investment in infrastructure
and industrial production. Under preferential policies, the local
authorities could establish their own trading companies in Hong
Kong. These companies could by-pass administrative controls in the
Mainland and seek financing from Hong Kong via their subsidiaries.
They have also become involved in real estate development, stock
market trading and other high-risk activities in Hong Kong and
overseas. However, the management of these large corporations have
cultural and educational constraints and failed to observe and
analyze the rapidly changing investment environment, such as the
Asian financial crisis, under the free market economy. They also lack
effective organization structures and good management and
accounting systems. Corruption is another problem. After the
financial crisis, many of the local authority owned corporations had
to suspend their business in Hong Kong. The Guangdong

International Trust and Investment Corporation (GITIC) and Guangdong Development Holdings Ltd. were two high-profile examples. The heavy debts they had accrued during the Asian financial crisis exposed the mismanagement as well as corruption problems of giant SOEs.

As for small and medium-sized TVEs in Guangdong, the major problem was the lack of supporting services and mechanisms from financial institutions, which hindered capital-intensive investments and long-term projects. Other problems included the lack of managerial personnel, modern management concepts and knowledge, government policy support and market information. The TVEs have many institutional problems to be resolved in order to remain competitive in a market economy.

The prospects for TVEs are not very bright, given that their competitive edge has been losing out to FIEs and private enterprises. The TVEs in Guangdong are suffering from the same problems as the SOEs in terms of management efficiency, constraints due to unclear property rights, lack of work incentives and knowledge of new markets. Some of the TVEs have been restructured into share-holding companies over the past few years. In Shunde, the municipal government privatized all but 20 public utilities, as an experiment of enterprise reform in the transition to a free market economy. At the same time, many local government officials have realized that improvements in productivity through using new technology is the right direction for TVE development.[8]

Reform of SOEs and Industrial Re-structuring

According to the Guangdong Statistical Bureau, in 1997 the corporate debts of state owned industrial enterprises in Guangdong reached a total of 211 billion yuan, which represented 29% of total industrial debts in the province.[9] Of the total debts, half of them were loans given to large-sized SOEs. The average asset-liability ratio reached 59%. In other words, more than half of the funding of capital in large-sized SOEs was loans financing, mainly from banks. Most of the SOEs with higher liabilities were capital-intensive, monopolized strategic industries, such as mineral mining and quarrying, petroleum extraction, tobacco processing, chemical fibre and gas production and supply. The major problem faced by these SOEs is that they borrowed short-term loans for long-term investment. The debts added to the heavy burden on principal and interest payments of the borrowing enterprises and subsequently caused liquidity problems.

Another factor contributing to the heavy debt burdens of large-scale SOEs is that they borrowed for long-term investments on low-yield assets. This was an error of judgment in investment decision-making by government officials who still had the "planned economy mentality". This problem will persist until government officials admit their mistakes, and respond to pressure to get rid of those loss-making assets by mergers, takeovers or bankruptcy. Only by doing so will they be able to stop the losses via fiscal subsidies or bank loans.

Small and medium-sized enterprises are mainly owned by local authorities and individuals engaged in producing light industrial products destined for both export and the domestic market. They rely on short-term borrowing as working capital. Due to economic fluctuations, sluggish market demand might affect their ability to settle debts immediately. Some of them might easily become insolvent. However, the scale of their debts has been limited because they could not borrow without collateral. Most important of all, the management was more flexible in the adjustment of their business strategies and decisions.

The Guangdong provincial government responded to the State Council on the decision to re-structure the textile industry in 1998.[10] The State Council set two targets which must be achieved by 2001; first, to dispose of 187,000 out-of-date textile spindles; and second, to dismiss 12,000 employees in the industry. In order to reduce losses and to increase the profit margins of SOEs, Guangdong adopted other measures formulated by the central government. Under the new system, SOEs are monitored and managed by a three-level organizational structure. The State-owned Assets Management Committee in the government is responsible for the monitoring of SOEs in terms of their planning and performance targets via the supervision and the management of the State-owned Assets Corporations which appoints the directors and managers of the SOEs.

Foreign Trade and Foreign Direct Investment

Foreign trade and foreign direct investment need to be discussed together because the Open Door Policy was extended only to FIEs engaged in industrial processing for exports. The average growth rate of Guangdong's exports from 1993 to 1998 was 15%, while the average growth by FIEs was 22%. The performance of FIEs has been better than that of domestic enterprises. As a result, the proportion of exports manufactured by FIEs has increased from 38% to over 50% in just five years.

The growth of exports from Guangdong has relied heavily on FIEs, mainly industrial processing by Hong Kong investors. For example, according to a survey conducted into the toy industry in 1999, Michael Goliestein, president of Toys-R-Us, said that the toy industry in China supplied about 60% of toys in the world market. In Guangdong, the industry employs more than 1.2 million workers, which is about 80% of the industry's total employment in China. Most of them are located in the PRD region, with foreign investment mainly from Hong Kong.[11] Both domestic and foreign invested exporting enterprises in Guangdong have targeted the same markets, mainly the United States, the European Union (EU), Japan, and Taiwan. Domestic firms and FIEs have become competitors in some of these markets.

After domestic enterprises in Guangdong acquired the know-how of running manufacturing and exporting businesses from joint ventures, many of them started their own operations. Their advantage was that they had a good knowledge of the domestic

Table 4.7
Foreign Trade of Guangdong

Year	Total Exports		Exports by FIEs		Total Imports		Imports by FIEs	
	Amount (US$ Mn)	Annual growth rate	Amount (US$ Mn)	% of Total Exports	Amount (US$Mn)	Annual growth rate	Amount (US$Mn)	% of Total Imports
1990	22,221.00	n a	5,481.00	24.7	19,677.00	n a	7,086.00	36.0
1993	37,394.00	11.8	14,366.00	38.4	40,950.00	26.8	19,814.00	48.4
1994	50,211.00	34.3	19,848.00	39.5	46,452.00	13.4	25,374.00	54.6
1995	56,592.00	12.7	25,759.00	45.5	47,380.00	11.4	27,451.00	57.9
1996	59,346.00	4.9	30,692.00	51.7	50,614.00	2.0	30,289.00	59.8
1997	74,564.00	25.6	36,794.00	49.3	55,556.00	9.8	32,748.00	58.9
1998	75,618.00	1.4	39,176.00	51.8	54,180.00	-2.5	31,725.00	58.6

Source: *Guangdong Statistical Yearbook, 1998 and 1999*(Beijing: China Statistics Press, 1998 & 1999).

Note: *Data based on Customs statistics*

Table 4.8
Guangdong's Exports by Country and Region
(US$ million)

Country/Region	1986		1990		1995		1998	
	Amount	%	Amount	%	Amount	%	Amount	%
Hong Kong	2,955	83.5	8,543	80.9	21,567	38.1	26,503	35.1
USA	284	8.0	403	3.8	12,793	22.6	18,951	25.1
Japan	104	2.9	288	2.7	6,489	11.5	6,930	9.2
Germany	71	2.0	117	1.1	2,166	3.8	2,686	3.6
UK	33	0.9	46	0.4	1,309	2.3	2,174	2.9
Netherlands	24	0.6	50	0.4	776	1.4	1,767	2.3
Taiwan	–	–	9	–	1,430	2.5	1,709	2.3
Singapore	84	2.4	140	1.3	1,192	2.1	1,637	2.2
France	27	0.7	45	0.4	753	1.3	1,155	1.5
Australia	16	0.4	38	0.3	587	1.0	977	1.3
Total	3,538*	100.0	10,5608*	100.0	56,592#	100.0	75,618#	100.0

Note: * Data from the Foreign Economic Relations and Trade Commission of Guangdong
   # Data from the Bureau of Customs

market. The domestic market would serve as the buffer for the excess output supply for exports. As for those FIEs which aimed at export markets, they prefer to operate on the basis of sole ownership or as majority shareholders. Yet many of them registered the enterprises as joint ventures so as to enjoy preferential treatment granted by the local authorities in terms of tax concessions and reductions, etc.

The major export commodities of Guangdong are garments, textiles, footwear, toys, plastic items, travel goods, furniture, telephone sets, watches and clocks. Each recorded an export value exceeding US$1 billion. These are also other major commodities produced by Hong Kong investors. Hong Kong is the most important business partner of Guangdong. The Guangdong provincial government recognizes the importance of maintaining close links with Hong Kong. In fact, Hong Kong and Guangdong have already integrated their production and manufacturing sectors. Together Hong Kong and Guangdong have expanded into the markets of the United States, the EU, Japan, Singapore and Australia. More than 70% of Guangdong's export commodities are sold to the US and EU markets. A high concentration in commodity items and export markets remain the characteristics of Guangdong's export manufacturing.

Foreign investment in industrial processing began in the 1980s, attracted by cheap labour and land costs. In the 1990s, China gradually opened its domestic market further to foreign investors. Many foreign investors have been smuggling raw materials for processing exported goods into China, or selling their exported products in the domestic market through their establishments for industrial processing in Guangdong. This practice caused losses to the Chinese government in lost customs duties and unfair trade practices between domestic firms. In 1998 Premier Zhu Rongji visited Fujian and Guangdong and tried to put a stop to these unlawful practices. His visit resulted in an investigation into smuggling and corruption among local government officials and customs officers, and the implementation of a depository system for importing raw materials for industrial processing. However, this measure has increased manufacturing costs, mainly in small and medium-sized enterprises from Hong Kong.

When China decided to apply for membership of the World Trade Organisation (WTO), it became clear that many administrative controls and trade restrictions would have to be

Table 4.9
Forms of Actualized Foreign Investment
(US$ million)

Form of investment	1985	1990	1995	1998
Foreign loans	289.60	441.32	1,840.28	2,044.74
Foreign direct investment	515.29	1,459.84	10,180.28	12,020.05
Equity JV	171.63	645.63	3,573.36	3,465.65
Contractual JV	335.15	453.15	4,064.61	4,547.96
Sole ownership	8.51	122.31	2,542.31	3,924.27
Compensation trade	30.56	69.11	29.05	20.85
Industrial processing	83.65	42.51	27.45	989.02
Leasing	–	10.69	23.31	1.79
Total investment	919.10	2,023.47	12,100.37	15,099.45

Source: *Guangdong Statistical Yearbook* (Beijing: China Statistics Press, various issues 1985–99).

Table 4.10
Employment in Guangdong

Year	Primary(%)	Secondary(%)	Tertiary(%)	Total
1980	70.6	16.8	12.5	23,678,000
1985	60.1	21.1	18.7	27,311,000
1990	53.0	27.2	19.8	31,181,000
1995	41.5	33.8	24.7	35,512,000
1996	40.7	33.4	25.9	36,413,000
1997	40.8	32.9	26.3	37,019,000
1998	41.1	32.1	26.8	37,839,000

Source: *Guangdong Statistical Yearbook* (Beijing: China Statistics Press, various issues 1984–99).

abolished. One of these is to allow foreign investors to operate as sole owners instead of joint ventures with Chinese parties. In Guangdong, many foreign investors actually solely own the joint ventures and the domestic parties have nominal shares only. Under the joint venture arrangement, it is easier for them to enter the domestic market.

Guangdong has an industrial policy to upgrade its industrial structure by developing its high-tech industries. Again, preferential treatment is given to investors who bring in high-tech industrial projects to the province, such as tax concessions and better access to the domestic market. However, foreign investors, including those from Hong Kong, have been slow in responding to the call from the Guangdong government.

Labour Force in the Industrial Sector

Over the past 20 years, economic development in Guangdong has created many jobs. Employment in the manufacturing sector has increased from 4 million to more than 12 million. Industrial development has not only absorbed excess rural labourers made redundant by agricultural reforms, but also created many jobs for migrants from the hinterland, such as Hunan and Sichuan provinces. Since the early 1990s, Guangdong has organized meetings for the arrangement and regulation of hiring migrant workers with eight other provinces. At the same time, the local authorities in Guangdong have recognized the status of migrant labourers and adopted more rational and flexible measures regarding the household management system (*hukou jidu*). The migrant workers can now receive housing benefits and their children can go to local schools.

Guangdong has to rely on the supply of labourers from other provinces for industrial processing. Further development in the industrial sector requires a labour force with a higher education. Guangdong has to hire management personnel, technicians and scientists from major cities in the northern provinces. The provincial authorities have incorporated the demand for migrant labourers in their planning since the early 1990s. This policy has helped Guangdong to solve the labour problem in the short run. However, in order to overcome the weaknesses in the long run, Guangdong has to increase its investment in education and scientific research. In the last ten years, the number of students enrolled in higher education has increased from 100,000 to 185,000.[12] Student enrolment in doctoral degrees has increased from 293 in 1990 to 1,539 in 1998 and in master degree programmes from 3,074 to 6,444 during the same period.[13] Funding for scientific and technological research has increased from 1.3 billion yuan in 1990 to 8.2 billion yuan.[14]

Administrative Reform of the Government

In the Ninth Five-Year Plan for 1996–2000, Shunde was chosen as a pilot city to test the policy of privatizing SOEs. The objective was to separate the management of the firm from the control of the local government. As a result, many local state firms were turned into shareholding enterprises, owned by shareholders, mainly private owners. Only public utilities and large enterprises were kept under the control of the local government. Nanhai was the first pilot city for the establishment of public administrative structure at village level. The provincial government followed the example of the State Council and cut down the establishment of the administration by half.[15] The objective was to improve the productivity and efficiency of the government. Nowadays, the Guangdong economy is mainly driven by market forces rather than by government planning.

Industrial Policy

The industrial structure of Guangdong has experienced a three-stage process over the past 20 years.[16]

(a) 1980–85: industrial processing for exports;

(b) 1986–95: infrastructure development, including investment in electricity, raw material production, transportation, communications, modernization of the agricultural sector, as well as education, science and technology, and social services;

(c) 1996–present: transformation of industrial structure and improvement in productivity.

In 1995, a policy paper produced by the State Council, entitled *Outline of National Industrial Policy*, identified six pillar industries for China's future industrial development. These six industries are machinery, electronics, communications, computers, petroleum and chemical products, automobile and construction. However, the light industries, such as toys, and textiles and clothing, which were the major contributing industries, were not mentioned in the province's strategic plan.[17] This policy has brought heavy losses to the province. For example, in order to support the automobile industry, Guangzhou has injected over a billion yuan into a Sino-French joint venture automobile assembly plant. After re-structuring by changing its partner to a Japanese firm, its output is still less than 100,000 cars per year and yet there is no market demand for the product.

Rapid changes in global technology and industrial structure have had a strong impact on political leaders in Guangdong. In a paper entitled the *Salient Points of the Industrial Policy in the Ninth Five-Year Plan* distributed within the government in 1998,[18] the government mapped out a development plan for the beginning of the twenty-first century. Energy, transportation and communications were identified as the sectors most in need of strengthening as the foundation for development. The major direction for development aims at high-technology industries, such as fibre optics and electronics, software technology, applied material technology, biotechnology, resource exploration and energy saving technology. The new industrial policy emphasizes three pillar industries; electronics and communication equipment, electrical appliances, machinery and specialized equipment manufacturing, and the petroleum and chemical industry. At the same time, the three major traditional industries, i.e., textiles and clothing, food and beverage processing, and the construction material processing industry, will be re-structured to improve the quality of their products and productivity. The tertiary industries will also be developed to support economic growth.

In an interview, Governor Lu Ruihua indicated that the provincial government would tackle two major issues; markets, and science and technology. Guangdong would develop both its domestic and overseas markets.[19] As for science and technology, the government would support the creation of software parks in Guangzhou, Shenzhen, Zhuhai and Nanhai. He forecast that by 2005, the value of high-tech industrial output would reach 600 billion yuan, accounting for 16–17% of gross industrial output, of which exports would be up to 40% of the output value.

In mid-1998, the Provincial Party Committee issued a document which outlined measures to encourage scientific research and technological development. Scientific research institutes were encouraged to co-operate with large enterprises in the development of technology for industrial production. Fifty large enterprises were selected to be technology bases in the province. The enterprises related to new technology, new products, new skill development and new equipment were granted preferential treatment in terms of tax rebates and autonomy in imports and exports. The provincial government appropriated budgetary funding of 35 million yuan for technological development and set up a risk capital fund. In agricultural research, the government allocated five million yuan for education and research. A total of 50 million yuan was appropriated for the development of science and technology.[20] The government also pledged to protect intellectual property rights. Most important of all, the fruits of scientific and technological development applied to industrial production would be well protected.[21] In mid-1999, the provincial government issued a notice on the proposals for the selection of 50 excellent large industrial enterprises and enterprise groups to build up their in-plant development centres for engineering technological research.[22]

Some cities have already reaped benefits from the new industrial policy.[23] For example, Shenzhen was the first to call for the development of high-technology industries. Many high-tech industries started their business in this border city and have become the most profitable non-state enterprises in the country, such as Shenzhen Huawei Technologies Co. Ltd. The enterprise is at the top of the list of Guangdong's 50 industrial enterprises with the largest gross output value at 24.3 billion yuan, and ranks second in terms of sales revenue at 7.1 billion yuan. Shenzhen ranks the third among all development areas in the country, after Beijing and Shanghai, in terms of gross output value and total revenue. It is not surprising that President Jiang Zemin paid an inspection visit to Shenzhen in February 2000 to show his approval.

For Guangdong province, six cities recorded remarkable achievements in high-technology development, among all the developed areas in the country. They are Shenzhen, Guangzhou, Zhongshan, Huizhou, Foshan and Zhuhai. In the coming years, Guangdong will have a new look to its industrial structure. Some scholars point out that the future development of high-tech industries requires supporting services, such as banking and finance, import and export services, transport and communications services.[24]

Conclusion

Since 1978, Guangdong province has benefited most from the economic reforms and Open Door Policy. Guangdong has successfully re-structured its economy and built a modern infrastructure for industrial development. The enterprises in Guangdong under public, collective, private or foreign ownership operate under free market conditions. The industrialization and urbanization of the PRD have turned the region into an external-oriented economic zone of China. With the benefits of foreign trade and foreign direct investment, it attracts both human resources and capital for the development of high-tech industries from other provinces as well as from abroad.

In the first ten years of the reform era, Guangdong developed its export-oriented manufacturing industries, with the support of foreign investors. Capital accumulation by industrial processing laid the foundations for investment in infrastructure to create a better investment environment. The sustained prosperity and improved income levels allowed people to save more and to seek investment opportunities in the capital market. In the Ninth Five-Year Plan, the PRD region of Guangdong has already built up the largest production base for modern industries such as electronic and communications. The liberal policies of the local authorities have provided incentives for people to develop ambitious high-tech enterprises in the PRD, especially the Shenzhen SEZ. The development of the financial sector and capital markets has also given support to the new industrial development.

During the second decade of the reform programme, Guangdong has been working hard to overcome the problem of recession.

However, new industries such as electronics and communications have blossomed. When China gains accession to the WTO, Guangdong will benefit further from increased access to international markets. The enterprises in Guangdong will have a competitive edge over the other provinces when dealing with foreign enterprises in a competitive business environment.

Guangdong has lagged behind in its investment in education and scientific R&D and lacks an efficient capital market. However, these weaknesses are being remedied by the local government. The Open Door Policy in terms of mobility of human resources and capital will help to overcome the problems in the short-run. As for the long-run, given its logistical and economic advantages, Guangdong will develop into a centre for new high-tech industrial development in the twenty-first century

Notes

1. *Guangdong Statistical Yearbook 1999* (Beijing: China Statistics Press, 1999), p. 110.

2. *Ibid.*

3. The PRD region includes Guangzhou, Shenzhen, Zhuhai, Huizhou, Dongguan, Zhongshan, Jiangmen and Foshan. The Northeast Region includes Shantou, Shaoguan, Heyuan, Meizhou, Shanwei, Chaozhou and Jieyang.The Western Region includes Qingyuan, Yangjiang, Maoming, Zhaoqing, Yunfu and Zhanjiang.

4. VAT is not included in the new statistical method.

5. Data in 1998 cannot be compared directly with that of 1997 due to changes in statistical classification.

6. *Guangdong Statistical Yearbook 1999*, *op. cit.*, p. 309.

7. *Guangdong Statistical Data* (*Guangdong Tongji Ziliao*) No. 67, 24 August 1998.

8. *Guangdong Statistical Data (Guangdong Tongji Ziliao)* No. 68, 26 August 1998.

9. *Guangdong Statistical Data (Guangdong Tongji Ziliao)* No. 59, 27 July 1998.

10. *Guangdong Gazette*, No. 20, May 1998. According to a directive from the State Council, in the three years starting from 1998, the industry has to cut down production capacity by 10 million spindles, to redeploy 1.2 million workers and to turn losses into profits.

11. Unpublished report, Chinghua University, Shenzhen "A Preliminary Survey Report on the Toy Industry in Guangdong", April 1999.

12. *Guangdong Statistical Yearbook 1999, op. cit.,* p. 549.

13. *Ibid.*

14. *Ibid.*

15. *Ta Kung Pao*, 24 February 2000.

16. *Statistical Data of Guangdong, op. cit.*

17. Guangdong Planning Commission, "The Outline Ninth Five-year Plan of Economic and Social Development in Guangdong", January 1996.

18. Guangdong Provincial Peoples' *Guangdong Gazette*, No. 1, February 1998.

19. *Ta Kung Pao*, 4 January 2000.

20. *Guangzhou Daily*, 23 February 2000.

21. Guangdong CPC, Provincial Government, "The Decision about Relying on Scientific and Technology Advancement to Improve Industrial Structure", *Guangdong CPC Gazette*, No. 16, 1998.

22. Guangdong Government, "Implementation Proposals for the Selection of 50 Excellent Large Industrial Enterprises and Enterprise Groups to set up Development Centres for Engineering Technology Research", *Guangdong Gazette*, No. 44, 1999.

23. Shenzhen Government, "Regulations on the Support for the Development of New and High Technology Industries", 1998.

24. Wang Jun, "Transformation of Industrial Structure and Economic Growth," in *Kua Shiji de Tansuo (Searches Across the Century)*, edited by Guangdong Economic and Social Development Research Centre, 1995, p. 16.

CHAPTER 5

Retrospect and Prospects of Foreign Direct Investment Inflow:

The Case of Guangdong Province

K. ZENG

Introduction

This chapter examines Foreign Direct Investment (FDI) inflows into Guangdong province in southern China. Guangdong has played an important role in China in terms of attracting FDI over the past twenty years. In the 1990s, the average annual growth rate of China's utilized FDI was 54%. In the 1990s, over one-third of the world's FDI flowing to developing countries was invested in China.[1] In 1997, China attracted US$45.3 billion in FDI. In the same year, Guangdong province accounted for over 25% of China's utilized FDI.[2] Guangdong, as the experimental province in the Open Door Policy, has occupied a significant position of utilized FDI among China's provinces since the 1980s, as shown in Table 5.1. It is also one of the most significant provinces in attracting FDI from Hong Kong, which has been one of the most prolific investors in China.

1992 was an important year for China's Open Door Policy, as economic growth was re-emphasized following Deng Xiaoping's southern tour. As a result, a large amount of FDI flowed into China's provinces. However, since then, both the internal and external

Table 5.1
Utilized FDI in China and Guangdong Province 1986–96
(US$ million)

Year	China's Total	Guangdong
1986	1874.89	722.68
1987	2313.53	602.99
1988	3193.68	957.86
1989	3392.57	1156.44
1990	3487.11	1460.00
1991	4366.34	1822.86
1992	11075.1	3551.5
1993	27514.9	7498.04
1994	33766.5	9397.08
1995	37520.5	10180.3
1996	41725.5	11623.6

Source: *Almanac of China's Foreign Economic Relations and Trade* (English version) (Beijing: China Economical Publishing House, 1989–97)

conditions of Guangdong province have changed. The province's share of the national utilized FDI in China has decreased due to the rapidly increasing amount of FDI flowing into other provinces. Although Guangdong's absolute amount of utilized FDI has increased. Another interesting phenomenon to note in terms of FDI is that Guangdong used to be the major destination for Hong Kong investors. In recent years, however, an increasing amount of Hong Kong's investments has been in other provinces in China.

Theoretical Review

FDI is the full or partial ownership of an enterprise located in one country by a foreign-investing firm. According to the US Department of Commerce, FDI is defined as "the movement of long-term capital to finance business activities abroad, whereby investors control at least 10% of the enterprise".[3] Therefore, FDI is distinguished from other types of foreign market penetration. It may take the form of a joint venture or a solely owned company. FDI is part of a company's global strategy. When the foreign-investing firm chooses to invest in a specific location, it needs to consider both internal and external factors. A foreign-investing firm's strategy is therefore viewed as how the firm responds to opportunities and threats in the new environment and deploys local resources in both tangible and intangible terms to achieve competitive advantages.

Theories relating to FDI need to answer three fundamental questions[4]:

(a) Why do firms, including multinational enterprises and small/middle size enterprises, undertake FDI?

(b) What determines where firms invest abroad?

(c) How can foreign investing firms compete successfully in an unfamiliar environment?

In the past most theories regarding FDI focused on the motivations, conditions, determinants and/or contributions. These theories try to explain why firms undertake FDI or why firms choose to invest in a particular geographic location.

One of the earliest analyses of FDI in the real (rather than monetary) sector was Hymer's ownership advantage theory.[5] Based on industrial organization theory, Hymer explained FDI as the result of market imperfections and firm-specific, or "ownership" advantages. The theory posits that foreign-investing firms possess firm-specific advantages which are not available to others on the open market. Therefore, this superior knowledge empowers the foreign-investing firm to create differentiated products/services and obtain an economic rent on its knowledge assets.

Internalization is another important approach in explaining FDI. Making use of Coase's transaction cost theory,[6] Buckley and Casson[7] arrive at "A long-run theory of the multinational enterprise" to explain FDI. They posited that firms may replace external markets with internal flows of factor services, technology and products when by doing so they can lower transaction costs. They argued that internalization generates benefits given the existence of market imperfections. Theories of ownership advantage and internalization explain FDI from different approaches. However, they have all ignored national economies. They fail to offer a full explanation of massive flows of FDI involving national economies.[8] What is needed is a new paradigm to explain FDI at both the national and enterprise level.

Dunning[9] provided an eclectic model for international production. He extends the framework repeatedly in 1981[10], 1988[11] and 1993.[12] According to Dunning's model, a firm goes to directly invest in a foreign country when three conditions are met simultaneously: (a) the firm possesses a firm-specific advantage. It is this firm-specific advantage, in some form or another, that gives investors the ability to compete with local firms; (b) the firm has the ability to internalize its firm-specific advantage. Dunning's idea of internalization relates to the firm's unique ability to insulate its firm-specific advantage from local firms. This can be achieved through trademarks and patents, but is also attainable by establishing foreign subsidiaries and enclosing the production and distribution process. If it is less beneficial for the firm to export or to lease, the firm that possesses these firm-specific advantages may internalize them through overseas production; (c) the host country has specific advantages. Once a firm has the ability and intention to internalize its firm-specific advantages, it must then consider the specific environmental factors in its target host country. Dunning summarized factors usually included in survey studies into four types: market factors, trade barriers, cost factors and the investment climate consisting mainly of political stability and policy.[13] As Dunning noted; "stress the host government's attitude to inward foreign investment, political stability, and the prospects of market growth as the most important considerations prompting foreign activities".[14] The main theories of the 1970s explain why FDI occurs. Dunning's eclectic paradigm includes the importance of a nation's specific environment. However, it does not go further to analyse the subsequent performance of FDI in an alien environment and explore the factors influencing the performance.

Another new paradigm of international competitive advantage emerged in the 1990s. Porter provided a model of national competitive advantage.[15] The central question in Porter's work is why a nation becomes the home base for successful international competition in an industry engaging in both trade and investment. His answer to this question is the so-called diamond model, which consists of four national attributes: (a) factor conditions, (b) demand conditions, (c) related and supporting industries, (d) firm strategy, structure and rivalry. In his complete system, the role of government and chance were included. The diamond model posits that industries gain competitive advantage when the national diamond is most favourable. It stresses the importance of the external environment to a firm's success. The model integrates trade and investment at the industry level where firms have a major role. However, Porter's work was based on the home of successful competitors. It is highly unlikely that his model can be directly applied to the impact of the host country on a foreign-invested firm. Moreover, other critiques (e.g., Rugman and Hodgetts[16]; Root[17]) have been offered since Porter's work was published.

Vernon's dynamic model of FDI relating to the stages of the product cycle may represent the developmental approach to explain foreign direct investment.[18] After Vernon, Kojima used a trade-increasing model to explain Japanese FDI.[19] Ozawa described Japanese investment in Asia as a result of industrial upgrading in Japan itself.[20] Dunning provided an investment-development cycle connecting the character of FDI outflows and the national stage of development of the source country.[21] This approach is typically served as a descriptive tool. Both the generality of the literature and its explanatory and predictive power are limited due to the character of their describing FDI outflows in particular countries during specific periods. This is particularly true when applying it to a region with a very different economic structure.

From the organizational perspective, the environment impacts on a firm's functioning because it does not operate in isolation. A firm has to understand the dynamics of its environment in order to adapt to changing demands from the outside world. The environment offers opportunities and threats which require a proactive move or a reactive response in a specific setting. The literature on strategic management provides an overview of the ideal procedure of a firm's strategic decision: goal setting; capability analysis; environmental analysis; competitor analysis; competitive strategy choice corporate strategy choice; strategy implementation; and performance evaluation.[22] It may conclude that environmental factors affect the decision of FDI in a specific geographic setting. Witteloostuijn summarized five types of environment based on the definition driven classification.[23] The five different types of environment are defined in terms of their reach of environmental variables: the resource pool that concerns input factors of an enterprise; the sub-environment that relates to the outside variables influencing an enterprise's specific division such as the R&D department; the task environment that is composed of the set of enterprise with which the focal enterprise has to interact directly in order to grow and survive; the aggregation environment that captures the parties outside the task environment; and the macro-environment that refers to broader societal factors influencing the performance of an enterprise as a whole. He also summarized a set of environmental factors based on the issue-driven classification. These environmental factors include economic factors, the capital market, the labour market, demographics, competition, government, supplies, technology, social-cultural factors and ecology.

There are many other perspectives explaining FDI in terms of environment. One of them is the international business perspective. Reuber identified one of the classifications of FDI as government-initiated investment (the other two are the export-oriented and market development-type FDI).[24] In Reuber's thinking, local government's incentives or subsidies may cause such kinds of FDI inflows. Following the path of the imperfect market, Calvet suggested that imperfections should include factors-markets and government-related environments, which may also explain FDI.[25] Other theories include Mundell's "factor endowment theory",[26] "location advantages", as reviewed by Caves[27] and Dunning[28], which covers many influencing factors such as production advantages (e.g., labour costs), market-related advantages, and productivity advantages (e.g., telecommunication infrastructure).

It must be understood that FDI takes place not only in an increasingly competitive and diversified global business environment, but also in a specific complex national environment. It is increasingly important to examine political, social, as well as economic factors which have profoundly influenced a foreign-invested firm. Research work needs to incorporate international ideas with new elements such as emerging environmental factors, firms' reaction and strategies, internationalized activities of entrepreneurship, etc. In Buckley's view, the theory of international business is the basis from which future theories and empirical studies should proceed.[29] He also indicated that the theory is not perfect in explaining all the issues of FDI. The external environment of the host country affects Foreign Direct Investment profoundly. This will require the integration of international business theory with other external changes and with other concepts or theories in a particular environment.

The Case of Guangdong Province

Guangdong province has practised the Open Door Policy since 1979. Guangdong, as the selected experimental province to attract foreign investment, was allowed to practise "special policies and flexible measures". Guangdong has a number of advantages in attracting FDI, but one of the most important factors is its geographical location. Guangdong is adjacent to Hong Kong. Its capital city, Guangzhou, was once the only port open to foreign traders in ancient times. Before 1979, the link between Guangdong and Hong Kong was viewed as the main channel for China to connect with the Western world. Before 1979, the Trade Fair held twice yearly in Guangzhou, was regarded as the main window for Westerners to look into China. Hong Kong, which is located in the outlet of the Pearl River Delta, served as the gate through which China's products could be shipped to the West and vice-versa. R. Mondejar viewed that; "Hong Kong has acted as China's window to the world. It also serves as the favourite drawing gate for foreigners entering China".[30] He demonstrated the importance of geographical proximity by pointing to the heavy traffic flow, both in vehicular and passenger terms, which traverse between Guangdong and Hong Kong.

The overseas Cantonese, who view Guangdong as their ancestral home, have their unique historical traits. Their language is different from Mandarin and other Chinese dialects. Compared to other Chinese people, the citizens of Guangdong have a much higher percentage of overseas relatives. During the 19th century, many Guangdong people went overseas to earn money. It is estimated that about 50% of the labourers recruited by European countries to work in Southeast Asia from 1870 to the early part of the 20th century came from Guangdong.[31] People in Hong Kong also formed part of the Cantonese migration in the 19th century. Today, Hong Kong people refer to "going home" or "returning to the mainland" when they visit Guangdong. Despite Hong Kong's status as a British colony before 1997, the English language is still very much a second language. It is estimated that around 95% of Hong Kong residents are Cantonese-speaking. Guangdong residents' overseas relations, plus their links with Hong Kong people, became one of the most important factors for Guangdong's success in attracting FDI.

Another reason put forward to explain Guangdong's success in attracting FDI is that the traditional centrally-plan economic regime in the province was comparatively weaker.[32] As a result, Guangdong was considered as an ideal experimental province to practice economic reform in the early stages of China's opening up to the outside world.

In the past twenty years, Guangdong province has gone through different stages of economic development in terms of attracting FDI. The period 1979–83 may be classified as the first stage of FDI inflow to Guangdong.[33] FDI mainly flowed into tertiary industries. The reason why tertiary industries were given priority was that Guangdong lacked basic infrastructure and its economic development level was low.[34] It was hoped that FDI could not only help improve Guangdong's economic conditions, but also help to establish basic infrastructure facilities which, in turn, would attract more foreign investors.[35] Accordingly, efforts were put into building hotels, forming taxi companies and entertainment projects that foreign investors were willing to invest in.

The second stage was 1984–90, a period when Guangdong's emphasis shifted to manufacturing industries. Small outward processing manufacturing firms began to take-off during this period, and it was estimated that a large percentage of FDI went to manufacturing firms. A very high percentage of foreign investment was from Hong Kong and Macau. Over 65% of FDI manufacturing firms were labour intensive and outward processing. Over 90% of foreign firms in Guangdong were small and middle sized. Most of the foreign-funded companies were located in the Pearl River Delta.[36] The inflow of FDI in this period was important to Guangdong's economic development and the reconstruction and upgrading of its manufacturing industries. Guangdong's economic position improved greatly during this period.

The third stage began in 1991. The Eighth Five Year Plan (1991–95) may be considered as representative of this period. Encouraged by Deng Xiaoping's southern tour in 1992 and the blueprint "to surpass the economic level of Asia's four little dragons",[37] the province attracted FDI at a much faster pace.[38] In this period, infrastructure problems, especially in transportation and electricity supply, became significant obstacles for the province to overcome. During this stage, the province put the development of infrastructure as the number one priority.[39] From 1992 to 1996, Guangdong invested a large amount of capital in infrastructure industries, including the transportation network.[40] In the 1990s, government investment was accompanied by a huge amount of foreign investment in the transportation network and other infrastructure projects.

Guangdong has enjoyed rapid economic growth in the past twenty years due to its successful and massive use of FDI. Its economic growth rate has ranked first in China for many years. The use of FDI has compensated for the shortage of capital in the province, updated its industrial technology, expanded the province's exports, created more employment opportunities and promoted tertiary industries.[41] A number of factors account for Guangdong's success in attracting FDI. One outstanding feature is that Hong Kong

Table 5.2

FDI from Hong Kong in 1990, 1995 and 1997

(US$ million)

Year	Guangdong's total	Inflow FDI from HK	Percentage
1990	1460.00	1985.00	67.46
1995	10180.30	7972.68	78.31
1997	11710.80	8431.90	72.00

Source: Statistical Bureau of Guangdong, *Guangdong Statistical Yearbook, 1998* (Beijing: China Statistics Press, 1998).

Table 5.3

Amount of Utilized Foreign Capital (including FDI)

in Cities Located in the Pearl River Delta

(US$ million)

	1996	1997
Guangdong's total utilized foreign investment	13899.43	14205.19
Guangzhou	2600.02	2740.33
Shenzhen	2422.42	2871.68
Zhuhai	908.14	1021.54
Donghuan	713.44	1166.35
Zhongshan	500.50	546.99
Jiangmen	642.62	479.97
Fushan	1159.39	1120.56
Huizhou	836.72	958.38
The percentage of inflow foreign capital in the selected cities to Guangdong's total.	70.38%	76.77%

Source: Statistical Bureau of Guangdong, *Guangdong Statistical Yearbook, 1998* (Beijing: China Statistics Press, 1998).

has been the key investor in Guangdong. Table 5.2 shows that Hong Kong has occupied the most important position in Guangdong's utilized FDI. Second, most of the FDI was in the Pearl River Delta. Statistics show that cities in this area accounted for over 70% of Guangdong's utilized FDI in 1996 and 1997 (see Table 5.3). Third, small and medium-sized firms with labour-intensive and outward-process-oriented traits hold a dominant position in the inflow FDI into Guangdong.[42]

FDI in Guangdong Province in the 1990s

In the early 1990s, nearly 40% of China's total utilized FDI flowed into Guangdong province.[43] However, many other provinces in China have also attracted an increasing amount of FDI since 1992. As mentioned earlier, 1992 was an important year for economic development in China and more opportunities emerged for foreign investors. The central government allowed a greater range of industries to use FDI, and all provinces were put on an equal footing when it came to competing for FDI. Accordingly, Guangdong needed to develop faster in order to compete successfully with other provinces in attracting FDI.

Guangdong's competitiveness has been challenged. According to the *Almanac of China's Foreign Economic Relations and Trade*, an increasing proportion of FDI has shifted to China's other provinces.[44] In 1990, the total amount of utilized FDI in Guangdong accounted for 41.87% of China's total. However, by 1997 it had fallen to 25.8 percent. This figure indicates that an increasing amount of FDI has flowed into other provinces. Guangdong used to be the major destination for investment from Hong Kong. However, in recent years an increasing amount of direct investment from Hong Kong has gone to other provinces in China.

Other phenomena relating to the inflow of FDI into the province can be seen in the 1990s. First, the completion Hong Kong's manufacturing industries move to Guangdong. Second, increasing production costs. Third, changed consumer markets. Finally, improved transportation.

The completion of Hong Kong's manufacturing industries move to Guangdong is probably the most obvious phenomenon in Guangdong's utilized FDI in recent years. Manufacturing industries used to be a major supporting pillar of Hong Kong's economy before the 1980s. Faced with rising production costs in the late 1970s and 1980s, Hong Kong needed a place with cheaper labour costs to relocate its manufacturing industries to.[45] Guangdong's opening and reform in the 1980s offered an opportunity for Hong Kong manufacturers to shift their production to a cheaper manufacturing base. Beginning from the mid-1980s, Hong Kong manufacturers transferred their low technology and labour-intensive production concerns to Guangdong, mainly to the Pearl River Delta. The large-scale transfer resulted in a massive inflow of FDI into Guangdong in the 1980s and early 1990s. The relocation process formed a "shop and factory" relationship between Hong Kong and Guangdong. Hong Kong remained the "shop" or "office" in dealing with manufacturing related activities such as product design, marketing and distribution, while the Pearl River Delta became the territory's "factory", the manufacturing base.[46] After more than 10 years of industrial transfer, the relocation process from Hong Kong to southern China was almost complete by the 1990s. Zhang Zhiyang and Fang Guangyi pointed out that Hong Kong has transferred 90% of its plastics industry, 85% of its electronics industry, 90% of its toy industry, and 90% of its watch industry to Guangdong.[47] Hong Kong has played a very important role in Guangdong's economic development. Hong Kong's manufacturing industry used to be the key factor in the province's utilized foreign investment. The completion this process means that Guangdong needs to exploit new sources of foreign capital.

Rising production costs accompanied the enormous inflow of FDI. These costs included the price of land, raw materials, energy resources, transportation and labour. However, the argument concerning the connection between rising production costs and the competitiveness of the province is not universally accepted. Arguments regarding the rise of the land and labour costs are good examples. One opinion is that "complaints about high land and labour costs may be a bargaining ploy by foreign companies eager for tax or other concessions" and "numerous surveys have shown that both domestic and expatriate labour is cheaper in Guangzhou and Shenzhen".[48]

Improvements in the transportation system is another achievement in Guangdong's development strategy. Transportation projects were given preferential treatment and government financial support. Super highways, ports and airports were all products of this policy. The improved transportation system makes it convenient not only for overseas investors to invest in Guangdong province itself, but nearby provinces such as Jiangxi and Guangxi. Similarly, other provinces have also prioritized the development of transportation to enable them to attract foreign investors and upgrade their economies.

The achievement of Guangdong's economic development can be seen in many areas. One of them is the changed consumer market. The supply and demand pole has changed since the introduction of China's reform policy. In the early 1980s, the province lacked daily necessities as a result of the centrally planned economic system. In the 1990s, however, the situation changed dramatically. Consumer goods have changed from a seller's market to a buyer's market. On the other hand, housing reform has begun and it requires urban residents to buy houses for themselves. Previously citizens were allotted houses by the local government or their working organizations.

The technological level of manufacturing in Guangdong should not be neglected. Since the introduction of the Open Door Policy, the technological level of the province's manufacturing industries has been upgraded substantially.[49] Considering the development of global technology, it is clear that the technological level of the province's manufacturing industries needs to be constantly improved. The technological level of the province's manufacturing industries today is, to the same extent, related to the inflow of FDI, especially the transfer of Hong Kong industries. The characteristics and level of technology used in the first half of the 1990s was comparable to that of Hong Kong manufacturing industries in the 1980s. Firstly, most small firms were labour-intensive. Small labour-intensive firms made up a large percentage of the total number of enterprises operating in the province.[50] Secondly, light industry played an important role. The competitiveness of Guangdong's manufacturing industries needs to be improved in the twenty-first century. The province needs to make greater efforts to attract technology-intensive and capital-intensive foreign investment.

The percentage of scientists, educated managers, technicians and skilled workers in the working population, a concept referred to as "the quality of the labour force" in Mainland China, is another factor which needs to be considered when examining the competitiveness of Guangdong. There is a great demand for high quality labour in the market. The provincial government recognizes the importance of continuously improving the quality of the labour force. Accordingly, capital has also been put to work in the educational sector.

In sum, the achievement of Guangdong province in terms of attracting FDI can be attributed to a number of factors including its geographic proximity to Hong Kong, and the special policies and flexible measures accorded to it by the central government. Environmental factors also play an important role in the case of Guangdong. These factors not only include government policy and production costs, but also socio-cultural factors, competition and the level of economic development.

Challenges in the Twenty-first Century

China's opening up to the outside world and economic reforms not only created new opportunities for the Chinese people, but also for foreign investors to enter China's huge market. Since 1992, foreign investors have been allowed to invest in a greater number of sectors such as transportation infrastructure, real estate and retail. Multinational enterprises possessing firm-specific technology and intensive capital have been encouraged to invest in China. The changing global marketplace has forced multinational enterprises to react positively in increasing competitive international business. For the purpose of gaining competitive advantage, multinational enterprises may view China as an ideal investment setting. An increasing amount of FDI has flowed into China's other provinces. This phenomenon is a result of China's economic development away from the coastal provinces and into the hinterland. As a result, Guangdong needs to attract FDI in a more efficient and effective way. On the one hand, the prospects for the province in the twenty-first century are bright. On the other hand, the province will certainly face challenges competing in the global marketplace.

Challenges in the Aftermath of the Asian Financial Crisis

In the past, Guangdong's utilized FDI relied heavily on East Asian countries, such as Hong Kong and Macau, Taiwan, Japan, the Philippines, Thailand, Malaysia, Singapore, Indonesia and South Korea. The inflow of FDI from these countries accounted for 87.93% and 86.06% of the total FDI inflows into the province in 1996 and 1997 respectively.[51] The Asian financial crisis and its aftermath cast a shadow over Guangdong's ability to attract FDI. The negative effects of the crisis can be seen from two aspects. Firstly, the amount of FDI inflow from the crisis-affected countries was reduced to a lower level because the capacity of, and incentive for, investors to operate overseas decreased. Secondly, in the aftermath of the crisis an increasing amount of FDI may flow to the crisis-affected nations. These crisis-affected countries may be strong competitors for Guangdong in terms of attracting FDI in the medium term due to their currency devaluation and lower property prices.

FDI inflow to Guangdong from crisis-affected countries in Asia such as Japan may fall even further in the first few years of the twenty-first century. This may be attributed to a number of factors. Firstly, to the currency depreciation in those affected countries. Investors from the affected countries may find that the devaluation of their currency results in increased overseas operation costs in US dollar terms. This may negatively influence their decision-making regarding ongoing operations and new investments. As a result, foreign investors may withdraw or suspend their investments, particularly those whose own countries have labour-intensive industries. The devaluation in currencies has reduced the cost differentials between producing in Guangdong and producing at home by so much that it is no longer worthwhile for investors to move their manufacturing plants to the province in the interests of competitiveness. The Asian financial crisis has severely curtailed the capacity of Asian investors to undertake outward FDI. Secondly, the lower amount of FDI inflow may also be explained by the difficult financial situation which the majority of firms located in the crisis-affected countries faced. In the aftermath of the crisis, Asian firms face such corporate financial problems as high interest rates, credit crunch at home, devaluation of stocks and difficulty raising funds abroad due to lowered credit ratings. Ongoing operations have been affected due to the shortage of cash. New overseas investment is certainly an extra burden for them.

Guangdong will also face strong competition in attracting investment from the crisis-affected countries due to their currency devaluation, lowered property prices and reduced barriers to FDI. Currency devaluation and reduced costs of production, in terms of US dollars, in the crisis-affected countries have a cause and effect relationship. Currency devaluation and falling property prices reduce the foreign currency costs of acquiring capital assets such as land, buildings, equipment, raw materials and other capital goods locally. Firms from unaffected regions require much lower amounts of capital, in terms of their home currencies, to obtain a given production capacity. Therefore, the attractiveness of the crisis-affected countries to foreign investors from Western Europe, North America, and other unaffected regions is increasing. Moreover, the depreciation of currencies is particularly important for export-oriented enterprises. As a result, some of the crisis-affected countries may become ideal sites for FDI inflow, especially the export-oriented multinational corporations. In addition, it can be seen that many local firms in the crisis-affected countries are faced with mature debt repayments, collapse of stock market prices, shortage of cash and high interest rates. Continuing with operations after the crisis in the affected countries is difficult for local firms. Those on the edge of bankruptcy become the target of overseas multinational corporations to undertake direct investments in the regions through mergers and acquisitions.

Challenges from the Shifting Key Factors Influencing FDI Location

Guangdong's economic development relies heavily on foreign investment. However, FDI location determinants are changing from those of the last few decades due to the emergence of the Knowledge Age. Guangdong will unavoidably have to face the challenges posed by the Knowledge Age and its affect on the key factors influencing FDI.

In the past, the important factors affecting the location of overseas investment included the following variables: market size and growth of host country; geographic proximity to world markets; the supply of natural resources; low production costs such as land and labour; and government policy and incentives. Investment decisions also included considerations of low costs of acquisition of production capacity, acquisition of technology and high quality infrastructure construction. However, the factors determining where firms invest abroad today are becoming more complicated, and especially reflect the rising importance of knowledge assets. It is believed that large multinational corporations are more sensitive to knowledge assets than small firms when they take location decisions about overseas investment. Poul Nyrup Rasmussen, the prime minister of Denmark, in his opening address to the conference on "Employment and Growth in the Knowledge-based Economy" claimed that; "New technologies, especially information and communication technologies, have already significantly affected the way our economies are organized and operate".[52] In *World Investment Report 1998: Trends and Determinants*, the secretary-general of UNCTAD wrote that technology and innovative capacities are "created assets" and possessing such assets is critical for competitiveness in the world economy. He wrote that; "It is precisely the rise in the importance of created assets that is the single most important shift among the economic determinants of foreign direct investment location in a liberalizing and globalizing world economy".[53]

Created assets can be both tangible and intangible according to the definition given by UNCTAD. Tangible created assets can be referred to as the stock of financial and physical assets such as communication infrastructure or marketing networks. In contrast, intangible assets refer to knowledge, in terms of the assets sought by transnational corporations, related to skills, attitudes to wealth creation and business culture, technological and innovative capacities, competencies of productivity, and relation capacities with governments and between firms, as well as the stock of information trade marks and goodwill.

The existence of created assets is increasingly important in location decision-making for overseas investments due to their ability to enhance a firm's competitiveness. Therefore, host countries possessing created assets can be more successful in attracting FDI.[54] Zimmerer, Alavi and Yasin suggested that some of the intangible assets have been translated into go/no-go decision variables in FDI.[55] These intangible assets include the education/skill level of the population, work experience with product/service, language skills, pool of technical talent, communications and information system infrastructure, cost of skilled labour/semi-skilled labour and protection of intellectual property rights. The authors pointed out that many of the traditional overseas investment decision criteria will become relevant only if the intangible considerations are positive.

In the Knowledge Age, Guangdong needs to improve the quality of its knowledge assets such as R&D capacity, the skills of its workforce, technical talents and auxiliary technology industries. Guangdong needs to acquire more knowledge assets if it is to compete with others in attracting FDI in the twenty-first century. The province may need to design, after analyzing the decision variables which firms use in searching for new investment opportunities, its competitive strategies towards the attraction of foreign investment.

The Challenge from Other Provinces

Guangdong province faces competition from other provinces and cities in terms of attracting FDI, as it is not the only place open to foreign investors. After the improvement of transportation and other infrastructures and the development of economies, other provinces have successfully attracted an increasing amount of FDI. It is reasonable to suppose that Guangdong will continuously face competition from other provinces in terms of attracting FDI in the twenty-first century.

An article entitled "Fourth Wave?" in *Business China* suggested that there have been four waves of FDI in China.[56] The first flooded Guangdong province. The second Shanghai, and the third Beijing and Tianjin. It predicted that the fourth wave of multinational investment will hit northeast China, specifically the provinces of Liaoning and Jilin because of their increasing economic growth, good industrial infrastructure and the potential huge industrial and consumer market. The article cites the examples of Canon and the Mabuchi Motor Company to demonstrate that they have attracted large foreign investors who were interested in low-cost outward processing. Recently, China has also been seeking foreign investment for its central and western regions. Provinces such as Sichuan, Hunan, Hubei and Jiangxi have successfully attracted large investors with long-term strategies in mind such, as Pepsi (in Chongqing, Sichuan province) and Citroen (in Wuhan, Hubei province). Though foreign investment in these provinces is still at an early stage, the competitiveness of these provinces in terms of attracting FDI is increasing.

There are many cities in China which have successfully attracted FDI. Two good examples are Shanghai and Beijing. Shanghai, and the surrounding provinces of Jiangsu and Zhejiang, is located in the Yangtze Delta, and has been China's important city in terms of finance, industry and commerce. From the point of view of most Chinese, Shanghai represents the engine of China's economic growth. The city's economic development also stands in the front position in China. Shanghai and its surrounding provinces have become one of the most significant locations in China for foreign investors, especially for those investing in the newly emerging sectors, due to its good quality labour force and industrial foundations.

Beijing and Tianjin are also good examples of Chinese cities which have attracted FDI. In 1996, the combined utilized FDI of the two cities reached US$3.9 billion.[57] The two cities are attractive for three reasons. Firstly, they possess a high quality labour force. The quality and quantity of university graduates in the two cities, when combined together, occupies an important position in China. Secondly, Tianjin is regarded as the one of the best manufacturing bases in China. The city not only has a sound industrial infrastructure, but also a good container port. Thirdly, the two cities and the areas between them are emerging as an important consumer and industrial market. In 1996, the combined amount of retail sales in the two cities was US$17 billion.[58] Moreover, the transport connections between Beijing and Tianjin and their surrounding regions are of a very high quality. This has not only strengthened the attractiveness of the region, but also improved the life of expatriates who lead comfortable lives there.

In sum, Guangdong province will face challenges not only from neighbouring regions, but also from the demands of the Knowledge Age. These challenges are unavoidable due to the dynamics of the global economy and the rapid development of knowledge based industries.

Suggestions

The great achievement of Guangdong's economic development and its success in attracting FDI can be attributed to a number of environmental variables. One of the most significant variables was the Open Door Policy. Other important variables include the province's geographical location, competitive production costs, resource supply and the domestic market. Today however, Guangdong faces competition from neighbouring provinces and other regions. It faces challenges posed by the Knowledge Age. Guangdong needs to upgrade its technological level, its innovative capacity, the quality of its labour force and its business environment in order to compete successfully in the next round of attracting FDI. Changes have occurred in the province's economic environment. These changes occurred not only in its external environment but also in its internal economic conditions. In order to maintain its competitiveness, Guangdong will need to address the following issues.

Cultivated Land and Utilization of FDI

Guangdong used to be regarded as rich in cheap land, and this was one of its strengths in attracting FDI. However, the amount of cultivated land is shrinking and has become a serious problem for the province's future economic development. Together with the growth of population, the cost of land has become much higher. The relationship between the protection of cultivated land and the utilizing of FDI needs to be treat carefully.

Protection of the Environment and Utilization of FDI

Ecology and the natural environment are significant determinants in the location choice of FDI. The natural environment may affect the future of Guangdong's competitiveness in attracting FDI. In the past, the overall inflow of FDI positively impacted on Guangdong's economic development. However, there are increasing concerns regarding the state of the natural environment due to low technology and polluting foreign investment projects. The polluted rivers and atmosphere serve as examples of the deteriorated state of the natural environment. It would be wiser to use FDI in a more selective way. A clean natural environment is an increasingly important factor for high-technology multinational enterprises when making investment location decisions.

The Improvement of Technology

Technology serves not only as an environmental variable in sub-environment considerations of location choice, but also a key factor for firms to acquire competitiveness in the global market. As a result of Hong Kong's manufacturing industries relocation to the province in the 1980s, many of Guangdong's manufacturing enterprises are small-scale and labour-intensive. This feature hinders the province's ability to attract capital-intensive and high-technology multinational enterprises, especially when the province has to compete with other regions. The province may improve its technological level through education and through co-operation with other provinces and Hong Kong. In sum, Guangdong needs to upgrade its technology and research capacity in order to meet the province's future needs.

Conclusion

The case of Guangdong adds to the body of FDI theory. First, FDI may be driven by government incentive policies. Second, FDI of small and medium-sized enterprises rely on, to some extent, the proximate geographic distance and the similarity of culture and language between the host and home. Third, FDI may be driven by the need to lower production costs.

Guangdong has achieved a great deal in terms of economic development and attracting FDI due to the Open Door Policy and the implementation of "special policies and flexible measures". Its geographic proximity to Hong Kong has also played an important role. Guangdong has employed outward-oriented economic development and maintained steady economic growth.

Competition and challenges cannot be avoided in the modern world, especially with the spread of modern technology. With heightening competition from other regions in China, Guangdong needs to attract FDI in a much more effective and efficient way. With challenges posed by the Knowledge Age, the province needs to upgrade its technology and the quality of its human resources. It is clear that Guangdong is no longer the only place for foreign investors to invest in China.

Guangdong's economic power is still strong after twenty years of rapid economic growth. With the co-operation of other provinces and Hong Kong and Macau, the province may be able to keep its competitive advantage and continuously serve as an ideal investment base for foreign investors.

Notes

1. *Changes Emerging in Foreign Investment into Asia*, UNCTAD Press Release (TAD/INF/2779), 2 November 1998.

2. Editorial Board, *Almanac of China's Foreign Economic Relations and Trade, 1998* (Beijing: China Economical Publishing House, 1998).

3. W. L. Hill, *International Business: Competing in the Global Marketplace* (Boston: McGraw Hill, 2000), p. 180.

4. F. R. Root, "International Trade and Foreign Direct Investment" in M. Warner (ed.), *International Encyclopaedia of Business and Management* (London: Routledge, 1996), pp. 2339–2354.

5. S. H. Hymer, *The International Operations of National Firms: a Study of Direct Foreign Investment* (Cambridge, MA: MIT Press, 1976).

6. R. H. Coase, "The Nature of the Firm", *Economica*, Vol. 4, pp. 386–405.

7. P. J. Buckley and M.C. Casson, "A Long-run Theory of the Multinational Enterprise", in P. J. A. Buckley and M. C. Casson (eds.), *The Future of the Multinational Enterprise* (London: Macmillan, 1976), pp. 32–65.

8. Hymer, *The International Operations, op. cit.*

9. J. H. Dunning, "Trade, Location of Economic Activity and the MNE: A Search for an Eclectic Approach", in B. Ohlin, O. P. Hesselnorn and P. J. Wijkman (eds.), *The International Allocation of Economic Activity* (London: Macmillan, 1977), pp. 395–431.

10. J. H. Dunning, *International Production and Multinational Enterprise* (London: Allen and Unwin, 1981).

11. J. H. Dunning, *Explaining International Production* (London: Allen and Unwin, 1988.

12. J. H. Dunning, *Multinational Enterprises and the Global Economy* (Wokingham: Addison-Wesley, 1993).

13. J. H. Dunning, "The Determinants of International Production", *Oxford Economic Papers*, Vol. 25, No. 3, 1973, pp. 289–336.

14. *Ibid.*, p. 295.

15. M. E. Porter, *The Competitive Advantage of Nations* (New York: The Free Press, 1990.

16. A. M. Rugman and R. M. Hodgetts, *International Business A Strategic Management Approach* (New York: McGraw-Hill, 1995), pp. 422–424.

17. F. R. Root, "International Trade", *op. cit.*

18. R. Vernon, "International Investment and International Trade in the Product Cycle", *Quarterly Journal of Economics,* Vol. 80, 1966, pp. 190–207.

19. K. Kojima, *Direct Foreign Investment* (London: Croom Helm, 1978).

20. T. Ozawa, *Multinationalism, Japanese Style* (Princeton, N. J., Princeton University Press, 1979).

21. J. H. Dunning, "Explaining the International Direct Investment Position of Countries: Towards a Dynamic or Developmental Approach", *Weltwirtschafiliches Archive*, Vol. 119, 1981, pp. 30–64.

22. G. Johnson and K. Scholes, *Exploring Corporate Strategy: Text and Cases* (Englewood Cliffs, NJ: Prentice Hall, 1993).

23. A. V. Witteloostuijn, "Contexts and Environment" in M. Warner, *International Encyclopaedia*, *op. cit.*, pp. 752–761.

24. G. L. Reube, *Private Foreign Investment Development* (Oxford: Clarendon Press, 1973).

25. A. L. Calvet, "A Synthesis of Foreign Direct Investment Theories and Theories of the Multinational Firm', *Journal of International Business Studies*, Vol. 12, No. 1, 1981, pp. 43–49.

26. R. A. Mundell, "International Trade and Factor Mobility", *American Economic Review*, Vol. 47, 1957, pp. 321–35.

27. R. E. Caves, *Multinational Enterprise and Economic Analysis* (Cambridge: Cambridge University Press, 1982).

28. J. H. Dunning, *Multinational Enterprises*, *op. cit.*

29. P. J. Buckley, "Problems and Development in the Core Theory of International Business", *Journal of International Business Studies*, Vol. 21, No. 4, 1990, pp. 657–65.

30. R. Mondejar, *Hong Kong and Guangdong: A Case of Organizational Integration*. (Kolu, Germany: Weltfoem Verlag, 1994).

31. Ezra Vogel, *Canton Under Communism*, (New York: Harper & Row, 1969).

32. Zeng Wuye, Zhang Yuanyuan, Guan Qixue, and Shong Zihe, *Guangdong Gaige De Jingjixue Sikao* (*The Economics of Guangdong's Reform*) (Guangzhou: Guangdong People's Press, 1993), (In Chinese).

33. See G. Yian, Z. Zhu, and P. Liu, "Analyses of Foreign Investment Development", in P. Liu (ed.), *Guangdong jing ji tou zi zong lan*, (Hong Kong: Shang Wu Yin Shu Guan, 1996, pp. 196–208.

34. See Wang Zhigang (ed.), *Zhou Xiang Shichang Jingji De Zhongguo* (*China: Going Forward to the Market Economy*) (Guangzhou, China: Guangdong Tourism Press, 1993), (In Chinese).

35. Yian et al, "Analyses of Foreign", *op. cit.*

36. *Ibid.*

37. The Asia's four little dragons refer to Hong Kong, Singapore, South Korea and Taiwan.

38. Lu Ruihua, "A Speech on the Conference of Guangdong Foreign Economy", in Economic Dept. of Zhongshan University (ed.), *Guangdong Waixiangxing Jingji Yanjiu* (*Guangdong Foreign Economic Studies*), (Guangzhou: Guangdong People's Press, 1993), (in Chinese), p. 1.

39. Lu Guoyi, "Guangdong Chanye Fazhan De Guiji Ji Taolue" (The Strategy of Guangdong's Manufacturing Industries), in Guangdong Government Development Research Centre (ed), *Guangdong Chanye Jishi* (*The Development of Guangdong's Manufacturing*), (Guangzhou: Guangdong Economy Press, 1997), (in Chinese), p. 5.

40. See Guangdong Government, *Guangdong Chanye Jishi, op. cit.*

41. Some researchers in Guangdong have studied the contributions of FDI in Guangdong and reached similar results. For example, see Liao Jianxiang. *Guangdong Duiwai Jingji Guangxi* (*Guangdong Foreign Economic Relations*), (Guangzhou: Guangdong Tertiary Education Press, 1988), (in Chinese); Wang Duo and Wen Wuhan, *Guangdong Gaige Yu Kaifang Pingshuo* (*Guangdong's Reform and Opening*), (Guangzhou: Guangdong People's Press, 1992), (in Chinese).

42. Many researchers in Guangdong have commented on this. See, for example, Zhang Zhizheng and Fang Guangyi. "Xianggang Huigui Yu Yue Gang Jingji Hezhuo Guangxi De Xinfazhan" (The Handover and the New Economic Cooperation between Guangdong and Hong Kong), (in Chinese), *Journal of Sun Yat Sen University Social Science Edition*, Vol. 38, 1998, 83–90.

43. Editorial Board, *Almanac of China's Foreign Economic Relations and Trade* (Beijing: China Economical Publishing House, 1991–96).

44. Editorial Board, *Almanac of China's Foreign Economic, op. cit.*

45. Zhang Bingshen, *Jingji Shehui Fazhan Yu Gaige Tuanshuo* (*Exploration of Economy and Society Development and Reform*), (Guangzhou: Guangdong People's Press, 1997), (in Chinese).

46. E. K. Chen, and K. W. Li, "Industry and Industrial Policy", in H. C. Y. Ho and L. C. Chau, (eds.), *The Hong Kong Economy in Transition* (Hong Kong: Asian Research Service, 1996, pp. 87–107).

47. Zhang and Fang, "Xianggang Huigui", *op. cit.*, pp. 83–90.

48. See "Contradictory Pressures", *Business China*, 19 January 1998, p. 12.

49. Wang Zhigang (ed.) *Zhouxiang Shichang Jingji De Zhongguo* (*China: Going Forward to the Market Economy*), (Guangzhou: Guangdong Tourism Press, 1993), (in Chinese), p. 84.

50. Statistical Bureau of Guangdong, *Guangdong Statistical Yearbook 1994* (Beijing: China Statistics Press, 1994).

51. *Ibid.*, 1997 and 1998.

52. OECD, *Employment and Growth in the Knowledge-based Economy* (Paris: OECD, 1996), pp. 7–9.

53. United Nations, *World Investment Report 1998: Trends and Determinants* (New York and Geneva: United Nations, 1998), p. xxx.

54. Thomas W. Zimmerer, Jafar Alavi and Mahmoud M. Yasin, "Developing Countries' Strategic Opportunities", *Thunderbird International Business Review*, Vol. 40, No. 3, 1998, pp. 315–332.

55. *Ibid.*

56. See "Fourth Wave?" in *Business China*, 19 September 1994.

57. See *China Statistical Yearbook* (Beijing, China Economical Publishing House, 1997), p. 690.

58. See "Investing in Beijing and Tianjin", *Business Asia*. 26 January 1998.

CHAPTER 6

Determinants for Foreign Direct Investment:

A Comparative Study between Guangdong and Beijing

ZHANG Xiaohe

Introduction

Foreign direct investment (FDI) in China increased dramatically in the 1980s and early 1990s, and since 1993 the People's Republic of China (PRC) has become the second largest receiver of foreign capital after the United States. Up to the end of 1998, the accumulated realized FDI amounted to US$235 billion. Foreign invested enterprises (FIEs) contributed about 50% of the country's total export value, 3.6% of tax revenue and employed 18 million workers.[1] However, FDI in China is unevenly distributed across the country. Guangdong, the largest province in hosting foreign capital, absorbed more than 26% of China's total FDI in 1998. In contrast, Beijing received less than 5% of FDI, ranking seventh place in the whole country after Guangdong, Jiangsu, Fujian, Shanghai, Shandong and Liaoning. It is interesting to note that if the Yangtze River is used to divide China into two parts, the top four largest destinations of FDI are all located south of the river, whilst the other four are all north of the river.

China is a huge country, and the business culture differs greatly from area to area, particularly between the north and south. Among Chinese, the popular perception is that the people in the south of the country are more market oriented, but lack a full understanding of Chinese culture and historical heritage, while the reverse is true for northerners. Clashes between the north and south occur frequently, not only in business strategies, advertisements and ethics, but also in different tastes and other consumer behaviour. This chapter focuses on a comparative study of the determinants of FDI in Guangdong and Beijing.

Between 1978 and 1997, FDI in Guangdong grew at an annual rate of 28%. The accumulated total number of FIEs was over 58,000. More than 80% of them were from Hong Kong and located in the Pearl River Delta and Shantou region, and about 67% were manufacturing firms.[2] There are several factors which are responsible for the concentration of foreign capital in the province. Firstly, Guangdong's geographical position, located on the southern coast and bordering Hong Kong and Macau, endows it with many advantages. For instance, sharing the same dialect and similar cultural values with its neighbours reduces transaction costs. The geographical proximity and relatively cheap labour costs allows Guangdong to attract many manufacturing firms from both Hong Kong and Taiwan. Another factor is that Guangdong is the ancestral homeland of 19 million overseas Chinese. As such, many overseas Chinese businessmen have chosen to invest in Guangdong.

Secondly, Guangdong, along with Fujian province, has benefited greatly from China's liberal economic policies, particularly those "special policies and flexible measures" which have been applied to them exclusively. These include substantial legal and administrative authority in managing the Special Economic Zones (SEZs) and FDI, and a wide range of fiscal incentives and supportive facilities. A range of preferential treatments, including a special contract regimes (submitting a fixed proportion of taxes to the central government), greater local autonomy, as well as the freedom to adopt market-oriented experiments, have all led to a surge of FDI in the province. Thirdly, preferential treatments provided by the local authorities has attracted FDI from other regions where such benefits are absent. These include measures such as tax holidays, long-term land leases, and greater flexibility in determining the variety of contract types signed with foreign partners.

Since the late 1980s, the determinants and regional allocation of FDI in China have attracted considerable attention. So far the most common explanations are based on economic factors: i.e., resource costs, external trade, infrastructure, location advantages and potential local market sizes.[3] Some scholars argue that the predominance of Hong Kong investment in China can be explained by the availability of social connections and familiarity with the idioms and practices of "Chinese capitalism".[4] It is posited that trust, friendship and personal networks are usually used in place of legal protection in China.[5]

Despite the great contribution offered by these studies, none of them has collected information at the company level, especially from foreign investors themselves. This leads to a lack of micro-level evidence to support hypothetical theories. In order to provide such evidence, the author has used a rather different methodology. An analysis of a survey of 106 FIEs conducted in the summer of 1995 is provided to establish the most important determinants and the differences among different foreign investors in different locations. This study is therefore complementary to that of Glaister and Wang,[6] and Zhang and Ho[7] in examining the determinants of FDI from the United Kingdom and Hong Kong respectively.

The rest of this chapter is set out as follows. The next section gives a brief introduction to how the survey was constructed and conducted, followed by a section outlining the main findings and a comparison of the differences of investors in different locations. Theoretical implications and conclusions are summarized in the final section.

The Characteristics of the Survey

A questionnaire was structured for interviews in Guangdong and Beijing. The interviews themselves were conducted by China's Urban

Socio-Economic Survey Organization of the State Statistical Bureau in the summer of 1995. The sampled firms were randomly chosen; half were located in Beijing and half in Guangdong. In order to examine the partner selection criteria of the investors, 90% of the total samples were made up of joint ventures, the main component of FIEs in China since the 1990s.[8] The questionnaire was written in both English and Chinese to avoid misunderstandings and misinterpretations. Each firm in the samples was first contacted and their agreement obtained before the interviews were held. A copy of the questionnaire was then sent to the firms before the interviewers called.

The questionnaire was divided into three parts. The first part required the respondents to give some background information about the firm. This included ownership details, the date of establishment, industry characteristics, size and length of the contract, etc. The second part asked questions about the motivations, objectives, and the selection criteria used to decide FDI location and partners, and is therefore the main focus of this chapter. The third part was designed to collect other information raised by the correspondents.

The sampling of the survey had several features. First, the samples covered all the major investment modes in China. The majority of the sampled firms (82%) were joint equity ventures, followed by wholly foreign-owned enterprises (9%), contractual/ co-operative joint ventures (8%) and other forms of investment (1%).[9] Second, a wide range of industries was covered. The samples vary from labour intensive light manufacturing industries (such as clothing and textiles, electronics, electrical and optical products) to capital intensive ones (such as chemical, metal and machinery). Using a previously established classification method of Chinese industries,[10] it was found that labour intensive industries accounted for 70%, while capital-intensive industries accounted for only about 9.4% of the total samples. Third, the time when the sampled firms were established was spread over the whole reform era, but mainly in the 1990s. Fourth, notwithstanding that more than half of the sampled ventures (53%) were small in size (with less than US$1 million in capital involvement) some giant conglomerates with over US$3 million capital involvement (26%) were also included. Fifth, a variety of investment means were found in the samples, including cash (65%), machinery and equipment (30%) and others (5%). Finally, the country distribution of the samples was kept in line with the general pattern of the aggregate data. Among the 106 sampled firms, 49 originated from Hong Kong and Macau, 14 from Taiwan, 15 from the United States, 16 from Japan, 7 from Europe and the remaining 15 from elsewhere in the world.

The Determinants of Foreign Investment

The key part of the questionnaire was to examine the determinants of FDI in China. Ten questions were asked with reference to the motivations, strategic and direct objectives, and location and partner selections. Resembling that of Glaister and Wang and Zhang and Ho,[11] the questions were designed on the basis of economic theory and business practice. Factors including market size, production costs, tax incentives, profitability, risks, economics of scale, availability of raw materials and technologies etc., were offered as the main determinants of FDI. The questions and results with regard to the motivations and objectives of the two groups of FIEs are summarized in Table 6.1.

The factors in the first column of the table were ranked by "weighted importance" which is the sum of the scores rated by the respondents. The managers (wherever possible the owner managers) of the firms were asked to rate the importance of the factors. If a factor was regarded as "important", a value of 2 was assigned; a value of 1 was assigned to a "relevant" factor; and a value of 0 was assigned to an "irrelevant" factor.[12] The figures shown in the three columns of Table 6.1 thus represent the average scores rated by the 53 respondents located in Beijing, 53 respondents in Guangdong and all the 106 respondents of the sampled firms respectively. The figures in brackets are the rankings of the importance scores rated by the correspondents.

Table 6.1

Motivations for Investing in China

Motivations and Objectives	Rated by FIEs in Beijing	Rated by FIEs in Guangdong	Overall Rating
Reasons for Investing in China			
Huge local market	62 (2)	75 (1)	137 (1)
Low labour costs	36 (2)	53 (2)	89 (2)
Preferential tax policies	27 (3)	30 (3)	57 (3)
High profitability	30 (2)	20 (4,5)	50 (4)
For understanding and friendship	13 (5)	20 (4,5)	33 (5)
Low cost of land and rent	10 (6)	150 (6)	25 (6)
Need to extend production scale	6 (6)	13 (7)	19 (7)
Advanced technology in China	4 (8)	8 (8)	12 (8)
Need raw materials from China	2 (9,10)	4 (9,10)	6 (9,10)
Others	2 (9,10)	4 (9,10)	6 (9,10)
Long Term Objectives			
To enter China's market	43 (1)	56 (1)	99 (1)
To achieve economics of scale	32 (2)	35 (2)	68 (2)
To expand to a third country market	31 (3)	29 (3)	60 (3)
To transfer production base to a lower cost location	21 (4)	27 (4)	48 (4)
To develop new products	13 (5)	21 (6)	33 (5,6)
To use local resources	11 (6)	22 (5)	33 (5,6)
To exchange technology	5 (7)	6 (7,8)	11 (7)
To reduce competition	3 (8)	4 (10)	7 (9)
To share risks	2 (9,10)	5 (9)	7 (10)
Others	2 (9)	6 (7,8)	8 (8)
Short Run Objectives			
To enter China's market quickly	39 (2)	71 (1)	110 (1)
To earn a profit quickly	48 (1)	39 (2)	87 (2)
To break even quickly	36 (3)	15 (4)	50 (3)
To enter a third market quickly	23 (4)	23 (3)	43 (4)
Others	4 (5)	2 (5)	6 (5)

Note: The figures shown in the three columns represent the average values of each factor rated by the 53 respondents in Beijing, 53 respondents in Guangdong and an overall rating by the 106 respondents of the sampled firms respectively. The figure in brackets is a ranking of the scores in ascending order.

As clearly shown in Table 6.1, the top four most important motivations for investing in China were (a) a huge domestic market, (b) low labour costs, (c) preferential tax policies and (d) high profitability. The two groups of foreign respondents both agreed that China's huge domestic market was the most critically important factor, and there was almost no difference in their ranking of importance in all the factors. Among the ten possible choices, the need to use China's raw materials and technology were ranked as the least important. For instance, only three firms emphasized a degree of importance in using China's raw materials, and only five firms showed an interest in using China's technology.

Referring to the long term objectives, the two groups of respondents both regarded entering China's market, exploiting economies of scale, expanding to a third foreign market (other than China) and transferring production to a lower cost location as the most important factors, while other objectives, such as developing new products, using local resources, exchanging technology, reducing competition and sharing risks etc., appeared to be less significant. Once again, there was no particular difference in ranking between respondents in Beijing and Guangdong.

The differences between the two groups of respondents can be seen more clearly in their short-run objectives ratings. Whilst respondents in Beijing ranked quick profit making as the most important goal, respondents in Guangdong gave the highest rating to entering China's local market. This suggests that when FIEs in Guangdong aimed at entering China's huge potential market, FIEs in Beijing regarded quick returns as their first priority. The reasons behind this may be that as the FIEs in Guangdong appeared to be more capital intensive and technologically sophisticated, they were able to substitute short run profits for long run market gains when China's market is heavily penetrated. In contrast, the FIEs in Beijing, due to their labour intensive nature and lack of monopolistic power, had to rely more on quick investment returns.

Location Specific Advantage

Location specific advantages have been considered as critically important for foreign investors in selecting geographical destinations for their capital and co-operative partners. In this survey, two questions referred to the selection criteria and each included ten factors for the respondents to rate. Table 6.2 summarizes the results of the scores and the ratings of the two groups of respondents.

The five major location specific advantages in choosing a particular destination were identified as, (a) the location of the

Table 6.2

Criteria for Choosing Location and Partners

Selection Criteria	Rated by FIEs In Beijing	Rated by FIEs In Guangdong	Overall Rating
Reasons for Investing in this City			
This is the location of the Chinese partner	33 (3)	51 (1)	84 (1)
Familiarity with the Chinese partner	38 (1)	35 (2)	73 (3)
Better preferential policies	36 (2)	28 (5)	75 (2)
Good infrastructure	25 (4)	30 (3)	55 (4)
Proximity to target market	16 (5)	29 (4)	47 (5)
Availability of skilled labour	12 (6)	21 (6)	34 (6)
Proximity to my residence place	8 (8)	5 (8)	14 (7,8)
Proximity to resources	6 (9)	6 (7)	14 (7,8)
Proximity to target market	9 (7)	2 (10)	11 (9)
Others	0 (10)	4 (9)	4 (10)
Reasons for Choosing this Particular Partner			
Mutual trust between managers from overseas and local managers	31 (1)	44 (2)	75 (1)
Good credit	13 (6, 7)	45 (1)	58 (2)
Capability in dealing with local Government	29 (2)	28 (4)	57 (3)
Industrial complementarity	20 (3)	34 (3)	54 (4)
Established market and distribution network	18 (4)	18 (6)	36 (5)
Reliable capital sources	10 (8)	25 (5)	35 (6)
Complementary in resources	16 (5)	11 (7)	27 (7)
Past co-operative experiences	13 (6,7)	10 (8)	23 (8)
Others	4 (9)	2 (9)	6 (9)

Chinese partner, (b) familiarity with the Chinese partner, (c) better preferential policies, (d) good infrastructure and (e) proximity to the target market. Since the location of the Chinese partner was identified as the most important factor in location decisions in both groups, it is suggested that the partner selection dominated the selection of geographical locations in our samples. This is consistent with the findings of Glaister and Wang for UK investors in China.[13] A difference in ranking reveals that respondents in Beijing appeared to emphasize familiarity with the Chinese partner, while respondents in Guangdong put more weight on the geographical location of the Chinese partner. Another difference was that whereas respondents in Beijing preferred preferential government policies, the respondents in Guangdong were more dependent on local infrastructure and proximity to the target market. This suggests that as the trailblazer of China's economic reforms, the environment for FIEs in Guangdong was more mature and healthier than for FIEs in Beijing.

In partner selection, the following five out of nine criteria were considered as the most important: mutual trust of managers between the two parties of the joint venture, capability in dealing with local governments, good credit, industrial complementarity, and established market and distribution networks. Some differences appeared between the two groups of respondents. While respondents in Beijing chose mutual trust between foreign and local managers, and capability in dealing with local governments as the two most important factors in partner selection, respondents in Guangdong chose good credit and mutual trust. This suggests that local governments played a more important role in Beijing than in Guangdong in forming Sino-foreign joint ventures.

Expectations, Problems and Prospects

The final part of the survey was designed to examine the level of satisfaction, and problems and prospects of the firms. It is clearly shown in Table 6.3 that more than half of the sampled firms (54%) were satisfied with the current situation. Of these, about 8% of the investors believed that the situation was better than expected. Among those respondents who were dissatisfied, Guangdong appeared to have a slightly larger share (45.2%) than Beijing (41.5%). This result is consistent with a recent survey released regarding multinationals in China,[14] which revealed that about 55% of multinationals surveyed had overestimated China's market.

The sources of dissatisfaction are recognized problems. The major difficulties included a poorly developed domestic market, time-consuming approval procedures, and the low quality of the labour force and management. While respondents in Guangdong appeared to be more concerned with government intervention, respondents in Beijing worried more about a poorly developed domestic market. The major investment and trade disputes included too many local charges and failures in contract fulfilment. Respondents in Guangdong complained more about local charges, while respondents in Beijing expressed a high degree of dissatisfaction with failures to fulfil contracts. In terms of prospects,

Table 6.3
Satisfaction, Problems and Prospects

	Rated by FIEs In Beijing	Rated by FIEs In Guangdong	Overall Rating
Satisfaction	(%)	(%)	(%)
As good as expected	45.2	45.2	45.2
Not as good as expected	41.5	45.2	44.6
Better than expected	7.5	7.5	7.5
Problems	Values	Values	Values
Poorly developed domestic markets	31 (1)	26 (4)	57 (1)
Time-consuming approvals	8 (8)	47 (1)	55 (2,3)
Quality of the labour force	22 (3)	33 (2)	55 (2,3)
Quality of the management	30 (3)	24 (6)	54 (4)
Frequent government intervention	19 (4, 5)	31 (3)	50 (5)
Inadequate infrastructure	13 (6, 7)	25 (5)	38 (6)
Inconvertibility of RMB	13 (6, 7)	11 (7)	24 (7)
Others	15 (4, 5)	10 (8)	25 (8)
Main Reasons for Business Disputes	Values	Values	Values
Excessive local charges	22 (2)	52 (1)	74 (1)
Fulfilment of contract	39 (1)	24 (2)	69 (2)
Employer/employee conflict	11 (3)	6 (3)	17 (3)
Prospects	(%)	(%)	(%)
Optimistic	64	70	70
Pessimistic	7	9	8
Uncertain	11	10	22

about 70% of investors were optimistic regarding the long term prospects of the Chinese economy, and expressed an interest in expanding their investments in China. Only 8% were pessimistic. Respondents in Guangdong were more confident about expanding their investments in China, suggesting that Guangdong is relatively more mature in hosting foreign capital than Beijing.

Summary and Conclusions

This chapter examines the determinants of FDI in China in general, and a comparison of FIEs in Beijing and Guangdong in particular. It is found that the main motivations for investing in the PRC were the country's huge potential market size, low labour costs and preferential governmental fiscal treatment. The main determinants for deciding geographical destination were the location of the Chinese partner, better preferential policies and familiarity with the Chinese partner. The main determinants for partner selection were mutual trust between the two parties, the Chinese partner's good credit and a capability in dealing with the local authorities. It is confirmed that the huge potential market and low labour costs were the most important factors in attracting foreign capital into China, as suggested by the literature. It also reveals that government preferential policies, which may not be easily identified by using conventional econometric approaches, also played a very important role.

According to the survey, there are more similarities than differences in the determinants of foreign investment between respondents in Beijing and Guangdong. It is found that there were no significant differences in motivations and long run strategic objectives, despite differences in short term objectives. In the long run, both groups aimed at entering China's huge potential market. In the short run, however, whilst respondents in Beijing were motivated to make quick economic returns, respondents in Guangdong attempted to enter China's local market and exploit low labour costs. This suggests that the FIEs in Guangdong were relatively more mature and longer term sighted than those FIEs in Beijing.

Differences also appeared in the selection criteria for geographical locations and partners. In location selection, whilst respondents in Guangdong emphasized good infrastructure and markets, respondents in Beijing were more concerned with the familiarity of the Chinese partner, and better preferential policies. In partner selection, whilst respondents in Beijing appreciated mutual trust and capability in dealing with local governments, respondents in Guangdong emphasized good credit. These differences, though appearing only marginal, may reflect different strategies and business cultures in hosting foreign investments between these two host destinations. In Beijing particularly, the representative of the top-down (government oriented) reform strategy in the north, foreign investors must place more weight on mutual trust or *guanxi* (personal relationship) and ability in dealing with local government than anything else. In Guangdong, a successful model of the bottom-up (market oriented) reforms of the south, economic relevance played a more important role in attracting foreign investors.

Notes

The author is grateful to Dr. Christopher Findlay of the Chinese Economies Research Centre, the University of Adelaide, and Dr. Hong Yang of the Swiss Federal Institute for Environmental Science and Technology. Financial support from the Faculty Research Grant of the Hong Kong Baptist University and the efforts of the Urban Socio-Economic Survey of the State Statistical Bureau are greatly acknowledged. Any remaining errors are my own.

1. *Yazhou Zhoukan* editorial, 18 April 1999.

2. Guangdong Statistical Bureau, *Guangdong Statistical Yearbook* (Beijing: China Statistics Press, 1998).

3. Wang Zhenquan and Nigel J. Swain, "The Determinants of Foreign Direct Investment in Transforming Economies; Empirical Evidence from Hungary and China", *Weltwirtchaftliches Archive*, 1995, pp. 359–382; Wang Zhenquan and Nigel Swain, "Determinants of Inflow of Foreign Direct Investment in Hungary and China: Time-series approach", *Journal of International Development*, Vol. 9, No. 5, 1997, pp. 695–726; Chen Chien-Hsun, "Regional Determinants of Foreign Direct Investment in Mainland China", *Journal of Economic Studies*, Vol. 23, No. 2, 1996, pp. 18–30; Liu, Xiaming, Song Haiyan, Wei Yingqi and Peter Romilly, "Country Characteristics and Foreign Direct Investment in China: A Panel Data Analysis". *Weltwirtschaftliches Archive*, Vol. 133, No. 2, 1997, pp. 313–329; Harry Broadman and Xiaolun Sun, "The Distribution of Foreign Direct Investment in China", *The World Economy*, Vol. 20, No. 3, 1997, pp. 339–362.

4. Josephine Smart and Alan Smart, "Personal Relations and Divergent Economies: A Case Study of Hong Kong Investment in South China", *International Journal of Urban and Regional Research*, Vol. 15, No. 2, 1991, pp. 216–233; Edward Gu and X. Gu, "Foreign Direct Investment and Restructuring of State-owned Enterprises", *China Information*, Vol. 12, No. 3, 1997, pp. 46–71; Simon Fan Chengze, "Why China Has Been Successful in Attracting Foreign Direct Investment: A Transaction Cost Approach", *Journal of Contemporary China*, Vol. 7, No. 17, 1998, pp. 21–32.

5. Tracy Lever, David Ip and Noel Tracy, *The Chinese Diaspora and Mainland China: An Emerging Economic Synergy* (London: Macmillan Press Ltd., 1996).

6. K. W. Glaister and Yu Wang, "UK Joint Ventures in China: Motivations and Pattern Selection", *Marketing Intelligence and Planning*, Vol. 11, No. 2, 1993, pp. 9–15.

7. Zhang Xiaohe and Ho Po-Yuk, "Determinants of Hong Kong Manufacturing Investment in China", *Marketing Intelligence and Planning*, Vol. 16. No. 4, 1998, pp. 260–267.

8. For instance, the share of the equity joint ventures had increased from accounting for about 39.9% in 1984 to 55.3% in 1995.

9. This indicates that our sample is biased to the equity joint ventures that have appeared to be more dominant in the 1990s.

10. Zhang Xiaohe, "Classification and the Dualism of China's Industries in the 1980s", *Industry and Development*, No. 34. UNIDO, 1994, pp. 61–91.

11. Zhang and Ho, "Determinants of Hong Kong", *op. cit.*

12. The assigned value follows the conventional custom of questionnaire survey and is used for comparison proposes only. See Glaister and Wang, "UK Joint Ventures", *op. cit.*, and Zhang and Ho, "Determinants of Hong Kong", *op. cit.* A arbitrarily change of the weighting scheme to (15, 10, 5) will not change the result significantly.

13. Glaister and Wang, "UK Joint Ventures", *op. cit.*

14. The Economist Intelligence Unit, *Multinational Companies in China: Winners and Losers* (Hong Kong: The Economist Intelligence Unit Limited, 1997), p. 4.

CHAPTER 7

Collective Contracts and
Chinese-style Collective Bargaining:
A Case Study of Guangdong

NGOK King-lun and Grace O. M. LEE

As a result of deepening economic reforms and the re-development of the labour market in China, labour relations within industrial enterprises have become tense, and labour disputes are getting more common.[1] The Chinese government realized that the issue of labour relations could not simply be solved by administrative measures, and hence introduced a system of collective contracts in the mid-1990s, hoping that such a system would help smooth industrial relations.[2] Moreover, the All-China Federation of Trade Unions (ACFTU) endorsed the introduction of collective contracts because it believed they would legitimize their existence in a market economy.[3] This chapter explores the implementation of collective contracts in Guangdong, and sheds light on Chinese-style collective bargaining. The chapter is divided into six sections. The first section gives a brief historical account of the progression of collective contracts from 1949 to 1994. Section two focuses on the development of collective contracts since the mid-1990s. The third section is an in-depth examination of the provisions relating to collective contracts. The implementation of collective contracts in Guangdong, with an examination of the issues and difficulties in two case studies, will be discussed in the fourth and fifth sections, followed by a conclusion.

The Development of the Collective Contract System in China

Although the practice of collective contracts only became common from the mid-1990s onwards, its origin can be traced back to the 1950s. The Common Programme (Provisional Constitution of the New China) enacted in September 1949 explicitly stated that for the benefit of both management and workers, the two parties (a trade union representing the workers) should enter into collective contracts in private enterprises (Article 32). In November 1949, the ACFTU drafted a *Provisional Regulation on the Establishment of Collective Contracts in Private Enterprises* to regulate the practice of collective contracts. The *Trade Union Law* enacted in June 1950 was the first legal embodiment which stipulated that trade unions could represent all employees in the management of production and the signing of collective contracts with management in all state-owned and collectively-owned enterprises (Article 5); and in private enterprises, trade unions could represent all employees to bargain with management, participate in labour-management consultations and enter into collective contracts with management (Article 6). Under the active promotion of trade unions, collective contracts flourished in the 1950s. However, the practice of collective contracts declined in the late 1950s as a result of Mao Zedong's criticisms and suspicions of trade union activities.

With the introduction of economic reforms and the Open Door Policy in 1978, the system of collective contracts was resurrected. In 1979, the ACFTU called for a revival of collective contracts. At the same time, individual contracts were also actively promoted. *The Procedures for Implementing the Provisions on Management of Labour in Sino-Foreign Equity Joint Ventures*, issued by the Ministry of Labour and Personnel (the predecessor of the Ministry of Labour) on 19 January 1984, stipulated that joint ventures could enter into collective contracts with their enterprise trade unions (Article 5). Article 9 of the *Regulations on the Congress of Workers and Staff Members in Industrial Enterprises Under the Ownership of the*

Whole People, enacted on 15 September 1988, stipulated that at congresses of workers and staff members, factory managers could represent management, while the chairs of the trade unions could represent employees in the signing of collective contracts or collective agreements.[4] Although collective agreements are not the same as collective contracts, they embody the shape of a collective contract and help pave the way for collective contracts.

The new *Trade Union Law* enacted on 3 April 1992 specified that "trade unions shall help and guide workers and staff members to sign labour contracts with the management of enterprises or institutions" and that "trade unions may, on behalf of workers and staff members, sign collective contracts with the management of enterprises or institutions. The draft collective contracts shall be submitted to the congresses of workers and staff members or all the workers and staff members for deliberation and approval" (Article 18). This was the first statutory provision for collective contracts since the introduction of economic reforms in 1978. However, such stipulations did not lead to the widespread adoption of collective contracts. Nevertheless, the first *Labour Law* enacted in July 1994, provided concrete regulations relating to the content of collective contracts, the procedures for setting up collective contracts, and the resolution of disputes.

The Collective Contract System in the 1990s

The 1994 *Labour Law* came into force on 1 January 1995. The Ministry of Labour (renamed the Ministry of Labour and Social Security in March 1998) and the ACFTU saw the collective contract system as a primary institutional arrangement to stabilize industrial relations, and adopted a range of top-down administrative arrangements to promote its development. On 5 December 1994, the Ministry of Labour issued a set of *Collective Contract Provisions* to regularize the signing and vetting of collective contracts, and outlined the dispute resolution mechanisms. At the same time, the Ministry of Labour issued a document called *Ideas on the Pilot Run of Collective Consultation and the Signing of Collective Contracts* to consolidate the principles, procedures and content of collective contracts. The Ministry of Labour suggested that collective contracts should begin in non-state-owned enterprises, including joint ventures and private enterprises, before being extended to other areas.[5] The trade unions and enterprises should sign collective contracts on the basis of voluntary consultation, equality and stability.

The ACFTU is another key player in promoting the collective contract system because it sees consultation on the basis of equality and collective bargaining as a tool to protect workers' interests, as well as a means to legitimize the union's existence.[6] The union will cease to exist if it cannot represent and protect the interests of workers. That is why the ACFTU fought for the provisions of collective contracts to be incorporated into the *Labour Law* at its drafting stage.[7] Once the *Labour Law* was enacted, the ACFTU decided in December 1994 to promote equal consultation and the signing of collective contracts as the crux of the law, and systematically set targets and plans to be fulfilled by their subordinate trade unions.[8]

The ACFTU saw 1995 as a trial period for the collective contract system. Joint ventures and pilot enterprises set for modern management were encouraged to adopt collective contracts. It also wished to transfer state-owned enterprises (SOEs) with collective agreements to the collective contract system. In early 1995, the ACFTU distributed a pamphlet called *Betterment of Trade Union Activities on Equal Consultation and Collective Contracts*, arguing that equal consultation and collective contracts should be applicable in all enterprises, prioritized and systematically introduced. The pamphlet also stated the principles, contents, scope and responsibility of superior trade unions, and drafted the *Methods for Trial Implementation of Equal Consultation and Signing Collective Contracts*. Incorporating the views of the Ministry of Labour, the ACFTU distributed the *Methods* through its trade union system in August 1995. The Methods consists of 42 articles separated into nine sections. *Inter alia*, it sets the principles to be adopted by trade unions in collective consultation and collective contracts; the system of equal consultation on an equal basis; the content of collective contracts, the procedures in signing collective contracts, steps to alter, dismiss and terminate collective contracts; supervision of collective contracts; the responsibilities of the trade union; and resolution of disputes arising from collective contracts.[9] The *Methods* became an important benchmark for trade unions in equal consultation and the signing of collective contracts. Under the active promotion of the ACFTU, the collective contract system was a remarkable success. By the end of October 1995, a total of 10,414 enterprises had entered into collective contracts, including 1,388 joint ventures.[10]

In summarizing the lessons of the 1995 pilot year, the ACFTU set equal consultation and collective contracts as the main priority for 1996. The following targets were set by the ACFTU: mandatory collective contracts in pilot enterprises with modern management practices; a minimum collective contract rate of 30% in foreign-owned enterprises with organized labour; another minimum collective contract rate of 30% in SOEs which had collective agreements; and identify private enterprises and township village enterprises to become pilot centres for equal consultation and collective contracts.[11]

A series of measures was adopted by the ACFTU to reach these targets. An Office for Collective Contracts was established in January 1996 to implement the collective contract system. Its aim was to promote the system of collective contracts by setting objectives and models, and conducting training and surveys.[12] In the first quarter of 1996, the Office for Collective Contracts organized two separate conferences in Hebei and Guangxi to promote a better understanding of the implementation of collective contracts in northern and southern China. After these meetings, it was decided that special offices should be established to fulfil the various targets set for collective contracts. Since then, the ACFTU has developed a quarterly reporting system to monitor the progress of the collective contacts system and to share experiences.[13] The ACFTU held three consecutive telemedia conferences in April, May and August 1996 to consolidate its experiences and raise performance demands.[14]

The ACFTU, the State Economic and Trade Commission, together with the Chinese Enterprises Directors Association, jointly issued an *Instruction on Gradual Implementation of Equal Consultation and Collective Contracts* on 17 May 1996. The *Instruction* established the consultative machinery among the three parties to work towards the promotion of equal consultation and collective contracts. To speed up the implementation of collective contracts and monitor their progress, eight secretaries of the ACFTU Secretariat led a total of nine small groups to visit 15 provinces, autonomous regions and municipalities between July and September 1996. The ACFTU Board of Chairs also conducted thematic research on collective contracts.

With encouragement from the ACFTU, federations of trade unions in 30 provinces, autonomous regions and municipalities, issued papers on collective contracts with their respective Labour Administrative Departments, and Leader Groups on Collective Contracts were established in many provinces. As a result, the collective contract system moved a huge step forward. By the end of 1996, 135,386 enterprises had entered into collective contracts, an increase of 1,201.79% when compared to 1995. The targets set by the ACFTU for 1996 had generally been met: 78 of the 100 pilot enterprises for modern management, 13,886 foreign enterprises (30.1% of foreign enterprises with organized labour), 3,270 private enterprises (61.5% of private enterprises with trade unions) had collective contracts.[15]

Apart from speeding up the implementation of collective contracts, the ACFTU enhanced the training of trade unionists in mid-1997. A *Handbook on Equal Consultation and Collective Contracts* was published, workshops were organized in Yunan, Beijing and Jiangxi, generating 1,010 collective contracts trainers,[16] and an *Instructions on Equal Consultation and Collective Contract Based on Regions and Trades* was issued to ensure that there would not be any regional and industrial differences in collective contracts.

By the end of 1997, 236,068 enterprises (including 169,235 state-owned and collectively-owned enterprises, and 23,147 foreign enterprises) had set up equal consultation and collective contract systems, covering a total of 60.72 million employees, and 46% of foreign enterprises that had trade union establishments.[17]

Judging from the number of collective contracts signed, the ACFTU has made significant progress. Interestingly, such impressive progress can partly be explained by two political reasons. The first reason is that the promotion of equal consultation and collective contract helps to legitimize the continued existence of the ACFTU through the representation of employees and protection of their interests in equal consultation and collective contracts. The ACTFU needs to change its role and functions to adapt to the economic reforms and the market economy. With the introduction of the collective contract system, the trade unions attained a standing on par with management, thus elevating their status in the enterprises and society. Thus, the ACFTU has been very active in promoting equal consultation and collective contracts. The second reason for the smooth implementation of the collective contract system has been the support of the central government. The collective contract system is regarded as a significant institutional mechanism to stabilize industrial relations, and stable industrial relations are seen as a conditioning factor for social stability. Since maintaining social stability is a top priority of the Chinese government, the collective contract system has received its full support and endorsement![18]

The Chinese Collective Contract System

The collective contract system is an institutional arrangement set up by the government to help adapt industrial relations to the market economy. The Chinese collective contract system is devised according to the *Labour Law* and its by-law, the *Collective Contract Provisions*. Its actors, content, procedures, dispute resolution, contract alteration, dissolution and termination will be discussed in the following sections.

Actors in Collective Contract

Article 33 of the *Labour Law* stipulates:

> "The staff of an enterprise as a whole may sign a collective contract with the enterprise to specify such matters as remuneration for work, working hours, rest and holidays, labour safety and sanitation, insurance and welfare, etc. The draft of the collective contract shall be submitted to the Congress of Workers and Staff Members or the entire staff for discussion and approval. The trade union shall sign the collective contract with the enterprise on behalf of the employees. If there is no trade union in the enterprise, the employees shall elect a representative to sign the collective contract with the enterprise."

Thus, the collective contract is signed between the trade union or, in the absence of a trade union, a duly elected representative of the employees. The factory managers represent the enterprise.

The Content of Collective Contracts

Article 6 of the *Collective Contract Provisions* stipulates:

> "A collective contract shall include provisions for the following: labour insurance; working hours; holidays and leave; insurance benefits; labour safety and hygiene; terms of the contract; consultation procedures for alteration, dissolution or termination of the collective contract; rights and obligations of both parties in the performance of the collective contract; arrangements for mediation when disputes arise in the performance of the collective contract; liability for breach of the collective contract; and other matters that both parties consider they must consult each other upon and that must be agreed upon."

According to the *Regulations on Collective Contracts in Enterprises in Guangdong Province*, the Provincial People's Congress added an additional item of "labour discipline" to the content of a collective contract.

Procedures in the Signing of Collective Contracts

The *Labour Law* does not specify any provisions for the procedures to be adopted in the signing of collective contracts. It was supplemented in Article 7 of the *Collective Contract Provisions*, that "the term 'collective consultation'[19] shall refer to the undertaking of discussions by a labour union or employee representative of an enterprise and the corresponding enterprise representative for the purpose of concluding a collective contract." A collective contract will therefore undergo different stages of consultation, signing, examination and promulgation. A draft collective contract can be initiated by the trade union or jointly between the trade union and the enterprise. The draft contract will then be discussed between the representatives of the two parties, the enterprise and trade union. Each party can include an equal number of representatives ranging from three to ten, and each party shall decide on a chief representative. The position of the enterprise representative shall be filled or designated by the legal representative of the enterprise; while the employee party shall be represented by the labour union. In enterprises that have not established labour unions, employees shall democratically elect representatives, and the agreement of 50% or more of employees must be obtained (Article 9, *Collective Contract Provisions*). Article 12 of the *Collective Contract Provisions* stipulates "the collective consultation process shall respect the laws and regulations, and the principles of equality and co-operation, etc. Neither party may exhibit extreme behaviour."

The draft of the collective contract is then submitted to the Congress of Workers and Staff Members for discussion and approval.[20] The trade union shall sign the collective contract with the enterprise on behalf of the employees (Article 33, *Labour Law*). Upon signing the collective contract, the enterprise involved should submit three copies of the collective contract to the labour administration authority within seven days (Article 22 of *Collective*

Contract Provisions). Articles 27 and 29 of the *Collective Contract Provisions* further stipulate that "where the labour administration authority has not advanced any objection within 15 days of receipt of the text of a collective contract, the collective contract shall go into immediate effect" and "both parties shall immediately promulgate a collective contract that has been examined by the labour administration authority to the entire membership that each party represents in an appropriate manner."

The Settlement of Collective Contract Disputes

The collective contract is legally binding on both the enterprise and employees. Where disputes arise in the conclusion of a collective contract and the two parties cannot resolve their differences through consultation, one party or both parties may submit an application in writing for mediation to the labour dispute mediation organization of the Labour Administration Authority. Even if no application has been submitted, the Labour Administration Authority may handle the mediation of the situation when it considers such action to be necessary (Article 32, *Collective Contract Provisions*). Disputes that arise in the performance of a collective contract shall be settled in accordance with the *PRC Regulations on the Handling of Labour Disputes in Enterprises* (Article 39, *Collective Contract Provisions*), namely, a party can apply to the arbitration commission for arbitration; and if a party is dissatisfied with the arbitration award, it may initiate legal action in the courts (Article 6, *PRC Regulations on the Handling of Labour Disputes in Enterprises*).

Alteration, Dissolution and Termination of Collective Contracts

The term of a collective contract shall be from one to three years. Within the stipulated term of a collective contract, representatives of both parties may review its performance. A collective contract may also be revised with the unanimous agreement of the parties after consultation (Article 16, *Collective Contract Provisions*). The collective contract shall terminate when a contract expires or when conditions for the completion of the contract, which have been agreed upon by both parties, are met (Article 17, *Collective Contract Provisions*). When, within the term of a collective contract, changes occur in the environment or the conditions under which it was concluded, which frustrate the performance of the contract, either party may submit a request to change or terminate the collective contract. When one party to a collective contract advances a request for discussion as to the implementation of or changes to the collective contract, the other party shall respond and both parties shall conduct consultation within seven days (Article 18, *Collective Contract Provisions*).

The Collective Contract System in Guangdong

As one of the first provinces to benefit from the Open Door Policy, Guangdong has the highest number of foreign enterprises. As different forms of economic investments co-exist, tensions in labour relations have intensified and labour disputes have become more frequent.[21] Hence, use of the collective contract system has been encouraged to stabilize industrial relations and protect the rights of employees. With the combined efforts of the ACFTU and the Ministry of Labour, all levels of governments and trade unions in Guangdong actively promoted equal consultation and collective contracts.

Before the enactment of the *Labour Law*, some foreign enterprises entered into collective contracts in accordance with the *Provisions on Labour Management in Sino-Foreign Equity Joint Ventures* which was enacted in 1980 by the State Council. The Guangzhou Peugeot Automobile Company, a Sino-French joint venture, set a precedent in collective contracts. A collective contract was signed between the enterprise trade unions and the enterprise on 31 March 1989. Their collective contract consists of 60 articles in 14 sections, specifying the duties and responsibilities of both parties, with explicit provisions on recruitment matters, working hours and rest days, labour insurance and employee protection.[22]

With the enactment of the *Labour Law* in 1995, the Guangdong Provincial Federation of Trade Unions followed the directives of the ACFTU by prioritizing equal consultation and collective contracts: concrete targets and plans were set, and Party and different ministries liaised closely. At the request of the Ministry of Labour and the ACFTU, the Guangdong Provincial Federation of Trade Unions and the Provincial Labour Bureau jointly issued an order to its cities and counties to identify all pilot enterprises with modern management, foreign enterprises and enterprises with collective agreements to be collective contract pilot studies. The Guangdong Provincial Municipal Federation of Trade Unions published a *Reference on Collective Contracts for Guangdong Enterprises* in June 1995 to instruct the enterprise trade unions on the signing of collective contracts.[23] In December 1995, the Guangdong Provincial Municipal Federation of Trade Unions called a meeting to recognize the achievements of the so-called "model enterprises" (*xianjin danwei*) in collective contracts. Under the active promotion of the different levels of trade unions, more than 800 enterprises signed collective contracts in 1995.[24]

The nation's first regional provision on collective contracts was also formulated in Guangdong. The *Regulations on Collective Contracts in the Enterprises in Guangdong Province* was enacted by the Provincial People's Congress on 1 June 1996 and came into effect on 1 September 1996. It consisted of 34 articles in five sections, covering the following principles: the signing and examination of collective contracts, the alteration, dissolution and termination of collective contracts; and the resolution of disputes. This regional regulation not only provided legal protection to equal consultation and collective contracts, but also reflected the Guangdong authorities' recognition of the collective contract system.[25]

All levels of Guangdong trade unions actively sought support from the local party organizations and governments. In mid-1996, all of the 21 city Party committees, municipal governments, trade unions and labour bureaux separately or jointly issued documents to "develop collective consultation and sign collective contracts". An example was the issuance of a *Notice on Equal Consultation and Collective Contracts in Enterprises in Our Cities* on 15 January 1996 by eight different departments including the Guangzhou Municipal Federation of Trade Unions, the Labour Bureau, the Economic Commission, the Foreign Economy and Trade Commission to work towards the attainment of targets set by the ACFTU for the year.[26] Furthermore, a Collective Contract Leader Group was formed, and the Guangzhou Municipal Federation of Trade Unions published and issued a *Model Collective Contract for Enterprises* to all enterprises in Guangzhou for reference.

As a result of interlocking support among the different departments, the collective contract system achieved significant progress. In 1996, a total of 4,822 enterprises (2,999 state-owned and collective enterprises, 595 enterprises changed from collective agreements to collective contracts, 1,029 foreign enterprises, 27 private enterprises and 141 pilot enterprises for modern management) entered into collective contracts, exceeding the set target by 160%.[27] As of August 1998, a total of 12,000 enterprises in the province had signed collective contracts, of which over 80% were state run enterprises.[28]

Case Studies in Guangzhou

By the end of 1997, 1,121 enterprises in Guangzhou had signed collective contracts. Among these were 909 SOEs (including 42 pilot enterprises identified for modern management practices), 185 foreign enterprises and 27 private enterprises.[29] In order to better understand the implementation of the collective contract system in Guangdong, the authors conducted a study of two enterprises in Guangzhou. Company A is an SOE selected as a pilot for modern management practices; Company B is a joint venture. The authors conducted field interviews with officials in the provincial Ministry of Labour, trade unions and the enterprises concerned in 1996, 1997 and 1998.

A Brief on the Two Cases

Company A was established in 1957. In 1995, it ranked ninety-eighth among the nation's 500 biggest enterprises, with 12,952 employees, 1.9 billion yuan in state assets, annual sales of over 3.5 billion yuan and an annual net profit of more than one billion yuan. It was chosen to be a pilot enterprise for modern management practices by the Guangzhou city government. Its first collective contract was signed on 26 October 1995. Company B is a Sino-Japanese joint venture that produces motorcycles. It started business in August 1992. In 1997, it produced 4.3 billion yuan worth of products. It employed 3,118 workers in 1998. A collective contract was signed in December 1998 in accordance with the *Labour Law*.

The Process of Signing the Collective Contracts

Company A

Company A was considered a "model enterprise" with a "model trade union". As it was chosen to be a pilot enterprise for modern management practices, it naturally became a test case for equal consultation and the collective contract system. In compliance with a request from the Guangzhou Municipal Federation of Trade Unions, a collective contract was signed. The whole process took six months, from April to October 1995.

Stage One: Preparation

In April 1995, the Party Committee, management and trade union of Company A held a meeting to decide that the trade union would be responsible for drafting a collective contract. A small group, including the lawyers of the enterprise and the Guangzhou Municipal Federation of Trade Unions, was called on to take up the task. They started off by familiarizing themselves with the business of the enterprise; the employees' views and wage demands, distribution of bonuses and welfare, and labour protection in general. To build up support for the collective contract, training sessions on the *Labour Law* and its relevant provisions were organized, and the rationale for the signing of a collective contract was publicized through various in-house publications and channels.

Stage Two: Consultation and Bargaining

Upon the production of a draft contract, the trade union began to consult the management of the enterprise. There were eight representatives from both sides. Management representatives included the General Manager (the chief signatory), the Deputy General Manager, the Deputy General Manager of Operations, the Personnel Manager, the Economics and Planning Manager, the Safety and Environment Manager, the Finance Manager, and the Director of the Company Law Office. On the trade union side was the chair (the chief signatory), the two deputy chairs, and five employee representatives. There were altogether three rounds of talks.

The bargaining process was conducted in a spirit of co-operation, respect and understanding, with the aim of reaching a consensus. To take two examples; the provision "service industries run by the union will be supported materially and financially by the enterprise" in the draft contract was amended to read "essential support will be provided by the enterprise to enable the trade union to organize its service industries under the laws"; and the clause "self learning in the form of part-time education" was amended to read "training and upgrading of technical skills will be provided by the enterprise in developing its employees". Hence, it can be seen that the trade union duly considered the suggestions raised by the management and was ready to amend the provisions in the draft contract.

Stage Three: Endorsement by the Congress of Workers and Staff Members

The draft collective contract was amended nine times during the three rounds of bargaining. The final draft was then forwarded to the Congress of Workers and Staff Members for discussion. Further amendments were made before the contract was endorsed. One example of the amendments related to the setting of quotas in the building of staff quarters. Originally, the trade unions set a quota for the building of staff quarters, but the management believed that the number to be built was subject to variables out of the enterprise's control and was hence reluctant to decide on a figure. The Congress of Workers and Staff Members were of the opinion that the enterprise should somehow show some commitment. Finally, a provision that read "the enterprise will build staff quarters according to the target set by the Congress after taking into account the productivity and efficiency considerations" was added to the collective contract.

Stage Four: The Signing of the Collective Contract

With the endorsement of the Congress of Workers and Staff Members, the collective contract was signed on 26 October 1995 by the two legal entities (the General Manager representing the enterprise and the chair of the trade union representing the employees).

Stage Five: Examination and Promulgation

Within seven days of signing the collective contract, it was submitted to the Guangzhou Municipal Labour Bureau for examination. The Labour Bureau offered no changes and the provisions in the collective contract were promulgated to all employees in the enterprise. The trade union published a special issue of its in-house newsletter and 4,000 copies of the collective contract were distributed to workers on the assembly line.

Company B

The first collective contract in Company B was signed in February 1993. It took only two weeks to finalize the contract. Its speedy completion can be attributed to three factors. First, the procedure was relatively simple when compared to the first case because joint ventures do not have a Congress of Workers and Staff Members, and hence can cut out one level of consultation. Second, the Japanese side of the joint venture was accustomed to the idea of trade unions and collective contracts, and actually provided samples of collective contracts for reference. Third, due to the fact that the enterprise was originally a state enterprise with well-organized trade unions, the new enterprise trade union was speedily formed. On the establishment of the joint venture, the enterprise issued two *Regulations on Employment and Welfare* in relation to labour discipline and provisions of wages and welfare which were detrimental to employees. Hence, the enterprise trade union intended to remedy such deficiencies with a collective contract. Its trade union paid many visits to other joint ventures to learn from their experience, and carefully studied the collective contracts of their Japanese counterparts. After two weeks of bargaining, based on the principles of mutual respect, trust and co-operation, a consensus was easily reached and the collective contract was signed on 2 February 1993.

In early 1998, the enterprise trade union decided to sign a new collective contract under the provisions of the *Labour Law* and *Regulations on Collective Contracts for Enterprises in Guangdong* because the original contract had been in operation for eight years and some terminology was found to be inconsistent with the new laws and regulations. The trade union drafted a new collective contract in July 1998, and sent it to the subsidiary assembly line trade union for discussion and amendment. Bargaining with management began in October and a new collective contract was signed in December 1998.

The Collective Contract

The collective contract of Company A consists of 61 articles in ten sections, covering recruitment and selection of employees; wages; working hours and breaks; rest days; social insurance and welfare; training; safety and health; trade union status; consultation, alteration, dissolution of contract; and resolution of disputes. Most of the provisions were copied from the *Labour Law* and the *Trade Union Law*, with very few provisions arising from bargaining (namely, the provisions on training and the building of quarters discussed above). The collective contract of Company A paid more attention to training, stating that the enterprise should spend not less than 1.5% of its total wage bill on training. However, contentious issues like "annual leave with pay" and "salary increases"[30] were not specified. On the issue of annual leave pay, Article 21 of the collective contract stipulated "the enterprise will follow the paid annual leave system and specifics in accordance with the nation's regulations". In fact, the State Council has never set any specifics on annual leave. On the issue of salary increases, Article 12 of the collective contract stipulated that "distribution of salary will follow the productivity of the year, and its annual distribution will be approved by the Congress of Workers and Staff Members", without specifying the details.

The 1993 collective contract for Company B consisted of 61 articles in nine sections, covering the status of trade unions; duties and responsibilities of both parties; work hours and rest periods; rest days; wages and allowances; social security and welfare; training; safety and health. Its 1998 collective contract contains 41 articles in seven sections. Its provisions are very similar to that of the old contract, but the terminology falls very much in line with official documents (the old one borrowed terminology from the Japanese contract). The most contentious issue in the old contract was on paid annual leave. The enterprise management only agreed to provisions on paid annual leave for section heads or above. After several rounds of bargaining, the trade union succeeded in winning the provision of paid annual leave according to the length of service. Workers are generally entitled to between five and eight days of paid annual leave, while section heads or above can enjoy 12 days. Such provisions were also transferred to the new collective contract. The issue of salary increases was neither addressed in the old nor the new contract. The new contract merely stipulated that "the enterprise will raise the employees' salary in relation to the productivity of the enterprise and living standards of society, details of which will be decided in accordance with other provisions". Nevertheless, some provisions of the collective contract reflect certain Japanese organizational culture, such as, "late marriagers will get 200 yuan on their first marriage" and "a fixed sum will be given to each employee on his or her birthday".

The Outcome of Collective Contracts

The chairman of the enterprise trade union in Company B had a positive opinion on the effect of the collective contract, stating "the signing and implementation of the collective contract regulates the direction and activities of the trade union, effectively protects the legal rights of employees, co-ordinates labour-management relations, motivates workers, and enables better development of the enterprise".[31] The deputy general manager of the enterprise also shared such positive views. He believed that "with the implementation of the collective contract, labour relations have been stabilized, productivity has risen, employees' welfare has improved, and the morale of staff raised".[32]

Yet, the trade unionists in Company B pointed out three preconditions for the success of collective contracts. First, the trade union must have a good image and effective authority. Their union leader was a veteran unionist appointed by headquarters, and there were four full-time union cadres. Twenty subsidiary unions were formed in different sections, covering 97% of all employees. They have also developed a good system to maintain close relations with their members. Union cadres are committed to four compulsory visits to members when they are sick, suffering from difficulties, absent from work for three days or hospitalized. Second, the trade union must be protective of employees' rights. According to their collective contract, the trade union has a big say on issues relating to overtime arrangements, employee dismissal etc. In Company B, applications for overtime work in the different sections need to be endorsed by the chair of the trade union, otherwise the manager dare not approve the application. On the other hand, the trade union is strict on employee discipline and management. Third, the trade union must assist the enterprise to improve its business. The trade union in Company B viewed that they had two basic roles: to protect the legal rights of employees, and to educate and mobilize the employees to fulfil their productive duties. Since they see the latter role as more crucial, they invite suggestions from employees on ways to improve efficiency and quality. The list of Party members was publicized by the trade union so that all employees can monitor their performance and exert pressure for good performance. The company's products were actively promoted through various channels that the trade union had access to. There have never been any industrial disputes, and the unionists even promised their Japanese partner that they would not resort to any industrial action. As a result of this co-operation, the Japanese manager had great trust in the union, assigned a company car for the chairman of the trade union, awarded the trade unionists benefits equal to that enjoyed by company executives, cared about the workers' livelihood, and participated and supported cultural entertainment and sports activities organized by the trade union. Hence, the collective contract system can be considered very successful in this particular enterprise.

Discussion

Under the active promotion of the ACFTU, many enterprises have established a system of equal consultation and collective contracts. Yet Warner and Ng opined that what is emerging inside China "is a system not yet comparable with the Western collective bargaining tradition".[33] Bearing in mind that such rapid developments were the result of "top-down" initiatives, in the form of targets being set for subsidiary trade unions, the whole process resembles a kind of "campaign". Even though the targets set for the quantity of collective contracts have been achieved, there is still the question of effectiveness. In practice, the provisions of most collective contracts were copied from the "model" contract and regulations set by the state, with very few provisions set as a result of bargaining. Success in consultation and its resultant collective contract depends, to a large extent, on the goodwill of the enterprise, particularly in cases of non-state enterprises (foreign and private enterprises). Company B in our case analysis was agreeable to the idea of a collective contract, but many other investors are not willing to enter into such an agreement.

Various reasons account for this reluctance. First, the signing of collective contacts is not compulsory under Chinese law. The *Labour Law* only stipulates that trade unions "may" sign a collective contract with the enterprise (Article 33, *Labour Law*), without specifying an obligation on the part of the enterprise. Second, there is no right to strike, and the laws even require consultation in line with the regulations and there can be no "extreme behaviour" (Article 12, *Collective Contract Provisions*). Third, the establishment of trade unions in the enterprises is not only subject to the consent of the enterprise but it must also provide the financing. Very often, the chair of the trade union is from senior management and other mangers are also trade union members, thus limiting the bargaining power of trade unions. As the salary and benefits of the unionists are derived from the enterprise management, they cannot possibly bargain with management on an equal basis.

Under such circumstances, the enterprise trade unions can only defend the employees in a marginal sense, and the interests of the enterprise will always come first. This idea was clearly demonstrated by the trade union in Company B when their trade unionists explained that employees must be mobilized to perform and contribute to productivity if the trade union were to protect the interests of employees. In simple terms, employees' interests are still subordinated to that of the enterprise.

Notes

1. Anita Chan, "The Emerging Patterns of Industrial Relations in China and the Rise of Two New Labour Movement," *China Information*, Vol. IX, No. 4, 1995; S. M. Karmel, "The Neo-authoritarian Dilemma and the Labour Force: Control and Bankruptcy vs. Freedom and Instability', *Journal of Contemporary China*, Vol. 5, No. 12, 1996; Zhu Ying, "Major Changes Underway in China's Industrial Relations", *International Labour Review*, No. 12, 1995; Ngok King Lun, *The Formulation Process of the Labour Law of the People's Republic of China: A Garbage Can Model Analysis*, unpublished PhD thesis, City University of Hong Kong, 1998.

2. Ministry of Labour, "Guanyu jinxing jiti xieshang qianding jiti hetong shidian gongzuo de yijian" (Ideas on the Pilot Run of Collective Consultation and the Signing of Collective Contracts), 1994, reprinted in Guangzhou Municipal Federation of Trade Unions, *Learning Materials on Equal Consultation and Signing of Collective Contracts*, Volume I, 1996.

3. Wei Jianxing, "A Speech at the Second Meeting of the 12th Executive Committee of the ACFTU", *Gongren Ribao (Workers' Daily)*, 13 December 1994, p. 1. Wei is the Chairman of ACFTU. Zhang Dinghua, "Jiji tuixing pingdeng xieshang he jiti tanpan zhidu" (Actively Implementing the Equal Consultation and Collective Bargaining System), 1995, reprinted in Guangzhou Municipal Federation of Trade Unions, *Learning Materials on Equal Consultation and Signing of Collective Contracts*, Volume II, 1996.

4. A collective agreement is a production contract which serves to shift the director's responsibility for production to be shared by all employees.

5. Ministry of Labour, "Guanyu jinxing jiti xieshang", *op. cit.*

6. Zhang Dinghua, "Jiji tuixing pingdeng xieshang", *op. cit.*

7. Anita Chan, "The Emerging Patterns of Industrial Relations", *op. cit.* Ngok King Lun, *The Formulation Process, op. cit.*

8. *Chinese Trade Unions Yearbook*, (Beijing: Zhonghua quanguo zonggonghui, 1995).

9. Guangzhou Municipal Federation of Trade Unions, *Learning Materials, op. cit.*

10. *Chinese Trade Unions Yearbook*, (Beijing: Zhonghua quanguo zonggonghui, 1996), p. 36.

11. *Gonghui Gongzuo Tongxun (Trade Union Activity Bulletin)*, No. 4, 1996, p. 21.

12. *Zhongguo Gongyun* (Chinese Labour Movement), No. 8, 1998, p. 9.

13. *Chinese Trade Unions Yearbook*, (Beijing: Zhonghua quanguo zonggonghui, 1997), p. 57.

14. *Zhongguo Gongyun* (Chinese Labour Movement), *op. cit.*, p. 9.

15. *Chinese Trade Unions Yearbook*, (Beijing: Zhonghua quanguo zonggonghui, 1997), p. 57.

16. *Zhongguo Gongyun* (Chinese Labour Movement), *op. cit.*, p. 9.

17. *Ibid.*

18. Li Qi, "A Survey on the Collective Bargaining System in the State-Owned Enterprises in China", paper submitted to the International Forum on Labour Law and Social Security, Peking University, 26–28 October 1998.

19. The ACFTU uses the term "equal consultation" instead of "collective consultation" adopted by the Ministry of Labour. According to the *Methods for Trial Implementation of Equal Consultation and Signing Collective Contracts* issued by the ACFTU, it sees equal consultation as a separate system that

co-exists with collective contracts. Article 3 of the *Methods* stipulates "equal consultation is a business dialog between the enterprise trade union representing its workers and the enterprise on matters relating to the legal rights of employees." The Collective contract is only one of the consequences resulting from equal consultation.

20. The requirement of the collective contract to be endorsed by the Congress of Workers and Staff Members has raised some discussion in Mainland China. The collective contract is a product of collective bargaining between the trade union and its enterprise, resulting in a legal relationship. On the other hand, the Congress of Workers and Staff Members is involved in democratic management of the enterprise and its members may differ from that of the trade union.

21. Chen Bing, "A Speech at the Discussion Meeting on Propagating and Implementing the Regulations on Collective Contracts in the Enterprises in Guangdong Province", internal memo, Guangdong Provincial Federation of Trade Unions, 1996.

22. Guangzhou Municipal Federation of Trade Unions, *Learning Materials Vol. II*, *op. cit.*

23. *Ibid. Vol. I.*

24. Guangdong Nianjian Bianjiweiyuanhui, *Guangdong Yearbook* (Guangzhou: Guangdong nianjian chubanshe, 1996).

25. Chen Bing, "A Speech", *op. cit.*

26. Guangzhou Municipal Federation of Trade Unions, *Learning Materials Vol. I*, *op. cit.*

27. Guangdong Nianjian Bianjiweiyuanhui, *Guangdong Yearbook*, (Guangzhou: Guangdong nianjian chubanshe, 1998), p. 468.

28. Field interview in Guangzhou, September 1998.

29. Guangzhou Nianjian Bianjiweiyuanhui, *Guangzhou Yearbook 1998*, (Guangzhou: Guangzhou nianjian chubanshe), p. 83.

30. Li Qi, "A Survey", *op. cit.*

31. Field interview in Guangzhou, September 1998.

32. *Ibid.*

33. Malcolm Warner and Ng Sek Hong, "The Ongoing Evolution of Chinese Industrial Relations: The Negotiation of 'Collective Contracts' in the Shenzhen Special Economic Zone", *China Information*, Vol. XII, No. 4, 1998, pp. 1–20.

CHAPTER 8

Labour Disputes in Shenzhen:
The Origin, Pattern and
Settlement of Workplace Conflicts

SUN Wen-bin

Introduction

Since the introduction of economic reforms in 1978, labour relations in China have experienced fundamental changes. In essence, these are that the degree of commitment among the state, enterprises and workers is weakening, and the interest relations between enterprises and workers are separating, if not totally conflicting. These changes were initially set in motion by two policy changes. One was the introduction of the Open Door Policy which led to the rapid growth of joint ventures, and more recently, Foreign Invested Enterprises (FIEs) on the Mainland, especially in the coastal cities and Special Economic Zones (SEZs). Thus, a new type of labour relations, i.e., capital-labour relations, was added to the general picture of industrial relations in China. The other policy change was the reform of State Owned Enterprises (SOEs), especially the reform of labour contracts beginning in 1986, and the enlargement of managerial autonomy in the 1990s. Therefore, the character of labour relations has changed from mainly state job assignment to contractual terms between labour and enterprises. With such changes, labour disputes and industrial unrest cases have increased rapidly. Table 8.1

Table 8.1

Labour Dispute Arbitration Cases in China, 1994–97

Year	Total no. of cases	Growth rate compared with previous year (%)	Total no. of workers involved	Percentage of enterprises which won the cases	Percentage of workers who won cases	SOEs	Growth rate compared with previous year (%)	J.V. and FIEs	Growth rate compared with previous year (%)	Other Types of enterprise	Growth rate compared with previous year (%)
1994	17,962	54.5	77,794	20.0	47.8	8,763	37.8	2,974	75.4	6,225	N/A
1995	33,030	73	122,512	19.7	51.8	13,689	56	5,740	93	13,601	118
1996	48,121	45	189,120	20.3	51.0	16,390	20	10,083	76	21,648	59
1997	71,524	48.6	221,115	16.2	56.6	18,546	13.2	23,244	131	29,743	37.4

Source: *Laodong zhengyi chuli yu yanjiu* (*Labour Disputes: Settlement and Research*) No. 4,
1995; No. 5, 1996; No. 5, 1997; and No. 4, 1998.

summarizes the official data available on registered arbitration cases of labour disputes on the Mainland as a whole, and indicates the scale and scope of workplace conflict.

From Table 8.1, several conclusions can be drawn. First, the total number of arbitration cases has been growing year by year. In fact, since the restoration of the labour dispute settlement system in 1987, the number of registered arbitration cases has grown rapidly.[1] The number of cases in 1997 was 12.8 times greater than that of 1987. Second, the percentage of workers who won their arbitration cases was usually much higher than that of enterprises. Also in terms of bringing disputes to arbitration, it was mostly the workers who had to rely on arbitration for fair treatment and justice. Taking 1997 as an example; among the 71,524 cases, 2,752 were appealed by enterprises to arbitration, only 3.8% of the total. The majority of cases (96.8%) were taken to arbitration by workers. This situation demonstrates the disproportional bargaining power of enterprises over workers in China today. Third, the number of dispute cases occurring in joint ventures and FIEs soared, both in terms of the actual increase by cases and the growth rate. This indicates that the geographic location of these cases was very uneven among the provinces, as most of the cases occurred in the eastern part of the country, particularly the coastal areas. For a number of years, most of the dispute cases have occurred in Guangdong province. According a report entitled *1997 Labour Dispute Settlement and Analysis*, Guangdong had the highest number of dispute cases at 24,704; Chongqing had 6,713 cases; Shandong 4,336; Shanghai 4,141; Fujian 3,628; Beijing 2,653; Zhejiang 2,496; and Jiangsu 2,493.[2] Fourth, it should be noted that before a dispute case goes to arbitration, it must first be mediated at the enterprise level and then at various administrative levels of the Labour Bureau. This means that among the total number of labour disputes, only a few go to arbitration. Therefore, the actual number of dispute cases is much bigger than the figures suggested in Table 8.1. However, due to the nature of the subject, more detailed data is unavailable.

This chapter examines the basic characteristics of labour disputes in Shenzhen, the cradle of economic reforms and the showcase of Guangdong. The data collected reflects the changes in labour relations in China during the transition from a planned economy to a "socialist market economy". This chapter is divided into three sections. Section one provides some background information on Shenzhen, the fieldwork undertaken and the data collected. Section two concentrates on the dispute cases, their origin, pattern and settlement. Finally, section three discusses the implications of the dispute cases in the context of institutional arrangements and workers' choices.

The Labour Bureau in Shenzhen and the Collected Data

The city of Shenzhen consists of two parts; namely, the SEZ, in which the municipal government is located, and the Baoan and Longgang districts, which lie beyond the formal boundaries of the SEZ. Before 1979, Shenzhen was a small agricultural town with a population of just over 300,000. Among these workers, 29,000 were employed in either state-owned or collectively owned enterprises. By 1998, the population of Shenzhen had risen to 3.5 million, 2.8 million of which were without a *hukou* (household registration).[3] Due to China's rising population, loss of cultivable land in the

Table 8.2
Complaints Related to Labour Issues by Letter and by Person to the Shenzhen Labour Bureau, 1990–95

	1990	1991	1992	1993	1994	1995
By Letter	1,275	1,479	2,340	2,129	4,350	3,825
By Person	2,134	2,181	2,620	5,031	15,172	33,470

Source: Office for Receiving Petition Letters and Appellant under Labour Relations Supervisory Brigade, Shenzhen Labour Bureau.

Figure 8.1
The Simplified Procedures for Settling Labour Disputes

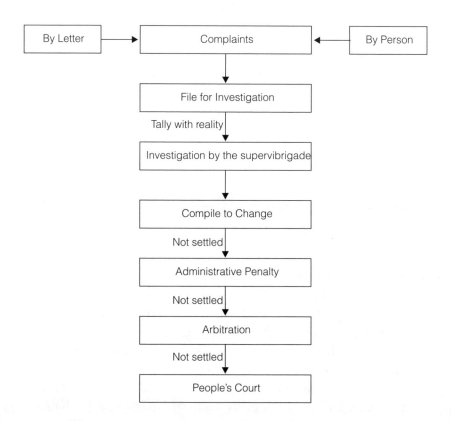

countryside, and the growing income gap between urban and rural areas, Shenzhen became an attractive place for surplus rural workers to seek jobs in. Therefore, abundant labour supply has been one of the characteristics of the labour market in Shenzhen.

The Labour Bureau in Shenzhen is mainly in charge of issues relating to employment, wages and social welfare, labour insurance, labour training, workers safety and labour protection, labour contract, and labour dispute and arbitration. The scope of the bureau is constantly expanding as it faces an increasing number of problems relating to labour issues.[4] The bureau consists of two divisions; the administrative division and the institutional division. In 1993, with reported dispute cases on the increase, each division set up a special branch to directly handle labour disputes; the Labour Dispute Arbitration Committee in the administrative division, and the Labour Relations Supervisory Brigade in the institutional division. These were the first of their kind in China. Subsequently, sub-branches at district and township levels were also established. Each administratively lower branch has to report to a higher one. The purpose of these branches is to "protect the legal rights of labour and to maintain the stability of society".[5] It is worth noting that under the Labour Relations Supervisory Brigade, different functions have been assigned to various offices. For instance, one office receives petition letters related to labour issues; another receives people who complain about or report labour disputes and ask for advice. There is also an office to investigate enterprises as soon as a complaint is received. Visiting in person and collecting petition letters are the most popular ways for workers to express their discontent in China today.

Generally speaking, one of the most striking aspects of the Chinese legal system is the unusual amount of importance placed on mediation in various dispute resolutions. This is partly due to the traditional perception of lawsuits, which are considered as shameful, but also because of the influence of communism on the Mainland for the last 50 years, whereby everything was controlled by the state or through the plan. Therefore all problems are viewed as administrative rather than legal disputes. Thus these problems should be resolved by mediation and co-operation rather than arbitration and

Table 8.3

Complaints by Letter and by Person between January 1996 to June 1996: By Industry

Reason	Salary Embezzled or Delayed	Over-time Work	Refuse to Sign Labour Contract	Consult Labour Law	Terminate Labour Contract without a Reasonable Reason	Compen-sation for Industrial Injury	Fail to Pay Social Insurance Premium	Other Matters	Total
Construction	242	6	2	15	8	43	1	44	361
Garment	230	41	3	11	15	7	3	49	359
Electronics	101	21	3	19	13	7	4	43	211
Service & Entertainment	190	7	11	15	31	7	2	52	315
Machinery	29	2	2	1	5	3	-	3	45
Trade	27	5	7	6	15	3	-	20	83
Others	412	51	32	85	89	55	10	277	1011
Total	1,231	133	60	152	176	125	2	488	2,385
% of Total	51.61%	5.57%	2.51%	6.37%	7.37%	5.24%	0.84%	20.46%	100%

Source: Office of Receiving Petition Letter and Appellant under Labour Relations Supervisory Brigade, Shenzhen Labour Bureau.

Table 8.4

Profile of Sample Enterprises

ID	Starting Year	Location	Ownership	Products	Number of Employees
1	1986	SEZ	China-US	PCs & computer components	1,510
2	1988	Outside the SEZ	Hong Kong-China	Bicycles	1,700
3	1983	SEZ	Japan	Audio products	900
4	1997	Outside the SEZ	Japan	Electric motors	700
5	1992	SEZ	China-US	PC hard disks	1,879
6	1987	SEZ	China-US-Japan	Glass	530
7	1986	Outside the SEZ	Hong Kong	Toys	700
8	1984	SEZ	Hong Kong	Electric wires	670
9	1993	Outside the SEZ	China-Australia	Shoes	1,049
10	1985	SEZ	China-Singapore	Power adapters	1,020

litigation. In other words, the emphasis on mediation often results in the settlement of labour disputes with an administrative nature. Figure 8.1 provides the simplified procedures for settling labour disputes.[6] All disputes are expected to be resolved at the enterprise level. An in-house mediation committee is formed to handle labour disputes as soon as they occur in most of the SOEs. Members of this committee are appointed by a workers' representative congress, the enterprise management and trade unions. For a joint venture, especially those small-sized ones, trade unions and in-house mediation committees are often not established. In such circumstances, petition letters and appellants are the major resources available to the workers. The system of labour dispute resolution uses a three-stage process — mediation, arbitration and litigation. As mentioned previously, it is rare for a dispute to move beyond the mediation stage to arbitration and then litigation, although the number of cases which do so is increasing.

The data employed in this chapter comes mainly from two sources. One is our own case studies which were undertaken collectively during the summer of 1997. The other is a databank of filed complaint cases by letter (petition letters) and by person (filed complaints) to the Shenzhen Labour Bureau during the period January 1996 to June 1996 (Table 8.3). With regard to the case studies, a profile of the enterprises visited is given in Table 8.4.

On average, two days were spent in each of the enterprises. The first meetings were with the top managerial and trade union staff to trace the development of the enterprise and to identify existing problems at the managerial level. Afterwards, individual interviews were conducted with representatives of the middle-level management and the workers. The interviews included questions regarding personal background, income, working and living conditions, previous experience of labour disputes, attitude towards work and authority, enterprise management and workers' participation in the decision-making process. In addition, a questionnaire survey was conducted in these enterprises with more detailed questions on the above mentioned aspects of labour relations. The questionnaire survey produced a data set of 399 valid responses. These studies provided the basic information of employment relations in joint ventures and FIEs, and workers' major short-term and long-term concerns. Although few dispute cases had actually occurred in these enterprises, the case studies contributed to the analysis and understanding of the pattern of labour disputes in general.

Table 8.5
Registered Arbitration Cases, 1994

		Collective Disputes	
No. of Registered Cases	**No. of People Involved**	**No. of Cases**	**No. of People**
19,098	77,794	1,482	52,637

Arbitration Cases Involving Contractual Workers by Reason of Dispute

No. of Cases	8,367
No. of Contractual involved Workers	41,532(Total)
Reasons of Dispute Related to:	
Dismisal	4,159
Resignation	812
Payment	263
Social Insurance Wellfare	2,078
Working Condition	208
Other Reasons	847

Arbitration Cases Involving Regular Workers by Reason of Dispute

No.of Cases	7,331
No. of Regular Involved Workers	20,155
Reasons of Dispute Related to:	
Dismissal	2,143
Resignation	1,011
Payment	1,843
Social Insurance Welfare	1,566
Working Condition	96
Other Reasons	672

Arbitration Cases Involving Other Types of Workers

No. of cases	3,074	No. of workers	9,357

Source: *Zhongguo laodong nianjian 1992-1994 (China Labour Yearbook 1992–1994)* (Beijing: China Labour Publishing House, 1994) p. 774.

The databank of the petition letters and the data of the complaint cases explain the reasons behind the disputes. Attached to each petition letter there is also a record of the suggested method of resolving the dispute from officials of the Labour Relations Supervisory Brigade. As mentioned earlier, due to the emphasis on mediation to resolve labour disputes, these petition letters and complaint cases, compared with arbitration cases, give a more accurate reflection of what is happening in reality. A general overview of the data is offered in Table 8.5. For the sake of convenience and later comparison, detailed information on the 1994 and 1997 registered arbitration cases is given in Tables 8.6 and 8.7.

The Labour Dispute Cases: Origins, Patterns and Settlements

The Origins of the Labour Disputes

Based on our interviews, there are three main reasons why migrants left their homes to seek work in Shenzhen. First, there is not enough land or jobs in the rural areas for young people. The workers we interviewed were mostly from Hunan, Sichuan, Shandong and Guangdong provinces. Second, the migrants hoped to earn more money in Shenzhen. Third, the migrants wanted to learn new skills for future self-enhancement. In contrast to workers in the SOEs, migrant workers in joint ventures and FIEs are usually young, educated and female, who have come from rural areas without a *hukou*. This means that they are not entitled to permanently settle down in Shenzhen. For those working outside the SEZ, the majority of them have not been able to go to the SEZ since a border pass is required to enter it. Consequently, the degree of workers' integration with the local society is very low. Second, the workers are poorly unionized and have no participation in the decision-making process with regard to their living and working conditions. The capital-labour relations in these enterprises manifest a very clear "us and them" feeling. Third, the labour turnover rate is quite high in

Table 8.6
Detailed Information Regarding 1997 Arbitration Cases by Reason and Types of Ownership

	Pay-ment	Insuran-ce and Welfare	Labour Protection	Training	Changing Contract	Dismis-sal of Contract	Termi-nate Contract	Others
Total cases	29,150	11,995	2,256	533	2,992	10,337	5,344	8,197
SOEs	5,624	3,931	624	220	735	3,869	1,127	2,416
Urban Collectively-owned Units	3,689	2,904	420	103	434	1,698	628	1,225
Rural Collectively-owned Units	2,111	1,969	464	28	127	649	147	470
Joint Ventures and FIEs	10,811	1,147	285	128	1,267	3,026	2,933	3,647
Jointly-owned and Share-holding Units	4,390	1,068	252	17	245	437	239	679
Private Enterprises	845	353	84	18	90	311	112	273
Individual Economy	496	231	86	8	18	44	26	65
State Institutions and Organizations	303	264	24	10	37	219	85	177
Other Ownership Units	867	98	16	4	39	58	47	77

Source: Zhongguo laodong nianjian 1998 (China Labour Yearbook 1998), (Beijing: China Labour Publishing House, 1998), p. 513.

Table 8.7
Dissatisfaction Expressed by Workers: By Different Scales of Enterprises

Scales Item	Below 50	50–100	100–300	300–500	Above 500
Frequency of expressing dissatisfaction	42	59	177	85	248
% of total	34.7%	20.6%	28.8%	20.9%	20.8%
Total responses	121	192	524	407	1,365

Source: Research Team of Survey on Moral State of Shenzhen Migrant Labour, "Report Two: The Development and Improvement of Healthy and Harmonious Labour Relations", 1996 an unpublished research report, p. 7.

joint ventures, especially in those small- and medium-sized enterprises located outside the SEZ. This suggests that the way workers express their discontent is rather passive, i.e., leaving their jobs rather than fighting for their own long-term interests.

Tables 8.4 to 8.7 reveal the origins of labour dispute cases in Shenzhen and in China as a whole. It is important to note the following differences by comparing these three tables. First, comparing Tables 8.5 and 8.6; the cause of disputes has showed a tendency of shifting from the implementation of labour contracts and handling dismissals to the distribution of payment and issues relating to social insurance and welfare. This indicates the changes of interest relations between enterprises and workers. Or more precisely, the sense of unified interest between enterprises and their workers, particularly in the SOEs, is gradually weakening. In joint ventures and FIEs, the concept of unified interest between enterprises and workers does not exist. Thus, disputes over payment and other economic interests are more likely to occur.

As shown in Table 8.4, disputes related to delayed and embezzled payments amount to more than half of the complaint cases in Shenzhen. The petition letters explain that migrant workers often borrow money to travel from their hometowns to Shenzhen, hoping to earn some money for future living or for paying family debts. Therefore, delayed payments often make their lives very difficult and cause a great deal of anxiety to the workers as well as their families. However, it is important to point out that the disputes over payment are not often triggered by trivial payment differences. In reality, it is only when disputes over delayed wages reach a serious extent that workers complain to the Labour Bureau. The following is a typical case:

> "We have been working in this factory for eleven months. However, we have only been paid for four months… Despite this, we haven't stopped working for a moment. In addition, we have been working for more than 12 hours a day without a day off. Our boss has never said anything to us about the delayed wages. It is almost as if nothing has happened. The boss seldom comes to the factory now. His relatives are helping to manage the factory. Several days ago, the boss removed some of the production equipment without any explanation. … Due to the delayed wages, many of us are penniless now. We can hardly meet our basic survival needs. In the meantime, the dormitories we are staying in will be closed due to delayed payment."[7]

The other major cause of disputes relating to payment is the embezzlement of workers' salaries. For those enterprises with high labour turnover rates, it often happens that the workers do not get their salaries for the first month (or two months in some enterprises). Instead they are given food tokens by the enterprise so they are able to survive for the first few months. When the workers have worked for the enterprise for two months, they receive their first month's salary. Consequently, it makes it difficult for the workers to leave their jobs if they are not satisfied with the pay or working conditions. Disputes over payment often occur when workers decide to leave but cannot get their full payment for the work they have already done. Enterprises normally give all kinds of excuses to embezzle the wages of workers who are leaving.

Embezzlement of workers' salaries frequently coincides with the problem of excessive overtime work, which is another root of many disputes in Shenzhen. Despite the codification of the *Labour Law* on working hours (eight hours per day, five days per week), rest days and holidays, and on the payment of overtime work, only a few joint ventures and FIEs comply with the law. According to our interviews, workers often have to work more than 12 hours per day. For those enterprises working on seasonal orders, workers often cannot have a day-off for several months. Due to financial considerations, workers do not often complain about overtime work (see Table 8.4). Thus, when disputes over overtime payment occur, it is the unfair payment which brings about the disputes and complaints.

According to the *Labour Law*, overtime payment should be 150% of the normal basic wage, 200% of work at weekends, and 300% for work done during public holidays. In reality, workers are only paid the basic wage for overtime work, and sometimes even less than the normal rate. There are all kinds of ways to reduce overtime payments. Some enterprises increase the intensity of the eight-hour shift. Some enterprises create very complicated ways of calculating overtime wages, which workers do not fully understand and cannot complain about. Some enterprises simply do not acknowledge the overtime work at all.

Related to the issue of overtime work, there were no arbitration cases over overtime work 1994 or 1997. Whereas there are cases in the Shenzhen data (see Table 8.4) specifically complaining about excessive overtime work, the number of cases is small compared with those over payment. It demonstrates the sheer intensity of work in some enterprises in Shenzhen. According to an investigation carried out by the Guangdong All-China Federation of Trade Unions in 1994, all 127 FIEs which were investigated had excessive working hours. At one enterprise, workers had not had any time off for eleven months.[8] Our interviews show that this was not a unique case at all.

Second, comparing the above three tables, there are fewer cases in the Shenzhen data related to labour contracts, be it related to the implementation, formation or termination of labour contracts. This can be understood from two aspects. One is that the economic power between enterprises and workers is so unbalanced. With an abundant labour supply, workers have limited bargaining power with enterprises. Therefore a labour contract for workers is usually a document simply listing their remuneration, working position and duties. In addition, a lot of contractual terms in the labour contracts are rather general and abstract. Thus, when there is a dispute, it is very difficult to use the contract as a method to resolve the dispute. In our survey, a large number of workers (81.5%) said that they had not signed contracts with their enterprises. In fact, they probably did have a collective contract with the enterprises signed by a representative, but they themselves did not know the details of the labour contract.

The other aspect is that even for those who have signed the labour contract by themselves, some of the contractual terms are quite irrelevant. For instance, given that most of the migrant workers are young and unmarried, there are less disputes over special protection for female workers during pregnancy or maternity leave, which is one of the main causes of disputes in SOEs.

Third, in the 1994 arbitration cases, there were disputes relating to working conditions.[9] In both the 1997 arbitration cases and the Shenzhen data, there were no disputes regarding working conditions.

In fact, dangerous working conditions, particularly in joint ventures and FIEs, has become a subject of serious concern in recent years. The well-known case of the Zhili Toy Factory fire, a Shenzhen joint venture owned by Hong Kong investors, claimed the lives of 87 workers. Again, this is not a unique case either. The list of severe factory fires in Guangdong is a long one: 93 killed and 160 injured at a Hong Kong-owned textile factory in Zhuhai SEZ in 1994; 7 killed and 4 injured at an electrical wire factory in Dongguan in 1995; and 22 killed and 33 injured at a Taiwan-owned factory in Shenzhen SEZ in 1996.[10] This is not to mention poor working conditions such as dim lighting, noise, dust, poor ventilation and so on. The major reason for the lack of disputes concerning safety conditions lies in the weak position of the workers in confronting their employers. Workers do not have any bargaining power, and have to either put up with dangerous and unhealthy conditions or leave their jobs.

Fourth, comparing the above three tables, the national arbitration data do not have specific items relating to disputes over compensation for industrial injuries. The explanation for this is twofold. One is that in the 1997 arbitration data, there is an item named "labour protection" — the official data for disputes over industrial injury might be included under this heading. Although they are related, labour protection and industrial injury do not overlap fully. The other explanation is that most serious cases normally end up in litigation. For some minor injuries, if enterprises are at fault, they might compensate the worker through medical treatment.

The Pattern of Labour Disputes

In general, many of the joint ventures and FIEs can be categorized into two groups. Group one enterprises are reminiscent of organizational features of Taylorism with systematic control and Fordism with automation and de-skilling jobs.[11] The other groups are purely "sweat shops" without any safety standards, guaranteed payment, or protection from trade unions.

Our fieldwork suggests that labour disputes are more likely to occur in small and medium-sized enterprises than larger ones. The "sweat shop" type toy factory was probably the worst case among all the ten enterprises we visited, both in terms of working conditions and labour relations. Since our visit, the Hong Kong owned toy factory has gone bankrupt and left all the workers without payment for two months. This pattern of disputes is also reflected by other research findings. For instance, the Shenzhen Labour Bureau conducted a questionnaire survey of 2,617 migrant workers in 1996. When asked about dissatisfaction towards their working conditions, dissatisfaction was highest in small-scale enterprises.

In the case of Shenzhen, most of the larger FIEs had investors from Japan, the United States, Australia, Singapore and other countries. These were more likely located inside the SEZ. The small and medium-sized factories were often set up by investors from Hong Kong, Taiwan and South Korea. The general impression was that employment relations are normally better in the larger FIEs, whereas those investors from Hong Kong, Taiwan, and South Korea treat their workers poorly. Some may argue that the styles of management with different cultural backgrounds explain this phenomenon. However, based on our fieldwork, it is really the types of industry and the perspectives of the investors that result in different labour relations, and thus different patterns of labour disputes. For instance, among the ten enterprises we visited, several of them were established in the 1980s. That means the owners have taken a longer-term perspective regarding their investment in Shenzhen. Therefore, their management is concerned with the long-term running of the enterprises and stable employment relations. Almost all of the FIEs visited had very detailed "Employee Manuals", which spelt out various regulations related to work; from confidentiality of their work, workers' responsibilities to telephone calls during working hours. Some enterprises even have their own regular newsletters to reinforce the rules of the enterprise and cultivate a sense of belonging for migrant workers. Most of these enterprises have their own training programmes for newly recruited workers to familiarize them with some "dos" and "don'ts".

All the workers who in these enterprises are completely powerless in the sense of being able to bargain for their own

Table 8.8
Workers' Preferences for Dispute-resolving Channels
Total: 399 valid

	Frequency	Missing Data	%	Rank
Enduring abuses	122	25	32.6%	4
Seeking help from related managerial staff	229	23	60.9%	1
Negotiating with the top managerial staff	177	23	47.1%	2
Seeking help from the in-house union	85	23	22.6%	6
Seeking help from the municipal union	37	23	9.8%	7
Seeking help from the Labour Bureau	169	23	44.9%	3
Going to court	13	24	3.5%	10
Telling the dispute to the media	25	23	6.6%	8
Still working but not hard	9	23	2.4%	11
A mass gathering	6	24	1/6%	12
Stopping production	14	23	3.7%	9
Quitting the job	92	23	24.5%	5
Other	5	23	1.3%	13

interests, since all the rules have already been made by the enterprises. They simply have to comply with the regulations or leave it. Thus, the number of labour disputes in these enterprises is very low. Also, these enterprises often employ an extremely de-skilled mass-production labour process. For the workers, they feel that most of the time they are confronted with machines rather than the managers of the enterprises. One more reason for fewer disputes in these enterprises is that they are often located in the Shenzhen SEZ, where the Shenzhen Labour Bureau is located. This means that they are subject to constant inspections from the Labour Relations Supervisory Brigade.

The other group of enterprises, i.e., the sweatshops, is often established outside the SEZ. These small or medium-sized enterprises are often engaged in processing, which means they take orders from regular or irregular customers. The garment industry operates many factories of this type. The investors often do not have to invest a lot in terms of capital or equipment. The local governments usually provide them with land or factories. They simply take advantage of the cheap and abundant labour supply. Therefore, the behaviours of these investors can be characterized as seeking a quick profit. In terms of businesses or labour relations, they focus only on the short term. When they have many orders, workers have to work excessive overtime. When their order books are empty, workers are fired without any compensation. It often happens that in this type of enterprise the investors simply disappear without paying their workers several months' salary. Due to local protectionism, local governments and local bureaux do not want to "upset" investors in case they move to another location. Therefore labour inspections are much more lax outside the SEZ, where most of the labour abuses and disputes take place.

The Settlement of Labour Disputes

From the collected petition letters, more than 80% of reported dispute cases were filed and investigated. In cases where the rights of workers were found to have been infringed, enterprises were often ordered by the Labour Bureau to correct their malpractices. According to the records of the Shenzhen Labour Bureau, normally more than 50% of disputes can be settled at the stage of complaining by letter or in person. Some serious cases may go to the arbitration committees, whilst some other cases may be declined, either because the people who complained had already left or been fired, or because other reasons made these cases very difficult to investigate.

Many joint ventures and FIEs do not set up in-house mediation committees, which is one of the reasons why the number of dispute cases in these enterprises is quite high. Thus, there is no established channel for the workers to express their discontent. Our questionnaire data show that when disputes occur, workers normally either negotiate with the managers or endure the hardship and unfair treatment. Table 8.8 lists the ways in which workers can express their discontent.

As shown in Table 8.8, when there is discontent or a dispute, the workers first seek help from their immediate managers or negotiate with the top managerial staff. If this does not result in a satisfactory outcome, then the workers either seek help from the Labour Bureau

Figure 8.2
The Actual Pattern of Settling a Dispute

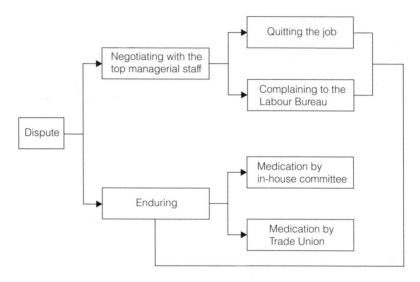

Source: Research Team of Survey on Moral State of Shenzhen Migrant Labour, "Report Two:
           The Development and Improvement of Healthy and Harmonious Labour Relations",
           1996 an unpublished research report, by the Shenzhen Labour Bureau, p. 19.

Figure 8.3
The Ideal Pattern for Settling a Dispute

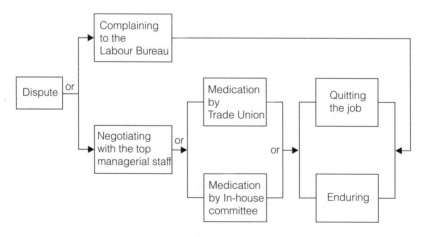

Source: Research Team of Survey on Moral State of Shenzhen Migrant Labour, "Report Two:
           The Development and Improvement of Healthy and Harmonious Labour Relations"
           an unpublished research report, by Shenzhen Labour Bureau, 1996, p. 19.

or simply endure whatever problems they are facing. Both of these methods leave very limited room for the workers themselves to bargain with their employers for long-term interests. Without mediation from the Labour Bureau first, the results of negotiations with the managers often end with two choices, either to leave the enterprise or to complain to the Labour Bureau.

However, by the time the Labour Bureau intervenes, labour relations have already entered a state of serious conflict. Eventually, many workers may leave their jobs. If they endure the hardship, the end result will be similar. This means that by the time workers can no longer tolerate the abuses, they would either negotiate with the managers or seek help from the Labour Bureau. In other words, no mechanism exists to buffer possible conflicts or to strengthen workers' bargaining power. This buffering role should be played either by a trade union or the mediation committee within an enterprise. As can be seen from Table 8.8, seeking help from the in-house trade union ranks rather late compared with other preferences. The role of the trade union will be discussed later in this chapter. This finding echoes research conducted by the Shenzhen Labour Bureau in 1996. In their research, workers listed two ways of handling discontent or disputes. The first was to negotiate with top managerial staff (68.8%). If this failed, 49.7% of workers chose to quit their jobs, and 30.3% chose to seek help from mediation committees. The second is to endure the hardship first (57.6%). When it becomes really unbearable, 38.8% of workers chose to complain to the Labour Bureau and 28.3% chose to seek help from their trade unions.[12] Both ways leave little room for equal discussion, and leaves the Labour Bureau or mediation committee to offer a final solution. If one side of the disputing parties is not satisfied with the solution, then the employment relationship is normally ended. This partially explains why the labour turnover rate is very high in some Shenzhen enterprises, but the rate of disputes remains relatively low. Figures 8.2 and 8.3 illustrate the ways of handling disputes in practice and in an ideal state.

Conclusion

In this chapter some preliminary observations regarding labour disputes in Shenzhen have been made since the reform era began in the 1980s. By examining the causes, patterns and settlements of the dispute cases, this chapter is an attempt to demonstrate the radical changes of the interest relations between workers and enterprises, i.e., from unified interest relations to diverging interest relations. However, the conflicts examined are not simply responses to the reforms; they often shape future reform policies at both central and local levels and they often lead to positive institutional arrangements. It is within this context that this chapter ends with the following three implications of the dispute cases at the institutional level, in the hope that these issues will draw due attention from both academics and policy-makers.

The Role of the Trade Union Needs to be Re-addressed

Before the economic reforms, the relationship between workers and enterprise management was basically co-operative in nature. The roles of trade unions then were mainly to facilitate the production of enterprises and to look after the welfare of their workers. This meant that all the real labour issues, such as wages, workers' safety, employment security and retirement, were all controlled by the state via related government departments. The trade union was only one of the strictly regulated departments of the state administrative system.

The reforms have brought some fundamental changes in labour relations with the decentralization of state-owned enterprises and the development of the private economy. The function of the trade union, particularly the role it should play in privately owned enterprises, has seldom been seriously discussed or redefined by the government. Although the *Labour Law* states that "A worker shall have the right to join and organize a trade union in accordance with the law. A trade union shall represent and protect the lawful rights and interests of workers, and organize its activities autonomously and independently in accordance with the law"(Article 7), the law does not mandate the establishment of trade unions at the enterprise level. Therefore few joint ventures or FIEs actually have functioning trade unions. For those enterprises which have established trade unions, the rights of union leaders have not been defined by government legislation. In fact union leaders often become the victims of mistreatment by enterprises.

Because the trade unions seldom address any real labour issues or represent workers' interests, workers have lost confidence in them. According to our questionnaire data, when asked about the necessity of establishing trade unions in their enterprises, most of the workers (86.1%) thought that it was unnecessary to establish a trade union; 9.5% were indifferent; and only 4.5% of workers thought that it was necessary to establish a trade union. Moreover, when there is a dispute, workers do not turn to trade unions first, as discussed above.

Giving Priority to the Protection of Workers

At this moment, some exiting institutional set-ups make it difficult to develop a long-term strategy to protect workers. The current *hukou* system is a good example. Without a *hukou*, migrant workers can only work in Shenzhen for several years. They do not have the right to become permanent residents of Shenzhen, which means they are not entitled to any social welfare or other beneficial policies provided for Shenzhen residents. Thus, for most of the migrant workers, they come to work in Shenzhen for three to four years on average, and then return to their own hometowns. Consequently, they place more emphasis on financial considerations. So long as they are able to earn some money, they choose to stay in their jobs rather than organize together to bargain with their employers for long-term interests. To some extent this explains why they choose to tolerate the hardships in the first place rather than negotiating for better living and working conditions. Most of the workers we interviewed expressed the view that when they are pushed into a corner, they would rather just return home earlier than expected. Moreover, with the high mobility of migrant labour, it is very difficult for migrant workers to organize themselves and protect their own rights.

If the issue of protecting labour is given a priority by the government, all kinds of positive institutional arrangements can be made. Two examples drawn from our fieldwork are worth mentioning here. One is that in enterprises which have a large number of migrant workers from one particular place, a person from that place's Labour Bureau will come with the workers to the enterprise. He or she may stay in the enterprise for the first two or three months to help the workers settle down and familiarize themselves with their work. He or she may also come to the enterprise every few months to represent the workers negotiating with the enterprise for improvements in working and living conditions. In this way, the workers are not simply voiceless and powerless in expressing their discontent to the enterprise. Another example comes from a town in the Longgang district. In this area many small and medium-sized joint ventures are located. Periodically some joint ventures go bankrupt, the owners disappear and leave their workers without payment. In view of this, the township government decided to send representatives from the government to participate in the daily running of the joint ventures so as to monitor the financial situation of these enterprises and to protect the interests of the workers.

Obstacles to Worker Organizations

The Chinese government has always considered industrial action as a threat to social stability and economic development. Since labour disputes have been considered as an indicator of labour relations, the government has applied administrative measures to reduce the number of dispute cases. Therefore mediation committees have been set up at all administrative levels of the Labour Bureau to reduce the number of labour disputes. In fact, local officials are very reluctant to report any serious dispute cases. Actual problems have been suppressed from their supervising authorities and the general public, which means that these problems will not be resolved through new policies or legislation.

By interfering and trying to control everything, the state also prevents workers from forming non-government organizations. Some have argued that the problem is also due to people's ignorance of their own rights. This could be true to a certain extent. For most of the workers we interviewed, they knew very clearly that they had been mistreated. It is mainly social control, institutional set-ups and government ideology that has made it impossible for these workers to organize and fight for their own interests.

Notes

Many arguments in this chapter are the result of collective discussions within the research team. I am grateful to Dr. Lin Yi-min, Professor Shi Xian-min and Dr. He Gao-chao for their insights and support. My thanks also go to the Hong Kong Research Grant Committee for funding the project "The Rise and Settlement of Labour Dispute in China: The Dynamic of Remaking the Chinese Working Class in the Post-Mao Era".

1. The restoration of the system of labour disputes settlement started in 1987. However, the full implementation of the system of labour dispute arbitration only came into practice in July 1993 when the State Council issued the *PRC Enterprises Labour Disputes Settlement Provisions*. This partially explains the reason why official data regarding labour disputes is available before 1994.

2. "1997 Labour Disputes Settlement and Analysis," *Labour Disputes: Settlement and Research*, No. 69, August 1998, pp. 10–15.

3. Shenzhen Yearbook Committee, *Shenzhen Yearbook 1999* (Shenzhen: Shenzhen Yearbook Publishing House, 1999).

4. The Shenzhen Labour Bureau, *"Shenzhen tequ laodong zhidu shinian gaige licheng"* (*Ten-year Reform of Labour System in Shenzhen Special Economic Zone*) (Shenzhen: Hai-tian Publishing House, 1991), p. 338.

5. Research Team of Survey on the Moral State of Shenzhen Migrant Labour, "Report Two: The Development and Improvement of Healthy and Harmonious Labour Relations", an unpublished research report, 1996, p. 15.

6. For detailed regulations on the procedures, particularly with regard to appeals to the courts, see the *Regulations on Labour Supervision and Inspection Procedure* [No. 457] issued by the Ministry of Labour in 1995, and *Regulations on Labour Supervision and Inspection* [No. 167] issued by the Ministry of Labour in 1993.

7. A petition letter to the Shenzhen Labour Bureau, 10 November 1996. Twelve people signed.

8. See A. Stevenson-Yang, "Labor Laments," *The China Business Review*, May–June 1994, pp. 32–33.

9. Regular workers (*Gudinggo*) are those with long-term work positions. Thus, they are normally workers in the SOEs.

10. For details see, *China Labour Bulletin*, No. 34 1997; and *Far Eastern Economic Review*, August 1994 and June 1994.

11. Fordism is a managerial approach based on the flow-line principle of assembly work. Every worker has a fixed work position along assembly lines. This enables closer supervision and control over the pace of production by the management. It is a further development of "scientific management". Related to this, de-skilling refers to the trend of systematic and further division of jobs so that they require increasingly less skilled workers, and the management can thus exercise more control over workers.

12. Research Team, "Report Two", *op. cit.*, p. 18.

CHAPTER 9

Guangdong and the Challenges of the Twenty-first Century:

The Legal Perspective

ZHANG Xianchu

Introduction

Since the introduction of the Open Door Policy in 1978, the economic take-off of Guangdong province has not only led the country's modernization process, but also attracted international attention as a striking phenomenon.[1] The statistics reflect this remarkable growth; Guangdong's GDP increased from 18.59 billion yuan in 1978 to 651.91 billion yuan in 1996, with an annual growth rate of 14.4%; in the same period, the amount of foreign investment in the province jumped from US$9.18 million to US$13.9 billion from more than 30 countries or regions; provincial exports rose from US$1.4 billion to US$59.35 billion, representing an annual increase rate of 21.3% and accounting for 40% of total national exports; provincial revenue grew from less than 4 billion yuan to 47.95 billion yuan; and the average annual salary for urban employees increased from 615 yuan to 9,127 yuan.[2] Guangdong has certainly come a long way in the last two decades towards completing the preliminary stage of industrialization.

Although rapid industrialization has turned Guangdong into the dynamo of economic development for China, the emergence of some side effects, also experienced by many other Newly Industrialized Economies (NIEs), has led to serious concerns regarding Guangdong's future development. Unstable political and economic conditions, such as the unsettled relations between the central and local governments and the undefined direction of the so-called socialist market economy, have added to these uncertainties. Moreover, as a market economy is being practised nationwide today in China, Guangdong no longer exclusively enjoys the special policies of the central government, including preferential treatment for foreign investment and export encouragement since the Open Door Policy was implemented. As a result, Guangdong is facing greater competition from other provinces. Finally, the issue of corruption, highlighted during the recent Asian financial crisis, has seriously damaged the regional economy as well as the confidence of foreign investors.

Against this backdrop, it is important to consider the issues concerning the further development of the province in the twenty-first century from the legal perspective. This chapter analyses the legal challenges to Guangdong's economic and social development in the new century. The first part of this chapter briefly reviews the development and current conditions of the province's legal infrastructure; the second part examines the major legal challenges facing Guangdong in the twenty-first century. The third part provides some analyses of the legal issues concerned, and the final part draws some conclusions.

The Development of Guangdong's Legal Infrastructure: An Overview

Unlike most parts of China, the path of Guangdong's development has been aided by certain special policies granted by the central government, together with large quantities of foreign investment from Hong Kong and Macau.[3] In 1979, the central government decided to vest in Guangdong, as well as Fujian province, more discretionary powers to develop its economy through international trade, import of modern technology and foreign investment. Meanwhile, Shenzhen, Zhuhai and Shantou were selected as the sites for three of the five Special Economic Zones (SEZs), areas designed to attract foreign investment and operate according to market forces. All these policy-based measures were soon codified into the *Provisions of the Special Economic Zones of Guangdong* by the Standing Committee of the National People's Congress (NPC) as the legal foundation for the province's economic take-off, which allowed more autonomy in its path to economic development than other parts of the Mainland.[4] By virtue of the *Provisions*, the Standing Committee of the NPC in November 1981 delegated Guangdong and Fujian legislative power to enact economic regulations applicable to the SEZs within their provinces in order to facilitate economic reform and growth.

As a sign of accelerating economic reforms and marketization following paramount leader Deng Xiaoping's famous southern tour of 1992, the Standing Committee of the NPC further authorized the people's congress and the government of Shenzhen to adopt and implement legal regulations applicable to the SEZ in accordance with its actual needs. These SEZ enactments had only to be in compliance with the provisions of the constitution and the basic principles of national laws as well as administrative regulations, and be reported to the central government and the provincial legislature for the record.[5] In 1996, the same legislative powers were extended to Zhuhai and Shantou, the other two SEZs in Guangdong.[6] As such, despite the lack of a constitutional basis,[7] the three SEZs have enjoyed legislative powers even greater than the provincial government because under the constitution local governments, including provincial governments and municipal authorities of their capital cities, may only adopt provisions consistent with the constitution, national laws and regulations.[8] As a result, a three-tier local legislative structure exists in Guangdong: provincial enactment, SEZs' special legislation, and the capital city's rule-making.

The local economic legislation played a crucial role in paving the way for rapid provincial development. The revolution started in 1982 when bold provincial legislation legalized the transfer of land use rights from the government to private enterprises for compensation. Previously the constitution had explicitly forbade the appropriation, purchase, lease of land, or any other land transactions.[9] Soon, right of land use was further liberated through transfer in the form of contract, bidding or auction under the 1987 *Regulations on Land Management of Shenzhen SEZ*. This legislation triggered a far-reaching constitutional and political controversy in China: to end the reform or to change the constitution.[10] Finally, the debate was concluded with an amendment to the constitution recognizing the transferability of the right of land use.[11] The implication of this legal and ideological victory cannot be fully understood without considering its financial impact on provincial development. According to an incomplete survey, the sum received by the Guangdong government from the transfer of land rights in 1992 amounted to 9.4 billion yuan, which alone accounted for 40% of the total annual provincial revenue and exceeded the annual revenue of most of China's provinces.[12]

The unprecedented legislation has had at least three important impacts on provincial reform. First, legislative power has been con-sciously and actively exercised as an effective weapon to hew out a path for the local economic take-off. The record demonstrates that since the 1980s, a large number of legislative measures have been adopted to guide local exploration of a market economy and to pro-tect economic achievements, particularly in the following areas: privatization of state public ownership, foreign investment protec-tion, incorporation and securitization of business enterprises, reform of the local financial and investment system, the transformation of the old labour and distribution regime, the modernization of agricul-tural production, market order supervision and the promotion of Guangdong–Hong Kong economic integration.[13] As a result, Guangdong has become the province with the most legal rules. Between 1978–96, more than 300 pieces of local legislation were promulgated, most of them economic regulations.[14]

Second, the local legislation has provided valuable experience for both national economic reform and legal modernization.[15] In the past, the central government used Guangdong as the trial field of national legislation for opening up to the outside world and marketization.[16] Thus far, many local regulations have been successfully adopted on a national basis, such as legal regimes concerning the real estate market, labour market, foreign investment, financial market and development of the private economy.

The third impact is the change of government function. The local legislation is leading to a transition from the traditional government domination under a socialist regime to a governance model under rule by law. In recent years, all provincial, SEZs' and other local governments have emphasized the rule of law as their long-term goal. The Shenzhen government, for example, has claimed that ten systems of the socialist market economy have been established with local rules: a property ownership system with public ownership as the leading body and equal competition; a state asset management and supervision system; a market-guided pricing system; a commodity market system; a social welfare protection system; a social service system; an accounting and auditing system; a fair distribution system; a macro-economic management system without direct government control; and a legal system serving the market economy.[17] Within these legal frameworks, the government has been trimmed, approval procedures have been simplified and reduced, and the subordinate relations between State Owned Enterprises (SOEs) and their upper level authorities have been disconnected. Currently the city government's functions are redefined as macro-planning and co-ordinating, market regulation and providing services.[18]

Along with this trend, the improvement of the legal infrastructure in the province has also been noticeable. In 1998, the peoples' courts in Guangdong tried 416,934 cases (a record high for the province), 17.9% up from the previous year.[19] In recent years, the number of commercial cases heard by the people's courts in Guangdong involving Hong Kong, Macau and other foreign parties reached over 500.[20] The number of law firms has increased from 146 firms with 1,816 lawyers in 1985 to 665 firms with 5,870 lawyers in 1997.[21] In addition, 1,915 legal services centres with 6,077 practitioners, who provide citizens with legal advice and mitigation services, have been established province-wide.[22] The first legal aid centre in China was opened in Guangzhou 1996.[23] In terms of legal education, the number of students in law schools within the province has jumped from 9,746 in 1985 to 17,779 in 1997.[24]

The return of Hong Kong to China has opened a new chapter in Guangdong–Hong Kong relations, as the ties have been expanded from civil and commercial relations to governmental co-operation in many aspects. Besides the extensive investment and trade, further economic integration of the two sides has been progressing well.[25] Moreover, the establishment of the Hong Kong–Guangdong Co-operation Joint Conference chaired by the Chief Secretary of Hong Kong and the Governor of Guangdong in March 1998 marked a new era in bilateral co-operation at the top governmental level. In a short period, progress has been made in longer border opening times, environment protection, promotion of tourism, and measures to assist Hong Kong businessmen's operations in Guangdong.[26] Furthermore, the co-operation in law enforcement and judicial affairs between the two sides has also proved successful in helping to curb smuggling, organized crime, drug trafficking and other criminal activities. In addition to a successful joint illegal immigrant exercise, border officers from Hong Kong and Macau met on the Mainland more than 170 times in 1997.[27] Both the Independent Commission Against Corruption (ICAC) and its Guangdong counterpart, the Guangdong People's Procuratorate have established mutual assistance schemes, including regular meetings, information exchanges, training, research, investigation and evidence collection.[28] In this regard, the arrest of the Triad leader "Big Spender" (Cheung Tze Keung) was a good example of increased cross-border co-operation.

Major Legal Challenges to Further Development

On the basis of the striking achievements over the past two decades, there is no doubt that in the long run the dynamic growth of the provincial economy will continue into the twenty-first century. In the short run, however, major obstacles present serious challenges, or even threats to the further success of Guangdong. The World Bank, for example, warned in 1997 that China might become the first East Asian victim of a phenomenon where a rapidly developing economy suffers setback and stagnation, as happened in Brazil and Mexico. To what extent these risks may be avoided will depend on the ability of the authorities to maintain the momentum of reforms.[29] This proved to be profound advice, particularly in the light of the recent Asian financial crisis.

Guangdong's economic take-off has primarily followed the so-called Asian Model, characterized by government intervention, export-orientation and labour intensive manufacturing. After 20 years of rapid growth, the dynamic for further development has significantly diminished. The provincial net GDP increase dropped by 12.5% between 1987 and 1997. In Guangdong today, large-scale enterprises account for only 1.4% of total businesses; technology-intensive products represent merely 25% of all provincial goods; overproduction has led to the suspension or half-suspension of 100 out of 204 major manufactured products; and investment in infrastructure has decreased since 1996.[30] With one third of products relying on investment from Hong Kong and export markets,[31] the provincial economy has suffered a great deal from the Asian financial crisis. Foreign investment, in terms of both project numbers and contracted value, has declined continuously for three years. For the first season of 1998, the actual utilization of foreign investment registered a shortfall of 13.2% and exports by foreign investment enterprises were only 23% of the provincial target.[32] Although the harsh reality may be well explained by various economic theories, this chapter will focus on the legal problems which contributed to these setbacks.

Excessive Government Control over Divided Markets

Local governments within the province have been playing excessive roles in the local economic development and pursuing their own

interests and goals. As a result, the provincial market has been irrationally divided, and a provincial development strategy has not been
successfully developed. Internal competition among cities and counties in the province with similar irrational structures has rendered
few industrial sectors capable of reaching sizable optimum production. It further hinders the upgrade of the provincial economy and
rational use of resources. At one time in the 1990s, approximately
100 assembly lines to produce refrigerators were established in the
Pearl River Delta and the cut-throat competition soon led to the closure of many.[33] Another good example is the provincial automobile
industry. Although the automobile industry was identified as one of
the pillar industries for future development, today more than 110 car
factories with a combined annual production capacity of less than
20,000 units belong to 17 different departments, including the military, the public security department and the judiciary.[34]

Excessive government control over provincial economic development has prevented the establishment of an economic structure
guided by the market. Since the 1990s, the overheated economy con-
vinced some leaders that the time of urbanization on a mature
industrial basis had arrived. Consequently a "gold rush" in real
estate development occurred, with many luxurious projects, built in
violation of national regulations, left unsold. These properties
amounted to 30 million square metres of housing space and had cost
more than 100 billion yuan by 1996.[35] Extensive illegal fund raising
fuelled the bubble economy further. In order to circumvent the state
measures on credit control, many county and township governments
tried to attract deposits with very high interest rates through their
own financial arms without the Central Bank's approval, despite
these activities being strictly illegal.[36] In a recent case, hundreds of
investors were left penniless when the Enping City Government
reneged on its promise to repay a public deposit of 6 billion yuan at
25% interest.[37] By 1997, the bad loans of provincial banks were
estimated to account for as high as 30% of their total lending.[38]

The local governments not only maintain excessive control over
macro-economic development, but are also often involved in
concrete commercial transactions. The sale of stocks of the Huabao

Company by the government of Shunde city serves as a good illustration in this regard. Huabao developed into a company from a collective enterprise without any government financial aid. In 1992 it was certified by the local government as the sole owner of its assets. However, in 1993, the local government, by presenting itself as the owner of the company, contracted with some Hong Kong investors to sell 80% of Huabao stock without observing the correct corporate procedures. Within a year, the company had suffered a loss of 300 million yuan, mainly due to the high price of the tender offer suggested by the local government to calm the anger of local shareholders. The poor performance also prevented the company from being listed. Finally, the Hong Kong investors withdrew and the company was repurchased by the former Huabao management.[39]

Another example of hindering development through excessive government enthusiasm was the unsuccessful attempt to upgrade the industrial structure of Shenzhen in the early 1990s. Starting in 1993, the city government stopped its approval process for labour intensive foreign investment enterprises in the belief that the condition for overall upgrading of its industrial structure was ripe. Some labour intensive factories were forced to move out or to upgrade their operations. However, the sharp decline of local exports, foreign investment and economic growth taught the government a lesson that an unrealistic push would not only hurt the city's further development, but even its means of livelihood.[40]

Further, the Communist Party, governments and legislative organs in Guangdong have commonly engaged in business operations. Such practices not only directly contradict the basics of a market economy, but also encourage corruption and abuse of power. Many cadres are found to be "too rotten to function effectively". As such, in following the central government's recent direction, the provincial leaders have ordered their subordinates to end their business activities by the end of 1999 and to hand over firms to the designated provincial authority. The decision also provides for severe punishment for officials found transferring, illegally selling or hiding assets from investigators.[41]

In the national competition for developing a market economy, Guangdong is falling behind. To a large extent, Guangdong's economic take-off has been supported by special policies which allowed it to forge ahead of the rest of the country in the 1980s. Since the 1990s, the operation of a market economy has no longer been a privilege enjoyed solely by Guangdong, but a goal that has been promoted and practised across China. As a result, as compared with the old days, Guangdong's competitive edge has been blunted. In terms of GDP growth, Shanghai, Jiangsu and Shandong have surpassed Guangdong since 1997.[42] In fixed asset investment growth, at least six other provinces accelerated ahead of Guangdong in 1998.[43] Although Guangdong has utilized foreign capital worth over US$10 billion in recent years, there is virtually no large project with investment over US$1 billion; whereas several such large foreign investment projects have landed in Shanghai. Moreover, 10,000 enterprises from other parts of the country with total capital of 20 billion yuan have been attracted to Shanghai. Among them are the headquarters of several listed companies.[44] By contrast, "wool wars" and "silk wars" burst out between Guangdong and its neighbouring province Hunan in the late 1980s when the two governments fought for local raw materials for their own industries with various administrative means. Since then, despite the conclusion of trade agreements between the two governments to open their markets,[45] Guangdong has not developed its own regional co-operative strategy.[46]

The Continuing Power Struggle

Since the economic reforms started at the end of the 1970s, the tension between the central and provincial government over local autonomy has long existed.[47] From the 1970s to the early 1990s, paramount leader Deng Xiaoping selected Guangdong as the trial province for national economic reform.[48] It has been suggested that the central government's only contribution to Guangdong's success was its tacit *laissez-faire* approach to regional issues that has allowed the Pearl River Delta to experience virtually self-motivated, self-sustained and market-oriented development.[49] However, Guang-dong's influential economic power and monopolized privileges have enabled it to resist Beijing's efforts to appoint local officials and to successfully negotiate a reduction in its payments to the central government.[50] As the economic reforms and marketization deepen, the liberated province has shown more reluctance to concede powers to or make sacrifices for the more political-motivated central government.[51] For example, in 1993 the provincial leaders did not agree to meet the tax demands made by then Vice Premier Zhu Rongji until a face-to-face meeting with President Jiang Zemin.[52]

The latest incident to show the clash between the central and local government over power allocation and political liberalization[53] is the controversy over the provision in the *Law of Legislation* on legislative power of the SEZ governments. Since 1995, in the draft of the *Law* the central government tried to limit the SEZ legislative power to "needs to institutional reform of (their) economy and opening up to the outside world".[54] The draft provision has been strongly opposed by local officials and scholars. They believe that the retreat of the central government will result in the SEZs losing their distinction and advantages.[55] In March 2000, the local governments celebrated their victory when the *Law* was adopted by the national legislature with all the restrictive words mentioned above being deleted.[56]

In most cases, the tension is solved by local circumvention. In Guangdong, local governments have earned a reputation for getting their own way when higher levels of the party and government impose ideological and institutional obstacles. Thus, devising strategies for circumventing certain central policies has been a major task of the Guangdong government.[57] However, in recent years, the central government has adopted a conservative approach by holding that over-decentralization disorients China's economic order and damages the national interests.[58] In 1998, to the surprise of many, Li Changchu and Wang Qishan were appointed by the central government to the posts of provincial party boss and the first deputy governor in charge of provincial financial matters respectively. However, top cadres in Guangdong have reportedly widely resisted them. For example, it is said that on 20 October 1998 five out of six resolutions slated for deliberation and passage were voted down in a meeting of the provincial Party committee. The conference originally scheduled for two days lasted for seven days without resolving anything. As a result, the central party was compelled to send Ye Xuanping, the former provincial governor, to mediate in the showdown. Thus, Guangdong's attempts to assert greater autonomy has been a major headache for the central government.[59]

In addition to installation of outsiders in senior provincial posts to break so-called "Guangdong Faction", recently the central government is turning the prosperous province into a base of ideological campaign to promote "Communist Origins" in order to relieve its anxiety that the province has veered from socialism in its embrace of practice based on Western values.[60]

Within the province, the power struggle continues unabated. For example, three years ago I was amazed by the deeply divided views of scholars and the attitudes of officials over the nature of provincial and SEZ enactments when I first studied local legislation in the Pearl River Delta.[61] At one extreme, it is held that the SEZ's legislation enjoys higher status than provincial enactments due to the direct delegation from the top national legislature.[62] This view is strongly opposed by some observers, who believe that SEZ legislation is subject to provincial law-making power because of its limited application and reporting for record to the provincial legislature.[63] The controversy has apparently not yet been resolved, but is inviting a new round of debate. After Zhang Yuqing, the Vice Chairman of the Standing Committee of the Shenzhen People's Congress, published an article outlining the establishment of a legal framework to fit the market development of the SEZ,[64] disagreement was immediately articulated from Guangzhou. For instance, in a recent article, Xie Xiaoyao openly opposed the establishment of such a legal framework in Shenzhen. He further held that it was wrong to legislate *ultra vires* in violation of documents of the upper level Communist Party committee and the government.[65] The sensitivity of the issue lies in the fact that the SEZ's special legislative powers is one of the few privileges left to them, after other regions have equalized their status with the SEZs in their own market development.[66] The newly adopted *Law of Legislation* fails to provide any answer to this debate. On the one hand, it classifies SEZ legislation into local legislation, indicating that by administrative rank, SEZ enactment is lower than provincial legislation.[67] On the other hand, the law re-emphasizes the SEZ enactment is based on the NPC's direct and special delegation.[68]

Also, the future of the SEZs in Guangdong is facing uncertainty. In 1994–95, a serious controversy was triggered by a proposal put forward by Dr. Hu Angang, an influential scholar in Beijing, to end the operation of SEZs. He argued that now a market economy was being practised nationwide, the SEZs had finished their historic function; otherwise, continuation of the special policies and treatment towards the SEZs[69] would only constitute an unfair privilege and monopoly against market principles and development of other regions of the country.[70] Hu's proposal was met with angry attacks, and to a large extent, the debate was politicized on the grounds that SEZs were supported by Deng Xiaoping and the Party's policy of creating windows for the country's opening up to the outside world.[71] The fight was brought to an end with President Jiang Zemin's reaffirmation of the Party's commitment to SEZs. However, since 1995, when most of the SEZ's preferential policies, except certain tax breaks and legislative powers, expired,[72] the SEZs have been struggling to redefine their functions in the context of the national market economy in order to justify the continuation of their special privileges.[73] Although the Shenzhen government developed a "three first" theory, namely international practice to be introduced into China being first tried in Shenzhen; new policies to be adopted for China's World Trade Organisation (WTO) bid being first applied in Shenzhen; and new reform measures being first used in Shenzhen,[74] it certainly cannot deprive other regions' right to embrace the market economy.

Extensive Corruption

During the reform era, unclearly defined ownership, multiple pricing, decentralization, and lack of legal institutions, including checks and balances mechanisms, have created an environment for some cadres to view marketization as their own private "gold rush".[75] Thus, some local officials have a vested interest in interfering with the market because they can gain financially from such interference.[76] In this regard, Guangdong, as the richest province in the country, has provided many shocking examples of how extensive government corruption threatens the province's continued development. In the period 1994–96, 7,085 people were found guilty of various corrupt business practices, mostly relating to financial matters; in government branches, 1996 alone recorded 4,255 cases of corruption.[77] In recent years, the trend has witnessed the downfall of higher-level officials.

After Ou Yangde, the Deputy Chairman of the Standing Committee of the Provincial People's Congress, was convicted of accepting bribes of 530,000 yuan in 1996,[78] another deputy chairman, Yu Fei, was dismissed from his post and stripped of his party membership. He was found to have used his position to acquire land for his children at unreasonably low prices, and then resold it for a sizeable profit. Through the power-backed transactions, his family easily pocketed 28 million yuan.[79] Another case that shocked Beijing recently was a smuggling syndicate in Zhanjiang, which involved the city party secretary, the head of the city's custom's department, and more than 140 other cadres in the city who took bribes averaging 500,000 yuan each. The head of customs collected as much as 10 million yuan.[80] A similar criminal group was found in Huidong county, including the party secretary, the head and a deputy head of the county, the heads of the Public Security Bureau and Industry and Commerce Bureau, and the director of the anti-smuggling office. They had allowed 16,000 carloads of smuggled goods through after receiving payments of 46 million yuan.[81] The latest high profile charge in the province was filed against Shao Rucai for bribe taking and misappropriation of public funds. He was arrested when he was holding three concurrent posts as the heads of the Financial Bureau, the Tax Bureau and the State Asset Management Bureau of Guangzhou.[82] All the aforementioned cases are widely regarded as merely the tip of the iceberg.

The judiciary has not been immune from corrupt practices. For example, Zhao Yongku and Zhong Naiting as head of the economic trial division and deputy head of the executive division of the Shenzhen people's court respectively were convicted of taking bribes amounting to 280,000 yuan and 440,000 yuan respectively in 1997.[83] To further add to the list, Zeng Sheng as a member of both the standing committees of the Party and political and legal affairs of Huazhou city, as well as the head of the city's Public Security Bureau, was sentenced to death after he was found to have received 3 million yuan in bribes.[84] Also, Cheng Yuwu as the head of the armed police squadron of Huilai county was sentenced to death suspended for two years for directing his squadron to protect smuggling operations.[85]

The Deteriorated Social Environment

Apart from official corruption, the overall public order situation in the province is grim. According to an investigation into certain cities within the province in 1994, more than 30 organized criminal gangs were found, including branches from Japan, Hong Kong, Macau and Taiwan.[86] The number of car stealing and looting cases jumped from 6,040 in 1990 to 52,020 in 1995, or 7.5 fold.[87] During the 1990s, Guangdong has become a wholesale centre for counterfeit currency. In 1995, the amount of counterfeit money seized by the Public Security Bureau accounted for 47% of the national total.[88] In 1998, smuggling cases in Guangdong made up 40% of the national total.[89] The province also ranks third in the nation in seriousness of drug trafficking and abuse. In 1997 alone, more than 3,000 drug cases and over 600 drug gangs were dealt with; 51,504 drug users were found.[90] In addition to domestic crimes, the number of crimes and violations committed by foreigners in Guangdong has also increased significantly. According to the Guangdong Public Security Bureau, in 1998, in the first nine months of the year, over 1,800 violations of unlawful entry, stay and employment were deal with; 19 criminal cases involving commercial fraud, border violations, and gang-controlled prostitution were cracked with 114 arrests of foreign criminals.[91]

Several million migrant labourers in Guangdong also pose a serious challenge to local development. On the one hand, they have been portrayed by the government as a desirable modern identity in the course of modernization; on the other hand, the identity is created on a basis of rural-urban disparities and regional and gender inequalities. Serious violations of labour laws and various abuses have made headlines of newspapers frequently. As such, the basic social justice and future development will inevitably require to eliminate the proliferation of the manipulated social division.[92]

At least, a partial explanation for this crime wave lies in the shortfall of social development. Much of the revenue generated in Guangdong has not been reinvested into society at large or used to augment the social development of the populace. Instead, the economic prosperity has induced new waves of consumerism, which have led to the proliferation of prostitution and pornography. Some military personnel have also been involved in criminal activities.[93] Also, closely related to the high rate of crime is the issue of population quality. According to 1996 figures, among all those employed in the province, only 1.9% received a college education, far lower than the 3.5% in Jiangsu, 13% in Shanghai and 50% in developed countries. Among the rural labour force, only 12.4% were high school graduates.[94] For those aged 15 and above, 15.6% were illiterate.[95] Moreover, in recent years 6.7 million rural migrant labourers with poor educational backgrounds came to Guangdong looking for work.[96] Without much chance to stay for long, they have little incentive to take any further studies. As such, in sharp contrast with the rapid economic growth and urbanization, the whole province has been struggling to develop learning opportunities for its people.[97] In fact, the number of universities and schools dwindled in the 1990s. Most of the northern hilly areas in the province today are still impoverished, particularly in education, medical and social facilities.[98]

Uncertainties Surrounding the Future Economic Integration of Guangdong and Hong Kong

Based on the successful co-operation between Guangdong and Hong Kong in the past, there is no doubt that the new century will provide more opportunities for the mutual development of the two sides. For example, the two governments have pledged to make the most of the advantages within the "one country, two systems" framework and fully explore their co-operative potentials by jointly creating a new competitive edge in the international market.[99] Also, businesses in Hong Kong continue to show their willingness to invest in Guangdong.[100] The construction of a Disney Park in Hong Kong is bound to bring in more business to the region, and the strategy of developing high-tech industries by the two sides will open a new field of co-operation. As Tung Chee-hwa, the Chief Executive of the Hong Kong Special Administrative Region (HKSAR) outlined in his 1999 Policy Address, the two sides will explore ways under "one country, two systems" to allow the pooling of manpower, goods, capital and other resources in response to economic challenges and to cope with the increase in cross-border traffic.[101]

However, to a certain degree, the future co-operation of Guangdong and Hong Kong faces some serious uncertainties. At a recent symposium attended by more than 100 experts, officials and scholars, some still felt unsure about the true meaning of "one country, two systems". The political sensitivity of the principle has not allowed a detailed definition of the rules governing relations between Guangdong and the HKSAR, and thus both sides worry about intervening in each other's affairs. Although the two sides believe such a definition is crucial for the orientation and future development of cross-border co-operation, they also agree that it is only a principle and that there are no clear answers to the questions yet.[102]

Today, both sides realize that Guangdong–Hong Kong co-operation has reached a stage where "the shop at the front, the factory at the back" model may no longer be suitable for the twenty-first century, and an upgrade based on the introduction and development of new technologies is urgently needed.[103] As Professor Victor Sit pointed out, Hong Kong and the rest of the Pearl River Delta already form a single economic entity. Nevertheless, further growth will be more difficult in the new international environment. Hong Kong–Guangdong infrastructure and cross-border links need to be improved.[104]

To date, extensive discussions have not produced any concrete plans or strategies to guide future co-operation, but have only identified differing opinions. For example, the issue of to what extent "the shop at the front, the factory at the back" model should be maintained has divided scholars and officials. Some claim that the model has lost its attraction due to its emphasis on small-scale production and the negative impact on delaying the transformation of Hong Kong's industrial structure.[105] Others believe that the industrial and trade development of the two sides, to a large extent, still depends on an increase of processing trade in the near future.[106] As such, certain negative impacts this model may have to be tolerated.[107]

With regard to co-operation in hi-tech development, Ji Chongwei of the Development Research Centre of the State Council holds that Guangdong should become a research and development base for upgrading Hong Kong's products. He further pointed out that many electronic technologies used by Hong Kong investment enterprises in Guangdong are becoming out-of-date, whereas certain Mainland inventions need to be marketed.[108] However, the recent Cyberport plan adopted by the HKSAR seems to suggest the government's top priority is to become a major international market player. As Tung indicated in his 1999 Policy Address, as the Mainland upgrades its economy from labour-intensive to service based industries, Hong Kong has to restructure its economy to become an innovative and knowledge-based economy.[109] As a result, some believe that the Mainland may only play a supplementary role by further utilizing the technologies developed or introduced by Hong Kong.[110]

Such uncertainties may have two legal implications. First, the lack of a co-operative strategy will prevent a legal framework from being developed. Professor Zhou Chengxin holds that the current legal gap between Guangdong and Hong Kong is so wide that the two systems cannot be linked up, but may only be co-ordinated.[111] Thus, bilateral development may not proceed smoothly if the necessary legal protection lags behind. Second, the lack of a co-operative plan may subject the two sides to some conflict of interests in their future development. For instance, to facilitate economic integration, Shenzhen has proposed that the border be opened 24 hours a day; to Hong Kong the implementation of such a plan will inevitably depress property prices and retail sales in the HKSAR.[112] Some worries about the potential competition between the two sides have been openly articulated.[113] Although such regional competition is normal in a market economy, the lack of a compatible legal basis would significantly change the mentality and environment of the past co-operation.

In addition to uncertainties regarding official relations, some problems revealed by the recent financial crisis have seriously affected Hong Kong investors' confidence in Guangdong province. The saga began when the Guangzhou International Trust and Investment Corporation (GZITIC), which was under the control of the city government, failed to repay US$30 million in October 1998.[114] Soon after, the Guangdong International Trust and Investment Corporation (GITIC), the commercial arm of the provincial government, together with its three wholly owned subsidiaries, filed for bankruptcy in January 1999.[115] Guangdong Enterprises and Guangnan Holdings, the two Hong Kong listed subsidiaries of GITIC, also became insolvent at the same time. The Hong Kong market was outraged at the two companies' losses of HK$18.8 billion and HK$5 billion respectively and demanded the HKSAR government thoroughly investigate the scandal.[116]

Although all the details of the scandal are far from clear, it appears that reckless speculation on risky securities and property trading was one of the main reasons for the parent company's debts and for dragging its subsidiaries into deep trouble. For example, Guangnan Holdings has announced that it will investigate whether its parent company used funds raised from the Hong Kong listing for speculative trading by taking advantage of inadequate legislation.[117] At the same time, Zhu Senlin, the Chairman of the Standing Committee of the People's Congress of Guangdong, has openly criticized Guangnan and Guangdong Enterprise for speculating in the securities market with the funds raised from Hong Kong.[118]

Recently, the GITIC liquidators concluded that only 6.5 billion yuan were likely to be recovered against 38.77 billion yuan in liabilities. They further discovered that reckless negligence, if not fraud or felony, was at the centre of the largest bankruptcy in China's history. The shocking findings included that the company books did not reflect the company's financial condition; there was no internal system to monitor the repayment of lending; several billion yuan in loans was either more than five years overdue or the debtors had ceased operation; and its overseas subsidiaries were also seriously insolvent.[119] During the investigation it was revealed that even the management of GITIC had no idea how many subsidiaries it owned. According to the approval documents, there should have been 36; the internal report showed 105; but the investigation found more than 240![120]

Although both the central and provincial governments have tried to put the series of collapses in a positive context by emphasizing their determination to streamline the operation of these financial companies for long-term orderly development, foreign institutions reacted to the incidents by immediately selling out,[121] downgrading GITIC's debts, and subjecting all China-funded companies to a credit-squeeze.[122] Moreover, they were stunned by the sudden government decision because the bankruptcy law does not contemplate such a situation where bankruptcy is used against creditors that wish to keep an enterprise afloat in an unfair way without allowing creditors an opportunity to reply.[123] Further they were deeply puzzled at how this type of massive violation could have happened under the direct control of the provincial government and the supervision of the People's Bank of China, and why the regulators waited so long to do anything about it.[124]

The GITIC case will have a deep impact on the future economic integration of the two sides. It has not only damaged the trust-worthiness of domestic financial institutions and investment projects, but also exposed the Hong Kong financial system to higher risks.[125] Some bankers have expressly stated that they have lost confidence in dealing with these government controlled trust and investment companies,[126] and some fund managers even held that "all of them [subsidiaries and their parents] are conspiring to con us of our money."[127] However, the worst time may not be over yet.

According to an early estimation, the bad debts in Guangdong may be as much as 100 billion yuan.[128] More recently, some high level banking officials have warned that, although most of the problems in the financial sector have been exposed, it may take three to five years to improve the financial system in the Mainland. Moreover, they made it clear that local governments should deal with local debts by themselves.[129]

The Potential Impacts of China's Entry into the WTO on Guangdong

After China concluded its negotiations for entry into the WTO with the United States in November 1999, its accession came closer to realization.[130] As a result, the potential impacts of China's entry into the WTO have generated a considerable amount of research and discussion. Generally, China's future membership of the WTO will further integrate it with the global market and close the gap with international business and legal practices. As a result, the development of the market, together with the corresponding political and legal reforms, is bound to accelerate. On the other hand, China's participation also means serious challenges to the current regime, particularly in trade freedom and the legal framework based on market discipline.

For example, in the past Hong Kong has been used as a stepping stone for many foreign investors to reach Mainland China and its huge market. Guangdong, as the contiguous region, has benefited a great deal from its geographical position, and cultural and people-to-people connections. China's entry into the WTO, which requires more openness in the domestic market and equal treatment to foreign investors, may lead not only to the reduction of Hong Kong's intermediary role in relation to Guangdong,[131] but also to severer economic competition between the two places.

Some scholars have correctly pointed out that the advantages of Guangdong's labour-intensive products on the international market and technology-intensive products on the domestic market have been created by national protective policies.[132] However, in the near future, foreign investors will gain access to the Chinese market with their advantages in technology, finance and information over domestic firms. Foreign products will enter China with much lower custom duties. In these circumstances, Guangdong's manufacturing and processing sector's ability to survive will be severely tested.[133] For example, a recent analysis warns that the earning and development capability of Guangdong enterprises has reached a dangerous level. In 1997, the average profit margin in the total production of local enterprises dropped to 6.67% from 11.42% in 1992, even lower than the bank deposit interest during the same period.[134]

Given the heavy reliance of Guangdong's products on the international market, the implementation of WTO rules will further streamline the provincial import-export practice. In the past, one of Guangdong's major means of competing on the international market was to damagingly undersell its goods. As a result, Guangdong's exports have borne the brunt of 172 anti-dumping actions by foreign countries in the period 1979–94. In some cases, the high anti-dumping duties imposed have forced Guangdong companies to withdraw from certain hard won markets.[135] Apparently, the harsh reality has put pressure not only on the efficiency of business operations and the foreign trade regime of the province, but also on the new round of reforms to allow enterprises more autonomy, including overseas investment, as a means to circumvent the trade barriers. Moreover, the over-relying on import-export manufacturing and processing has hindered the development of service sector in Guangdong since foreign investors' sales, finance and information gathering all take place outside Mainland China. A recent statistical report shows that as compared with 1992, the export output in the total provincial production jumped from 23.75% to 43.2%. However, the increase of service using against the export booming in the same period was merely 0.06%.[136] If the trend continues, the competitive edge created by Guangdong in its early take-off will become a problem for its future development.

The highlighting of the above-mentioned legal challenges does not represent a thorough coverage of all the legal issues and concerns to be solved in the province. Limited space prevents some equally urgent problems from being discussed here, including the effective enforcement of laws and execution of judicial judgments, the transformation of SOEs, the establishment of social welfare and insurance systems, and environment protection.[137]

Analysis

The phenomenon in Guangdong that combines dynamic economic growth and legislation on the one hand and extensive violations and crimes on the other hand may confuse many. However, what has been happening in Guangdong, like other parts of the country, provides some good illustrations of the transition from rule of man, to rule by law, and further to rule of law in the context of Chinese conditions.

Since the establishment of the People's Republic of China (PRC) in 1949, law for a long time was considered as just the expression of the will of the "ruling class" and an instrument of the "dictatorship of the proletariat" to safeguard the socialist regime.[138] After the Cultural Revolution, the tendency towards legal nihilism was broken by the top leaders who held that "there must be law for people to follow and the laws must be strictly observed." As a result, the last two decades have seen a long wave of law-making nationwide. Guangdong, as the pioneering province of national openness and reform, has been taking the lead. However, Deng Xiaoping and other leaders did not want to see a swift change of the legal system or the introduction of democracy, and found themselves in a dilemma between upholding the Party's role and the application of legal rules.[139] Thus law is still viewed as a means to stabilize the policies of the Party in a legal form.[140] It is agreed by some scholars that despite the dynamic legislation, the Party and the government have not entirely accepted the notion of the market economy, and the law is still used as a pragmatic means to promote economic development.[141]

Indeed, the development of a market economy in China has seriously challenged the fundamentals of the notion of law as perceived by the Party and the government. In 1993, when the socialist market economy was legitimized through an amendment to the constitution,[142] the slogan of "market economy is an economy governed by rule by law" became popular to further justify the government's law making. However, its merits were soon questioned, particularly on the substantive fairness and justice of law. The debate led to a break-through in PRC legal history: the constitution was amended again in 1999 to establish the concept of rule of law as the country's goal.[143]

Nevertheless, the recent amendment to the constitution may not be able to immediately change the social and political conditions of China. In particular, there is still a considerable gap between the notion of law in China as a tool of administration and the one held in developed countries where laws are defined as those forms of social consciousness or institutionalized social relations that have as their generic function the expression, regulation, or maintenance of dominant social relations within the social formation.[144] Application of this concept to Guangdong, as well as to other parts of China, will be hindered by the lack of both basic elements: consciousness and institutions.

Despite the government's hard promotion, a legal tradition cannot take root within two decades in a country with a feudal history of over 3,000 years and 50 years of Communist Party governance. Thus far, what has been established in Guangdong in the past two decades is a legislative framework for the so-called socialist market economy that still needs to be supplemented with a lot of important contents, or in some Western scholars' term, an inefficient legal system which would associates with uncertainties and additional costs.[145]

The study of legal developments in Guangdong since the 1970s seems to endorse Professor Hayek's belief that law and legislation are not interchangeable concepts, since legislation does not necessarily lead to a state of law.[146] In a recent report sponsored by the Asian Development Bank (ADB), a key finding was that in major Asian economies the law and legal institutions should not be viewed as technical tools that once adopted will produce the desired out-come.[147] In the case of Guangdong, the increased legislation has not seen the conscious abidance, effective enforcement and establishment of certain necessary formal institutions, such as checks and balances, clear ownership rights, market disciplines and fiduciary duties as well as informal institutions, including customs conventions and professional ethics. As a result, the existing legal rules are not able to prevent local government officials from continuing to interfere with business operations and to fight for local or even personal interests; nor effectively deter other violators. For instance, an investigation into eight harbours in Shenzhen in 1995 found that various duties and fees created by different government authorities numbered as many as 689 items in 82 categories, which made Shenzhen's collection 3.37 and 5.18 times higher than Hong Kong and Singapore respectively.[148] As Professor Zhu Suli correctly holds, the legal evolution includes not only the development of a modern economy, but also conditions that support social transformation.[149] In this regard, the legal construction in Guangdong may represent a national development in living epitome.

Another concern closely connected with the discussion above is the relationship between economic reforms and political reforms in China. Presently, it is beyond any doubt that the achievements of economic reform in China have earned international recognition. However, the efforts in promoting political reforms have been very limited. The disorganized growth and extensive violations in Guangdong particularly reflect the resistance of corrupt ideology and the bureaucratic system, which have viewed political pluralism and power sharing as threats to their traditional monopoly.[150] Even Deng Xiaoping realized that economic reform would not succeed without political reform when he stated; "the final success of all our reforms depends on political reforms."[151] Nevertheless, under the socialist market economy, also known as the market economy with "Chinese characteristics", rule by law always occurs under the party tutelage and remains limited to the extent that the supreme status of the Party leadership cannot be challenged.[152] In this regard, as scholars observed, China is faced with a dilemma between developing the rule of law and preservation of the powers of the Party and the government.[153]

In Guangdong's context, it is interesting to note that on the one hand, widespread corruption derives from the powers subject to no checks and balances; on the other hand, in terms of control, the methods used by the province to circumvent the central government have been widely used by city governments to deal with the provincial authorities. Consequently, *Zhuhou Jingji* (feudal princes' controlled economy) has in fact existed for a long time with localities' own policy, economic systems and barriers against other parts of the province and the country. All these struggles may create more uncertainties to the province's future development.

As such, Professor Stanley Lubman has pointed out, "among the many differences between the Asian newly industrialized countries and China is that China has been travelling an uncertain path leading from totalitarianism to as yet undefined goals involving inconsistently, both establishment of a market economy and maintenance of the continued rules of a Leninist party".[154] His view is shared by Professor James Feinerman, another well-known scholar on Chinese law. He holds that in fact, what the Party and the government have tried to achieve is to exercise "rule by law", rather than "rule of law" since the latter requires the distinction between the state and society.[155]

As the reforms deepen, the relationship between the central and provincial governments will become more complicated and sensitive. In the past two decades, the main themes played in Guangdong have been decentralization and more local autonomy. Recent developments, however, have showed some retreat, not only on tightening up of financial matters, but also on policy and personnel control. Historically, the tension between the central and local governments has never been successfully solved. A study of the evolution of the market economy suggests that the development of a uniform market in China must start with division of powers between the governments at the two levels.[156] Although China's local development is distinguished by its reliance on the existing bureaucratic network and the central government's policy, concrete conditions have made each local government have its own goals, resources and accounting. Thus far, the constitutional question of how the localities can continue to grow in power without fatally damaging the strength of the central government has not been well settled.[157] Thus, to a large extent, the further success of Guangdong in the twenty-first century depends on a satisfactory solution to this problem.

The central-local relationship also has significant impacts on Guangdong–Hong Kong relations because many important issues may not be decided by the two local governments. For example, the establishment of the Guangdong–Hong Kong Co-operation Joint Meeting as a permanent forum needed approval from the State Council as the central government.[158] Moreover, the recent "Big Spender" and "Fung Shui Master" trials have raised concerns of the practical meaning and implementation of the "one country, two systems" principle.[159] In the "Fung Shui Master" case, except for the suspect being a Guangdong resident, the crime was committed in Hong Kong. As such, the Mainland's refusal to allow the trial to take place in Hong Kong led some scholars to question whether Hong Kong was considered part of China under Mainland criminal law.[160] The incidents clearly demonstrate that Hong Kong–Guangdong relations are not of a purely local nature, but part of the Hong Kong–Mainland connection subject to the control of the central government. Thus, uncertainties over future co-operation between Guangdong and Hong Kong as being out of their hands are further compounded by the complex relationship between the central government and Guangdong government. As Professor Stanley Lubman pointed out; "as long as the ultimate goals of the reform remain both vague and self-contradictory the legal rules applicable to foreign investment are likely to continue to reflect more basic Chinese dilemmas".[161]

Guangdong's development also resembles that of other Asian NIEs. The common features underlying the economic transformation of the NIEs are the implementation of market-orientated reform, the adoption of export-orientated industrialization strategies, inflow of foreign capital and technology, and selective intervention by the government.[162] However, the prosperity also brings similar challenges, including tension for political pluralism, corruption, poor enforcement, organized crime, labour abuse, environment pollution and illegal migration.[163] Recent events further prove that the legal systems are insufficient to tackle these problems, rendering the NIEs vulnerable in international competition and financial crisis. Since Guangdong has followed the NIE's development strategy for two decades and has limited autonomy to choose its own legal and political institutions in a centralized state, it seems impossible for Guangdong to skip this painful development stage.

Up to this point, it should be noted that the contents of this chapter are bound to discuss the problems rather than the achievements. However, it would not be fair to leave readers with such a negative impression. Rather, opportunities stand side-by-side with the challenges. At the end of the twentieth century, Guangdong and other local governments had adopted ambitious development plans for the twenty-first century through legislative procedures. According to the Guangdong government's plan, the provincial economy should reach the level of a moderately developed country by the year 2010, with a GDP of 1,970 billion yuan, or 20,800 yuan per capita, representing an annual rate of growth of 12.4%.[164] More specifically, by 2010, the provincial industrial structure shall be transformed from one based on manufacturing to a service led model; import-export volume will go up by 14.8% every year; and actual foreign investment is targeted at US$190 billion between 1990–2010.[165] For provincial officials, the real economic goal behind all these figures is to catch up with Asia's "Four Little Dragons" — South Korea, Taiwan, Hong Kong and Singapore by 2015.[166] Recently, the provincial government announced that the Pearl River Delta shall reach the national goal of modernization ahead of other parts of China by 2005, with Shenzhen as the model city in this evolution.[167]

Moreover, the plans have particularly emphasized the development of provincial democratic and legal systems under a market orientation.[168] The governments at different levels in the province have identified all the problems discussed above and are taking measures to deal with them in a new round of reforms. For example, recently in Guangdong, a township governor was elected based on residents' free nomination for the first time in the PRC's history. The election was considered as a significant breakthrough because in the past, all elections had to be based on the Party's nominations and direct elections in China thus far have been limited to village administrations.[169] Thus, the reform indicates an encouraging future development of democratic politics in the province.

In addition to some recent enactments on anti-corruption and criminal activities, education promotion and reform of SOEs, the provincial Party committee and government jointly promulgated *Certain Opinions on Further Opening* on 11 February 1999. The *Opinions* map out Guangdong's development strategy in all areas, including promoting hi-tech industries with Hong Kong, co-operation to tackle cross-border crime, and raising capital from Hong Kong's securities market. In order to achieve these goals, the *Opinions* promises to improve the investment environment by fostering market institutions in accordance with international standards, increasing transparency in policy-making and enforcement, accelerating national treatment of foreign investment enterprises, and improving people's moral standards and working skills.[170] The promulgation clearly reflects the government's firm commitment to a market economy and orderly development heading to rule of law and thus, the full implementation will surely ensure Guangdong a better future.

Conclusion

Guangdong has made very impressive progress in the past two decades in building up its legal infrastructure, which has facilitated and protected to the province's economic achievements. However, the province, like other parts of the country, is also facing serious legal challenges, including excessive government control over economic affairs, the continuing power struggle among governments at different levels, corruption and high levels of crime, and uncertainties regarding further co-operation and integration with Hong Kong. The reasons for such a sharp contrast between dynamic legislation and extensive violations are multi-fold. The lack of necessary institutions, the resistance of the old ideology, lack of experience and defective market conditions combine to make the transition and exploration more difficult and complex than the course in other NIEs. As such, the legal challenges to Guangdong are the same across the whole country. In addition, the loss of preferential treatment by the central government and the suffering caused by the Asian financial crisis have subjected Guangdong to tougher conditions for its further development.

Nevertheless, given the early pioneering of the market economy, a well-established infrastructure, the governments' firm commitment to the rule of law[171] and its close connection and co-operation with the HKSAR, one may have good confidence in Guangdong's success in dealing with these challenges and exploring new opportunities in the twenty-first century.

Notes

Part of this chapter was presented at the "Conference on Social Development and Legal Construction of Guangdong, Hong Kong and Macau" on 9–11 December 1999 in Shenzhen.

1. Jane Khanna, "The Cultural of Interests in the Subregional Economy of Southern China, Hong Kong, and Taiwan", in Jane Khanna (ed.), *Southern China, Hong Kong, and Taiwan – Evolution of a Subregional Economy* (Washington D.C: The Center for Strategic & International Studies, 1995), p. 1.

2. The data is quoted from Zeng Muyie and Li Kehua, "Guangdong Jingji 20 Nian Fazhan Chengjiu Jiqi Zhanwang" (20 Year Achievements of Guangdong's Economy and Perspectives), *Guangdong Shehui Kexue* (*Social Science in Guangdong*), No. 5, 1998, pp. 24–27.

3. In Guangdong, as much as 80% of foreign investment has come from Hong Kong. The province alone has received more than US$50 billion in investment from Hong Kong firms which now directly employ five million workers.

Geoffrey Murray, *The Next Superpower: Dilemmas in Change and Continuity* (Richmond: China Library, 1998), p. 14.

4. See the *Provisions on the Special Economic Zones of Guangdong* adopted by the Standing Committee of the NPC on 26 August 1980. Printed in The Legislative Affairs Commission of the Standing Committee of the NPC (compiled), *The Law of the People's Republic of China (1990–92)* (Beijing: Science Press, 1993), p. 524.

5. *Ibid.*

6. The Decision of the Standing Committee of the NPC to Delegate the People's Congresses, their Standing Committees and the People's Governments of Zhuhai and Shantou the Powers to Adopt and Implement Regulations and Provisions in the SEZs of 17 March 1996. *Ibid.*, (1996), p. 361.

7. Professor Zhou Wangsheng pointed out that neither the Constitution nor the organic laws of local governments include any provision of SEZ delegated legislation. Zhou Wangsheng (ed.), *Lifa Xue Jiaocheng (A Textbook of Legislative Study)* (Beijing: Legal Publishing House, 1995), pp. 157–158.

8. Article 100 of the 1982 Constitution.

9. Article 10 of the 1982 Constitution.

10. Jiang Yaping, *Gaige Kaifang de Luongtou — Guangdong (The Vanguard of the Opening and Reform — Guangdong)* (Hong Kong: Mirror Cultural Enterprise Ltd., 1993), p. 225.

11. Article 2 of the Amendment to the Constitution of 12 April 1988.

12. Jiang Yaping, *The Vanguard of the Reform*, *op. cit.*, p. 224.

13. The Study Group of the Planning Committee and the Scientific and Technology Committee of Guangdong, *Zhongguo 21 Shiji Yicheng Guangdong Sheng Shishi Fangan Yianjiu Baogao (Part I) — Guangdong Sheng Jinghi Shehui Kechixu Fazhan Zhanlue Yianjiu (Study Report of Implementing Plan of China 21st Century Agenda in Guangdong — A Strategic Study of Economic and Social Sustainable Development of Guangdong Province)* (Guangzhou: Guangdong Economic Publishing House, 1997), p.9. For a detailed survey, see Xianchu Zhang, "Economic Legislation in the Pearl Delta", in Joseph Y. S. Cheng (ed.), *The Guangdong Development Model and Its Challenges* (Hong Kong: City University Press, 1998), pp. 111–145.

14. Liu Guixing, "Guangdong Difang Lifa de Lilun yu Shijia" (Theories and Practice of Guangdong Local Legislation), *Guangzhou Daxue Xuebao (Journal of Guangzhou University)*, No. 3, 1999, p. 14.

15. For a discussion, see Xianchu Zhang, *Economic Legislation*, *op. cit.*, pp. 117–118.

16. See the speech made by Qiao Shi, then President of the Standing Committee of the NPC in Guangdong in *Guangdong Nianjian 1994 (Yearbook of Guangdong 1994)* (Guangzhou: Guangdong Yearbook Publishing House, 1995), p. 155.

17. For a very extensive discussion in this regard, see Zhang Jianguo and Zhou Chengxin (ed), *Shenzhen Jingji Tequ Shichang Jingji Lifa de Lilun yu Shijian* (*Theory and Practice of Shenzhen SEZ Legislation on Market Economy*) (Beijing: Mass Publishing House, 1999); also Luo Musheng, "Guangdong Jingji Tequ de Fazhuan Daolu" (The Developing Path of the SEZs in Guangdong), *Guangdong Shehui Kexue* (*Social Science in Guangdong*), No. 5, 1998, p. 20.

18. Zhang Siping and Gao Xinglie, *Shida Tixi* (*Ten Big Systems — the Basic Framework of Socialist Market Economy in Shenzhen*) (Shenzhen: Haitian Publishing House, 1997), pp. 248–250.

19. See the summary of the 1998 work report of the High People's Court of Guangdong Province, *Nanfang Ribao* (*Southern Daily*), 1 February 1999.

20. The number for 1997 was 528. See *Guangdong Nianjian 1998* (*Yearbook of Guangdong 1998*) (Guangzhou: Guangdong Yearbook Publishing House, 1999), p. 181.

21. *Guangdong Tongji Nianjian 1998* (*Statistical Yearbook of Guangdong 1998*), (Beijing: China Statistical Publishing House, 1998), p. 567.

22. *Ibid.*

23. Yan Junxing (ed.), *Falu Yuanzhu Gongzuo Shouce* (*Handbook of Legal Aid*) (Beijing: Guangming Daily Press, 1997), p. 123.

24. *Statistical Yearbook of Guangdong 1998*, *op. cit.*, p. 567.

25. For a brief review, see Lin Shuwen, Jiaqiang Yuegang Jingji Hezuo, "Strengthening Economic Co-operation between Guangdong and Hong Kong", in *Yearbook of Guangdong 1998*, p. 125.

26. Tung Chee-hwa, Section 13 of the 1998 Policy Address, *South China Morning Post*, 8 October 1998.

27. *Yearbook of Guangdong 1998*, *op. cit.*, p. 180.

28. For a recent discussion on these developments, see Fu Hua-ling, "Cross-Border Co-operation in Criminal Law Matters", *Policy Bulletin of Hong Kong Policy Research Institute*, Feb/Mar Issue, 1999, pp. 7–9.

29. World Bank, *China 2020 — Development Challenges in the New Century*, (Washington D. C: The World Bank, 1997), pp. 97–104.

30. Huang Defa, "Zengchuang Xin Yiushi, Yingjie Xin Shiji" (Looking Forward to the New Century by Re-gaining the Upper Hand — The Challenges and Choices of the Knowledge-based Economic Era to Guangdong) in *Guangdong Statistical Yearbook 1998*, *op. cit.*, pp. 22–25.

31. *Ibid*, p. 22.

32. Zhuao Yufang, "Dangqian Liyong Waizi Gonzuo de Liangda Yiaodian" (The Two Focuses of Current Foreign Investment Utilization) Guangdong *Da Jinmao* (*Economy and Trade of Guangdong*) No. 4, 1998, p. 26.

33. For a discussion in this regard, see Joseph Y. S. Cheng, "Guangdong's New Development Strategy", in Joseph Y.S. Cheng, *The Guangdong Development Model*, *op. cit.*, pp. 15–16.

34. Jiang Zuozhong *et al*, "Zhaozhuen Fangxiang, Zengchuang Huihuang" (Selecting the Right Direction and Creating More Excellence — A Comparative Study of Guangdong with Shanghai, Jiangsu and Shandong), *Guangdong Shehui Kexue* (*Social Science in Guangdong*), No. 4, 1998, p. 28.

35. The Study Group, "Guangdong Jingji: 1996 Nian Huigu ji 1997 Nian Zhanwang" (The Economy of Guangdong Province — 1996 in Respect and 1997 in Prospect) in Li Chao and Li Hongchang (eds.), *Guangdong Jingji Lanpi Shu — Jingji Xingshi yu Yuce 1997* (*Guangdong Economic Blue Paper: An Analysis and Forecast of Economy in Guangdong*) (Guangzhou: Guangdong People's Publishing House, 1997), p.9. According to this study, since 1996 the irrational investment in real estate market has not been effectively stopped.

36. Article 79 of the *Commercial Bank Law* of 1995 and Article 176 of the *Criminal Law* of 1997.

37. See the report in *Ming Pao*, 9 May 1997, A10. The city's party boss and the head of the bank branch were dismissed due to the incident.

38. The Study Group, *Guangdong Economic Blue Paper*, *op. cit.*, p. 7.

39. For a detailed report and discussion, see Tang Zongkun *et al.*, *Guoyiu Qiyie Chanquan Jiaoyi Xingwei Fengxi* (*The Analyses of Behaviours of State Owned Enterprises in Property Right Transactions*), (Beijing: Economic Science Publishing House, 1997), pp. 17–18 and pp. 34–45.

40. For a more detailed discussion, see Xianchu Zhang in Joseph S. Y. Cheng, *The Guangdong Development Model*, *op. cit.*, pp. 133–134. Also, Fang Yitao and Luo Jiansui, "Cong Gangchang Beiqian Kan Jingji Tequ Laodong Mijixing Chanye de Tidu Zhuanyi" (Eventual Transfer of Labour Incentive Industry From Shenzhen SEZ to Northern Areas by Hong Kong Investment Enterprise), *Yatai Jingji* (*Asian and Pacific Economy*) No. 10, 1998, pp. 36–38.

41. Vivien Pik-kwan Chan, "Guangdong Cadres Told to Drop Business", *South China Morning Post*, 27 March 1999, A10.

42. Jiang Zuozhong, "Selecting the Right Direction", *op. cit.*, pp. 24–25.

43. Chen Jie and Li Chao, "Guonei Xingshi dui Guangdong de Tiaozhan Jiqi Duice" (The Domestic Challenge to Guangdong and the Counter-Measures), *Guangdong Fazhan Daokan* (*Guangdong Development Journal*), No. 4, 1998, p. 33.

44. Jiang Zuozhong, "Selecting the Right Direction", *op. cit.*, p. 29.

45. Yasheng Huang, "Why China Will Not Collapse", *Foreign Policy*, No. 99, 1995, pp. 65–66.

46. Chen and Li, "The Domestic Challenge to Guangdong", *op. cit.*, p. 36.

47. Feng-Cheng Fu and Chi-keung Li, "Disparities in Mainland China's Regional Economic Development and Their Implications for Central-Local Economic Relations", *Issues and Studies*, No. 11, 1996, p. 3.

48. The central government granted some special preferential policies to Guangdong in the late 1970s. In the early 1980s, more local autonomy was granted through the establishment of SEZs in Guangdong In 1988, Guangdong was authorized to go ahead of the rest of the country in financial, foreign trade, labour, and other market reforms. In 1992, Deng Xiaoping made his famous tour to Guangdong with gave his firm support to the local experience and made a vigorous call for further bold reforms. Since then, the establishment of a socialist market economy has been set up as the national goal. For a detailed historical review, see Shao Hanqing, *Deng Xiaoping Llun yu Shenzhen Shijian* (*Deng Xiaoping's Theory and Its Practice in Shenzhen*) (Shenzhen: Haitian Publishing House, 1998).

49. George C. S. Lin, *Red Capital in South China Growth and Development of the Pearl River Delta* (Vancouver: UBC Press, 1996), p. 189.

50. Khanna, *Southern China, Hong Kong and Taiwan, op. cit.*, pp. 2–5. It should be noted that the two areas are of historical contention between the central and local governments in China.

51. Gerald Segal, *China Changes Shape: Regionalism and Foreign Policy*, Adelphi *Paper 287* (London: International Institution for Strategic Studies, 1994), p. 55.

52. Dali L. Yang, *Beyond Beijing: Liberalization and the Regions in China* (London and New York: Routledge, 1997), p. 104.

53. For a recent discussion, see Zhong Zhu Ding, "Decentralization and New Central-local Conflicts in China", *American Asian Review*, No. 4, 1998, pp. 63–93.

54. Article 64 of the *Draft Law of Legislation* submitted to the Standing Committee of the NPC for deliberation on 18 October 1999.

55. The latest concerns were articulated by Professor Cheng Xinhe of Zhongshan University in his speech made at the "Conference on Social Development and Legal Construction of Guangdong, Hong Kong and Macau" on 9 December 1999 in Shenzhen.

56. Article 65 of the Law of Legislation of 2000 reads: The people's congress and its standing committee of a SEZ may adopt legal regulations by virtue of the delegated power by the NPC and apply them within the SEZ concerned. The text of the Law is available at:
    http://www.peopledaily.com.cn/200003/15/0108.html.

57. John Fitzgerald, "Autonomy and Growth in China: County Experience in Guangdong Province", *Journal of Contemporary China*, Vol. 11, No. 5, 1996, pp. 7–22.

58. Jian Zemin, "Zhengque Chuli Shehui Zhuyi Xiandaihua Jiashe zhongde Jige Zhongyao Guanxi" (Correctly Handling Some Important Relations in the

Socialist Modernization Construction), *Xinhua Wenzhai* (*Xinhua Digest*), No. 12, 1995, p. 4.

59. See Profile of Li Changchun as Guangdong Provincial Party Committee Secretary, *Inside China Mainland*, January 1999, p. 85. Also see Willy Wo-Lap Lam, "A Power Play Shaking Guangdong", *South China Morning Post*, 3 February 1999, A15.

60. Willy Wo-Lap Lam, "Guangdong Crusade for 'Jiang Thought'", *South China Morning Post*, 12 April 2000, A9.

61. Xianchu Zhang in Joseph Y. S. Cheng, *The Guangdong Development Model*, *op. cit.*, pp. 129–132.

62. Quoted from Li Yahong, "Dui Zhuanxing Shiqi Zhongyang yu Difang Lifa Guanxi de Sikao" (Thoughts on Legislative Relations between the Central and Local Governments during the Transitional Period) *Zhongguo Faxue* (*Chinese Legal Science*), No. 1, 1996, p. 26.

63. Cheng Xinhe, *Jingji Fa Xinlun* (*New Theories of Economic Law — Certain Legal Issues in the Reform*) (Guangzhou: Zhongshan University Press, 1993), pp. 191–194.

64. Zhang Yuqing, "Renzheng Xingshi Lifaquan, Zengchuang Tequ Xinyushi" (Consciously Exercise of SEZ Legislative Powers to Create New Edges of the SEZ), *Faxue Pinglun* (*Wuhan University Law Review*), No. 2, 1997, pp. 67–71.

65. Xie Xiaoyao, "Jingji Tequ Shouquan Lifa Tanxi" (A Study of SEZ Legislation), *Zhongshan Daxue Xuebao* (*Journal of Zhongshan University*), No. 1, 1998, pp. 106–108.

66. As Li Peng, the Chairman of the Standing Committee of the NPC, pointed out, the SEZ legislative power should be one of the principal means to further develop the SEZs in the new circumstances. See the report of his speech, *Renmin Ribao* (*People's Daily*), 5 April 1996, p. 1.

67. See Chapter 4 of the *Law of Legislation* of 2000 dealing with local legislation, where provincial law-making power is provided on the top.

68. Article 65 of the Law.

69. For a recent discussion of these policies and treatment, see Li Xueling, *Tebie Jingjiqu Fa* (*Law of Special Economic Zones*) (Beijing: Legal Publishing House, 1997), pp. 36–52.

70. The summary of Hu's argument is printed in Zhang Wenmin (ed.), *Zhongguo Jingji Da Lunzhan* (*The Great Economic Controversies in China*) (Beijing, Economic Management Publishing House, 1997), Vol. 2, pp. 234–236.

71. Zeng Qing, "Gunzi xiang Shui Dalai" (The Chastising Rod to Whom?) *Shenzhen Tequ Bao* (*Shenzhen SEZ Daily*), 14 September 1995.

72. The preferential treatment lost by the SEZs included favourable or flexible measures in taxation, land use, foreign exchange, banking credit, employment,

border crossing, investment and trade and management autonomy. Shao, *Deng Xiaoping's Theory and Practice in Shenzhen*, *op. cit.*, pp. 184–185.

73. It has been realized that the SEZs' fate shall depend on whether they can adapt themselves to changing conditions, redefine their functions and develop suitable development strategies. "Zhan Du, Zhuazhu Xingde Lishi Jiyu, Buduan Fahui Duo Fangmian Yushi" (Catching the Historical Opportunity and Further Play Multi-sided Advantages) in Wu Yumin (ed.), *Zhongguo Jinji Tequ 21 Shiji Fazhan Zhanlue Yanjiu* (*A Strategic Study of Development of Special Economic Zones in China in 21st Century*) (Guangzhou: Southern China Polytechnic University Press, 1996), p. 59.

74. Zhao Yining, "Tequ Zenmo Te Zhenglun de Beihou" (Behind the Debates Concerning SEZs' Specialty), *Liaowang* (*Outlook*), 9 October 1995, p. 13.

75. Margaret Y. K. Woo, "Legal Reforms in the Aftermath of Tiananmen Square", *Review of Social Law*, No. 1, 1991, p. 58.

76. Lynn T. White, III, *Unstately Power, Vol. I: Local Causes of China's Economic Reforms* (New York and London: East Gate, 1998), p. 295.

77. Investigation and Research Group of Disciplinary Committee of Guangdong Province, the Main Issues Concerning Current Anti-corruption Campaign and Their Counter-measures in Research Office of the Disciplinary Committee of the Central Committee of the Communist Part (ed.), *Wunian Jinji, Wunian Sisuo* (*Five Years' Campaign, Five Years' Thinking — Review of Anti-corruption Campaign since 14th National Congress of the Party*) (Beijing: Fangzheng Publishing House, 1997), pp. 52–53.

78. For a report of the case, see Compiling Group, *90 Niandai Chengzhi Fubai Daan Yaoan Jishi* (*Major Anti-corruption Cases in 1990s*) (Beijing, Fangzheng Publishing House, 1998) pp. 53–67.

79. See the report in *Liaowang* (*Outlook*), 22 March 1999, p. 5.

80. See the report in *Ming Pao*, 13 March 1999, A15.

81. See the report in *Liaowang* (*Outlook*), 22 March 1999, pp. 3–4.

82. See the report in *Nanfang Ribao* (*Southern Daily*) 2 February 1999.

83. Liu Zhifeng (ed.), *Zouxiang Cifa Gongzheng* (*Towards Judicial Justice*), (Beijing: Material Publishing House of China, 1998), pp. 287–288.

84. *Ibid.*, pp. 282–287.

85. *Ibid.*, p. 465.

86. Cao Feng, *Diwuci Gaofeng—Dangdai Zhongguo de Fanzui Wenti* (*The Fifth Wave — Contemporary Criminal Issues in China*), (Beijing: Today's China Publishing House, 1997), p. 29.

87. *Ibid.*, p. 47.

88. *Ibid*, pp. 54–55.

89. See the report in *Ming Pao*, 8 March 1999, A14.

90. *Yearbook of Guangdong 1998, op. cit.*, pp. 176–177. For an extensive treatment, see Wai-kin Che, "The Drug Problem in Guangdong Province: an Unexpected By-product of Development", in Joseph Y. S. Cheng (ed.), *The Guangdong Development Model, op. cit.*, pp. 335–378.

91. *Ming Pao*, 13 November 1998, A20.

92. For a recent discussion in this regard, see Pun Ngai, Becoming *Dagongmei* (Working Girls): the Politics of Identity and Difference in Reform China, *The China Journal*, No. 42, July 1999, pp. 1–18.

93. Simon X. B. Zhao and Chun-Shing Chow, "Disparities Between Social and Economic Development in Guangdong", *Journal of Contemporary China*, Vol. 19, No. 7, 1998, p. 481.

94. Huang Defa, *Looking Toward the New Century, op. cit.*, p. 25.

95. The Study Group of the Guangdong Social Science Academy, "Xin Fazhanguan yu Guangdong Gaige Fazhan Xin Jieduan" (The New View on Development and the New Stage of Guangdong's Reform and Development), *Guangdong Shehui Kexue (Social Science in Guangdong)*, No. 5, 1997, p. 41.

96. Cao Feng, *The Fifth Wave, op. cit.*, p. 132.

97. For a detailed discussion, see K. H. Mok, "Education Development in Guangdong in the Context of Educational Reform in China", in Joseph Y. S. Cheng, *Guangdong's Development Model, op. cit.*, pp. 251–274.

98. Zhao and Chow, "Disparities", *op. cit.*, pp. 480–481.

99. See Tung Chee-hwa, Section 14 of the 1998 Policy Address.

100. According to a survey conducted by the Hong Kong Trade Development Bureau in 1997, among 751 trade and manufacturing firms, 52% answered positively for the continuation of their investment in Guangdong. Fei Yue, "Tuegang Xieshou Gongchuang Xin Jiyuan" (Jointly Creating A New Era by Guangdong and Hong Kong), *Gangau Jingji (Hong Kong and Macao Economy)*, No. 5, 1998, p. 1.

101. See Tung Chee-hwa, Sections 48 and 49 of the 1999 Policy Address.

102. Zhao Daying, "98 Yuekong Jingji Hezuo Zuotan Hui Zongshi" (A Summary of 98 Symposium on Economy), *Zhujiang Sanjiaozhou Jingji (Pearl River Delta Economy)*, No. 1, 1999, p. 16.

103. See Li Xiuheng, "97 Nian Yuegong Jingmao Hezuo de Fangxiang yu Jianyi" (The Direction and Proposals of Economic and Trade Co-operation between Guangdong and Hong Kong after 1997), *Zhujiang Sanjiaozhou Jingji (Pearl River Delta Economy)* No. 2–3, 1997, pp. 11–12. Also Yan Xiaojiang, "Huigui houde Xianggang yu Tequ de Chanye Hezuo" (Industrial Co-operation between Hong Kong and Special Economic Zones after the Handover), *Tequ yu Gangao*

Jingji Yuekan (*SEZs and Hong Kong–Macao Economy*), No. 8, 1998, pp. 46–47.

104. Quoted by Dick Wilson, "Safeguarding a Symbiosis", *Hong Kong Business*, March 1999, p. 6.

105. Tsang Shu-ki and Cheng Yuk-shing, "The Economic Link-up of Hong Kong and Guangdong: Structure and Development Problems", *Working Paper Series*, No. 54 (10/97), Faculty of Social Science, Lingnan College, Hong Kong, 1997, p. 8. Also, see Yuan Yiming, "Certain Issues to Be Solved Concerning Expansion of Technology Cooperation between Hong Kong and the Mainland", in Li Rongbin, Feng Subao and Jiang Weiping (eds.), *Xianggang yu Zhujiang Sanjiaozhou Gongye Fazhan: Jiyu yu Celue* (*Industrial Devepment of Hong Kong and Pearl River Delta: Opportunities and Strategies*) (Hong Kong: jointly published by Polytechnic University of Hong Kong, Shenzhen Institute of Comprehensive Development, and Science and Technology Promotion Association of Hong Kong, 1997), pp. 105–109.

106. Mo Shixiang, "Shenkong Hezuo de Huigu yu Qianzhan" (Review and Prospective of Shenzhen–Hong Kong Co-operation), *Shenzhen Daxue Xuebao* (*Journal of Shenzhen University — Humanties and Social Science*) No. 3, 1999, p. 36.

107. Chen Wenhong, "Shenzhen Jingji Jinyibu Liyong Gangzi Yanju Baogao" (Study Report on Further Utilization of Hong Kong Investment in Shenzhen's Economy), *Ziben Zazhi* (*Capital*), No. 10, 1997, p. 106.

108. Ji Chongwei, "Xianggang yu Zhujiang Sanjiaozhou Hezuo Fazhan Gaoxin Jishu Chanye de Qianjing" (The Perspective of Hi-tech Development Co-operation between Hong Kong and the Pearl River Delta) in Li, Feng and Jiang, *Xianggang yu Zhujiang sanjiaozhou Gongye Fazhan*, *op. cit.*, pp. 95–104.

109. See Tung Chee-hwa, Section 41 of the 1999 Policy Address.

110. See the report in *Guangdong Da Jingmao* (*Guangdong Great Economy and Trade*), No. 10, 1998, p. 24.

111. Zhou Chengxin, "Lun Zhengque Rishi Shengang Liangdi Falu de Xianghu Guanxi"(Correctly Recognizing the Relations between the Legal Systems of Shenzhen and Hong Kong) in Wang Zhengming and Zhou Chengxin (eds.), *Shenzhen Tequ Jiejian Xianggang Fazhi Yanjiuji* (*Collection of Essays on Shenzhen's Borrowing from Hong Kong's Legal System*) (Shenzhen: Haitian Publishing House, 1996), pp. 1–10.

112. Sung Yun Wing, "Hong Kong's Economic Integration with the Mainland: Beyond Guangdong", a conference paper presented to the "Conference on Hong Kong in China: A Year Later", Singapore, 29–31 October 1998, p. 17–18

113. Report on *Guangdong Great Economy and Trade*, *op. cit.*, p. 24.

114. Lana Wong and Christine Chan, "GITIC Fails on US$30m Payment", *South China Morning Post*, 16 October 1998, B1.

115. Christine Chan and Matthew Miller, "GITIC Forced into Bankruptcy", *Ibid.*, 11 January 1999, A1.

116. Editorial, "The Hong Kong Government Must Thoroughly Investigate the Debt Scandal", *Ming Pao*, 3 March 1999, A3.

117. "Securities Law: a Good Beginning", *China Economic Review*, March 1999, p. 18. Professor Anthony Neoh, the former Chairman of the Hong Kong Securities and Futures Commission, points out that the existing legislation in China is inadequate in dealing with these parent companies which potentially play a make-or-break role in listed companies. *Ibid.*

118. See the report in *Ming Pao*, 29 January 1999, B1.

119. Matthew Miller and Lana Wong, "GITIC 'Grossly Negligent'", *South China Morning Post*, 23 April 1999, B1.

120. Hu Shuli and others, "The Rise and Fall of GITIC", in Hu Shuli (ed.), *Yinbao cong 1998 Kaishi (Touching-off from 1998)* (Beijing: World Knowledge Publishing House, 1999), p. 104.

121. See the report on "Foreign Funds Cleared their "Red Chip" Holdings", *Ming Pao*, 13 January 1999, B2.

122. *Ming Pao*, 12 January 1999, A2. It was reported that in the first six months after the closure of GITIC, Hong Kong banks' loans to Mainland companies was reduced by HK$23.5 billion. *Dongfang Ribao (Oriental Daily News)*, 7 May 1999, B3.

123. Gordon G. Chang, "Examination of Technical Bankruptcy Issues Crucial for GITIC Creditors", *China Law & Practice*, February 1999, pp. 67–72.

124. For example, the investigation shows that only 132 out of 240 investment projects were on GITIC's book; the company's assets were only 60% of what it declared; and large amount debts were not present in the accounts. As one foreign investor opined, "it appears GITIC was a golden valley for people to enrich themselves." Matthew Miller, "Questions of Felony Emerge in GITIC Crash", *South China Morning Post*, 23 April 1999, B3.

125. Lana Wong, "Debt Trouble at Guangdong Investment Arm Threaten SAR", *South China Morning Post, China Business Review*, 11 March 1999. Recently, it is estimated that the bad debts of China-funded companies would drive the problematic loans of Hong Kong banks up to 6%. Huang Shaozhen, "Zhongzi Qiye Budao Shenhua Pomie" (Falling of Mainland Enterprises' Fairy Tale), *Ziben (Capital)* No. 3, 1999, p. 106.

126. Matthew Miller and Christine Chan, "GITIC Debt Decision Dismays Creditors", *South China Morning Post*, 11 January 1999, B1.

127. *China Economic Review*, p. 18.

128. *Ming Pao*, 20 May 1998, A13.

129. *Ming Pao*, 29 April 1999, A21.

130. Since the details of the agreement between China and the US have not been disclosed at the time of writing, the discussion here can only touch on some general concerns.

131. Xu Zhuoyu, "Zhongguo Jiaru WTO dui Yuegang Jingji de Yingxiang ji Yinying Cuoshi" (The Impacts of China's Entry into WTO on Guangdong and Hong Kong Economy and Handling Measures), *Zhujiang Sanjiaozhou Jingji (Pearl River Delta Economy)*, No. 3, 1999, p. 7.

132. Pan Li, "Zhongguo Jiaru WTO yu Guangdong de Chanye Tiaozheng" (China's Participation into WTO and the Restructuring of Guangdong's Industries), *Nanfang Jinji (Southern Economy)*, No. 7, 1999, p. 18.

133. Chen Honglei, "Jiaru WTO dui Guangdong Jiadianyie de Yingxiang ji Duice" (Impacts of TWO entry on Guangdong's Household Electronic Industry and the Counter-measures), *Zhujiang Sanjiaozhou Jingji (Pearl River Delta Economy)*, No. 3, 1999, p. 42; Zhang Xiujuan and Mao Yianhua, "Zhongguo Jiaru WTO dui Guangdong Jiadian Chanye de Yingxiang he Tiaozhan" (Impacts and Challenges to Household Electronic Appliance Industry of China's Entry into WTO), *ibid*, p. 36–37.

134. Bu Xinmin *et al*, Yuhua Jiegou Shi Dangwu Zhiji (The Current Urgency Is To Rationalization of the Economic Structure), *Zhongguo Guoqing Guoli (China's National Conditions and Strength)*, No. 1, 2000, p. 29.

135. Sui Guangjun, *Guangdong Chuyu Zhuanzhedian (Guangdong at the Turning Point—A Study of Guangdong's Development in the New Century)*, (Guangzhou: Guangdong's People's Publishing House, 1997), p. 210.

136. Bu Xinmen, Yuhua Jiegou Shi Dangwu Zhiji, *op. cit.*, p. 20.

137. In his recent Policy Address, the HKSAR Chief Executive expressed his deep concern regarding environment protection in the Pearl River Delta. He further identified six areas where Guangdong's co-operation is needed. The two sides have agreed to set up a joint working group to deal with the relevant problems. See Tung Chee-hwa, Section 120 of the 1999 Policy Address.

138. Albert H. Y. Chen, "The Developing Theory of Law and Market Economy in Contemporary China", in Wang Guiguo and Wei Zhenying (eds.), *Legal Developments in China — Market Economy and Law* (Hong Kong: Sweet & Maxwell, 1996), p. 7.

139. Carlos Wing-hung Lo, *China's Legal Awakening* (Hong Kong: Hong Kong University Press, 1995), especially Chapter Two: Deng Xiaoping's Ideas on Law, pp. 33–41.

140. Chen Jiafu, "China: Constitutional Change and the Legal Reform", in Alice E.S. Tay and Conita S. C. Leung (eds.), *Greater China: Law, Society and Trade* (Sydney: The Law Book Company Limited, 1995), p. 142.

141. Li Lin, "Shishi Yifa Zhiguo de Tedian he Xuyao Jiejue de Wenti" (The Characteristics of Rule of Law Implementation and Problems to Be Solved),

Faxue (*Legal Science*), No. 9, 1998, pp. 7–8; and Ronald C. Keith, *China's Struggle for Rule of Law*, (New York: St. Martin's Press, 1994).

142. Article 7 of the 1993 Amendment to the Constitution.

143. Article 13 of the 1999 Amendment stipulates that China shall be governed by law and developed into a socialist country governed by the rule of law. For a discussion of the background to the amendment, see Albert H. Y. Chen, "The Developing Theory of Law", *op. cit.*, pp. 4–7; Li Buyun and Li Qing, "Cong Fazhi dao Fazhi" (From Rule by Law to Rule of Law) *Faxue* (*Legal Science*), No. 7, 1999, pp. 2–5; and Guo Daohui, "Zhiguo Fanglue de Genben Gaibian" (The Fundamental Change of the Governance of the Country) in Liu Hainian, Li Buyun and Li Lin (eds.) *Yifa Zhiguo, Jianshe Shehui Zhiyi Fazhi Guojia* (*Governing the Country by Law, Constructing a Socialist Country under Rule of Law*) (Beijing: Legal System Publishing House, 1996), pp. 111–112.

144. Francis G. Snyder, *Capitalism and Legal Changes: An African Transformation* (London: Academic Press, 1981), p. 10.

145. Robert Brown and Alan Gutterman, *Asian Economic and Legal Development—Uncertainty, Risk, and Legal Efficiency* (London: Kluwer Law International, 1998), pp. 129–145.

146. Friedrich A Hayek, *Law, Legislation, and Liberty* (Chicago: University of Chicago Press, 1973), Vol. 1.

147. Katharina Pistor and Philip A. Wellons, *The Role of Law and Legal Institutions in Asian Economic Development 1960–1995*, (Oxford: Oxford University Press, 1999), p. 19.

148. See the report in *Guangzhou Ribao* (*Guangzhou Daily*), 9 March 1995.

149. Suli Zhu, "Paradoxes of Legal Development in 20th Century China from the Perspective of Modernisation", *Hong Kong Law Journal*, Vol. 28, Part 3, 1998, p. 429.

150. Wang Yuesheng, "What does Eastern Europe Tell Us?", in Dong Yuyu and Shi Binhai (eds.), *Political China—Facing the Time selected by the New System*, (Beijing: Today's China Publishing House, 1998) p. 87.

151. *Ibid.*, the title page.

152. Carlos Wing-hung Lo, "Socialist Legal Theory in Deng Xiaoping's China", *Columbia Journal of Asian Law*, No. 2, 1997, p. 486.

153. Zheng Yongnian, "From Rule by Law to Rule of Law? A Realistic View of China's Legal Development", *China Perspective*, October 1999, pp. 31–43; and Pitman B. Potter, "The Chinese Legal System: Continuing Commitment to the Primacy of State Power", *The China Quarterly*, No. 3, 1999, pp. 673–83.

154. Stanley Lubman, "Introduction: the Future of Chinese Law", in Stanley Lubman(ed.), *China's Legal Reform* (Oxford: Oxford University Press, 1996), p. 8.

155. James Feinerman, "Introduction: The Rule of Law … with Chinese Socialist Characteristics", *Current History*, September, 1997, pp. 278–81.

156. Zhou Weilin, *Zhongguo Difang Zhengfu Xingwei Fenxi* (*Analyses of Economic Behavior of Local Governments in China*) (Shanghai: Fudan University Press, 1997), particularly, p. 11.

157. Jean C. Oi, "The Role of the Local State in China's Transitional Economy", in Andrew G. Walder (ed.), *China's Transitional Economy* (Oxford: Oxford University, 1996), pp. 170–87.

158. Fei Yue, "Jointly Creating a New Era", *op. cit.*.

159. H. L. Fu, "The Battle of Criminal Jurisdictions", *Hong Kong Law Journal*, Vol. 28, Part 3, 1998, pp. 273–281.

160. Cindy Sui, "Verdict 'Put SAR's Status in Doubt'", *South China Morning Post*, 21 April 1999, A3.

161. Stanley Lubman, *China's Legal Reform*, *op. cit.*, p. 8.

162. Gerald Tan, *The Economic Transformation of Asia* (Singapore: Times Academic Press, 1997), p. 342.

163. For a recent detailed examination, see James Shinn (ed.), *Fires Across the Water: Transnational Problems in Asia* (New York: Council on Foreign Relations, 1998).

164. Huang Weihong, "Zhanwang Xin Shiji, Zaichuang Xin Huihuang" (Looking Forward to the New Century for New Glorious Achievements), *Guangdong Fazhan Daokan* (*Journal of Guangdong Development*), No. 5, 1998, p. 16.

165. Study Group, "Study Report of Implementing the Plan of China 21st Century Agenda in Guangdong", *op. cit.*, p. 6.

166. Harry J. Waters, *China's Economic Development Strategies for the 21st Century*, (Connecticut: Quorum Books,1997), p. 71.

167. The speech made by He Jinghuan, the Deputy Mayor of Shenzhen at the "Conference of Social Development and Legal Construction of Guangdong, Hong Kong and Macau" on 9 December 1999 in Shenzhen.

168. Study Group, "Study Report of Implementing the Plan of China 21st Century Agenda in Guangdong", *op. cit.*, p. 6.

169. See the report in *Ming Pao*, 30 April 1999, A 10.

170. The *Opinions* were printed in *Nanfang Ribao* (*Southern Daily*), 23 February 1999.

171. It should be noted that in the recent amendment to the Constitution, Article 13 explicitly stipulates that China shall be governed by law and shall commit itself to the construction of a socialist country by rule of law. Amendment made on 15 March 1999 to the 1982 Constitution. *Zhonghua Renmin Gongheguo Xianfa* (*Constitution of the PRC*) (Beijing: Legal Publishing House, 1999), p. 48.

CHAPTER 10

Legal Developments and New Challenges in Guangdong Province

GU Minkang

Introduction

At the beginning of the reform process in China, Guangdong was given wider law making powers to promulgate rules and regulations provided they did not contradict to Chinese constitution, national laws and regulations.[1] The underlying reason behind this special treatment was that Guangdong has the geographical advantage of being next to Hong Kong and Macau,[2] enabling it to increase business contacts between these two regions and learn from their experiences. Guangdong started business relations with Hong Kong and Macau very early on in the form of two-way trade and investment.[3] This relationship was strengthened after 1 July 1997, the day Hong Kong was returned to China's sovereignty, and 20 December 1999, the day Macau became reunited with the People's Republic of China (PRC). Regarding the development of the legal system, Guangdong has gained much experience since the reform process began, especially from Hong Kong where business laws are well developed. A good example is the 1992 *Shenzhen Provisional Regulations for Limited Joint Stock Companies*, in which many of the provisions were borrowed from Hong Kong company law.[4] For this reason, many of Guangdong's regulations have become "pilot-studies" for national legislation.[5] And it is not surprising to see that many new local regulations first emerged in Guangdong.

In China, Guangdong has promulgated the most comprehensive set of legislation among all the provinces. Beginning 18 years ago, Guangdong has made remarkable progress in enacting local legislation, and has become the model of "walking first" (*Xian Xing Yi Bu*) in China.[6] From 1979 to 1996, Guangdong passed 769 rules and regulations. During the period 1993–96, 124 pieces of local legislation were passed, amounting to 55.36% of all legislation within the past 18 years.[7] The amount of legislation is obviously more than other provinces and cities.[8] These local rules and regulations cover various areas, including: (1) the Special Economic Zones (SEZs); (2) the economy; (3) public security, justice and civil administration; (4) nationalities and overseas Chinese; (5) education, culture and sanitation; and (6) local people's congresses.[9] Much of the legislation has been experimental in nature, and used as a reference point by the central government and other provinces.[10]

When discussing legal developments in Guangdong, it can be argued that many of the legal measures have been quite innovative. Since the 1980s, Guangdong has solicited public opinion during the legislative process. This is deemed as the "democratization of legislation", i.e., the legislation will reflect actual needs, and the will and intelligence of the people (*Ti Min Qing, Biao Min Yi and Ju Min Zhi*).[11] Furthermore, Guangdong was the first province to pass legislation on the management of prices. Starting on 1 July 1999, Guangdong began to enforce the *Implementation Measures for the Price Law of the PRC*. This is regarded as the first piece of local legislation performing a gap-filling function.[12] The Guangdong authorities implemented a public hearing system on 9 September 1999. The public hearing concerned the *Amendment Draft of Bidding of Guangdong Construction Projects*, and was the first public hearing since the establishment of the PRC in 1949, and hence is regarded as an important milestone in the development of Chinese democracy.[13]

However, the province's rapid economic development requires the provincial government to focus on further legal development that will guide Guangdong into the twenty-first century, especially in view of the "Big Triangle Economic Co-operation Programme" put forward by the Chief Executive of the Hong Kong Special Administrative Region (HKSAR), Tung Chee-hwa in his 1999 Policy Address.[14] According to Guangdong's 1998–2003 legislative plan, the provincial government plans to promulgate 104 rules and regulations in 35 categories.[15] These include regulations on the joint stock co-operative system, environmental protection and labour rights.[16] Nevertheless, much more needs to be done before China can realize the goal of "a country under the rule of law" (*Fa Zhi Guo Jia*). This can be illustrated through two aspects. First, it is not enough to pass legislation without considering its implementation. In Guangdong, as well as across the whole of China, the main problem is enforcement of laws and regulations due to local protectionism and corruption. Second, even though the Guangdong government has done a great deal of work to improve its legal system, many other problems need to be considered in order to fulfil the concept of a county under the rule of law. According to some sources, the major problems existing in Guangdong can be summarized into four main areas:

(a) There is conflict between the need to continue economic growth and a shortage of resources, overpopulation and environmental issues;

(b) There is conflict between the need to improve industry, social development and educational development;

(c) There is conflict between the organic or co-operative development of the economy and the existing local interest structure;

(d) There is conflict between high-speed economic development and the relatively slow social development.[17]

Certainly, the reconciliation of these conflicts requires further legal development in order to facilitate a well-organized environment. The existing or potential legal problems are obstacles to the future development of Guangdong province. If Guangdong is to move smoothly into the twenty-first century and maintain its leading legislative role in China, these challenges must be met. Readers must bear in mind that the legal challenges and legal developments can be discussed from various aspects, as they involve issues of culture, economics and science. All these elements will affect legal developments. Considering the nature of this book, however, readers should consult the other chapters in order to understand the whole picture of Guangdong's legal development. For this reason, this chapter will limit its discussion to several topics rather than trying to examine every aspect. Even though there is a good relationship among Guangdong, Hong Kong and Macau, it is an onerous task for the former to learn from the legal framework of the latter. Guangdong needs to pay attention to the following areas:

(a) First, Guangdong has serious problems in the financial sector. Therefore, the management of financial institutions should be further regulated;

(b) Second, Guangdong has the country's most serious smuggling problem, as well as endemic corruption. Therefore, the government should organize an effective force to crackdown on these illegal activities;

(c) Third, due to its geographic location, Guangdong is an ideal location for investment and tourism from Hong Kong and Macau. Therefore, more regulations concerning foreign investment and tourism activities are needed, especially regarding investment and tourism from the HKSAR;

(d) Fourth, the idea of a country under the rule of law, put forward by the central government, should be given serious attention by the provincial government.

Regulating and Supervising Financial Institutions

As mentioned earlier, Guangdong is well known for its flexible policies and regulations regarding economic reform. Some of the policies and regulations carried out in Guangdong have not been formally endorsed by the central government. For this reason, some observers have strongly criticized Guangdong for going too far, a situation summed up by the phrase "walk faster when the green light is on; make a detour when the red light is on; manage to walk when there is no light on" (*Jian Le Lu Deng Gan Jin Zou; Jian Le Hong Deng Lou Zhe Zou; Mei You Deng Shi Xiang Fa Zou*).[18] On the one hand, this phrase may be considered as praise for Guangdong province. In China, even though the central government adopted a policy of economic reform and opening up to the outside world in 1978, and that China should move towards a "socialist market economy", no one actually has a clear concept of how economic reforms should be carried out. Because of this situation, China's former paramount leader, Deng Xiaoping, encouraged people to "touch stones when crossing a river" (*Mo Zhe Shi Tou Guo He*). This implies that many unsuccessful experiments would have to take place if progress was to be made, but that the persons responsible would not usually be punished.[19] Due to its learning experiences from Hong Kong, Guangdong has played an important role in offering the central government many new and successful initiatives, including the privatization of state-owned enterprises (SOEs) through auctions. Guangdong's implementation of bankruptcy, merger and acquisition laws has also been highly praised by the central government.[20]

On the other hand, however, this kind of practice has caused serious problems due to a lack of control and supervision. This has led to many violations of laws and rules promulgated by the central government. In this regard, the financial sector in Guangdong offers a good illustration. Generally speaking, violations of financial institutions can be categorized as follows:

(a) Disregarding the standard interest rates provided by the central government and soliciting deposits by offering interest rates several times higher than standard rates. The result of this kind of practice enlarged the costs and directly affected the economic benefits of the banks;

(b) Deducting the interest from loans when offered to enterprises. This increased the heavy economic burdens of enterprises and led to bad debts;

(c) Allowing enterprises to open multiple accounts in order to earn more management fees. The result of this kind of practice increased the possibility of financial violations by enterprises.[21]

It is clear that Guangdong has encountered many serious financial problems.[22] It was reported that Guangdong had bad debts of over 100 billion yuan (more than US$80 billion), the highest in China.[23] As this was a major concern for the central government it urged strong action. From 1996 to 1998, several financial institutions were ordered to investigate illegal activities among their personnel. As a result, one deputy director of a city bank co-operative was arrested.[24] In the Yunfu city branch of the People's Bank of China (PBOC), seven personnel were found to have misappropriated money amounting to US$100 million. Among those seven personnel, three were members of the Chinese Communist Party.[25] On 26 August 1997, two high-ranking officers at the Zhongshan branch of the PBOC were sentenced to death. In addition the director and deputy director were sentenced to five years in prison.[26] In 1998, five financial institutions were punished for violating state foreign currency regulations.[27] In November 1998, nine companies were ordered to cease operation because of financial irregularities on the Hong Kong Hang Seng Index (Futures).[28]

The most shocking story was the shutdown of the Guangdong International Trust and Investment Corporation (GITIC), the second biggest trust and investment corporation in China, due to a serious financial crisis mainly caused by corrupt management practices. In this incident, the general manager, Huang Yantian, was detained. More than 10 senior personnel were also placed under investigation.[29] At first the Chinese government promised that GITIC's foreign creditors would be paid back, but later reneged on this promise.[30] Shortly afterwards, the Guangzhou International Trust and Investment Corporation also experienced financial difficulties. It was estimated that it had assets worth approximately 20 billion yuan, but debts amounting to 19 billion yuan. The vice-mayor of Guangzhou, Sheng Bonian, warned that the city government would not provide the company with any financial assistance. He said that if the company could not pay its debts, it should be bankrupted.[31] These examples demonstrate the need for greater regulation over Guangdong's financial institutions.

Further Regulating the Financial Institutions in Guangdong

Financial institutions in Guangdong should be subject to greater regulation, rather than de-regulation. During the recent Asian financial crisis, many people speculated as to the main causes of the financial turmoil. One strongly held view was that many countries in Asia had misunderstood the idea of de-regulation. De-regulation does not mean that there are no regulations or that financial institutions can do whatever they want.[32] Instead, de-regulation should be interpreted as giving greater autonomy to financial institutions while the government retains macro-control and is responsible for general policies. Under this system, financial institutions must follow the general rules and policies of the central government. Interestingly, one author has pointed out that the financial market in Guangdong is still falling behind, because it is still subject to strict control.[33] The vice mayor of Guangzhou has again recently expressed the same view.[34] This opinion may be misled by the "irrelevance hypothesis", i.e., law as a formal legal system is irrelevant for economic and social development as no detectable link between different legal arrangements and intermediate economic growth factors has ever been found. In fact, as Albert Chan has noted, "law made an important contribution to Asia's economic development and was most effective when it was congruent with economic policies".[35]

The regulation of financial institutions in Guangdong can only be effectively enforced by establishing a good legal framework. In fact, a general regulatory framework has been provided by the central government:

(a) On 13 July 1998, the State Council promulgated the *Measures Regarding Banning Illegal Financial Institutions and Illegal Financial Activities.*[36] By its terms, those who establish illegal financial institutions or conduct illegal financial activities will be subject to fines, administrative sanctions or criminal punishment;

(b) In November 1998, the State Council abolished the branch banks of the PBOC at the provincial level and established nine branch banks which have jurisdiction over several provincial areas. For example, the Guangzhou branch of the PBOC now has jurisdiction over Guangdong province, Guangxi Autonomous District and Hainan province.[37] It is clear that the central government wants to put all the financial institutions under the tight control of the PBOC;

(c) The head of the PBOC published an article in the *People's Daily* arguing that financial supervision must adopt the principle of management and supervision of different businesses.[38] This conclusion was reached after considering the situation of the Chinese financial market;

(d) The PBOC has made it very clear that a bankruptcy mechanism should be established for financial institutions;[39]

(e) The Chinese financial market is not well regulated. For this reason, Chinese law clearly stipulates that banks, security firms and insurance companies should be operated separately.[40] Therefore, Chinese commercial banks should not be allowed to engage in trust investment and stock operation and should not be permitted to invest in immovable property within the territory of the PRC that is not for their own use.[41]

It is understandable that the decision to separate the various financial markets was due to the immaturity of the Chinese financial markets. In the long run, however, this kind of limitation will eventually be overcome. The new movements of financial institutions in developed countries support this conclusion. For example in the United States, the NationsBank Corporation, which owns Boatmen's First, recently announced a US$1.2 billion acquisition of

Montgomery Securities. According to Ed Brown, the president of NationsBank Global Finance; "This combination is going to enhance our ability to provide one-stop financial services to our clients".[42] This statement indicates that US banks are going to extend the scope of their business to include insurance and securities. Certainly this can be done in the US because the financial markets are well developed. Even though commercial banks in China are not allowed to conduct insurance or securities transactions at the moment, this situation will change greatly in the twenty-first century when Chinese financial markets become more developed. The Guangdong government should foresee this possibility and try to provide some good experiences for the central bank.[43]

Taking Secured Interests While Making Loans

Commercial banks usually have two major financial activities. One is to attract deposits and the other is to offer financial loans in order to earn interest payments. In Guangdong, as well in the rest of China, financial loans are usually a source of loss for commercial banks. As will be discussed in this section, it is very important to emphasize the concept that financial loans should be made more securely.

Before China embraced the market economy, commercial banks were instructed by governments at various levels to make loans to designated enterprises without requiring any guarantees, since both banks and most enterprises were subject to the control of the central government. Under that kind of system it was almost certain that the loans would not be repaid. When debtors failed to repay these loans, commercial banks could not foreclose on the properties of those enterprises because the loan contract did not give banks that right. Ultimately, commercial banks had to treat those non-guaranteed loans as bad debts, resulting in heavy economic losses.

Today, however, commercial banks can now protect their legal interests by taking secured interests. On 30 June 1995, the *Secured Interests Law of the PRC* was promulgated. It provides that secured interests can be taken in the form of a guarantee, mortgage, pledge, lien or deposit. If a commercial bank fails to take secured interests from its debtors, it may run the risk of becoming an unsecured creditor and may receive nothing from its debtors during bankruptcy proceedings. In practice, in order for a commercial bank to do so, it should not only require borrowers to provide a guarantee, but also assess the guarantor's ability to repay, rights attached to and the value of the mortgaged or pledged property, and the feasibility of the realization of rights under a mortgage or pledge. However, commercial banks should be careful of the suggestion that by law "if, after examination and valuation by a commercial bank, the bank considers that the borrower is creditworthy and is able to repay, the borrower need not provide a guarantee".[44] In the author's view, commercial banks should always ask for a guarantee whenever they provide financial loans.

On the other hand, all people's courts should strive to protect the legal interests of commercial banks. In China, particularly in Guangdong, a major headache is that debtors often refuse to pay back loans even when there are judgments against them. In 1998, the courts in Guangdong province received 144,530 applications for enforcement of judgements. It was estimated that this figure would increase by 30% every year.[45] Courts are the last hope to fight for the interests of creditors, and they must exercise their power fairly. For this reason, various measures should be taken to ensure repayments. Furthermore, debtors should be educated to be more responsible for their debts. Suggestions have been made to personally bankrupt individuals who fail to repay their debts. Unfortunately, this kind of legislation does not yet exist in China. However, the newly promulgated *Contract Law*[46] may offer some guidelines. For example, the *Contract Law* introduces a novel term called the "subrogation power". Subrogation power in common law countries usually refers to a situation whereby after a guarantor has paid the debt he can exercise power of the debtor. Contrarily, Article 73 provides that in case a debtor fails to collect the debt owed to him and causes harm to the creditor, the creditor can apply for subrogation power from a people's court and collect the debt from the third party who owes money to the debtor. This provision may help commercial banks get back their loans from third parties.

Guangdong should take this opportunity to promulgate trial measures of individual bankruptcy and other rules.

Creating a Competitive Environment for Domestic and Foreign Financial Institutions

The Guangdong government should prepare for more competition between local commercial banks and foreign-funded financial institutions.[47] So far, at the national level, there are several regulations governing foreign-funded financial institutions. On 25 February 1994, the State Council published the *Administrative Regulations of the People's Republic of China Governing Foreign-funded Financial Institutions*. On 30 April 1996, the PBOC issued the *Detailed Implementation Rules for the Administrative Regulations of the People's Republic of China Governing Foreign-funded Financial Institutions*, and on 29 April 1999 the *Administrative Measures for Representative Agencies of Foreign Financial Institutions*. According to these legal documents, foreign banks, foreign bank branches, joint equity banks, foreign finance companies and joint equity finance companies are allowed to engage in financial activities in China. Furthermore, Shanghai was the first city in China to give licenses to foreign-funded financial institutions to deal in Chinese Renminbi (RMB).[48] Following its efforts to join the World Trade Organization (WTO), China will allow foreign-funded financial institutions in Shenzhen, as well as in other cities, to operate RMB businesses.[49] Guangdong needs to grasp this opportunity to become a major financial center through co-operation with Hong Kong and Macau.[50]

On 15 November 1999, after 13 years of negotiations, China reached a bilateral agreement with the United States regarding entry into the WTO. Under the agreement, China will allow foreign banks to engage in RMB business with Chinese enterprises two years after China becomes a member of the WTO; China will completely open its banking sector to foreign businesses five years after entering the WTO.[51] Therefore, it is anticipated that foreign financial institutions will strive to enter the relevant markets. Experts predict that foreign currency transactions and RMB savings will move from Chinese financial institutions to foreign financial institutions. Foreign financial institutions will try to operate businesses such as individual loans and credit cards.[52] Guangdong is an attractive place for foreign financial institutions. The Guangdong authorities should foresee these changes and promulgate relevant rules and regulations accordingly.

Promoting New Legislation

Even though the Guangdong government intends to promulgate 35 rules and regulations between 1998 and 2002, it is surprising to see that none of them are directly related to financial management and supervision. It may be that the Guangdong government had not yet foreseen the problems facing financial institutions when it produced the list of rules and regulations. For this reason, Guangdong should re-examine its existing financial regulations and re-organize its financial institutions in a better way. Most importantly, Guangdong should learn the lessons from Hong Kong during the recent Asian financial crisis. During the crisis, many problems emerged in Hong Kong regarding the financial sector. Many financial companies committed fraud and cheated their customers. However, the Hong Kong authorities felt that the activities of these companies were outside the control of its legal framework. For this reason, the relevant authorities in Hong Kong decided to amend the current securities regulations. The "Consultation Document on the Securities and Futures Bill" was released in order to invite views and comments.[53] Guangdong should work on regulations that can effectively control all financial institutions. It has been suggested that Guangdong should try to establish mortgage companies. This is a good suggestion, but it should be accompanied with tight regulations too.

The Guangdong government should adopt further measures to give financial support to private enterprises. Even though Guangdong allowed private entrepreneurs to develop their businesses in various areas beginning in 1989,[54] privates enterprises were often given unfair treatment in the areas of finance, taxes, import, export and so on.[55] Nevertheless on 15 March 1999, the National People's Congress published an amendment to the Constitution. Article 11 provides that private enterprises are an important component of the socialist market economy.[56] Under the Constitution and new government policies towards private enterprises, it is foreseen that China will take further steps to regulate and protect private enterprises.[57] In August 1999, the National People's Congress Standing Committee promulgated the *Law of the People's Republic of China on Individual Proprietorship Enterprises*.[58]

Financial reform in Guangdong should also take into consideration supportive policies for private enterprises. Most importantly, private enterprises should be granted equal status with other business enterprises. Nevertheless, Guangdong is still the leading province in terms of developing individual or private businesses. Recently the *Regulations Regarding Protection of Interests of Individual Commercial and Industrial Household and Private Enterprise* was put forward for discussion at the 9th Guangdong People's Congress. These regulations target existing unfair policies, random fee collection and infringement of independent operations. Individual businessmen or private businessmen will be given a special card to register fee collection. They shall have the right to refuse payments if the payment amount is not shown on the card, or if the fee collectors refuse to sign their name on the card.[59] The Guangdong authorities made another remarkable decision recently. Individual commercial and industrial household and private enterprises are permitted to hold shares in SOEs and collectively owned enterprises. They may take controlling shares in other regular enterprises.[60] Furthermore, private enterprises are permitted to engage in foreign trade and organize joint ventures, joint co-operation or business relationships with foreign investors directly.[61]

The 4th Session of the 15th Party Congress was held during 19–22 September 1999. One of the major tasks facing the congress was the further reform of the SOEs through four measures, i.e., (a) retain control over the large-sized SOEs but sell-off the small-sized SOEs;[62] (b) convert the debts of SOEs into shares (debt for equity), thus easing their heavy economic burden; (c) personnel who are in charge of managing SOEs will be given higher salaries; (d) strengthening the supervision of SOEs.[63] Among these measures, the most important one related to financial reform is debts for equities. As mentioned earlier, SOEs owe a huge amount of money to commercial banks and are not be able to repay them. In order not to simply write-off these debts, the government decided to convert debts into shares, so commercial banks, through their financial capital management companies (*Jinrong Zichan Guanli Gongsi*), change their legal status from creditors to shareholders.[64] This measure is intended to give SOEs a new lease of life. By listing shares, purchasing other enterprises, and other methods, commercial banks hope to recover their investments.[65]

This is certainly an attractive and bold idea. However, the measure may contain some potential risks. Firstly, even though the central government tried to set several preconditions in order not to bar most poor and hopeless SOEs from taking advantage of this measure, many SOEs may manage to "satisfy" the preconditions in order to get rid of their heavy economic burden.[66] In addition, local protectionism may further damage the implementation of this measure.[67] Secondly, it is hoped that some SOEs will be given a fresh start under the new measure. However, without other serious reorganizations, it is unrealistic to expect targeted SOEs to achieve success. Thirdly, even though the financial capital management companies are expected to be independent legal entities, the legal relationship between commercial banks and those companies needs to be further clarified in order to avoid legal confusion between creditors and shareholders. The policy of "debt for equity" will give the Guangdong government a new chance to restructure its SOEs. Because of its geographical location, Guangdong will try to implement this policy through co-operation with Hong Kong investors. In addition, Guangdong needs to promulgate new regulations to implement the measure of debt for equity. It is important to clarify the relationship between the commercial banks and the financial capital management companies. Otherwise, commercial banks may violate the 1995 *Commercial Bank Law*.[68]

The Fight against Smuggling and Corruption

Establishing Effective Anti-smuggling Taskforces

Guangdong's contiguous geographical location with the HKSAR has led to a high rate of smuggling activities. In fact, Guangdong has the most serious smuggling problem in China.[69] The most worrying aspect of smuggling in Guangdong is that some customs officers have actively participated in the smuggling trade. It has been reported that some customs officers have even organized special forces to protect their smuggling operations. If this situation continues, not only will the state suffer serious economic losses, but the goal of "country under the rule of law" will be jeopardized.

In 1999 Premier Zhu Rongji urged the Guangdong authorities to seriously crackdown on smuggling activities in the province. A number of investigations were carried out and during one the head of Zhanjiang customs, Cao Xiukang, was arrested for smuggling steel, oil and cars worth 30 billion yuan (US$3.6 billion dollars).[70] After the trial, Zao and other six offenders were sentenced to death. Another 25 offenders (including some Hong Kong residents) were also punished.[71] From August 1998 to January 1999, the Guangdong authorities dealt with 3,324 smuggling cases involving goods worth 2.18 billion yuan.[72]

In response to the smuggling problem, Guangdong established a special police task force, the Guangdong Smuggling Investigation Bureau (GSIB) on 8 January 1999. The GSIB has 2,700 special policemen in eight branch bureaux. The GSIB has the power to investigate any smuggling cases and detain, arrest and question any suspects.[73] However, its unique leadership may cause some problems. Since the GSIB is under the leadership of both the General Customs and the National Public Security Bureau, it is uncertain whether the GSIB can function well as the two authorities have conflicting interests.[74] Nevertheless, the establishment of the GSIB was a step in the right direction. The Guangdong authorities should realize that they must wage a sustained war against the smugglers rather than carry out sporadic campaigns. Statistics show that smuggling activities increased in 1999. During the period from January to July 1999, the Guangdong authorities investigated 6,069 smuggling cases. Compared to the same period of 1998, smuggling cases have increased 1.1 times.[75] As is well known, the huge profits to be earned motivate the smugglers. The only way to deal with smuggling activities is to continuously fight against those criminals and for the courts to impose stiffer penalties. Furthermore, the Guangdong authorities should increase co-operation with the Hong Kong and Macau authorities in order to eliminate cross-border smuggling activities.

Anti-corruption in Guangdong

Guangdong has a bad reputation for corruption.[76] However, corruption is endemic across the whole of China. In a recent survey, 2,000 foreign invested enterprises were asked about the investment environment in China. The aspect they were most satisfied with was infrastructure; however, corruption topped their list of concerns.[77] One American observer has commented; "corruption is almost institutionalized in China, and payoffs, kickbacks, graft and bribery.... And becomes a daily feature of doing business with China".[78] Since Guangdong is close to Hong Kong and Macau, and exercises a large degree of autonomy from the central government, it is an ideal breeding ground for corruption. As a result, corruption not only damages the good image of Guangdong, but also impedes its economic development. Corruption itself will certainly affect the implementation and enforcement of laws and regulations.

Guangdong established an anti-corruption force, the Guangdong People's Procuratorate Anti-Corruption Bureau (GPPACB), ten years ago, the first of its kind in China.[79] This body has made some headway in the fight against corruption in Guangdong. Since it was established, the GPPACB has arrested 800 criminals and recovered 2.36 billion yuan.[80] During the same period, the GPPACB investigated 20,000 corruption cases. Among those cases, 25% involved bribes, and each case involved kick-backs worth over 10,000 yuan.[81] It was also reported that during 1998, the GPPACB investigated 1,700 government officers involved in corruption.[82] These statistics indicate how serious the problem is in Guangdong, and how further work is needed to eliminate this corrosive phenomenon. It should be noted that a high percentage of corruption cases occur in enterprises. For example, from 1982 to 1989, the GPPACB estimated that 76% of corruption cases took place in enterprises. From 1992 to 1994, 70% of cases occurred in enterprises.[83] These corruption cases usually involved the loss of state-owned assets.

Guangdong should learn from Hong Kong's Independent Commission Against Corruption (ICAC). On 22 March 1999, the ICAC held an international conference regarding the elimination of corruption in the twenty-first century. The Mainland Chinese officials who attended the conference pointed out that corruption was a global problem and that international co-operation should be stepped up to tackle the phenomena.[84] One important area of co-operation is the transfer of suspects among different jurisdictions. One international treaty regarding the fight against corruption was signed on 29 March 1996. It provides that those involved in corrupt activities be extradited.[85] In southern China, anti-corruption co-operation between Hong Kong and Mainland China should be increased. Guangdong should take advantage of its location to formalize its relationship with the ICAC and to learn from its experiences. As one scholar pointed out, even though the ICAC and the GPPACB have similar functions, the ICAC is stronger in three aspects. Firstly, the ICAC can carry out its own investigations. Secondly, the ICAC has more powers authorized by relevant laws, but is subject to no outside influences. Thirdly, the functions of the ICAC are much clearer.[86]

Improving Investment Conditions in Guangdong

China resumed sovereignty over Hong Kong on 1 July 1997, and over Macau on 20 December 1999. The relationship among

Guangdong, the HKSAR and the Macau Special Administrative Region (MSAR) is becoming much closer, even though Hong Kong and Macau citizens will continue to be treat as "foreigners" when making investments in China.[87] It is true that Guangdong needs to develop its economy further. It is also true that Hong Kong has a significant interest in increasing its investments in Guangdong due to the provinces good location and cheap labour costs. In his 1999 Policy Address, the Chief Executive of the HKSAR, Tung Chee-hwa, emphasized the importance of building closer ties with Mainland China, especially with Guangdong province. In October 1999, the HKSAR government announced that the Kowloon Canton Railway Company (KCRC) would open a new route from Sheung Shui to Lok Ma Chau which would connect with the Shenzhen Mass Transit Railway.[88] It was estimated that an increasing number of Hong Kong residents would choose to shop and buy homes in Shenzhen.[89] For this reason, the Hong Kong and Guangdong authorities intend to increase cross-border co-operation. As long as the central government preserves the special status of Hong Kong and Macau, it is reasonable to foresee that the Guangdong authorities should make Guangdong more like (a) the processing factory of Hong Kong (b) the back garden of Hong Kong and (c) a residential area for Hong Kong and Macau people. However, the following legal issues should be addressed in order to perfect this idea.

A Legal Framework to Ensure Guangdong as a Processing Factory

"Shop" and "processing factory" are terms which are often employed to describe the special relationship between Hong Kong and Guangdong. Certainly this kind of relationship is not based on any agreement between the two governments. Rather it has developed through market forces.[90] Comparatively speaking, Guangdong is attractive for Hong Kong businessmen not only because it has been given special treatment by the central government, but also because it has a cheap labour market. However, the legal framework in relevant areas is still lacking. For example, China promulgated the *Labour Law* on 5 July 1994; this law is intended to apply to all enterprises regardless of whether they are domestic or foreign-invested enterprises. Under the *Labour Law*, an employee with over ten years employment in a unit is entitled to opt for an indefinite term contract if both sides agree to extend the employment beyond the original fixed terms (Article 20). However, the 1994 *Administration of Labour in Foreign Investment Enterprises Provisions* provides that an employment contract shall be terminated upon expiration, or when the terms for termination stipulated in the contract are met. The contract may be renewed by mutual agreement (Article 10).[91] How to reconcile these differences is an urgent matter for the Guangdong government.

It has been reported that foreign invested enterprises in Guangdong have a serious problem of unpaid workers' wages. In some small-sized enterprises, workers have had to work overtime but often had their overtime payments delayed.[92] The Guangdong government should pay close attention to this kind of violation. In practice, workers' interests are less protected because local government officials are afraid of foreign investors withdrawing their investments. The author is of the opinion that the legal interests of workers should be better protected. It is one way to show that foreign investors and Chinese workers are equal before the law. Moreover, the government should be aware of the potential for instability to society posed by angry workers. In addition, the provincial government should pay close attention to the illegal activities of foreign businessmen. For example, it was reported that the Dongguan authorities arrested six Taiwanese businessmen for engaging in smuggling activities.[93] Another serious problem is that many businessmen have transferred high polluting industries to Mainland China through direct investment.[94]

Another big issue is whether foreign investors (including Hong Kong and Macau investors) should be granted special treatment. There is no doubt that many foreign investors have been attracted by the special treatment accorded to them, such as generous tax breaks. However, this puts domestic investors in an unfair situation with foreign investors. It is very encouraging to see that Guangdong has led the way in granting foreign investors the status of "national treatment" (*Guomin Daiyu*). Following this policy, foreigners are accorded the same treatment as local people regarding transportation, management of real estate, medical care, etc.[95] For example, in the Shenzhen SEZ, foreign invested enterprises and foreigners have been granted national treatment in broad areas since 1 January 1997. The Guangdong authorities should learn from the experiences of Shenzhen and implement this practice in other areas of Guangdong in order to attract more foreign investors. This is also consistent with Chinese efforts to enter the WTO.

Last, but not least, it is not certain whether the Guangdong government should strictly follow the unified national policy regarding the management of foreign investment. After a one-year investigation, the relevant Chinese authorities cancelled 36 foreign invested enterprises due to reasons such as failure to contribute to the registered capital or pass the authorities' annual examination.[96] In response to the call from the central government, the Guangdong government also reexamined foreign investment supermarkets before the end of October 1998. The central government made it very clear that in any foreign invested business enterprise, Chinese partners must control more than 50% of the contribution. Regarding chain stores or wholesale stores, the Chinese partner must hold the controlling shares. Moreover, such joint ventures should not be run for more than 30 years.[97] As China is seeking membership of the WTO, the central government has promised fewer restrictions on foreign investors. In this regard, the Guangdong government needs to reconsider whether more flexible regulations should be promulgated in order to encourage more foreign invested business enterprises.

A Legal Framework to Guide Guangdong as a Back Garden

Guangdong is moving towards providing more tourist areas in order to attract Hong Kong people. Taking Shenzhen as one example, there are many theme parks and leisure resorts, such as the Window of the World, the Happy Valley, Future World, the China Cultural

Village, Splendid China and so on. Shenzhen also has an extensive range of restaurants and nightclubs. More and more Hong Kong people are spending their weekends in Shenzhen.[98] For this reason, the HKSAR government considered various methods to dissuade Hong Kong residents from spending their money on the Mainland, but these have not been very effective. One survey conducted in August 1999 showed that 3.5% of those Hong Kong residents questioned had visited Shenzhen recently; 10% of people had a habit of going to Shenzhen twice a month. Most Hong Kong residents travel to China for eating, recreation, massage and beauty treatment, and shopping. Among those questioned, 80% spent below HK$500, while the rest spent more than HK$1,000.[99] Due to the price difference, more than one million Hong Kong residents who have lower incomes intending to live in Shenzhen.[100]

Providing Healthy Entertainment Conditions in Guangdong

Guangdong should strive to provide people from Hong Kong and Macau with healthy entertainment conditions. The most urgent thing is to solve the prostitution problem. Surveys reveal that many Hong Kong males go to Guangdong for the purpose of visiting prostitutes. Unfortunately, many of these males engage in unprotected sex.[101] This not only increases the risks of contracting AIDS and other venereal diseases, but also damages the reputation of Guangdong. Family disputes in Hong Kong are rising due to husbands taking mistresses or second wives on the Mainland, especially in Guangdong province. The "second wife" problem has become a serious problem since 1994. In 1994–95, a woman's hotline in Hong Kong received 493 phone-calls regarding husbands who had mistresses on the Mainland. This figure increased by 5% during 1995–96.[102] Guangdong has a serious "second wife" problem, and even local people have started to take mistresses. Many middle-aged or elderly people have sought a "second wife" based on three reasons; (a) they were too honest in the past and should compensate themselves now; (b) a man who has no "second wife" is deemed as having no ability, and will be looked down on; (c) they were afraid of not being promoted in the past if they were discovered, but are now "free" after retirement.[103] The major reason for the "second wife" problem is the lack of enforcement in Guangdong. The provincial government has published a legal document on how to deal with illegal activities relating to marriage for more than a year, but no further progress has been made.[104]

Tackling Organized Crime

Guangdong should pay particular attention to the problem of organized crime. A concern existed that after the handover of Hong Kong and Macau, more and more criminal organizations (i.e., triad gangs) would extend their activities to Mainland China. Due to its geographic location, Guangdong is susceptible to criminal activities.[105] It was reported that in Zhuhai, many criminal organizations have connections with the triad gangs in Macau (including the "Fuqing Bang" and the "Dongbei Bang").[106] During the latter half of 1998, the Zhuhai police arrested more than 160 members of criminal organizations, among them 62 triads from Hong Kong, Macau and Taiwan.[107] On 21 June 1998, the Public Security Bureau (PSB) of Guangdong province launched a crackdown on triad gangs. During the crackdown, 108 suspects were arrested, including 12 triad members from Hong Kong and Macau.[108] The head of one triad gang, the so-called "Big Spender" (Zheung Tzekeung) was arrested and later sentenced to death. One very important phenomenon is that most organized crime involves the use and trafficking of weapons. In Dongguan, a police crackdown on organized crime led to the seizure of 21 guns and nearly 2000 rounds of ammunition.[109] The use of guns in criminal activities is, unfortunately, on the increase throughout China.

Another major activity of organized crime is prostitution. The problem of prostitution and second wives in Guangdong is becoming more and more serious. Many criminals see Guangdong as an ideal place to make huge profits from prostitution. For this reason, criminal gangs have offered females from other parts of China domestic work in Guangdong. Once those females arrive in Guangdong, they are forced into prostitution. On 25 April 2000, the Guangdong police announced it had broken up one gang involved in coercing females into prostitution. Fifteen gang members had forced 105 young females (some under 14 years of age) into prostitution. This was the biggest case in China to date.[110] Control of prostitutes is a lucrative business in China. One organized crime gang was recently uncovered in Shenzhen. The gang had forced several women into prostitution for over a year, earning themselves 300,000 yuan.[111] Some criminals have conspired with their counterparts in Hong Kong to bring prostitutes into Hong Kong through tourist channels.[112] Even though the police forces in Guangdong and Hong Kong have smashed several organized crime gangs through close co-operation, there is no sign of a reduction in this kind of crime.

Since many crimes are cross-board crimes, it is important for the Guangdong authorities co-operate more closely with the police in Hong Kong and Macau. In September 1999, based on information from the Guangdong PSB, the police in Macau successfully smashed a criminal organization and seized a large amount of firearms and explosives. According to the Macau police, this arsenal had the highest number of weapons and explosives ever discovered.[113] Further work needs to be done in order to reach an agreement regarding the quick exchange of information and extradition of criminals. However, in line with the policy of "one country, two systems", it is plausible to extradite criminals based on some internationally recognized principles, such as the exception to the non-extradition of political offences, and no double punishments and so on. Certainly, the agreement should be reached based on mutual understanding and respect.

Legal Framework for Improving Residential Areas

Due to substantial price differences and a convenient location, more and more Hong Kong people are interested in buying residential property in Guangdong. In 1993, there were only 201 property transactions but this increased dramatically to 6,000 in 1999.[114] Following the judgment of Hong Kong's Court of Final Appeal, it was estimated that around 2 million Mainland Chinese were entitled to right of abode in Hong Kong.[115] It was suggested that a special residential area should be built in Shenzhen in order to deal with this massive influx of people. This special residential area would look and feel like Hong Kong in order for residents to familiarize themselves with Hong Kong society.[116] Furthermore, the Hong Kong Education Authority is considering the possibility of opening Hong Kong style schools on the Mainland. These schools would provide Hong Kong teaching materials to children of Hong Kong residents who were born on the Mainland.[117]

The Guangdong government should take this opportunity to develop real estate according to international standards. This will certainly be attractive to investors from Hong and Macau and simulate the local economy. Several years ago, real estate development in Guangdong faced severe problems. Many of the real estates under development were in the form of joint co-operatives. Some investors complained that they had paid for their properties but that the buildings were unfinished or of poor quality. In 1996, the provincial authorities received 120 complaints regarding unfinished projects or substandard building. The problematic buildings were mainly located in Guangzhou, Shenzhen, Dongguan, and Zhuhai.[118] If the quality of buildings is not improved, fewer Hong Kong people will want to live in Guangdong. For the same reason, they will not spend money in Guangdong either. In 1999, the Guangdong authorities promulgated two rules to mitigate this situation. One was the *Regulations Regarding Management of Pre-sale of Commodity Houses in Guangdong Province* and the other one was the *Regulations on Management of Real Estate in Guangdong Province*.[119] According to the regulations, if a seller breaches the contract by selling substandard houses, the buyers will be entitled to take back the prepaid deposit money plus 10–20% of the deposit money as compensation.[120]

Promoting the Concept of a "Country under the Rule of Law" in Guangdong

The slogan "country under the rule of law" was officially promoted by President Jiang Zemin at the 15th Party Congress in 1997. On 15

March 1999, at the 2nd Session of the 9th National People's Congress, the concept of "rule of law" was written into the Constitution.[121] In Western countries, the rule of law usually refers to the concept that the law is supreme. It includes elements such as (a) the law must be published and available; (b) it utilizes an adversarial approach to court proceedings; (c) judges are trained in the law; (d) the administration of justice is open and impartial; and (e) citizens are entitled to "due process". Compared to the situation in China, the concept of rule of law is far from satisfactory. Many scholars maintain that China is currently at the stage of a "country with rule by law" (*Yi Fa Zhi Guo*). Nevertheless, it is possible to interpret the meanings of rule of law in line with China's conditions. On the one hand, every one should obey the law and nobody should be above the law; on the other hand, justice should be done when there is a violation of law and no preference should be given to anybody. Furthermore, the Chinese government believes that the most important thing is to enforce laws fairly,[122] and to adjudicate cases in accordance with the law.[123]

In China, the corruption of law enforcement refers to unfair law enforcement, abuse of power, and violation of the law by law enforcement officers. Unfair law enforcement means that sometimes relatives or friends of law enforcement officers can escape prosecution. They do this in order to seek personal benefit, or in favour of local protectionism. Abuse of power means that some law enforcement personnel become illegally involved in economic or administrative disputes. Furthermore, they disregard the legal rights of other people, recklessly arrest people who disobey them, or extort confessions by torture. Finally, law enforcement personnel violate the law themselves by engaging in illegal activities.[124]

In Guangdong, efforts have been made to restore the good image of law enforcement departments. It was reported that in 1999 the PSB corrected 876 cases which had been improperly handled; 5,671 who had been detained had their cases re-examined. Furthermore, 365 members of law enforcement agencies were assigned to other non-law related duties. In addition, 507 policemen were investigated for violating the law. Among them, 31 were arrested, 21 were transferred to other duties, and 102 were dismissed from the force. In order to enhance the supervision of law enforcement personnel, 138 report centres have been established across Guangdong.[125] It should be noted that legal education should not only extend to ordinary people, but also extend to law enforcement personnel. General speaking, the quality of law enforcement personnel in Guangdong is not very high, and needs to be improved. Many of them have poor educational backgrounds. It is encouraging to note that Guangdong is paying more attention to the legal education of law enforcement personnel. For example, in September 1998, 1,778 new prosecutors were required to take judicial examinations. Those who failed to pass the examination were not allowed to serve as prosecutors.[126]

The Guangdong government should realize that one of its major tasks is to establish a clear connection between legal education and legal practice. In China, those who do not have a legal education from university can still serve as judges, prosecutors and lawyers. Some personnel may have some legal training, but are still far from legal professionals. The Guangdong authorities need to reform the existing legal educational system and show a willingness to move towards "rule of law".

Regarding the reform of the trial system, Guangdong was the first province in China to put forward the *Interim Rules Concerning Exchange of Evidence Before Trying Civil and Economic Dispute Cases* on 31 August 1999. The rules contain five major points:

(a) Parties shall submit evidence within 15 days after they are notified that their cases have been established or they shall give their plea. Third parties shall do so within 15 days after receiving notice to join the cases. In foreign related cases, the duration of submitting evidence is 30 days. Only in exceptional situation can parties apply for an extension;

(b) If parties have difficulties collecting evidence through investigation, examination, appreciation or audit, or due to evidence involving national security or trade secrets, they can apply in writing and ask the people's courts to collect the evidence;

(c) When the people's courts receive submitted evidence, the courts shall require both parties to exchange the evidence within a limited period.

(d) If parties fail to submit evidence within a limited period, they shall be deemed as giving up their rights and will be responsible for the relevant legal consequences;

(e) If parties can find new evidence which would overrule the original decision, the people's courts shall examine that new evidence.[127]

These five points indicate that from now on, those who want to bring civil or economic cases to court in Guangdong should be aware of the new rules. Otherwise, their chances of winning will be substantially reduced. As for the evidence system, more creative legislation can be expected in the near future.

Conclusion

Guangdong has been referred to as the pioneering province in developing new legal systems in China. Since 1979, Guangdong has shown a strong intention to build up a legislative system in response to the call of the central government to create a "country under the rule of law". The Guangdong government should meet the new challenges in order to keep its role as "pilot province" and move smoothly into the twenty-first century. The Guangdong government should pay particular attention to developing new legal regulations governing individual commercial and industrial household and private-run enterprises. It is clear that Guangdong has implemented this kind of practice long before the amendment of the Constitution.[128] Therefore, the next logical step is to pass more legislation and regulations concerning the protection and management of private businesses. In addition to this, the Guangdong government should pay close attention to increasing co-operation with Hong Kong and Macau and offer a suitable environment for investment, residence and entertainment. This will not only help to develop Guangdong's economy, but also help to extend legal co-operation among those areas.

Notes

1. In China, the purpose of local legislation is to implement or supplement national laws and regulations. Therefore, almost all the local legislatures adopt the forms of regulation [*tiaoli*], rule [*guiding*], measure [*banfa*], decision [*jueding*] or detailed implementing rule [*shishixize*]. See Susan Finder, "Changes in the Legal System" in Y. M. Yeung and David K. Y. Chu (eds.), *Guangdong: Survey of a Province Undergoing Rapid Change* (Hong Kong: The Chinese University Press, 1994), p. 356. Others have viewed this situation differently. According to Brian Hook; "the central government can overrule legislation by the local units, impose decisions upon them, and negate any polices felt to be inappropriate. National policies decided at the center are applicable to all the local units and they must abide by them. Since the introduction of the Four Modernizations, however, there is clear evidence that the rapidly modernizing provinces have increased their informal power of decision-making, particularly in the economic sphere, at the expense of the centre. There is, therefore, a clear mismatch between the informal powers of the local units and the formal constitutional relationship, leaving a grey area which the local units have been quick to exploit." See Elfed Roberts and Winston Ng, "Government and Politics" in Brian Hook, (ed.) *Guangdong, China's Promising Law* (Oxford: Oxford University Press, 1996), p. 61.

2. "The Pearl (Zhujiang) River Delta has long been the most affluent area in the province. It has, of course, the navigable river that divides Hong Kong and Macau, a position close to the South China Sea, a relatively good communications system and long historical and cultural connections with the outside world." Roberts and Ng, "Government and Politics", *op. cit.*, p. 50.

3. David Faure, "History and Culture", Yeung and Chu, *Guangdong, op. cit.*, p. 12.

4. *Ibid.*, p. 357.

5. *Ibid.*, p. 356.

6. The Research Group for Theory and Practice of 'A Province Under the Rule of Law', "Deng Xiaoping's Theory of Democracy and Legal System and the Practice of A Province Under the Rule of Law in Guangdong (Deng Xiaoping

Minzhu Yu Fazhi yu Guangdong Yifa Zhisheng Shijian)"; The Department of Propaganda of the Chinese Communist Party Committee of Guangdong Province (ed.) *The Theory of Deng Xiaoping and New Period of Development of Guangdong Reform (Deng Xiaoping Lilun yu Guangdong Gaige Fazan de Xin Shiqi)* (Guangzhou: Guangdong Economic Press, 1997), p. 472.

7. *Ibid.*, p. 473.

8. Taking Shanghai as an example, from 1983 to 1998, there were only 124 pieces of local legislation. See the *Compilation of Shanghai Local Legislation* (1983–97) and (1998) that are compiled by the Commission of Legislative Affairs, Standing Committee of the Shanghai People's Congress. On file with author.

9. For detailed information see Mai Chongde (ed.), *The Complete Book of Rules and Regulations in Guangdong* (Guangzhou: Guangdong People's Press, 1995).

10. Department of Propaganda, *The Theory of Deng Xiaoping*, *op. cit.*, p. 473.

11. Internal Material edited by the Standing Committee of Shanghai People's Congress on 22 December 1998. The document is on file with the author.

12. "Guangdong promulgating local regulations in order to ensure the effective implementation of the Price Law of the PRC (Guangdong Zhiding Difangxing Fagui Quebao Jiagefa Youxiao Shishi)", *South China News* (Hua Nan Xin Wen), 24 June 1999, p. 1.

13. "Guangdong: The first province to start public hearing of legislation (Guangdong Shou Kai Lifa Tingzheng Hui)", *Ming Pao*, 31 August 1999.

14. In his 1999 Policy Report, Tung Chee-hwa suggested that Guangdong, Hong Kong and Macau should form a Big Triangle Economic Cooperation. The 1999 Policy Address is available on the World Wide Web at http://www.info.gov.hk/rthk/cepa1999.

15. The legislation list is on file with the author.

16. The Legislation Plan of Guangdong Province, 1998–2002 is on file with the author. The joint stock co-operative system is a new system following the further development of the shareholding system in China. It is applicable to an enterprise formed by a certain number of farmers or workers based on the principle of share contribution and co-operation, with registered the capital provided mainly by themselves. Shareholders adopt the articles of association of the enterprise based on the principles of joint stock and co-operation among the workers. They enjoy the rights and bear the duties. The enterprise is a legal entity that pursues profits and common interests. For details see Gu Gongyun, *Standard Operative Guidelines on Joint Stock Cooperative Enterprises (Gu Fen He Zuo Zhi Qi Ye Gui Fan Yun Zuo Zhi Ying)* (Shanghai: Shanghai Academy of Social Science Press, 1998).

17. The Research Group of the Guangdong Academy of Social Science, "New Ideas For Development and the New Stage for the Development of Reform in

Guangdong (Xin Fazhan yu Guangdong Gaige Fazhan Xin Jieduan)";
Department of Propaganda, *The Theory of Deng Xiaoping*, *op. cit.*, pp. 48–50.

18. Cao Siyuan, *Say When You Should Say* (Dang Shuo Ze Shuo) (Guangzhou: Guangdong Economic Press, 1998), p. 60.

19. For detailed information see Liu Jian, *The Loss of Chinese Property* (*Liushi de Zhongguo*) (Beijing: China City Press 1998).

20. "Guangzhou adds 13 enterprises for bankruptcy, merger and acquisition (Guangzhou Xin Zeng Jianbing Qiye 13 Jia)", *Guangzhou Daily* (*Guangzhou Ribao*), 5 August 1998.

21. Liu Shihang, "Financial violations should not be overlooked (Jinrong Weigui Burong Hushi)", *Market Newspaper* (*Shi Chang Bao*), 19 October 1998.

22. The major financial scandals in Guangdong included:

    (a) The Guangdong Branch of China's Construction Bank used 1.7 billion yuan to purchase real estate in Hong Kong (1996);

    (b) The Guangdong Branch of China's Agriculture Bank illegally collected funds to buy and sell futures amounting to 4 billion yuan (1997);

    (c) Guangdong Overseas Trust, Guangzhou Trust, Fushan Trust and other trust companies could not pay the due debts (July 1998);

    (d) The GITIC was shutdown (6 October 1998);

    (e) The Yue Hai Company failed to pay due debts (October 1998);

    (f) The Central Government ordered the Guangdong Development Bank to takeover the Enping Credit Cooperative (7 December 1998); and

    (g) Guangzhou State Investment Company after it failed to pay due debts and faced bankruptcy (January 1999).

    "The list of major financial problems in Guangdong (Guangdong Zhuyao Jinrong Wenti Shijian Bu)", *Ming Pao*, 8 December 1999.

23. "Central government paying attention to the financial risks in Guangdong (Zhongyang Zhongshi Guangdong Jinrong Fenxian)", *Ming Pao*, 20 May 1998.

24. *Ibid.*

25. Li Li, "Anti foreign currency crime (Fan Pian Hui: Zhong Bang Chuji)", *Legal System and News* (*Fa Zhi Yu Xin Wen*), February 1999, p. 4.

26. Liu Yuanyuan: "Examining the big financial case involving 1.1 billion yuan (Toushi 11 Yi Yuan Jinrong Daan)", *Human Man and the Law* (*Ren Yu Fa*), No. 12, 1997, p. 7.

27. "Five financial institutions in Guangdong are subject to punishments due to their illegal operation of foreign currency (Weigui Jingying Waihui Yewu, Guangdong Wujia Jinrong Jigou Shou Chufa)", *Huanan News* (*Hua Nan Xin Wen*), 21 September 1998, A1.

28. "Guangdong shutdowns nine companies engaging in black market for Hong Kong futures index (Yue Chafeng Jiujia Heishi Gang Qizhi)", *Hong Kong Economic Daily (Jing Ji Ribao)*, 13 November 1998. A3.

29. "The smart capture of corrupt officials shocked officialdom of Guangdong (Qiaoji Zhua Tuanguan, Jin Zheng Yue Guanchang)", *Yazhou Zhoukan*, pp. 73–74, 16–22 November 1998.

30. *Ibid.* However, at a recent news conference, Dai Xianglong, the head of the PBOC, made it clear that the liquidation procedures should be done by the people's courts in accordance with the law and foreign creditors' interests should be protected. See "Dai Xianglong urges implementation of proper monetary policy and to strengthen financial supervision (Dai Xianglong: Shixing Shidang Huobi Zhengche, Dali Jiaqiang Jinrong Jianguan)", *People's Daily*, 28 January 1999, p. 2.

31. "Guangzhou International Trust and Investment Corp. is facing bankruptcy (Guangzhou Guotou Mianlin Pochan)", *Ming Pao*, 27 January 1999.

32. Cao Jianming and Hou Xiaoyong, "Global Economy and Legal Regulations", *Journal of the East China University of Politics and Law*, No. 1, 1998, p. 43. Also see Cao Jianming, "Financial Security and Legal Construction", *Shanghai Securities News (Shanghai Zhengquan Bao)*, 9 June 1998.

33. Zeng Muye et. *al*, (eds.), *The Economic Thinking of Guangdong's Reform*, (Guangzhou: Guangdong People's Publishing House, 1993), pp. 94–95.

34. Shen Bonia, the Vice Mayor of Guangzhou, told *Ming Pao* that "due to the policy of strict financial control by the central government, local financial institutions are lacking of autonomy and flexibility". *Ming Pao*, 15 November 1999.

35. Citing from Albert H. Y. Chen, "Law and Development: A Commentary on the Asian Development Bank's Report on the Role of Law and Legal Institutions in Asian Economic Development 1960–1995", paper presented at 4th Annual Conference of the Asia Pacific Economic Law Forum, 3–5 December 1998, City University of Hong Kong.

36. *Fei Fa Jin Rong Ji Gou he Fei Fa Jin Rong Ye Wu Huo Dong Qu Di Ban Fa.* Articles 22 to 27.

37. Dai Xianglong, "The historical responsibility of the PBOC (Zhongguo Renmin Yinhang de Lishi Zeren)", *People's Daily*, 30 November 1998, p. 10.

38. "The establishment of bankruptcy mechanism in financial industry (Jinrongye Jianli Pochan Jizhi)", *Ming Pao*, 31 October 1998.

39. It was reported that the Guangdong government initially wanted to keep GITIC alive, but the central government gave the order to close it. See *Ming Pao*, 31 October 1998.

40. *Ibid.* But in the United States, the banking industry does have the ability to do banking, securities and insurance together.

41. *Commercial Bank Law of the People's Republic of China*, Article 43.

42. "National banks continue to diversify financial operations", see http://businessjournal.net/stories/081197/national.html

43. It was reported that the State Council is going to allow insurance companies to invest in mutual funds. See "The insurance industry is allowed to buy mutual funds (Baoxianye Jiang Huozun Gou Jijin)", *Ming Pao*, 11 September 1999.

44. *Commercial Bank Law of the People's Republic of China*. Article 36.

45. "Courts and banks are researching a proper policy to handle loan cases (Fayuan Yinhang Gongshang Duice, Qinli Jiedai Huajie Fenxian)", *People's Daily*, 17 March 1999, p. 1.

46. *The Contract Law of the PRC* which was promulgated on 15 March 1999 and became effective as of 1 October 1999.

47. "Chinese banks need a massive injection of competence", *South China Morning Post*, 23 April 1998, p. 7.

48. See the *Tentative Procedures of Administration of Pilot Operation of Renminbi Business by Foreign-funded Financial Institutions in Shanghai Pudong New Development Zone* issued by Shanghai Government in 1997.

49. In November 1999, the China-US Bilateral agreement was signed. Under the agreement, foreign banks will have "full market access within five years and to permit them to engage in RMB business with Chinese companies within two years and within five years in the case of Chinese individuals. They would also be permitted to conduct business without geographic restrictions within five years." Gary Lock, "China, WTO and the future for foreign investors", *Asian Lawyer* (*Business Law Asia*), Vol. 5, No. 2, 2000, p. 6.

50. Li Huaji, Xu Long, Zhou Weiping (eds.), *Economy In the Area of Guangdong, Macao and Hong Kong in the Century* (*Kua Si Ji de Yue Gang Au Qu Yue Jing Ji*), (Guangzhou: Guangdong Higher Education Press, 1996), p. 182.

51. "China opens 10 big areas (Zhongguo Kaifang 10 Da Lingyu)", *Ming Pao*, 16 November 1999.

52. "Sino-foreign banks will have full competition (Zhong Wai Yinhang Quanmian Jinzheng)", *Ming Pao*, 23 November 1999.

53. The document is published in Chinese and English, and can be found on the website of the Financial Services Bureau at www.info.gov.hk/fsb and that of the Securities and Futures Commission at www.hksfc.org.hk

54. For detailed information see Xianchu Zhang, "Economic Legislation in the Pearl River Delta" in Joseph Y. S. Cheng (ed.), *The Guangdong Development Model and Its Challenges* (Hong Kong: The City University Press, 1998), pp. 119–120.

55. "China decides to give further support to private enterprises (Zhongguo Jueding Jingyibu Fuzhi Siying Qiye)", *Hong Kong Economic Journal*, 30 April 1999, p. 13.

56. "The amendment of the Constitution of the PRC (Zhonghua Renmin Gongheguo Xianfa Xiuzhengan)", *People's Daily*, 17 March 1999, p. 1.

57. "Less limitations to private economy (Jingyibu Fangkai Dui Geti Jingji de Xianzhi)", *ibid.*, 24 May 1999, p. 9.

58. Zhonghua Renmin Gongheguo Geren Duzi Qiye Fa was adopted at the 11th Session of the Standing Committee of the 9th NPC on August 30, 1999 and was effective as of 1 January 2000.

59. "Guangdong adopts card system in order to protect individual industrial and commercial households and private enterprises (Guangdong Jiang Dui Getihu he Siying Qiye Shixing Jiaofeika Zhidu)". The information is downloaded from http://www.cwi.gov.cn/private/brother2-7.htmwhich is also on file with author.

60. "Guangdong private enterprises could hold controlling shares in SOEs (Yue Siying Jingji Ke Konggu Guoqi)", *Huasheng Bao* (*Electronic Edition*), 9 August 1999.

61. *Ibid.*

62. That is to say that about 25% of SOEs will be kept while the rest will be reorganized through merger, sale, or joint stock co-operative system.

63. "Zhu Rongji gains a stable position due to the effectiveness of enterprise reform (Qi Gai Jian Xiao Zhu Rongji Diwei Wen)", *Ming Pao*, 20 September 1999.

64. "The 'debt for equity' offers developing chances to investment industry (Zhai Zhuan Gu Gei Tou Hangyi Danlan Fazan Jiyu)". This source is available on the World Wide Web at
http://kangxi.online.tj.cn/caijinghot/cjhot/1999081273520.htm

65. "'Debt for equity' is an ideal weapon to resolve the financial problem of state-owned enterprises (Zhai Zhuan Gu: Guoqi Tuo Pin de 'Xiashoujian')", *Hai Mai Economic Journal* (Electronic Edition), 9 August 1999. This source is available on the World Wide Web at
http://www.hermes.com.cn/economy/990809.htm.

66. Five preconditions are required by the government in order to take advantage of the measure: (1) the products of the SOEs should meet market demands and have the ability to compete with similar products; (2) equipment and technologies should reach national or international standards. Furthermore, production should satisfy environmental requirements; (3) there is higher level management with a clear list of debts and credits; (4) there should be a good management team comprising a chairman of the board of directors and a general manager; and (5) the plan to change operational systems meet the requirements of modern enterprise systems. This information is available on the World Wide Web at http://kangxi.online.tj.cn/caijinghot/cjhot/19990912073520.htm.

67. "China should not fully rely on debts for equity (Zhongguo Guoqi Gaige Bunen Ba Shuoyou de Bao Dou Ya Zai Zan Zhuan Gu)", this source is available on the World Wide Web at http://www.cq.cei.gov.cn/jjrd/99082002.htm.

68. Article 43 provides that "commercial banks shall not be permitted to engage in trust investment and stock operation and shall not be permitted to invest in immovable property within the territory of the People's Republic of China that is not for their own use. Commercial banks shall not be permitted to invest in non-banking financial institutions and enterprises within the territory of the People's Republic of China. ... "

69. "Guangdong formally establishes smuggling investigation bureau (Yue Zousi Zhenchaju Zhengshi Gua Pan)", *Sing Tao Daily*, 9 January 1999.

70. Later on, the Vice Governor of Guangdong province said that the total amount of smuggled goods amounted to is 10 billion yuan. See "The smart capture of corrupt officials shocked the officialdom of Guangdong (Qiaoji Zhua Tuanguan, Jin Zheng Yue Guanchang)", *Yazhou Zhoukan*, 16–22 November 1998, p. 73.

71. "Li Shen sentenced to death for involvement in Zhanjiang smuggling case (Zhanjiang Zousi An Gang Fan Li Shen Pan Si)", *The Oriental Daily* (*Dong Fang Ribao*), 13 May 1999.

72. "Fight against smuggling is a permanent war (Fan Zousi Shi Chijiu Zhan)", *Guangzhou Daily*, 3 November 1999.

73. "Guangdong formally establishes smuggling investigation bureau (Yue Zousi Zhenchaju Zhengshi Gua Pan)", *Sing Tao Daily*, 9 January 1999.

74. In theory, the GSIB is under the direct leadership of the General Customs. But in practice, it is quite difficult to say that the PSB will have no involvement, and this may create some inconsistencies.

75. "The dramatic increase of smuggling cases in Guangdong in the first seven Months (Shou Qi Ge Yue Guangdong Zousi An *Beizeng)* ", *Ming* Pao, 30 August 1999.

76. "Corruption in Guangdong (and the rest of China) has flourished under an economic system which gives significant authority to officials with little checks and balances, and draws a fuzzy line between government and business and which controls the movement of persons within and outside China". See Finder, "Changes in the Legal System", Yeung and Chu (eds.), *Guangdong*, *op. cit.*, p. 367.

77. "Foreign investors like to make their investments in Shanghai (Waishang Zui Xi Touzi Shanghai)", *Ming Pao*, 15 September 1999).

78. Delia Poon, "Exposure to the Foreign Corrupt Practices Act: A Guide for U.S. Companies with Activities in the People's Republic of China to Minimize Liability", *Hastings International and Comparative Law Review*, Vol. 19, 1966, p. 330.

79. "Remarkable achievements made by Guangdong anti-corruption bureau during ten years (Zhonghua Diyi Fantanju Shinian 'Dahu' Jian Qigong)", *Legal Daily* (*Fa Zhi Ribao*), 21 August 1999, p. 1.

80. *Ibid.*

81. *Ibid.*

82. "Guangdong investigates 1,700 corrupt officials (Guangdong Chaban 1700 Ming Tanguan)", *Huasheng Bao (Electronic Edition)*, 24 January 1999.

83. Cited by He Qinglian, *The Pitfalls of Modernization: Economic and Social Problems in Current China (Xian Dai Hua de Xian Jing)*, (Beijing: Today's China Press, 1997), pp. 145–146.

84. "Anti-corruption co-operation between China and Hong Kong will be expanded (Zhong Gang Fan Tan Hezuo Lingyu Jiang Kuoda)", *Ming Pao*, 23 March 1999, A 12.

85. Huang Fen, *Research On the Extradition System In China (Zhongguo Yindu Zhidu Yanjiu)*, (Beijing: Chinese University of Politics and Law Press, 1997), pp. 79–80.

86. Shan Min, "Comparative Research on Anti-Corruption Organs in Hong Kong and the PRC". Paper represented at the Conference on Legal Systems in Hong Kong and the PRC organized by the Hong Kong Legal Education Trust Fund on 19–20 November 1999 in Hong Kong.

87. Regarding investors' legal status, it is worth mentioning two documents: (1) *The State Council Regulations Concerning Encouragement of Foreign Investment* which was promulgated 11 October 1986 by the State Council; and (2) *The State Council Regulations for Encouraging Investment by Overseas Chinese and Hong Kong and Macau Compatriots* which was promulgated 19 August 1990 by the State Council. In accordance with these two regulations, investors from Hong Kong and Macau enjoy special treatments as "foreign investors".

88. "Futian will be a new consumer area for Hong Kong people (Futian Jiang Chengwei Gangren Xin Xiaofei Qu)", *Apple Daily*, 2 July 1999.

89. "Hong Kong residents purchase 7,000 flats a year in Shenzhen (Gang Ren Nian Gou Qi Qian Shenzhen Danwei)", *Apple Daily*, 10 April 2000.

90. Li *et. al*, *Economy In the Area*, *op. cit.*, pp. 12–13.

91. Andreas Lauffs (ed.), *China Update: The PRC, Labour Law* (Hong Kong: Asia Law & Practice Ltd. 1995), p. 31.

92. Li Xiuheng, "Foreign invested enterprises have serious problems owing wages (Waiqi Tuoqian Gongzi Wenti Yanzhong)", *Xinpao Financial News*, 27 January 1998, p. 20.

93. "Dongguan arrests 6 Taiwan businessmen involved in smuggling (Dongguan Zousizui Ju Liu Taishang)", *Ming Pao*, 25 August 1999.

94. Liao Guansheng (ed.), *Worries and New Chances In the Economic Exchange between Taiwan and China (Liang An Jing Mao Hu Dong de Yin You yu Sheng ji)*, (Hong Kong: Chinese University Press, 1995), p. 124.

95. Foreigners must acquire resident cards or temporary resident cards issued by the Shenzhen Public Security Bureau in order to get such treatment. For this reason, foreign tourists will not be granted such special treatment. See "Shenzhen offers national treatment to foreigners", *Nanfang Weekend Newspaper* (Guangdong), 21 February 1997, p. 4.

96. "Maintaining the unification and seriousness of foreign investment policy, 36 foreign-funded enterprises were cancelled (Weihu Xishou Waizi Zhengce de Tongyixing he Yansuxing, 36 Jia Waizi Shangqi Bei Zhuxiao)", *Market Daily* (*China*), 27 October 1999, P1.

97. "Guangdong cleans up unqualified foreign-funded businesses (Yue Yuedi Qingsao Bu Hege Waizi)", *Hong Kong Economic Daily*, 16 October 1999, A55.

98. Interestingly, the Hong Kong government announced a 10% income tax refund intended to stimulate the retail market. However, most Hong Kong people preferred to spend their refunded money in Shenzhen or other places in Guangdong, despite various tax-refund-sales in Hong Kong.

99. "80% Hong Kong people consume 500 yuan in Shenzhen (Ba Cheng Gang Ke Shanzhen Xiaofei 500 Yuan)", *Appledaily*, 30 August 1999.

100. "The price of products in Hong Kong is too expensive, residents with lower income feel difficulty to live, 1.09 million people intend to move to Shenzhen (Gang Wujia Da Gui, Di Shouru Nan Ai, 109 Wan Ren Yi Qianju Shenzhen)", *Apple Daily*, 10 April 2000.

101. "1/3 of Hong Kong males visited prostitutes on the Mainland (1/3 Fan Neidi Gang Han Piaoji)", *Sing Tao*, 12 September 1997.

102. "The deathknell is sounded to people who have second wives (Bao Ernan Qiaoxiang Shangzhong)", *The Nextmedia* (*Yi Zhou Kan*), 27 January 1999.

103. "To have a lover becomes popular in Guangdong (Yue Shixing Qixing 'Huanghun Lian')", *The Oriental Daily* (Hong Kong), 23 June 1999, A34.

104. "Guangdong hands over an empty answer sheet in dealing with 'second wife' Problems (Hui Daji Bao Ernan Jiao Banjuan)", *Ming Pao*, 25 May 1999.

105. "Guangdong police forced 'snakes' out of holes (Guangdong Jingfang Gan 'She' Chu Dong)", *Yazhou Zhoukan*, 10–16 August 1998, p. 32.

106. "Zhuhai is mopping up mafia from Hong Kong and Macau (Zhuhai Zhongdian Saodang Gang Au Yuejing Fanzui)", *Zaobao* (Internet Edition), 5 August 1999.

107. *Ibid.*

108. "Guangdong police forced 'Snakes' out of holes (Guangdong Jingfang Gan 'She' Chu Dong)", *Yazhou Zhoukan*, 10–16 August 1998, p. 32.

109. "Guangdong starts mopping-up operation against Macau mafia (Guangdong Daju Saodang Jingnei Au Heibang)", *Ming Pao*, 11 September 1999.

110. "Guangdong police destroy one organized crime gang forcing women into prostitution (Guangdong Jingfang Cuihui Yige Zuzhi Qiangpo Maiyin Teda Tuanhuo)", *China News Agency*, 25 April 2000.

111. "Control females to conduct prostitution: One organized crime made illegal profits of 300,000 yuan within one year (Caozhong Funu Maiyin, Yi Fanzui Jituan Juli 30 Wan)", *Nanfang Doushi Bao*, 29 April 2000.

112. "Police forces in Guangdong and Hong Kong jointly crack down on cross border prostitution (Yue Gang Jingfang Lianshou Daji Kuajing Maiyin Piaochang Huodong)", China News Agency, 26 April 2000.

113. "Macau uncovers an arsenal based on information from Guangdong (Yue Tigong Xiansou Au Po Junhuoku)", *Ming Pao*, 25 September 1999.

114. "Hong Kong people are interesting in buying second hand buildings in Shenzhen (Gangren Rezhong Gouzhi Shenzhen Ershou Lou)", *People's Daily*, 26 August 1999, p. 2.

115. The HKSAR government estimated the figure was 1.6 million people. For this reason, the Hong Kong government sought a re-interpretation of the Basic Law (Articles 22 /4 and 24/2). See *Ming Pao*, 27 June 1999, p. 1.

116. "Tang Yingnian suggests to let Hong Kong children to stay in Shenzhen temporarily (Tang Yingnian: Rang Gangren Zinu Zan Ju Shenzhen)", *Ming Pao*, 11 February 1999, A10.

117. "The Education Authority of Hong Kong intends to run schools in the Mainland (Jiao Shu Yi Neidi Ban Xue Shu Gang Yali)", *Ming Pao*, 7 April 1999.

118. "Guangdong has taken effective measures to cure 'problematic buildings' (Guangdong Zhili 'Lanweilou' Jian Chengxiao)", *People's Daily*, 22 November 1998, p.4.

119. "Guangdong drafts the rules in order to control problematic buildings (Yue Ding Guanzhi 'Lanweilou' Fagui)", *Wen Hui Pao* (Hong Kong), 26 May 1998.

120. *Ibid.*

121. The amended Article 5 states that China shall adopt the policy to run the country in accordance with laws and to build a socialist country with the rule of law.

122. In China, law enforcement (Si Fa) refers to legal activities conducted by law enforcement personnel, prosecutors and judges.

123. On 16 September 1998, the Chairman of the NPC pointed out that adjudication should be subject to supervision in order to have fair judicature in accordance with the law. See Li Peng Urges to Strengthen the Supervision in order to Ensure the Fair Adjudication in line with Laws (Li Peng Zai Quanguo Renda Huiyi Shang Zhichu Jiaqiang Jiandu Baozheng Gongzhengsifa Yifa Banan), *People's Daily*, 17 September 1998.

124. Liu Min, "Rooting out corruption of law enforcement (Chanchu Sifa Fubai)", *People's Daily*, 8 August 1998

125. "Guangdong rectifies teams of law enforcement and makes good progress (Guangdong Zhengfa Duiwu Zhengdun Chengxiao Da)", *Guangzhou Daily*, 16 August 1998.

126. "Those who fail to pass the examination cannot be procurators (Kaoshi Bujige Bunen Dang Jianchaguan)", *Guangzhou Daily* (Guangdong), 21 September 1998.

127. "Parties shall pay attention to new rules when they are involved in civil or economic trials (Zai Guangdong Da Guansi Qing Zhuyi Xin Guiding)", *South China News* (*Hua Nan Ri Bao*), 1 September 1999, p. 1.

128. Article 11 of the PRC Constitution states that the non-public owned economy, such as individual businesses, privately-run businesses, is a very important part of the socialist market economy. The state will protect the legal rights and interests of individual businesses and private-run businesses. The state will guide, supervise and manage those individual businesses and private-run businesses.

CHAPTER 11

The Decentralization of
Higher Education in Guangdong:
Challenges and Opportunities

Nixon K. H. MOK

Introduction

Since the mid-1980s, the Chinese Communist Party (CCP) has instituted a policy of decentralization in the educational sphere to allow more flexibility for governments and educational practitioners at local levels to run education. With this policy context in mind, this chapter examines how decentralization has affected the running of higher education in Guangdong, with particular reference to strategies adopted in reforming the financing structure, instituting joint development programmes to enhance the competitive edge of higher educational institutions (HEIs), merging universities and reforming the management structure of HEIs. With the introduction and implementation of "Project 211", the CCP introduced "internal competition" in its university sector in order to bring about substantial improvements. A close examination of developments in Guangdong's higher educational sector reveals that even though the role of the state in higher education has changed, the policy of decentralization has in fact strengthened the state's role in higher education. One significant consequence of this change is that the public-good functions of education, of which the state has taken the primary role as a reliable guarantor, have diminished. Nonetheless, the state's role as a regulator and overall service co-ordinator has been strengthened rather than weakened under the policy of decentralization.

A Changing Policy Context: The Policy of Decentralization

Before economic reforms started in the late 1970s, China's higher educational system was guided and run by the "centralist model".[1] This meant that the central government held five key functions in education, namely:

(a) Provision of core funding;

(b) Setting student enrollments for each institution;

(c) Approving senior staff appointments;

(d) Authorizing all new academic programmes; and

(e) Managing the student assignment process.[2]

With the rapid expansion of higher education, the central government felt that this model was no longer appropriate to meet the needs of higher education.

Acknowledging that over-centralization and stringent rules were killing the initiatives and enthusiasm of local educational institutions, the CCP thus called for "resolute steps to streamline administration, devolve powers to units at lower levels so as to extend the schools' decision-making powers in the administration of school affairs"[3] and thus reduce the rigid controls over schools at all levels as stipulated in the 1985 document *Decision of the Central Committee of the Chinese Communist Party on the Reform of the Educational System*.

One of the major themes of this document was related to reform in the higher education sector and devolving decision-making power from the central government to individual HEIs. Realizing the importance of professional knowledge and technical know-how to the success of China's modernization programme, and conscious of the state's insufficient financial resources to create adequate higher education opportunities for its citizens, the state allowed more autonomy and flexibility to local governments and educationalists in directing the course of educational development.[4] The state, in providing a framework necessary for educational development, deliberately devolved responsibility and power to local governments, local communities and other non-state sectors to involve themselves in creating more learning opportunities.

The promulgation of the 1993 *Mission Outline of the Reform and Development of China's Education* (*Zhongguo Jiaoyu Gaige he Fazhan Ganyao*) reassured people that the state still supported the decentralization policy and diversification of educational services. Moreover, the *Mission Outline* stated very clearly that; "the national policy is to actively encourage and fully support social institutions and citizens to establish schools [including higher educational institutions] according to laws and to provide correct guidelines and to strengthen administration"[5], and that the "Government has to change its function from direct control to managing schools [including HEIs] through legislation, funding, planning, advice on policies and other necessary means".[6] In sum, the principles behind the new approach were to deepen reform of China's higher education system "by gradually setting up a system under which the government exercises overall management while institutions are run independently and geared to the needs of society".[7] Most important of all, the new approach furthered the policy of decentralization, allowing individual institutions to exercise more managerial autonomy in deciding matters related to student enrollment, adjustment of specialties, appointment and dismissal of cadres, use of funds, evaluation of professional titles, distribution of wages and pursuing international co-operation and exchanges.[8]

Within this policy context, there was a significant change in the relationship between the central government and provincial/local governments. Instead of exercising "micro control", that is, imposing very tight control over the details of the operation of higher education, the central government would henceforth maintain "macro control" by giving policy directions and issuing policy principles. The Ministry of Education (formerly the State Education Commission) became responsible for supervising the implementation of the plans and policies whilst directly governing the 35 national universities; higher educational institutions at the provincial and local levels became directly managed and run by governments at lower levels. At the same time, the central government also encouraged local governments to participate in "joint-development programmes" to run the universities and colleges affiliated to the central line ministries by means of a joint-management system by both the provinces and the ministries (*Gongjiang*).[9]

More recently, the promulgation of the *Higher Education Law* in August 1998 again stipulated that the development of higher education must cater for emerging social needs. Once more, the *Higher Education Law* reconfirms the general principles behind the policy of decentralization, calling for more diversified modes of educational services and allowing greater flexibility for local and provincial governments to run higher education.[10] Openly recognizing that the state alone can never satisfy the pressing needs of higher education, Jiang Zemin, the General Secretary of the CCP, repeatedly called for the joint efforts of every sector in society to engage in creating more educational opportunities. More importantly, he even openly endorsed the role of *minban* (people-run) higher educational institutions and urged further development in *minban* institutions of higher learning to train people for China's modernization.[11]

The "211 Project" and "Internal Competition" in the Higher Education Sector

Although the central government adopted a policy of decentralization in running higher education, the CCP has never withdrawn entirely from the higher education domain. Instead of being the sole direct provider of educational services, the central government now performs the new roles of policy facilitator and regulator of higher education. Even though the central government has delegated its authorities to local/provincial governments and individual HEIs to take charge of their operational matters, the central government has introduced "internal competition" and "review exercises" to regulate the higher education sector. Drawing comparative insights from leading universities in other countries, the CCP has begun to realize the importance of bringing about substantial improvements in its university education system. Early in the 1993 *Mission Outline*, the State Education Commission (SEC) (now the Ministry of Education) initiated a concrete plan to bring resources together to operate 100 universities and selected academic disciplines to meet world standards. The *Mission Outline* states clearly that:

> "In order to meet the challenges coming from the global technological revolution, both central and local authorities should concentrate resources and powers on operating around 100 main point universities and a group of main point professions and disciplines. It aims at enhancing the quality of teaching, scientific research and institutional management in selected HEIs as well as their academic disciplines to recognized world standards during the twenty-first century."[12]

Based upon the framework of the *Mission Outline*, the SEC issued a document introducing the 211 Project in July 1993, five months after the promulgation of the *Mission Outline*.[13] Pursuant to the goal of reforming and restructuring China's higher education system, central to the 211 Project is the training of high quality professionals for future economic modernization, and constructing a solid base for scientific, technological and social development. In addition, the 211 Project is meant to promote "quality education" in both scientific research and management to recognized international standards.

In order to select the top 100 HEIs to be included in the 211 Project, the SEC set out a stringent set of regulations. In brief, the criteria for being selected depends on the quality and achievements of individual HEIs' performance in teaching and research, as well as their ability to achieve leadership status in both the national and international academic arenas. Therefore, universities are assessed by quantifiable, objective criteria on staffing, buildings, libraries, laboratories, research, funds, etc. to determine whether they are "qualified" to be included as top higher educational institutions.[14] Moreover, the 211 Project also calls for a high quality institutional management by its repeated emphasis on managerial reforms within HEIs along the line of the 3Es; namely efficiency, effectiveness and economy.

Between 1994 and 1996, 30 HEIs submitted their applications with detailed review reports. Thereafter the SEC assessed these HEIs with great care, and the first stage of the assessment was completed in 1996.[15] Up to 1998, the setting up of 100 national main point laboratories and 25 research centres for national engineering and technology has marked the progress of the 211 Project. Two hundred and fifty universities have been included in the China Educational Scientific Research Computing Network (*Zhongguo Jiaoyu Keyan Jisun Jiwan*). Meanwhile, nearly 100 HEIs submitted their applications to be included in the project pending assessment by the then SEC and the 211 Project Office.[16]

Responses to Changes:
Higher Education in Guangdong[17]

Reform in the Financing of Higher Education

Under the policy of decentralization, one of the major transformations in China's higher education sector is related to the financing system. In order to alleviate the pressure on the government's finances and to strengthen the institutions' capacity for self-reliance, sources of financing in higher education have been increasingly diversified. In spite of the fact that public expenditure on education in real terms has grown by 6.19 times, from 22.8 billion yuan in 1985 to

141.16 billion yuan in 1995, and its percentage of total government expenditure from 12.35% to 16.05% during the same period, it is nearly impossible to meet the pressing needs for higher education dependant on the state's limited financing abilities.[18]

In order to diversify the sources of educational financing, educational institutions have looked to surcharges in both urban and rural areas, tuition fees, profits from school-run enterprises and voluntary tax allowable contributions from businesses and individuals, and other sources of alternative funding.[19] As part of the overall economic reform initiatives to allow provinces to retain a higher portion of their revenues, the central government has allowed provincial governments more flexibility in exercising their financial autonomy. In Guangdong, the provincial government has allocated additional financial resources to develop its higher education on top of the legally stipulated educational surcharges. For instance, the provincial government of Guangdong has invested massively in higher education by raising teachers' wages and improving the learning environment of HEIs. Another way of upgrading the HEIs in Guangdong has been by matching the allocation from the central government to universities under the Ministry of Education and HEIs located within the province.[20]

Another major structural change in financing higher education was the introduction of a "fee-paying" principle. Early in the 1980s, the plan for charging students a fee was regarded as an "ultra-plan", implying that the intake of these "self-supporting" students was beyond the state plan.[21] However, after the endorsement of a socialist market economy at the CCP's Fourteenth Congress, in 1992 the SEC officially approved HEIs' admitting up to 25% of their students from the "commissioned training" or "fee-paying" categories. In 1993, 30 HEIs were selected for a pilot study known as "merging the rails", whereby students were admitted either because of high public examination scores or because they were willing and able to pay a fee, even though their scores were lower than that which was required. In 1994, more institutions entered the scheme and the fee-charging principle was thus legitimized.[22] From 1997 onwards, all HEIs in Mainland China began charging all students tuition fees.[23]

During field visits to Guangdong, the author was told that all students were required to pay tuition fees. Beginning in 1995, Zhongshan University started to "merge the tracks", signifying that there were no longer any differences among "publicly-funded students", "self-paying students" and "commissioned students". Professor Cai He, Head of the Department of Sociology, and Professor Zhang Minqiang, Director of the Institute of Higher Education of Zhongshan University, told me that students had begun to accept the self-paying principle. In the 1998/1999 academic year, the range of tuition fees varied between courses, with students paying from 2,500 to 3,500 yuan. Despite the fact that some students still have difficulties in accepting the notion of paying tuition fees in higher education, most students are relatively sympathetic. Wu Yechun, Deputy Director of the Office of Administration at the South China University of Technology (SCUT), told me that students had far more incentives to study hard after the adoption of a "fee-charging" principle in the university sector. According to Wu:

> "In the past, university education was entirely supported by the state and students seemed to take higher education for granted and thus their motivation was low once they were admitted. But this situation has changed since the adoption of the "self-paying" principle in the university sector. Students are strongly motivated to study because they have to pay for their courses, and they are eager to learn a wider range of subjects to broaden their knowledge base. Despite the fact that some students, particularly those who are from poor families, may have difficulties in paying tuition fees, many of them are able to secure financial support to obtain higher education. More fundamentally, people are generally supportive of the "fee-paying" principle in higher education because they believe that higher education is an investment. With higher qualifications, university graduates would find it

easier to get jobs in the open labour market. "Value" is thus added to the students after university training."[24]

In addition to allowing HEIs to charge students tuition fees, the central government also encourages HEIs to generate their own revenue through research and consultancy, commissioned training programmes, school-run enterprises and other services to industry and society. HEIs are also encouraged to receive private donations and overseas contributions.[25] According to Professor Wu Fuguang of the Institute of Higher Education of Zhongshan University, it has become increasingly popular for faculty members and departments to venture into the commercial and business fields to generate additional revenues. In the face of limited financial resources from the state, the university authorities have had to diversify their sources of financing. Obviously, those departments with the skills and knowledge demanded by the market have formed their own enterprises or collaborated with the private sector to generate more income. University-run enterprises are not unique to Zhongshan University. Jinan University has also has set up a special office for co-ordinating work related university-run enterprises. The Economic and Technology Development Company, one of the subsidiary companies of Jinan University, has established a close partnership with industry in order to promote its products developed in research projects. In addition, paid consultation services are offered in the fields of law and accounting.[26]

Similarly, a variety of ways have been employed by different HEIs in Guangdong to attract additional funding. For instance, the South China Normal University (SCNU) has tried to generate additional income by leasing out some of its university-owned property. Professor Wang Guojian, Vice-President of SCNU, commented:

"Revenue generation in universities is increasingly popular. Without adequate funding for educational development, we should search for our own ways to get additional income. I think what has been done in revenue generation in this university is not sufficient, and we must work harder in this endeavour. In the midst of a market economy, there should be a fundamental transformation of the way a university is managed and operated. Obviously, enhanced economic position would enable the university to develop new frontiers and other related activities."[27]

In spite of the fact that SCNU has only limited financial means, the university has successfully established a new Kangda School in collaboration with, and funded by, a local enterprise in Guangzhou. Affiliated with SCNU, Kangda School has attracted students, and therefore the university can obtain additional income from this collaborative project. All in all, different strategies have been adopted by HEIs in Guangdong to gain additional funds to finance educational developments in the region. As the policy of decentralization has actually delegated financial authority from the central government to local/provincial governments and even to individual HEIs, the financial capacity of HEIs now depends entirely upon whether they can attract sufficient income to finance their institutions. Since one of the performance indicators is closely related to the financial conditions of individual HEIs, it is therefore not surprising to see that different HEIs in Guangdong have eagerly diversified the channels for educational financing.

Joint Development Programmes to Enhance the Competitive Edge of HEIs

In order to further develop HEIs in Guangdong, the provincial government and the State Education Commission decided to pool their resources to strengthen the academic standards of HEIs in Guangdong. For instance, SCUT was one of the HEIs in Guangdong selected to enjoy "joint development" by both the central authorities and the local government. It is reported that such a reform initiative has greatly improved the research and learning environment at SCUT. Under the reform directives, the School of Communications and the School of Electrical Power have been developed jointly by the university and the relevant departments of the provincial government. Other examples include the Automobile and Engine Research Centre, the Chemical Engineering Science and Technical Research Centre, and the Ultrasonic Electronic and Information Equipment Engineering Research Centre which have been jointly developed by the university and relevant local organizations and industrial conglomerates. In addition, joint development projects also include those between SCUT and other institutions of higher learning and research institutes in Guangdong.[28]

By making use of the joint development programmes, SCUT succeeded in being selected as one of the top 100 universities in 1995. In its mission statement, SCUT is committed to become:

> "A university of science and technology that stands in the front rank of the key universities of China with respect to its comprehensive strength and overall standards. By that time its academic standards will have approached those of the first-rate universities in the world and some disciplines will have reached advanced world standards, making it an important base for the training of highly-qualified students for Guangdong and the nation as a whole and also an important base for scientific research and technical development."[29]

With very good connections to the business and industrial sectors, SCUT should have few problems in attracting additional funds. The Deputy Director of SCUT's Administration Office told me that the university had engaged in projects funded by enterprises in Guangzhou. According to him:

> "Under the concept of *"Gongjiang"* (joint effort of the SEC and Guangdong Provincial Government to run universities), SCUT has a very clear mission to train people for the modernization project in Guangdong. Therefore, we have extended our contacts and established a very close relationship with local enterprises. We are sensitive and responsive to the needs of the enterprises. In order to capitalize on the knowledge and skills possessed by our

faculty members, it is extremely important for the university to develop a partnership with industries and enterprises in the Guangdong area."[30]

Similar experiences can be found at Zhongshan University in Guangdong to jointly develop the institution in collaboration with the central authorities, local governments and other local non-state sectors. Zhongshan University has been allocated 108 million yuan from both the central and provincial government. Even though Zhongshan University has enjoyed the privilege of the "joint development programme", depending upon state and provincial support does not satisfy the development goals of the university. Like other universities in Guangdong, Zhongshan University has to look for other sources of income to meet its own ends.[31]

Merging Universities and the Establishment of a "University City"

As the CCP seeks to recruit its best 100 institutions of higher learning into the 211 Project, the state is going to attach a new financial and strategic importance to about 100 universities and some subject areas in order to try and ensure that these universities will become "world-class universities" in the early twenty-first century. Central to the scheme is the introduction of "competition" among universities, rewarding the top 100 higher educational institutions which have attained international benchmarks.[32]

In 1997, the SEC issued a new direction for higher education in which universities were encouraged "to share resources and facilities among universities; to merge universities to enhance research and teaching quality; to consolidate and strengthen the existing good work, and to establish new universities in collaboration with local governments".[33] In accordance with this policy, local universities in Guangzhou have attempted to merge with others in order to enhance their common strengths, hoping that such an undertaking may enable them to be selected for the top 100. In order to upgrade Guangzhou's city-run higher educational institutions, the present Guangzhou Normal University, together with the Guangzhou

Institute of Education and the Guangzhou Teacher College, will merge to form a new Guangzhou Normal University. At the same time, the Guangzhou Medical College, the South China Construction College and Guangzhou University are committed to the improvement of their research and teaching, while establishing closer links with local industries and businesses in order to make their courses more attractive and competitive in the market.[34]

Another growth area will be the establishment of a "University City" in Guangzhou. Realizing the limitations faced by Guangzhou's city-run higher educational institutions (particularly in terms of small student population size, limited space for school buildings and inadequate resources and faculty members), it is proposed that a University City be developed composed of various local institutions of higher learning such as Jiaotung College, the Vocational College, the Industrial and Business College, the College of Arts and Law, and the College of Finance. The proposed merger would draw resources and strengths together. Coupled with the existing 100 college-run research centres and enterprises, students would very much benefit from sharing more resources, better facilities, well-qualified faculty members and enhanced research and teaching in the future University City.[35]

Like these locally run higher educational institutions, the publicly run institutions of higher learning have already started a similar process by allowing students to enrol in courses offered by sister universities. For instance, Professor Wu Yunfeng, Deputy Registrar of Jinan University, informed the author that his university has an agreement with six nearby universities, such as the South China Polytechnic University and the South China Normal University, to allow their students to enrol in courses outside their universities and transfer credits. In addition, libraries and other facilities are also commonly shared among these universities. It is hoped that this scheme will not only encourage students to broaden their scope of knowledge, but also pull more resources together to facilitate quality education.[36] Similar experiences are found at SCUT and SCNU where the university authorities identify outstanding students and allow them to enrol in "double degree" programmes. With a broader knowledge base and specialty, graduates would find themselves more competitive in the labour market.[37] More importantly, it is also hoped that the merging of universities will lead to stronger institutions, thereby improving their competitive edge in the selection process of the 211 Project.

The Reform of HEIs Management Structure

As discussed earlier, the policy of decentralization has delegated authority to individual HEIs so that they can manage their own affairs. Various reforms of the management structure of individual HEIs have been introduced and implemented gradually and incrementally.[38] One of the reforms is to empower university presidents to take charge of the overall affairs of their institutions. Under the leadership of the Party Committee of the HEIs, the presidents of individual HEIs are held responsible for the development and operation of the institutions. Like other *minban* HEIs which are run by a new management system of "Presidential Responsibility", under the supervision of a Board of Advisors,[39] some public universities have attempted to establish similar management structures by forming Boards of Trustees to develop closer links with the industrial and business sectors, as well as cultivating fruitful relationships with other sectors of society. According to Wei:

> "There was no common expectation from the creation of the Boards. Most institutions used the Boards to give them access to a wide range of enterprises and to mobilize funds. Some of them stressed the involvement of the related officials, while only a few actively involved the Boards in their management, expecting the Boards to review the universities' development plan and to provide suggestions to the authorities of the universities."[40]

During field visits to various HEIs in Guangdong, the author also learned that similar bodies are in formation. As the state encourages the establishment of Boards of Trustees at universities and colleges, one would therefore expect that the system of trustees would play a role in the internal management of the institutions of higher learning in the future.

In addition to reforming the management structure by allowing the presidents of HEIs more flexibility in running their institutions, another major area of reform is related to the restructuring of academic organizations. To transform the conventional "two-level-model" of university and academic departments, some universities in Guangdong have taken the initiative by establishing a "three-level-model", whereby the relationship among the university, colleges and departments is made clearer. With the intention of reducing the overall workload of university presidents and streamlining university/HEI administration, the restructuring process has allowed the college and departmental levels far more autonomy to run their business. Being the central governance body in the university, university presidents are therefore held responsible for the formulation of policies and the development of long-term development plans and objectives. The colleges have now become management entities which enjoy considerable powers to deal with their teaching and research matters, the management of personnel and resource allocation.[41]

The recent management reforms and academic re-organization of HEIs in Guangdong are timely and appropriate methods of adapting to the new context of the market economy. No doubt, such reform strategies have empowered the college and department levels to exercise responsibility over their own operational matters. But it is also true that the delegation of power implies that these entities have to struggle to survive. Similar to their Western counterparts, academic departments in Chinese universities nowadays are managed with a one-line budget, thus suggesting individual departments have to find ways of sustaining themselves. It is therefore easy to imagine that those academic departments or colleges which possess market-friendly skills and knowledge would have no problem in surviving; while others without the same market appeal will lose out. Hence, all academic departments and colleges have been trying hard to ride the "strong tide of marketization". In order to survive, HEIs have sought either to make their courses more "market-friendly" to attract more "customers" (i.e., students) or to engage in various kinds of activities to generate additional income.[42]

Challenges from Other Regions in the Mainland

Under the policy of decentralization and diversification, students are now granted far more freedom to select the institutions and disciplines for which they wish to apply, providing that they can perform well in the national HEIs entrance examination. It is not surprising to see that students with high academic achievements choose those institutions with high academic prestige, like Beijing University, Tsinghua University in Beijing and Fudan University in Shanghai, all considered the top universities in Mainland China. This is particularly true when all Chinese universities are required to collect students' tuition fees. It is not difficult to imagine that when students have become the "users" and "customers" of educational services, they would choose universities and courses they consider to be "value for money". In order to attract students of higher quality, universities have to enhance their teaching and research programmes as a means of maintaining their prestige and academic achievements. Obviously, whether the academic standards and research performance of individual HEIs can be enhanced and advanced depends upon whether they can obtain sufficient financial resources.

There is no doubt that the most prestigious universities have no problem in recruiting top students because they have no difficulty in securing funds from both the central government and other non-state sectors (including the market) to improve their teaching and research environments. Nonetheless, the second-tier universities or, even worse, the universities located in local areas, may encounter problems in admitting students. No one can deny that the 211 Project acts as a catalyst to arouse HEIs' motivation to enhance quality so as to earn a place in the top 100. However, it is also true that those second-tier and locally run universities may find themselves in disadvantageous positions when competing with the top universities.

For instance, the Shanghai City Architecture College and the Shanghai Architecture College, with a total staff of 2,000 and 6,000 students, merged with Tongji University. After the merger, these three HEIs pooled their resources to strengthen their teaching and research profiles. Similarly, Sichuan Lianhe University merged with other local HEIs to strengthen its application for inclusion in the 211 Project. The strategy of merging has proved effective enough to improve the operations of Tongji University and Sichuan Lianhe University. Both of them have successfully passed the first stage of the 211 Project assessment.[43]

More recently, the Ministry of Education (MOE) announced a new scheme to strategically develop only two universities, namely Beijing University and Tsinghua University, as the top universities in Mainland China by allocating additional funds to establish these two HEIs as internationally recognized "Top Class" universities. Meanwhile, the MOE has also called for all provincial and local governments to identify one or two universities for strategic development. In response to the MOE's call, the Shanghai municipal government has identified Fudan University as the primary target for strategic development.[44] Undoubtedly, with such "preferential treatment", these selected institutions will have little difficulty in becoming world-class universities. But what is also true is that there will be disparity and inequality of development within the university sector in the Mainland.

Putting such new developments in perspective, it is pleasing to hear the success stories of some universities. However, it is regretful that some local universities and colleges in Guangdong have experienced difficulties in recruiting students. How these second-tier universities and local colleges can secure sufficient financial resources to improve their teaching and research in order to compete with the strengthened and properly restructured universities as mentioned above has posed a big problem for them. Unquestionably, the MOE's new policy of identifying a few universities for strategic development may weaken the position of those universities without the same "preferential treatment". It is conceivable that one of the great challenges which HEIs in Guangdong will encounter is how to improve their competitive edge in the emerging "internal market" within China's university sector. The central government seems to be intent on developing Beijing and Shanghai as the leading centres of cultural and academic exchange in the Mainland. Whether the HEIs in Guangdong can be established as centres of excellence in academic and research endeavour will prove to be one of the most challenging tasks ahead.

Discussion: Decentralization without Deregulation in Higher Education in China

Despite the fact that the policy of decentralization was adopted by the CCP in the 1980s, the state's role in the control of education has actually been strengthened instead of being weakened. Even though the state has realized that its own capacity to provide people with sufficient higher educational opportunities is severely limited in the present social and economic context, it would be incorrect to say that the CCP has entirely withdrawn from the educational arena. What has really happened in Mainland China is a transformation of the state's role as a sole provider or a reliable guarantor of educational services to a regulator or service purchaser, even when education has become more marketized and privatized.[45] China has moved in a direction similar to that of some Western countries where their policies "amount to a 'hollowing out' of the state[46] with the loss of some activities "upwards" to supranational bodies and the loss of others 'downwards' to sub-national or non-state bodies".[47] China's education system has been going through the processes of marketization and decentralization whereby the state has gradually reduced its subsidy and provision in education. The shift from direct state control to governance has caused fundamental changes in the state's role in education. As Hirst and Thompson suggested when talking about a wide range of government activities in the public sector:

> The tendency in common usage (is) to identify the term "government" with the institutions of the state that control and regulate the life of a territorial community. [For] Governance — that is, the control of an activity by some means such that a range of desired outcomes is attained - is, however, not just the province of the state. Rather, it is a function that can be performed by a wide variety of public and private, state and non-state, national and international, institutions and practices.[48]

One point that deserves attention here is that during the process of transformation, the state does not "go away" in the Chinese context. Rather, the nature of the work it does has changed, broadly speaking, "from carrying out most of the work of the co-ordination of education itself to determining where the work will be done and by whom".[49] Seen in this context, decentralization and devolution do not necessarily mean that the state has reduced its control over the educational sphere. In the Chinese case, it can be argued that the central government in Mainland China has gradually forsaken its major role in the provision of educational opportunities, adopting a wider fee-charging principle to recover a large proportion of costs through tuition fees and other means. Re-emphasizing the importance of individual responsibilities and encouraging local communities and social organizations to create additional educational opportunities, the Chinese government is continuously reducing its educational subsidy and provision. As pointed out earlier, multiple channels of financing include educational surcharges, local government subsidies, tuition and miscellaneous fees and funds raised from overseas Chinese and compatriots in Hong Kong and Macau.[50] These developments demonstrate the shared responsibility of the state and non-state sectors in providing educational services. Above all, the efforts to recover costs in education and the expansion of private and *minban* (people-run) education reveals that China's education system is going through a process of "privatization" or "marketization".[51]

Marketization means "education becomes a commodity provided by competitive suppliers, educational services are priced, and access to them depends on consumer calculation and ability to pay".[52] The above discussion on Guangdong's higher education system in particular, and higher education in Mainland China in general, has suggested that "internal competition" is institutionalized among universities. Seemingly, "internal markets" have gradually evolved, whereby the state becomes the "purchaser" while universities become "providers" of educational services. Although the split between purchaser and provider is still not as clear as it is in many other countries, recent developments in China's higher education sector in moving from the state's role as sole provider or co-ordinator of educational services to that of a regulator and monitor are very important for China's future.

Conclusion

Clearly commercial influences, the establishment of tuition fees and a limited role for private provision in China suggest a reduced state role in educational provision and financing, but this process does not constitute a total withdrawal from state control. Despite the fact that the state has tried to "roll back" from the direct provider role, the CCP has taken different forms of state intervention. Moving from direct control to governance, other actors and non-state sectors have emerged to engage in educational provision. Roger Dale is correct when he opines that as far as co-ordinating institutions are concerned, in relation to different governance activities in education like funding, regulation and provision/delivery, the role of the state, market and community would normally be identified. However, as far as the processes of "marketization" and "decentralization" in China's higher education sector are concerned, "the state has never done all these things alone, the market and especially the community have been indispensable to the operation of the educational systems".[53] What really interests us is how to formalize and contract the areas of their involvement in the Mainland.

Notes

1. Wei Xin, "Reform and Development of China's Higher Education System in the Past Decade", paper presented at the International Conference on Academic Reform in the World: Situation and Perspective in the 'Massification' Stage of Higher Education, 6–7 February 1997, Hiroshima, Japan.

2. *Ibid.*, p. 8; China National Institute of Educational Research, *A Study of NGO-Sponsored and Private Higher Education in China* (Beijing: UNESCO, 1995).

3. Keith M. Lewin, *et al.*, *Educational Innovation in China* (Harlow, UK: Longman, 1994), p. 233.

4. Wei Yitong and Zhang Guocai, "A Historical Perspective on Non-governmental Higher Education in China," paper presented to the International Conference of Private Higher Education in Asia and the Pacific Region, November, 1995, the University of Xiamen, China; Zhu Yiming, "Perspectives on Minban Schools in China," paper presented at the Shanghai International House for Education, 15–20 August 1994, Shanghai.

5. Chinese Communist Party Central Committee, *The Programme for Reform and Development of China's Education* (Beijing: State Education Commission, 1993).

6. State Education Commission Policies and Law Department, *Law and Regulation on Basic Education of the People's Republic of China* (Beijing: Beijing Normal University Press, 1993), p. 6.

7. Cited in Wei, "Reform and Development", *op cit.*, p. 9.

8. Kai-ming Cheng, "Markets in a Socialist System: Reform of Higher Education", in K. Watson, S. Modgil and C. Modgil (eds.), *Educational Dilemmas: Debate and Diversity*, *Vol. 2, Higher Education* (London: Cassell, 1996); Wei, "Reform and Development", *op cit.*

9. State Education Commission, *Guojia Jiaowei Guanyu Zhongdian Jianshe Yipi Gaodeng Xuexiao he Zhongdian Xueke de Ruogan Yijian* [*Some Opinions on Constructing a Group of Main Point Higher Education Institutions and a Group of Main Point Academic Disciplines by the State Education Commission*] (Beijing: State Education Commission, 1993).

10. Central Committee of Communist Party of China, *Higher Education Law* (Beijing: Ministry of Education, 1998).

11. *Guangming Daily*, 16 June 1999, p. 1.

12. Central Committee of the Chinese Communist Party, *Outline for the Reform and Development of China's Education* (Beijing: Central Committee of the Chinese Communist Party, 1993), Part II, para. 9.

13. See note 9.

14. Flemming Christiansen, "Devolution on Chinese Higher Education Policy in the 1990s: Common Establishment and the '211' Programme", *Leeds East Asia Papers*, No. 36, pp. 1–23; Ka-ho Mok, and King-yee Wat, "The Merging of the Public and Private Boundary: Education and the Market Place in China", *International Journal of Educational Development*, Vol. 18, No. 3, 1998, pp. 255–267.

15. Beijing Normal University Editorial Committee, *Maixiang 21 Shiji de Zhongguo Gaoxiao [China HEIs in the Coming 21st Century]* (Beijing: Beijing Normal University Press, 1996).

16. Zhu Kaixuan, *Zai Guojia Jiaowei 1998 nian Jiaoyu Gongzuo Huiyishang de Jianghua [Commissioner of State Education: Speech on the State Education Commission Annual Work Conference of 1998]* (Beijing: State Education Commission, 1998).

17. The discussion below is mainly based upon my field visits to various HEIs in the Guangdong area. Much of the material reported here is based upon intensive interviews, otherwise additional sources will be specified.

18. Wei, "Reform and Development", *op. cit.*

19. Stanley Rosen, "Recent Developments in Chinese Education," *Chinese Education and Society*. Vol. 30, No. 3, 1997; Ka-ho Mok, "Retreat of the State: Marketization of Education in the Pearl River Delta," *Comparative Education Review*, Vol. 41, No. 3, 1997, pp. 260–276.

20. Wei, "Reform and Development", *op. cit.*

21. Kai-ming Cheng, "Markets in a Socialist System", *op. cit.*

22. *Ibid.*

23. Ka-ho Mok, "Professional Autonomy and Private Education," in Ka-ho Mok, *Social and Political Development in Post-Reform China* (Basingstoke,UK: Macmillan, 2000).

24. Field interview, Guangdong, 1998.

25. Hu Ruiwen, *Jiushi Niandao Zhongguo Jiaoyu yu 2010 Nian Zhanwang [China's Education in the 1990s and the Prospects in the Year of 2010]*, paper presented to the Fifth International Conference on Chinese Education "Towards the 21st Century", August 13–19 1997, at the Chinese University of Hong Kong; Julia Kwong, "The New Educational Mandate in China: Running School, Running Business," *International Journal of Educational Development*, Vol. 16, No. 2, 1996, pp. 185–194; Ka-ho Mok, "Education and the Market Place in Hong Kong and Mainland China", *Higher Education*, Vol. 37, 1999, pp. 133–158.

26. Field interview, Guangdong, 1998.

27. *Ibid.*

28. *South China University of Technology Leaflet, 1998*, p. 1.

29. *Ibid.*

30. Field interview, Guangdong, 1998

31. *Ibid.*

32. Ka-ho Mok and King-yee Wat, "The Merging of the Public and Private Boundary", *op. cit.*

33. Wu Ziyin, "Guangzhoushi Jiaoyu Fazhan Zhanlue Yanjiu de Huigu Jiqi Renshi" [Review and Study of the Strategies of the Education Development in Guangzhou] in Ng Ziyin *et al.* (eds.), *Zhanshe Xindaihua Jiaoyu Jiangsi Guangzhousi Jiaoyu Fazhan Zhanlue Yinjiu [Building a Strong Educational Province — Strategies of the Education Development in Guangdong]* (Guangdong: Guangdong Higher Education Press, 1997)

34. *Ibid.*

35. *Ibid.*

36. Field interview, Guangdong, 1998

37. *Ibid.*

38. Wei, "Reform and Development", *op. cit.*

39. Ka-ho Mok, "Marketization and Quasi-Marketization: Educational Development in Post-Mao China," *International Review of Education*, Vol. 43, No. 5–6, 1997, pp. 547–567.

40. Wei, "Reform and Development", *op. cit.* p. 19.

41. Field interview, Guangdong, 1998.

42. Julia Kwong, "The New Educational Mandate", *op cit*; Lin Jin, "Private Schools in China", *Chinese Education and Society*, March–April 1996; Ka-ho Mok, "The Resurgence of Private Education in Post-Mao China," in Ka-ho Mok and Kar-ming Yu (eds.), *China in Transition: Social and Political Transformation in Post Reform China* (Hong Kong: Hong Kong Humanities Press, 1998).

43. Wu Ziyin, "Guangzhoushi Jiaoyu Fazhan Zhanlue", *op.cit*; *Gaojiao Wenzhai*, October 1994, pp. 6–7.

44. Field interview, Shanghai, 1999.

45. Ka-ho Mok, "Marketization and Quasi-Marketization", *op cit.*, "Education and the Market Place", *op. cit.*

46. See B. Jessop, "Towards a Schumpeterian Workfare State? Preliminary Remarks on Post-Fordist Political Economy", *Studies in Political Economy*, Vol. 40, 1993, pp. 7–39.

47. Roger Dale, "The State and the Governance of Education: An Analysis of the Restructuring of the State-Education Relationship", in A. H. Halsey, Hugh Laude, Phillip Brown and Amy Stuart Wells (eds.) *Education: Culture, Economy & Society* (Oxford: Oxford University Press, 1997), p. 274.

48. P. Hirst and G. Thompson, "Globalization and the Future of the Nation-state", *Economy and Society*, Vol. 24, No. 3, (1995), p. 422.

49. Dale, "The State and the Governance of Education", *op cit.*

50. Ka-ho Mok, "Private Challenges to Public Dominance: The Resurgence of Private Education in the Pearl River Delta", *Comparative Education*, Vol. 33, No. 1, 1997, pp. 43–60.; Ka-ho Mok, "Education and the Market Place", *op. cit.*

51. Ka-ho Mok, *Ibid*; Ka-ho Mok, "Private Challenges to Public Dominance", *op. cit.*, Ka-ho Mok and King-yee Wat, "The Merging of the Public and Private Boundary", *op. cit.*; see also note 50.

52. Yin Qiping and Gordon White, "The Marketization of Chinese Higher Education: A Critical Assessment," *Comparative Education*, Vol. 30, No. 3, 1994, p. 217.

53. Dale, "The State and the Governance of Education", *op cit.*, p. 275.

CHAPTER 12

China's Challenges in Services for the Elderly in the Twenty-first Century:
Reflections from Guangdong

Alex Yui-huen KWAN

Introduction

The term "demographic transition" refers to a gradual process whereby a society moves from a situation of high fertility and mortality rates to low ones.[1] This transition is characterized by a decline in infant and childhood mortality rates as infectious and parasitic diseases are brought under control. Whole populations begin to age when fertility rates decline and mortality rates for all age groups improve. Successive birth cohorts may eventually become smaller and smaller, as seen in the more developed nations. If projected declines in fertility and mortality rates in less developed countries proceed as expected, the overall population age structure will lose its strictly triangular shape, and the elderly portion of the population will increase. According to the definition used by the United Nations (UN), a country with 10% of its total population aged 60 and above, or 7% aged above 65, can be classified a country with an aged population.[2]

At the 34th Conference of the Social Development Committee convened in 1997, the UN warned its members that population aging would be a major challenge to every society in the twenty-first century, and that particular attention should be paid to this issue.[3] The rapidly expanding number of older people represents a social phenomenon without historical precedent. The world's elderly population — defined here as persons aged 60 and above — reached 550 million in 1996 and is expected to approach 1.2 billion by 2025.[4] According to UN estimates, at the beginning of the twenty-first century, the elderly population will exceed 600 million, or about 9.8% of the global population. The world's population will increase by 0.6 times from 2000 to 2050; during the same period, the elderly population will increase more than 2.3 times. The ratio of elderly people will increase from 9.8% to 20%, representing a demographic change throughout the world by the middle of this century.[5]

Of the approximately 580 million elderly people in the world today, around 355 million live in developing countries. By 2020 the number of elderly people worldwide will reach more than a billion, with over 700 million of them living in developing countries. It is projected that in China it will take only 27 years (2000–27) for the proportion of the population aged 60 years and over to increase to 20%.[6]

The numerical growth of older populations around the world is indicative of major achievements — reductions in infant and maternal mortality rates, decreases in fertility rates, reductions in infectious and parasitic diseases, improvements in nutrition and education — that have occurred, albeit unevenly, on a global scale. At the same time, the growth of older populations poses challenges to national public policies because a society's needs change as the proportion of the elderly population increases.[7] In the following sections an examination will be made of the challenges encountered by China in general, and Guangdong province in particular, in the face of population aging.

The Challenge of Population Aging

As reported by Hong,[8] according to China's Fourth National Census of 1990, out of a total population of 1.13 billion, there were

96.97 million elderly people, accounting for 8.58% of the total population. As a result of the projected changes in the age structure of the population, the process of aging (since 1982 and over the next several decades) may be divided into the following three stages:

(a) The first stage (1982 to 2000). These years cover the beginning of the aging process. During this period, the elderly population increased from 76.64 million to 127 million, an increase of 7.6% to 9.81%. This represents an annual elderly growth rate of about 2.9%.

(b) The second stage (2000 to 2020). The development of population aging is sustained. The elderly population will increase from 127 million to 229 million, and their proportion will rise from 9.81% to 15.23%, with an average growth rate of 3% per year.

(c) The third stage (2020 to 2040). During this period the development of population aging will reach its peak. The population born during the two baby booms of the 1950s and 1960s will enter the cohort of older people. The elderly population will increase from 229 million to 374 million, representing an increase from 15.23% to 24.28% — namely, one elderly person in every four people in the total population. The annual growth rate will slow down to 2.5%. Thereafter, the aging process in China will tend to stabilize, with projected small increases in the elderly population between 2060–90 (see Table 12.1).

As reported in a special issue of China Development Briefing,[9] the President of the China National Committee on Aging identified the following features of population aging in China:

(a) The absolute number of elderly people is large and are rising quickly;

(b) The advanced aged population has increased rapidly;

(c) China's population aging occurs within a relatively undeveloped economy;

Table 12.1

The Demographic Structure of China's Aging Population

Year	Total Aging Population 60+ (million)	Percentage of Total Population (%)	60–69 (%)	70–79 (%)	80+ (%)
1990	98	8.6	62.2	29.9	7.9
1995	117	9.3	61.8	31.5	6.7
2000	132	10.5	60.2	32.9	6.9
2010	176	12.7	58.7	33.5	7.8
2020	252	16.8	61.9	30.8	7.3
2030	372	23.5	60.3	32.6	7.1
2040	419	25.7	50.2	40.9	8.9
2050	468	27.8	49.4	37.7	12.9

Sources: Yu Xuejun, *The Economic Study of China's Aging Population* (Beijing: China Demography Publisher, 1995), p.30 (in Chinese); Jiang Zhenghua and Zhang Lingquang, *A Report on China's Population* (Liaoling: Liaoling People's Publisher, 1997), p. 337, Table 11.6 (in Chinese).

(d) The development of population aging is unevenly spread across the country;

(e) Population aging is more pronounced in rural areas.[10]

Within populations, different age groups may grow at very different rates. Over time, the elderly population itself may grow older on average as a larger proportion survives to 75 years and beyond. The oldest old constituted 23% of the world's 60-and-over population in 1996, among which 17.9% lived in China.[11] As indicated by the US Bureau of the Census,[12] China had 10.46 million people aged 80 and above in 1998 (3.87 million males and 6.59 million females); this will increase to 29.96 million in 2025 (10.15 million males and 15.81 million females). In 1998, the population aged 80 and above as a percentage of the 60 and over age group was 6.5% for males and 10.4% for females. It is predicted that in 2025, the number will increase to 7.7% for males and 10.8% for females. The numerical growth and increasing heterogeneity of the oldest old challenge social planners to seek further information about this group since they consume disproportionate amounts of health and long-term care services.

In 1995, the sex ratio among the older population was 92.85 men for every 100 women. With the increase of age, the sex ratio decreases. The sex ratio among the highly aged population, aged above 80, is 55.4 men for every 100 women.[13] As reported by the US Bureau of the Census,[14] the proportion of female persons aged 60 and above in China in 1998 was 52%, and the proportion of females aged 80 and over was 63%. In 1996, the average life expectancy at birth was 70.8 years, with 73 years for women and 68 years for men. Those people reaching 60 years old have an average life expectancy of an additional 17.4 years (18.8 years for women and 15.9 years for men).[15]

The rapid pace of the aging process and the absolute and relative increase in the number of the elderly will inevitably have important social and economic implications for China's development. The growth in the population aged 60 and above entails a heavier burden on the working population and a further commitment from the government. The elderly dependency ratio (which relates the size of the elderly population to the number of people aged 15–59) was 12.99 in 1982; it will increase to 15.97 by 2000, 23.68 in 2020 and 37.90 in 2040.[16] Data issued by the Chinese State Statistics Bureau shows that among the 80.91 million elderly Chinese aged 65 and above, 25.71 million have stable incomes, representing 31.78% (13.80 million are still engaged in salaried work and 11.91 million live on retirement pensions) (see Table 12.2). The remaining 55.2 million people (68.22%) mainly depend on their children, relatives or friends. Among the 80.91 million elderly people over 65, 60.91 million (about 75%) live with their children who provide care. A total of 20 million elderly people (about 25%) live independently without children around providing direct care. This indicates that the support and care of the elderly at present in China mainly depend on the family.[17]

The 1990 census showed that 75% of those aged 60 and above lived in the countryside. However, the aging of the urban population is expected to become more pronounced than that of the rural

Table 12.2

A Comparison of Labour Population Ratio and Overall Dependency Ratio
after Adjusting the Maximum Working Age

Year	Aging Population Ratio (%)		Labour Population Ratio (%)		Overall Dependency Ratio (%)	
	Age 59	Age 64	Age 59	Age 64	Age 59	Age 64
1991	8.8	5.7	63.7	66.7	57.0	49.8
2000	9.8	6.7	63.1	66.2	58.5	51.0
2010	11.8	7.7	66.8	70.9	49.7	41.1
2020	15.6	10.9	65.4	70.1	52.9	42.6
2030	21.9	14.6	60.0	67.3	66.6	48.5
2040	25.1	19.6	58.8	64.4	70.3	55.4
2050	27.5	20.4	56.6	63.6	76.8	57.3

Source: Zhao Lixin, "Facing the Challenge of Population Aging Rationally", *Population Research*,
           Vol. 4, 1997, pp. 43–47(in Chinese)

Table 12.3

The Population Structure of Guangdong Province
(%)

Year	0–14	15–64	65+
1990	29.9	64.5	5.6
1995	29.1	64.2	6.7
2000	25.9	66.6	7.5
2010	20.5	71.0	8.5
2015	20.3	70.0	9.7
2020	20.2	68.8	11.0

Sources: Zhou Guangfu, "The Development Trend of Guangdong's Population", *Southern
           Population*, Vol. 3, No. 6, 1997, Table 4, (in Chinese). Zhang Jianming, "A preliminary
           analysis of the characteristics of Guangdong's aging population", *Southern Population*,
           Vol. 1, 1998, pp. 46–49, (in Chinese).

population in the next few decades, an effect of the very different
levels of fertility. In 1982, 4.38 million (8.2%) of Guangdong's 59
million people were aged 60 or above. The 1990 census enumerated
5.65 million elderly persons, 9% of Guangdong's 62.9 million
people. In 1995, there were 7.22 million (10.5%) elderly persons
aged 60 or above in Guangdong province.[18] The overall population
of Guangdong increased from 27.83 million people in 1949 to 62.83
million in 1990; to 68.38 million in 1995; to 69.61 million in 1996;

and to over 70 million by May 1997.[19] In Guangzhou city alone there are already 850,000 elderly people.[20]

The Challenge of Aging Policy

As a socialist society steeped in a unique cultural tradition of filial piety, China is strongly committed to promoting the well being of the elderly. In order to meet the severe challenges posed by the aging population and to protect the interests of the aged, in 1996 the Chinese government passed the *Law of Protecting the Rights and Interests of the Aged*. This law makes clear that the government will introduce policies "providing for the aged, medical services for the aged, voluntary devotion to the aged, continuous learning for the aged, and offering pleasure to the aged".[21] The legislative intent of this law is as follows; *lao you suo yang* (that the elderly have appropriate material and financial support), *lao you suo yi* (that they have appropriate medical care), *lao you suo xue* (that they have educational opportunities), *lao you suo wei* (that they have a sense of accomplishment) and *lao you suo le* (that they have entertainment and enjoyment). This idealized strategy of *wu you* (five haves) relies on resources from all aspects of society by integrating the contributions of the state, the collective and the family.[22] It lays the foundations for care of the elderly in China in the twenty-first century.

Examined and approved by the Standing Committee of the National People's Congress of the People's Republic of China on 29 August 1996, the *Law of Protecting the Rights and Interests of the Aged* came into force on 1 October the same year.[23] The basic characteristics of the law are: the role of the family in offering support to the elderly is emphasized; the function of the social security system is reinforced; the identification of the "five guarantees for the elderly"; to advocate active aging; and that inputs from the government should be increased. Its main purpose is to help meet the needs of elderly people who have lost their ability to work. The services provided for elderly people include provision of clothes, food, housing, and medical, health and funeral services. The formulation and implementation of this law has greatly improved the protection of the rights and interests of elderly people. The government's commitment to the elderly can be seen in the increased investment in welfare institutions for the elderly such as apartments and care centres. The social security system has also been improved. The work of promoting education and cultural activities has been speeded up, and the elderly have more opportunities to develop their potential. The law has also raised society's awareness with respect to supporting the elderly.

The traditional meaning of supporting the old entails three major aspects: taking care of the elderly; respecting the elderly; and burying the elderly. Supporting the elderly is a component of Chinese culture and was integrated into the state supportive pattern of family support for the elderly.[24] Today, China is moving towards the concept of home care for the elderly. This means that family care remains the core, but is supplemented by community services, and safeguarded by state constitutions.[25]

In one of the recent issues of *China Social Work*, the concept of "socializing social welfare" was identified as the guiding principle for future welfare policy in China.[26] The new approach to welfare work includes; an integrated social welfare network for urban and rural areas, one welfare institute and two systems, socialization of raising social welfare funds, and special teams for social services.[27] Community support therefore has five basic functions; security support, service and solution, medical care, spiritual well-being, and participation in society. It should be people-focused, with the family as the basic unit, but supported by community resources.[28]

Finally, looking at the work of the China National Centre on Aging (CNCA), their policy objectives are centred around five principles, which Pennekamp considers as the main preconditions for a Chinese policy on the elderly:[29]

(a) The elderly should be supported where needed and basic needs should be fulfilled;

(b) The elderly should be medically cared for in a proper way;

(c) The elderly should have a chance to continue contributing to society;

(d) The elderly should be engaged in life-long learning;

(e) The elderly should lead a happy life.

In order to meet the challenge of population aging and maintain sustainable economic development, it is necessary to carry out the following measures: to formulate a population development strategy for controlling the birth rate and rationalizing the age structure, to establish a support system for the aged with Chinese characteristics, to raise the upper limit of the working age, and to utilize manpower resources among the elderly.[30]

The Challenge of Aging Welfare

In the wake of social and demographic changes (see Table 12.4 for the size of potential welfare recipients), the primary issue emerging is the provision of support for the elderly (see Table 12.5 for old people's service needs), in particular the economic implications which arise (see Table 12.6 for Civil Affairs' budget). Moreover, due to the projected decrease in the population of younger age groups (15–59) and shrinking household sizes, the main support for the elderly traditionally provided by family members is bound to weaken. For example, with the increasing number of retirees, there has been a staggering rise in welfare expenditures. Expenditures on social insurance and welfare for retirees jumped from 1.73 billion yuan in 1978 to 181.78 billion yuan in 1996. During the same period, the expenditure on retirees swelled from 22.2% of the total welfare budget to 66.7% (see Table 12.7). As a result of this demographic transition, other compensatory sources of support have to be found for the elderly. Essentially, the burden must be shared between the social partners, in a collective effort at complimentarity according to their mutual role and function in the reform era. The introduction of Family Planning Old-Age Insurance by a county

Table 12.4
Forecast of the Social Security Population in 2000
(million)

Year	Total Population (billion)	Social Security Total Population (billion)		Handicapped		Priority Treatment		
		Total	Civil Affairs	Total	16-59 yrs.	Total	Fixed No.	Public Discount
1985	10.45	4.48	2.99	5,225	1,045	4,163	325	1,784
1990	11.19	4.38	3.15	5,595	1,120	4,516	340	1,920
2000	12.48	3.90	3.40	6,240	1,248	5,032	390	2,130

Year	Difficult Household		Disaster Population			60+ Aging Population		
	Total	Severe Case	Disaster Population	Relief Population	Unemployment Population	Total	Urban	Rural
1985	10,939	3,900	10,000	6,000	5,933	8,569	1,970	6,599
1990	6,000	4,140	10,000	5,000	7,778	9,959	2,680	7,281
2000	4,620	4,620	10,000	3,000	986	12,979	4,932	8,047

Source: Mao Hai-po "The Forecast of China's Civil Affairs' Social Security in 2000", *China Civil Affairs*, No. 229, April 1998, p. 10.

Notes: (1) The percentage of social security population to total population: in 1985 was 42.9%, in 1990 was 39.1%, in 2000 is 31.2%.
(2) Civil Affairs social security population includes: handicapped, priority treatment, severe difficult households, disaster population, elderly in rural areas.
(3) Urban population: in 1985 was 23%, in 1990 was 26.9%, in 2000 is 38%.
(4) The handicapped population is estimated to be about 5% of the total population: the 16–59 handicapped age group is about 20% of the total handicapped population.
(5) The priority treatment group is about 4% of the total population: severe difficult household is about 3.7% of total population.
(6) 60+ aging population: in 1985 was 8.2% of total population, in 1990 was 8.9% of the total population, 2000 is 10.4% of total population.

Table 12.5
Older Persons' Service Needs (%)

Types of Service	Already Receiving Service	Need Service	Service Gap
Home help	3.2	18.7	15.5
Volunteer service	1.8	26.2	24.4
Emergency service	4.0	45.1	41.1
Health care knowledge	9.3	36.8	27.5
Telephone hot-line	0.8	17.4	16.6
Meals service	0.7	13.9	13.2
Geriatric beds	14.6	42.4	27.8
Senior citizen card	39.7	46.5	6.8
Day-care centre	0.5	18.9	18.4
Periodical physical checkup	27.6	57.8	30.2

Table 12.6
Forecast for Civil Affairs Budget in 2000
($RMB billion)

Year	Civil Affairs Social Security Budget (CASS)				Proportion of CVSS Expenses to Revenue		Proportion of PA to National Expense		Proportion of CVFI to National Investment	
	Total	Public Assistant (PA)	Public Discount	Fixed Invest-ment (FI)	National Revenue	(%)	National Expense	(%)	National Total Invest-ment	(%)
1985	45.9	30.0	14.7	1.2	6,822	(0.67)	1,844.8	(1.63)	2,543.2	(0.05)
1990	80.7	40.7	20.0	1.8	7,610	(1.08)	2,567.0	(1.59)	2,007.0	(0.09)
2000	153.8	111.8	36.8	5.2	14,499	(1.06)	4,800.0	(2.33)	2,895.0	(0.18)
Average annual increase rate in 15 years (%)	8.4	9.2	6.3	10.3			6.6			

Source: Mao Hai-po, "The Forecast of China's Civil Affairs' Social Security in 2000", *China Civil Affairs*, No. 229, April 1998, p. 12.

Notes: (1) In 2000, national average income is RMB14,499 billion, is 3.9 times of 1980s RMB 3688 billion, average annual increase is 7%, average per person is RMB 1,161.8.
(2) The basic investment ratio within national fixed investment: in 1985 was RMB1,822 billion, 74%; in 1990 was RMB 1,466.9 billion, 73%; 2000 is RMB 2,0882.2 billion, 72%.

Table 12.7
Social Insurance and Welfare Funds for Retirees, 1978–96

Year	Total Welfare Expenditure (Billion RMB)	Welfare Expenditure for Retirees (Billion RMB)	Percentage of Expenditure for Retirees in the Total Welfare Expenditure
1978	7.81	1.73	22.2
1979	10.73	3.25	30.3
1980	13.64	5.04	37.0
1981	15.49	6.23	40.2
1982	18.05	7.31	40.5
1983	21.25	8.73	41.1
1984	25.77	10.61	41.2
1985	33.16	14.98	45.2
1986	42.01	19.47	46.4
1987	50.87	23.84	46.9
1988	65.31	32.06	49.1
1989	76.80	38.26	49.8
1990	93.79	47.24	50.4
1991	109.47	56.20	51.3
1992	130.95	69.52	53.1
1993	167.02	91.37	54.7
1994	195.81	121.89	62.3
1995	236.13	154.18	65.3
1996	272.53	181.78	66.7

family planning association in Heilongjiang province is a good example.[31]

The needs of the elderly depend on supply and demand. This involves the need for support and care from the elderly, the function of the family in this regard and the scale of institutional support services. The factors which influence the needs of the elderly include the following:[32]

(a) The increasing needs of the elderly is the major driving force behind the development of community services;

(b) Changes in the family structure make it more difficult for the elderly to receive comprehensive day-to-day care as once an only child starts his or her own family, the situation will worsen.

(c) The existing institutional care provided for the elderly is far from satisfactory — the expansion of community services will be an effective means of solving this problem.

In a study conducted in 11 major Chinese cities regarding citizen's major social concerns, Yuan discovered that concerns associated with old age ranked sixth after unemployment, corruption, the condition of state enterprises, social order and pollution.[33] For those who needed help the most, the elderly ranked number 4 (out of 15 groupings) after uneducated children, orphans, and disaster victims.[34]

Furthermore, the growth of the elderly population suggests that not only will their health needs increase proportionately, but also that their individual health problems may multiply and become more complex as persons survive to an older average age. The health needs of older persons, either unmet or expressed in actual utilization of health services, are much greater than that of the rest of the population.[35] This expected rise in demand for health care is intensified by both the increasing proportion of the elderly and by the aging of the older population itself, that is, the growing number of older persons who are living longer. The elderly are particularly vulnerable to chronic debilitating diseases and severe disabilities, and are more likely to need long-term care. As all these conditions are expected to increase, it becomes necessary to plan for the appropriate levels and types of services required for older people. Hence, there is an urgent need for more innovative approaches to the organization and financing of health care against rapidly aging population trends. As such, demographic changes have far-ranging implications for the elderly in socio-economic terms and health considerations, and in the nature of care and security systems planned for their support, not to mention the psycho-social care aspect.[36]

Social welfare for the elderly has undergone rapid development in the past few years (see Table 12.8 for demands of welfare beds). At present, there are more than 20,000 service facilities for the daily living needs of the elderly in urban areas (see Table 12.9 for the development of old people's homes). More than 8,300 universities for the elderly have been established and have enrolled 600,000 elderly students. Across the country, there are more than 100,000 activity centres for the elderly, 30,000 clinics and more than 40 hospice care hospitals.[37] According to statistics complied by the Ministry of Civil Affairs, China has 1,029 welfare institutions and 40,000 homes for the elderly (18,000 in urban areas, 22,000 in rural areas) which look after 658,000 aged people. In addition, there are 1,326 institutions for retired cadres. There are also a certain number of terminal patient care hospitals and care centres, but they cater for only 0.4% of the elderly who are in need.[38] By the year 2000, Shenzhen will have a total of 2,500 beds for the elderly, an average of 2.3 beds per 100 older persons.[39] Major issues to be addressed in Guangzhou and other big cities in China such as Shanghai and Beijing include both quantity and types of care provided and also the quality of care.[40]

As clearly suggested by Chong,[41] for China to be able to tackle the challenge of population aging in the next few decades, a comprehensive long-term care policy on the development and provision of a wide spectrum of services in institutional, community, and in-home care is required. As concluded by Kwan and Chen,[42] community care for the elderly in urban China is neither a myth nor a reality, but a promising undertaking which demands more serious

Table 12.8
Forecast of Demands of Welfare Beds in 2000

Year	No. of beds (10,000)	Forecast of Lone Elderly, Handicapped, and Dependent Population (10,000)				No. of Beds to No. of Dependent Population (%)
		Total	Urban	Rural	Lone Elderly	
1985	49.1	397	91	306	300	0.4
1990	80.0	500	135	365	400	16.0
2000	160.0	750	285	465	650	21.3
Average annual increase rate in 15 years (%)	(8.2)					

Source: Mao Hai-po, "The Forecast for China's Civil Affairs' Social Security in 2000", *China Civil Affairs*, No. 229, April 1998, p. 10.

Note: (1) The number of lone elderly, and handicapped population is about 5% of the total population.
(2) The number of lone elderly is about 4% of the total aging population of 60 and above.
(3) The staff and bed average ratio is 1:2.5 in general.

Table 12.9
The Development of Old Folks Homes in Urban China

Year	Total Number of Old People's Homes	Total Number of Beds	Total Number of Elderly Admitted
1984	319	5,254	4,574
1985	3,481	58,646	42,284
1986	6,114	104,013	74,670
1987	7,001	119,642	84,913
1988	8,123	142,124	99,595
1989	7,746	137,681	97,590
1990	11,495	188,811	136,711
1991	10,753	205,806	150,149
1992	14,310	277,093	200,988
1993	15,741	279,864	202,998
1994	17,315	282,663	205,028
1995	19,046	285,490	207,078
1996	20,951	288,345	209,149
1997	23,046	291,229	211,240
1998	25,350	294,141	213,352
1999	27,885	297,082	215,486
2000	30,674	300,052	217,641

Sources: Financial Planning Bureau, *A Collection of Civic Affairs Statistics and Historical Data 1949–92* (Beijing: China Social Publishers, 1993); Jiang Shangqun, "The Social Services and Future Direction of China's Elderly," *Population Research*, Vol. 19, No. 4, 1995, pp. 13–17.

Note: The figures from 1993 to 2000 are based on an estimate of a 10% annual increase rate.

and tremendous social efforts, including active policy-making, more state commitment, the maintenance of the traditional care functions of the family, and the improvement of community services as well as local governmental provisions. China should immediately set up a support system for the elderly.[43] For example, frail elderly females in urban areas need more help than their male counterparts.[44] Moreover, to develop community services for the elderly is a major step towards healthy aging.[45] Overall, the community services in China's urban areas can be classified into six types: elderly; disabled persons; children and young people; home help; citizen daily living; and sports and recreation.[46]

As for Guangdong, up to 1997 a total of 2,010 old people's homes with 5,800 beds were established and supported by the Ministry of Civil Affairs. In May 1997 the Guangdong provincial government passed the *Regulations of Managing Non-government Organizations in Guangdong Province* in order to effectively promote, govern, and support elderly welfare service development. In 1981, Guangzhou became the first city to implement the concept of private homes for the elderly. Today, more than 16 homes with over 3,000 beds are in operation.[47] According to Xu,[48] currently Guangzhou has 175 various kinds of institutions for the elderly, with a total of 8,578 beds. Among them seven homes are government operated (with 1,883 beds); 50 homes are operated by street committees (with 565 beds); 99 homes are in rural areas (with 3,880 beds); and 19 are private homes (with 2,250 beds). The Guangzhou Committee on Aging constructed a multi-service centre for the elderly with a building area of 10,000 square metres. Another Guangzhou project (頤老園) occupies 350,000 square metres, and includes a park, a hostel, recreational facilities and medical clinics. Zhuhai Leisure Villas Garden (頤樂園) occupies 200,000 square metres, with 388 cottages plus other facilities. The Guangzhou Firm Pine Garden (勁松園) occupies 73,000 square metres and the Guangzhou Elderly Respect Association (尊老協會) constructed a 10,000 square metre 700-bed nursing home.[49] Other homes for the

Table 12.10
The Judgement on Personal Gains from Various Reforms
(%)

Reform Item	1998 (N=2,278)		1997 (N=1,748)	
	Will Gain	Will Lose	Will Gain	Will Lose
Elderly Welfare Reform	60.5	11.6	53.2	14.0
Housing Reform	42.6	23.4	35.1	27.9
Political System Reform	41.3	4.1	37.6	5.5
Education System Reform	40.8	5.0	36.2	6.0
Medical Reform	34.6	39.1	33.3	40.7
Labor/Employment Reform	33.7	18.9	33.9	19.7
State Enterprise Reform	33.2	13.5	30.3	17.3
Organization/Personnel Reform	29.6	9.4	28.5	7.3
Economic Reform	29.1	9.0	20.5	16.9

Source: Xu, Yinyin, "1998–1999: Chinese citizen's major concerns and future expectations", Ru
Shun, et al. (eds.). 1999: Analysis and Prediction of Social Situation's in China (Beijing:
Social Science Publication, 1999), p. 88, Table 3 (in Chinese).

elderly include the Kato Home for the Aged (嘉濤耆康之家) in
Shenzhen with 100 beds, and the Oriental Old People's Land
(東方老年樂園) in Zhuhai has 56 apartments with 150 rooms and
286 beds. The Civil Affairs Bureau in Shenzhen is still in the process
of testing new elderly care models,[50] and Foshan recently
implemented a community building scheme.[51] Through socializing
social welfare, Zhongshan has also established 34 elderly homes, and
invested 41 million yuan in the last three years.[52]

China's Strategies to Provide Services for the Elderly

The elderly population of China is growing very fast, both in terms
of proportion and absolute numbers, and is one of the most serious
social problems facing China in the twenty-first century. A recent
study of Chinese citizen's attitudes towards various reforms showed
that most of the respondents considered they would gain from
elderly welfare reform (see Table 12.10).[53] Zhang Wenfan suggests
that; (a) the radical way to overcome aging problems is to further
develop the economy and enhance its sustainability; (b) China should

pay more attention to family support for the elderly, actively developing community services for the elderly and combining family care and society support for the elderly; (c) China should perfect its social security system to reflect current realities; (d) China should pass further legislation protecting the rights and interests of the elderly and (e) China should raise the living quality of the elderly to create a healthy aging environment.[54]

Other proposals for developing community services for the elderly include:

(a) Maintaining traditional modes of care while introducing new models;

(b) Formal and informal care should be combined to provide multi-layered services for the elderly in need;

(c) Community care should be combined with family support;

(d) Development should be made according to the changes in the structural framework of the industry;

(e) The development of community care and services should be given a place in the macro social development plan, and taken into consideration while developing social security for the elderly.[55]

Throughout the world, the vast majority of care for the elderly is provided by females — wives, daughters, daughters-in-law and even maids. In the best of circumstances, this family support system and the formal care system work together. Family caregivers provide day-to-day support and emotional aid, while formal service institutions offer health care and specialized services. However, as more people are surviving to a very old age, families are becoming smaller, thus providing fewer potential caregivers who are themselves likely to be old. A recent study concluded that the social-psychological stress level of urban residents was on an upward trend (see Table 12.11).[56] Population-based health promotion strategies may be the only feasible means of addressing the underlying common causes of the major health problems that

Table 12.11

**The Changing Pattern of Social-psychological Stress of Urban Residents
(1995–98)**

Year	Consider Stress in Life (%)	Consider Stress in Life Increased (%)
1995	65.4	69.7
1996	68.6	67.7
1997	79.2	68.6
1998	79.7	74.1
Average	73.2	70.0

Source: Sun Li and Zheng Weidong, "The research report on social-psychological aspect of China's social situations and reforms", in Ru Shun, *op. cit.*, p. 54, Table 6 (in Chinese).

adversely affect the health of aging women.[57] Therefore, specific strategies are needed to support family care giving. Heyzer suggests the following strategies:

(a) Day care that enables caregivers to continue employment and meet other obligations;

(b) Housing adaptations are needed that are added to existing family homes to accommodate the elderly;

(c) In-home services for the elderly are needed — for example, household help, networks, self-help groups and specialized training;

(d) It is possible to create foster care in which about four to five elders live as a group with a paid caregiver;

(e) There has to be support for family care giving that includes care benefits or financial strategies such as workplace benefits, including family leave or care leave for care of the elderly;

(f) Direct payments or care allowances can be given to families to compensate for the cost of care or for losses in economic productivity. Tax incentives or credits can also be extended for family care.

(g) Long-term care insurance or financial planning strategies would enable the working generation to plan for their own probable period of late life dependency;

(h) It is important to give a clear signal of the true value of care giving — for example, by improving the pay scales of the caring professions, especially among nurses;

(i) It is crucial that we build up and support local, national, regional and international networks of older persons in pursuit of the goals of education, work, companionship, health and well-being.[58]

The China National Committee on Ageing has stressed the following strategies in dealing with the aging population:

(a) To further promote, through publicity, society's awareness of the aging population and its implications for social and economic development. To promote the Chinese tradition of respecting and supporting the elderly which should be included as an important component in the construction of the socialist spiritual civilization;

(b) To strengthen policy-oriented studies in order to improve policies related to the aged. The priority of study should be the support system and care system for the elderly. A long-term development plan on aging will be drafted in accordance with the China National 9th Five-Year Social and Economic Development Plan and the Long-Term Targets for 2010 so that the work on aging can be incorporated in the overall national development plan;

(c) To formulate a social insurance system which brings together the four components of the state, community, family and individual. Family support for the elderly will be kept as the core of the system over a considerably long period of time, and the community based social services for the elderly will be greatly improved to assist in family support;

(d) To improve the social welfare for the elderly in order to meet their special needs and raise their quality. Except for the government input on aging, society, including groups and individuals, should be mobilized to support the work on aging and invest in the areas targeted at the elderly such as building homes, nursing homes, hospitals, activity centres and universities/schools for the elderly;

(e) To protect the elderly in accordance with the *Law of Protecting the Rights of the Elderly*;

(f) To organize a group of highly qualified scientific researchers;

(g) To strengthen the existing network of committees on aging by raising the quality of the working staff.

Conclusion

Aging is an irreversible process, and China in the twenty-first century will have some 200 million persons 60 years of age and older, or close to 20% of its total population. The progressive aging of Chinese society (both national or local) and the continuing increase of its elderly population is an expected event resulting from its population policies (one-child) and its national development efforts (economic reform). The demographics of aging in China have produced a range of discussions and responses. At one extreme are the alarmist calls for action and deep concern about the lack of attention given to aging-related policy and planning issues. At the other end of the spectrum are the critiques of the ethnocentric demographic imperative and the accompanying imposition of Western models to solve the problem.

Considering the aging process in its totality, and recognizing that all aspects of aging (physical, psychological and social) are interrelated, imply the need for an integrated approach within the framework of overall economic and social planning, including cultural factors, and a co-ordinated approach to policies and programmes in aging. Policy-makers in China (especially in

Guangdong province) are urged to consider a multi-level approach in planning for the elderly population: short-term planning to meet immediate and urgent needs of today's elderly, particularly the very old disabled and females; medium-range planning to meet the needs of the active elderly population; and long-range planning for future generations in the latter part of the twenty-first century.[59]

1999 was chosen as the International Year of Older Persons by the United Nations. The Asia-Pacific Regional Conference for the International Year of Older Persons (with the theme Towards a Society for All Ages) was held in Hong Kong in April 1999. The conference organizing committee produced a conference declaration as the statement of vision of all the attending delegates. Large aging populations pose both opportunities and challenges to all societies, and policy-makers in China should also address the related social concerns. China's accelerated socio-economic development and its aim of improving the general living standards, health, education and well-being of its population at large are repeatedly witnessed in the past decade. The Chinese government, in this respect, is urged to ensure a balanced and integrated development to guarantee a decent living standard for the dramatically increasing numbers of its elderly people foreseen in the next few generations. The following principles in the above-mentioned conference declaration could possibly provide a good working guideline for the future welfare of the elderly in China:

Older Persons

(a) Should have access to adequate food, water, shelter, clothing and health care through the provision of income, family and community support and self-help;

(b) Should have the opportunity to work or to have access to other income-generating opportunities;

(c) Should remain integrated in society, participate actively in the formulation and implementation of policies that directly affect their well-being and share their knowledge and skills with younger generations;

(d) Should be able to pursue opportunities for the full development of their potential;

(e) Should have access to the educational, cultural, spiritual and recreational resources of society.

Families with Older Persons

(f) Should be supported and strengthened in providing care and to respond to the needs of its dependent aging members;

(g) Should be encouraged to have all family members collaborate in care giving.

Governments:

(h) Should work with non-governmental organizations and the older persons themselves to make efforts to overcome negative stereotyped images of older persons as suffering from physical and psychological disabilities, incapable of functioning independently. These efforts, in which the media and educational institutions should also take part, are essential for achieving a society that champions the full integration of the elderly.

National and International

(i) Should make efforts to promote research on the biological, mental and social aspects of aging and ways of maintaining functional capacities and preventing and delaying the start of chronic illnesses and disabilities.

Notes

1. T. R. Ford and G. F. DeJong, *Social Demography* (Englewood Cliffs, N. J.: Prentice-Hall, 1970), pp. 623–669.

2. Kun Yan, "Socio-economic Problems Led by Population Ageing and Their Solutions", *Almanac of China's Population 1997*, pp. 165–173.

3. Zhang Wenfan, "Population Ageing in China and its Strategic Options", *Population and Economics*, Vol. 1, 1998, pp. 55–58.

4. National Institute on Aging, *Global Aging into the 21st Century* (Washington, D. C.: U. S. Census Bureau, 1996).

5. Feng Guishan, "Meeting the 21st Century Challenge on Aging", in Feng Guishan (ed.), *Proceedings of the International Conference on Aging into 21st Century* (Shanghai: Shanghai Science and Technology Publisher, 1998), pp. 1–15.

6. World Health Organization, *Population Aging — A Public Health Challenge* (Geneva: WHO, Health Communication and Public Relations Fact Sheet No. 135, 1998); A. Kalache, "The Health Status of Older Women", (paper presented at the International Conference on Women's Health — The Nation's Gain, 5–7 July, 1999 in Singapore).

7. "Population aging — The biggest worry", *Ming Pao*, 3 February 1999, p. B15 (in Chinese).

8. Hong Guodong (ed.), *Proceedings of the Conference on the Support Systems for China's Elderly* (Beijing: China Research Center on Ageing, 1994), p. 3; Hong Guodong, "Population Aging in the Mainland: Trends, Characteristics and Strategies", *Hong Kong Journal of Gerontology*, Vol. 10, 1996 (supplement), pp. 55–57.

9. "Population Ageing in China and its Policy Implications", *China Development Briefing*, Vol. 12, 1998, pp. 9–14.

10. Zhang Wenfan, "Population Ageing", *op. cit.*, p. 56.

11. National Institute on Aging, *Global Aging, op. cit.*

12. V. A. Velkoff and V. A. Lawson, *Gender and Aging — Caregiving* (Washington, D. C.: U.S. Bureau of the Census, 1998), p. 7, Table 1.

13. China National Committee on Ageing, *The Elderly Population in China* (Beijing: China National Committee on Ageing, 1997).

14. K. Kinsella and Y. J. Gist, *Gender and Aging — Mortality and Health* (Washington, D. C.: U. S. Bureau of the Census, 1998), p. 7, Table 2.

15. China National Committee on Ageing, *The Elderly Population, op. cit.*

16. Hong Guodong, (ed.) *Proceedings, op. cit.*, p. 7.

17. China National Committee on Ageing, *The Elderly Population, op. cit.*

18. Zhang Jianmeng, "A Preliminary Analysis of the Characteristics of Guangdong's Aging Population", *Southern Population*, Vol. 1, 1998, pp. 46–49 (in Chinese).

19. Zhou Guangfu, "The Development Trend of Guangdong's Population", *Southern Population*, Vol. 3, 1997, pp. 4–6 (in Chinese); Statistical Bureau of Guangdong, *Guangdong Statistical Yearbook* (Beijing: China Statistics Press, 1999), p. 134, Table 4.3.

20. Yang Chunfeng and Feng Jie, "Towards 21st Century's Elderly Care Services", *Guang Dong Min Zheng*, Vol. 3, 1999, pp. 8–10 (in Chinese).

21. Jiang Baojiang and Qin Dekui, "The Five Points about the Aged is the Foundation of Serving the Aged Well", *Conference Proceedings (Volume 1) of Asia-Pacific Regional Conference for the International Year of Older Persons* (Hong Kong: Hong Kong Council of Social Service, 1999), pp. 224–228.

22. Chen Sheying, *Social Policy of the Economic State and Community Care in Chinese Culture* (England: Avebury, 1996), p. 57.

23. Zhang Tongchun, "Basic Characteristics of the Old Age Law in China", *Conference Proceedings (Volume 1) of Asia-Pacific Regional Conference for the International Year of Older Persons* (Hong Kong: Hong Kong Council of Social Service, 1999), p. 229.

24. Yao Yuan, "Elderly Support: A Special Component of the Traditional Culture", *Population Research*, Vol. 20, No. 6, 1996, pp. 30–35 (in Chinese).

25. Xiang Guangren and Zeng Bizhong, "Insist on the Integration of Family Care and Social Care for the Elderly — A Unique Feature of Chinese Pattern of Elderly Care", (paper presented at the *Asia-Pacific Regional Conference for the International Year of Older Persons* in Hong Kong, 26–29 April, 1999), p. 2.

26. See *China Social Work* No. 4, 1998, eight different articles on socializing social welfare, pp. 1–28 (in Chinese).

27. Luo Ping, "New Approach to Welfare Work — Independent of the Government", *Journal of Foshan University*, Vol. 16, No. 3, 1998, pp. 45–51 (in Chinese).

28. Li Tiansheng and Xu Liju, "On the Community Support", in Feng Guishan (ed.) *Proceedings of the International Conference*, *op. cit.*, pp. 406–423 (in Chinese); Fu Huilin, "Perfecting the Residential Support System with Chinese Characteristics", in *ibid.*, pp. 424–432 (in Chinese); Wang Zhenhua, "About the Social Supporting System of Residential Support", in *ibid.*, pp. 467–476 (in Chinese).

29. H. B. Pennekamp, "Growing Older towards the 21st Century", in *ibid.*, pp. 70–93.

30. Xiong Bijun, "On China's Population Aging and Sustainable Development of Economy in the 21st Century," in *ibid.*, pp. 661–675 (in Chinese).

31. He Xiangya, "Family Planning Old-age Insurance: A Means of Helping Ageing Farmers in China", *People and Development Challenges*, Vol. 6, No. 11, 1999, pp. 4–5.

32. Cheng Yong, "Develop Community Care for the Elderly as the Best Choice", *Conference Proceedings (Volume 1) of Asia-Pacific Regional Conference for the International Year of Older Persons* (Hong Kong: Hong Kong Council of Social Service, 1999), pp. 319–322.

33. Yuan Yue, "1998–1999: Chinese Cities Citizen's Psychological Assessment", in Ru Shun, *et al.* (eds.) *Analysis and Prediction of Social Situations in China* (Beijing: Social Science Publication, 1999), p. 103, Table 1 (in Chinese).

34. *Ibid.*, p. 116, Table 8 (in Chinese).

35. Y. H. Kwan and S. C. Chan, "A Comparison Study on the Medical and Health Quality of Old Age Homes in Beijing, Shanghai, Taiwan and Hong Kong", in Y. S. Wu and H. Y. Luk (eds.), *Economic Liberalization and Social Structure Transformation in China* (Beijing: Social Science Publication Co., 1998), pp. 501–515 (in Chinese); Y. H. Kwan and S. C. Chan, "The Challenge of Health Care in Institutions for the Elderly in Urban China", in Zang Xiaowei (ed.), *China in the Reform Era* (New York: Nova Science Publishers, Inc., 1999), pp. 81–101.

36. Y. H. Kwan and S. C. Chan, "The Psycho-Social Care in Institutions for the Elderly in Beijing, Shanghai, Taiwan and Hong Kong", (paper presented at the *Asia-Pacific Regional Conference for the International Year of Older Persons* in Hong Kong, 26–29 April, 1999).

37. China National Committee on Ageing, *The Elderly Population, op. cit.*

38. Cheng Yong, "Develop Community Care", *op. cit.*, p. 321.

39. Wang Yaobo and Zhang Jianmeng, "Shenzhen's Civil Affairs Developments in 21st Century", *Guang Dong Min Zheng*, Vol. 73, No. 8, 1999, p. 6 (in Chinese); Zhang Jianmeng, "The Development of Community Services in Shenzhen", *ibid.*, Vol. 74, No. 9, 1999, p. 9 (in Chinese).

40. H. Bartlett and D.R. Phillips, "Ageing and Aged Care in the People's Republic of China: National and Local Issues and Perspectives", *Health and Place*, Vol. 3, No. 3, 1997, pp. 149–159.

41. M. L. Chong, "Residential Care for the Elderly in Urban Areas: A Future Challenge for China", in T. W. Lo and Y. S. Cheng (eds.), *Social Welfare Development in China: Constraints and Challenges* (Chicago: Imprint Publications, 1996), p. 194.

42. Y. H. Kwan and S. Y. Chen, "Community Care for the Elderly in Guangdong", in Y. H. Kwan and Y. S. Cheng (eds.), *Capitalistic Welfare Development in Communist China: The Experience of Southern China* (Chicago: Imprint Publications, 1996), p. 53.

43. Yi Jiayan, "China Should Immediately Set up a Support System for Elderly", *Population Journal* Vol. 6, 1996, pp. 49–53 (in Chinese).

44. Xu Qin, "The Formal and Informal Support of China's Aging Population", *Population Research*, Vol. 19, No. 5, 1995, pp. 23–27 (in Chinese); Xu Qin, "Elderly Women — The Most Vulnerable Group in the Female Population", *Population Journal*, Vol. 5, 1995, pp. 3–10 (in Chinese).

45. Guan Siufang, "Developing Community Services for the Elderly is a Major Step towards Healthy Aging", *Southern Population*, Vol. 4. 1997, pp. 38–42 (in Chinese).

46. Xia Jianzhong, "The Urbanization of Community Organizations and Community Services in Chinese Cities", (paper presented at the *International*

Conference on China's Economic Reform and Adjustment of Social Structure at Hong Kong Shue Yan College, 8–10 July, 1999) (in Chinese).

47. Yang and Feng, "Towards 21st Century's", *op. cit.*, pp. 8–10 (in Chinese).

48. Xu Chi, "The Development of Social Care Services for the Elderly and the Responsibility of the Government", (paper presented at the 1999 *Shanghai International Seminar on Social Services to the Elderly*, 22–24 November, 1999 in Shanghai, China).

49. Xiang Guangren and Zeng Bizhong, "Insist on the Integration of Family Care and Social Care for the Elderly — A Unique Feature of Chinese Pattern of Elderly Care", (paper presented at the *Asia-Pacific Regional Conference for the International Year of Older Persons* in Hong Kong, 26–29 April, 1999), p. 7.

50. Zhang Jianmeng, "A New Elderly Care Model in Shenzhen Special Region", *Guang Dong Min Zheng*, Vol. 59, No. 6, p. 14 (in Chinese).

51. Liu Hai, "Foshan Fully Implements its Community Building Scheme", *Guang Dong Min Zheng*, Vol. 74, No. 9, 1999, p. 10 (in Chinese).

52. Cai Zeqiang and Wang Yingkang, "Zhongzhan Speeds up Socializing Social Welfare", *ibid.*, pp. 11–12 (in Chinese).

53. Xu Yinyin, "1998–1999: Chinese Citizen's Major Concerns and Future Expectations", in Ru Shun, *et al.* (eds.) *1999: Analysis and Prediction of Social Situations in China* (Beijing: Social Science Publication, 1999), pp. 84–100 (in Chinese).

54. Zhang Wenfan, "The Selection of Strategy on China Population Aging", in Feng Guishan (ed.) *Proceedings of the International Conference, op. cit.*, pp. 16–27 (in Chinese).

55. Cheng Yong, "Develop Community Care", *op. cit.*, pp. 321–322.

56. Sun Li and Zheng Weidong, "1998: The Research Report on Social-psychological Aspects of China's Social Situations and Reforms", in Ru Shun, *et al.* (eds.) *1999: Analysis and Prediction of Social Situations in China* (Beijing: Social Science Publication, 1999), pp. 43–62 (in Chinese).

57. R. Bonita, Women, *Ageing and Health — Achieving Health across the Life Span* (Geneva: World Health Organization, 1998), pp. 48–50.

58. N. Heyzer, "Healthy Ageing in a Caring Society: Women's Health and the Nation's Gain", (paper presented at the *International Conference with a Special Focus on Older Women in Asia* in Singapore, 5–7 July, 1999), pp. 3–4.

59. Jiang Xiangqun, "The Development and Model for Socializing the Elderly Care System", *Guang Dong Min Zheng*, Vol. 71, No. 6, 1999, pp. 4–5 (in Chinese); Xu Daosheng, "Speedup the Socialization of Social Welfare", *ibid.*, p. 6 (in Chinese); Xu Hua, "Care for the Elderly via Business", *ibid.*, pp. 8–10 (in Chinese); Ou Weitong and Li Gengmeng, "A Review of Guangdong's Socio-economic Development since 1949", *Social Sciences in Guangdong*, Vol. 79, No. 5, 1999, pp. 34–39 (in Chinese); Bai Ping, "An Exploration of Elderly

Care Model and Strategy in Urban China", *ibid.*, pp. 120–125 (in Chinese); Wong Nianhua, "How to Face Population Aging", *Guang Dong Min Zhang*, Vol. 71, No. 6, 1999, p. 7 (in Chinese).

CHAPTER 13

The Crime Scene
in Guangdong Province

CHE Wai-kin

The Crime Scene in China

Since the mid-1980s, the people of Guangdong province have enjoyed rising prosperity due to economic reform and development. As a result, the per capita income of its population now ranks number one in the People's Republic of China (PRC). The most economically advanced part of the province is the Pearl River Delta region, which includes Guangzhou, Shenzhen, Zhuhai, Foshan, Jiangmen, Zhongshan, Huizhou and Dongguan. The total population of this region stands at just over 19 million, which accounts for about 30% of the total population of Guangdong province. However, about 70% of the province's criminal offences also occur in this region.

Guangdong province is, of course, a part of China, and it has been influenced by political, economic and social events in the nation as a whole. Therefore, in order to understand the crime situation in Guangdong, it is necessary to understand the overall pattern of crime in China and the foundations of the criminal justice system.

The High Crime Waves in China

Since the establishment of the PRC in 1949, the country has experienced several waves of high crime. Wang Da Wei of China's

Table 13.1

Criminal Cases filed by the PSB in China in 1997

Types of Criminal Cases	No. of Cases	%
Murder	26,070	1.62
Wounding	69,071	4.28
Robbery	141,514	8.77
Rape	40,699	2.52
Kidnapping and Sale of Persons	6,425	0.40
Larceny	1,058,110	65.57
1) Serious theft	448,917	27.82
2) Theft of bicycles	56,607	3.50
Deceit	78,284	4.85
Smuggling	1,133	0.07
Manufacture and Sale of Counterfeit Money	5,422	0.34
Others	186,901	11.58
Total	1,613,629	100.00

Source: *Law Yearbook of China* (Beijing: Law Yearbook Press, 1998) p. 1,244.

People's Public Security University has identified four high crime waves since 1949.[1] The first wave of high crime began at the beginning of the 1950s and ended in 1956. The main characteristic of the criminal cases during that period was that they were anti-governmental and reactionary in nature. The remnants of the Kuomintang (KMT) were opposed to the rule of the Chinese Communist Party (CCP) and engaged in various types of criminal activities. The second high crime wave occurred between 1961 and 1963, when the Chairman Mao Zedong launched the Great Leap Forward Movement and established people's communes. Criminal acts committed at this time were mainly against property — largely theft and larceny, such as the theft of food, farming tools and animals. The third high crime wave occurred between May 1966 and October 1976, during the Cultural Revolution. In that decade, China was in a state of chaos and anarchy. The national economy collapsed, social order was disrupted, there was no functioning government, the public security and judicial organs collapsed, and human rights were not protected. Most of the criminal cases were political in nature.

The fourth high crime wave occurred between 1978 and 1989, after the Chinese government adopted the Open Door Policy. The reform policy led to rapid economic development and progress, as well as ideological and social changes. As a result, the government's power of social control was weakened. Given such drastic changes, new management, social norms and moral codes needed to be developed to meet the new situation and social needs. Also, there were many loopholes in the legal code for criminals to exploit, especially in the financial and commercial area. As a result, corruption became widespread and a new high crime wave took place. In order to curb high crime, the central government launched a serious clampdown on criminal activities beginning in 1983, and severely punished criminal elements. However, another serious crime wave emerged in 1989. In that year, 1,970,000 criminal cases were recorded, including 412,000 serious cases.

In order to examine the current crime rate in China, it is necessary to consult statistical records filed by the police, and criminal cases brought to trial at the different levels of judicial courts. Based on the *People's Republic of China Yearbook, 1998–1999*, the number of criminal cases filed by the Public Security Bureau (PSB) in 1997 was still very high, amounting to 1,613,629 cases. Included in this figure were 1,058,110 larceny cases and 142,000 robbery cases, accounting for 74.3% of the total criminal cases. There were 578,000 burglary cases, an increase of 5.9% over 1996. There were 122,000 cases of vehicle theft, an increase of 24.8% over 1996. Economic crimes were also more serious in 1997, as fraud cases increased by 14%. The police investigated 5,422 cases of printing and trafficking counterfeit money, an increase of 5.6% over 1996, and confiscated about 300 million yuan in counterfeit Renminbi (RMB), an increase of 40% over 1996. The production and trafficking of drugs also worsened. Organized crime in China also demonstrated new features. Some criminal groups started to recruit grassroots officials in order to receive official protection.[2]

The Criminal Justice System in China

In China, the criminal justice system is composed of four elements. The first is the PSB which is responsible for maintaining law and order, investigating criminal cases and arresting suspected criminals. The second is the procuratorial organs which screen and decide which cases should be sent to the judicial courts for prosecution. The third is the judicial courts where suspects are tried and judged. The fourth is the correctional organs which are responsible for the incarceration of offenders. Criminals convicted by the courts are sent to prison to serve their sentences. However, in addition to prison, another type of organ for confinement is the Institute of Reform Through Education. Minor offenders, that is those who have violated the law but whose violation is not serious enough to constitute a criminal act but is counted as a minor offence, such as drug abuse, gambling, prostitution, minor theft, and civil offences, are sent to the Institute of Reform Through Education without going through the judicial process in court. Suspects can be sent to the Institute of Reform Through Education by order of the PSB.

The PRC Courts and Crime

On 10 March 1998, the President of the People's Supreme Court, Yen Ken-Hsin, gave a report to the 9th National People's Congress on the work of the people's courts. He summarized the work of the judicial courts in four points.[3]

(a) From 1993–97, 22,417,744 criminal, civil, commercial, administrative and marine cases were closed after trial, registering an 11.47% annual increase.

(b) Judicial workload increased. Due to the strengthening of the law and the promulgation of new laws, the courts handled many types of new cases.

(c) There were a larger number of serious cases brought to trial. Also, the amount of money involved in commercial crimes increased. The amount of money involved in civil, commercial, marine and administrative lawsuits increased annually up to 951.5 billion yuan.

(d) All the cases were handled properly, both in quality and quantity. In 1997, about 97.52% of cases were brought to trial and closed on time.

Yen also stated that cases of serious violent crimes against persons and property, organized crime syndicates (such as triad societies), smuggling, drug trafficking, and the manufacture and sale of pornography were on the increase. Corruption and other commercial crime cases grew rapidly and involved a huge amount of money. From 1993–97, 2,437,426 cases of this nature were submitted to judicial courts for prosecution and trial, an increase of 0.75% annually and 2,742,133 suspects were convicted. Among them, 40.08% received sentences of 5 years imprisonment or above, including life imprisonment and the death sentence; 57.07% were imprisoned for less than 5 years; 1.42% of defendants received no criminal punishment and 0.43% were released. The courts recovered 26.6 billion *yuan* in criminal assets. The number of serious criminal cases, such as murder, manslaughter, robbery, kidnapping, rape, armed robberies, organized crime, highway robbery, the sale of women and children, prostitution, forgery, and the counterfeit of money, goods, CDs, etc., was 1,022,326 and a total of 1,413,051 suspects were convicted.

Regarding commercial (white collar) crime, a series of clampdowns took place against corruption, bribery and other economic crimes. The crackdown targeted corrupt government officials in the Party, administrative, judicial and financial sectors. A total of 169,433 suspects were put on trial and 158,806 were convicted.

The Causes of High Crime in China

Criminologists in China have attempted to examine the causes leading to the sharp increase in the number of criminal cases and the crime rate since the mid-1980s. Dai Yi-sheng argues that the unequal distribution of wealth has been a major factor in the sharp increase of crime since the 1980s.[4] He found that in 1994, China's Gini Coefficient was 0.445, and was expected to increase in the future. Also in 1994, the richest household group, which accounted for 20% of the population, owned 50.24% of the total national income. At the same time, the poorest household group, which also accounted for 20% of the population, owned only 4.7% of the total national income.

Another important cause has been the large increase in unemployment in China. In the early 1950s, China adopted a planned economy, and state-owned industries and enterprises employed nearly all the available workers. However, after the introduction of economic reforms in 1978, each industry or enterprise had to be responsible for its own budget. Enterprises which lose money had to lay off workers or even close down. Because of this new economic policy, millions of workers have been made redundant. In addition, since 1980 more than 100 million rural labourers have been laid-off. It is estimated that more than 80 million of these workers have moved to the cities in search of work — the so-called "floating population". About 60–70% of criminals arrested in the cities are classified as part of the floating population. The Ministry of Labour reported that by the year 2000, 130 million more peasants would join the floating population, plus 16 million laid-off workers from State Owned Enterprises (SOEs). Thus it seems likely that the growing population problem, the unequal distribution of income and economic hardship have been the leading causes of the rising crime in the PRC since the mid-1980s.

The Crime Scene in Guangdong Province

As Guangdong was the first province in China to adopt economic reform policies, it has reaped the greatest fruits of economic growth and prosperity, especially in the Pearl River Delta Region. Consequently, millions of workers and labourers have come from less developed provinces looking for employment. For those who do not find work, many resort to illegal activities to survive.

Unfortunately, criminals and other bad elements have also been attracted to Guangdong in search of rich pickings. Therefore, from the early 1980s the number of criminal offences began to increase and accelerated in the mid-1990s. For the purposes of reviewing the crime scene in Guangdong, the author will examine the rising crime rate first, especially that of violent crime, which has shocked the general public, and cross border crime between Guangdong and Hong Kong. Finally, criminal activities in Guangzhou, which has the highest crime rate in the province, will be examined in detail.

The Rising Crime Rate in Guangdong Province

The extent and severity of the crime wave in Guangdong province can be gauged from a paper presented at a symposium by two researchers who highlighted a number of key trends.[5] First, the number of criminal offences rose drastically in the mid-1990s. For example, in 1994, 163,000 criminals cases were reported to the PSB, which represented a 10.6% increase over 1993, and 4.9 times that of 1987. Among these cases, 107,000 were serious offences which showed a 16.3% increase from 1993 and were 13.7 times that of 1987. In 1995, about 150,000 cases were reported to the police including 100,000 serious criminal cases. In 1994, crime cost the nation 2.8 billion yuan, an increase of 18% from 1993. Moreover, 2,241 victims were killed, and 8,998 persons were injured, a 12.3% increase from 1993.

Second, the types of criminal offences have also changed. Before the reform era, the main types of criminal offences were larceny, theft and homicide (mainly caused by domestic disputes). However, after the economic reforms began, new types of criminal offences emerged. In the early 1980s, prostitution, pornography, kidnapping and the sale of persons re-emerged. In the mid-1980s, triad activities began to increase in the province. Other types of crime appeared including highway robbery, and white-collar and commercial crimes such as credit card and computer crimes. In the 1990s, the manufacture and sale of illicit drugs began to rise. Triad related criminal gangs began to strengthen their position. Robbery cases also increased significantly; in 1994, 26,000 robbery cases were reported (including 23,000 serious cases). Murder, kidnapping, and armed robberies also increased in number. Because of the establishment of the market economy, conflicts among different sectors of society also arose creating social instability. Criminals from other provinces and countries, such as Hong Kong, Macau and Taiwan, also arrived. As a result, criminals could escape to other places after committing crimes and the police had difficulties in pursuing them.

Third, the activities of criminal gangs increased rapidly. About half of the offenders arrested by the police were members of criminal gangs; and about one-third of criminal cases were committed by criminal gangs. Triad societies from outside the province, including Hong Kong, Taiwan and Macau, have established bases in Guangdong. At the same time, local triad gangs were formed. They began to penetrate the entertainment business and engaged in various types of criminal activities, such as collecting protection fees, blackmail, robbery and controlling prostitutes and drug trafficking. In 1994, 468 organized criminal syndicates were eliminated and 2,213 criminals were arrested. In the following year, 381 syndicates were eliminated and 1,381 criminals arrested.

Fourth, criminal activities flourished in the Pearl River Delta region. The region is the most developed economically; it has an efficient transportation network and a large number of new immigrants arrive daily from other provinces. Although the region has about 30% of the province's population, it has recorded about 74% of the criminal offences committed in Guangdong. About 60% of the criminals arrested came outside Guangdong. In some cities, such as Shenzhen, Zhuhai, Foshan and Dongguan, "outsiders" constituted 80% of arrested offenders. The discharged prisoners from the Institutes of Reform Through Education constituted a large number of the criminals arrested. A large number of unemployed people, including those laid-off from SOEs and former peasants who had lost their farmland, wandered around the region with nothing to do. In 1994, about 37,000 such people were arrested by the police.

Offenders

According to a statistical report of the PSB in Guangdong, criminals in the province are composed of three main types; namely, the floating population from other provinces, ex-offenders released from prison and Institutions of Education through Labour, and unemployed people.[6] By 1994, there were 12 million mobile people in Guangdong, of which 6.6 million came from other provinces. Most were concentrated in the Pearl River Delta (PRD) region. In 1994, people from other provinces accounted for 58.4% of the suspects arrested in Shenzhen, Zhuhai, Foshan and Dongguan.

As for ex-offenders, many learned criminal techniques from other prisoners, and developed strong anti-social attitudes and behaviour. After release, no follow-up services were provided to ex-inmates, such as counselling, rehabilitation or helping them secure suitable employment. As a result, the rate of re-offences was very high. In addition, juvenile delinquents composed about 70% of those arrested. They have been badly influenced by capitalism, and only interested in material gain without working hard for a living. They wish to get rich quickly and live an easy life. As a result, a large number of primary and secondary school students have dropped out from school, as they believe that study cannot bring them financial success. They are easily induced by bad elements to commit criminal offences.

The PSB in Guangzhou is concerned about the crime problem in the province, especially in the PRD region.[7] Accounting to PSB officers, although the population in the PRD region makes up only one-fourth of the province, it produces 48% of all criminal cases and 44% of serious crimes. Since the early 1980s, violent crimes such as armed robbery, kidnapping, theft of motor vehicles, drug trafficking, computer and commercial crimes began to emerge in Guangdong and in the PRD region as a whole. In the early 1990s, murder, robbery and drug trafficking became serious threats to the law and order situation in the province.

In order to tackle rising crime, the PSB have adopted various tactics to respond quickly to crimes and pursue follow up investigations. They have also tightened the supervision and investigation of many rented apartments and houses, motels and hotels, karaoke bars, etc. where vice establishments operate. In each district, the police request local government and citizens to establish patrol teams to maintain law and order. Also, the police have instituted street patrols as well. PSB officers say that about 120,000 criminal cases were reported to the police in the province in 1997; these constituted 7.5% of all criminal cases in the nation.

According to the PSB, the majority of criminals arrested in the province's developed cities came from other provinces and were usually former rural labourers. They constituted about 80–90% of the criminals arrested. Even the local suspects arrested were mainly agricultural labourers from Guangdong province. This group of local deviants and offenders are officially classified us "peasants". However, the great majority of the peasants in the well-developed cities are not engaged in farming anymore as their farmlands were taken away by the government for building industrial enterprises, factories, residential houses, etc. These marginal "peasants" have no work to do but they receive a substantial amount of compensation and rent from the apartments they lease to outsiders. These well to do pseudo "peasants" — especially the young — have engaged in various type of deviant activities, such as drug abuse, gambling, prostitution and participating in delinquent gangs. They participate in gang activities, such as collecting protection fees and gambling debts, and gang fights. However, the PSB officers believe that the number of these kinds of criminal activities will remain stable in the years to come.

Violence in Guangdong Province

Violent crime has shocked the citizens of Guangdong province in recent years. The most notorious case was that of the "Two Pistols and One Axe" gang of armed robbers who started their criminal career in December 1993 when they used only butcher's knives and axes. Their first robbery took place in Panyu city during which they killed one person and seized 70,000 yuan. The gang was composed of 16 members, 9 of whom were natives of Hunan province. Most of them were in their twenties, with little or no education. All of them were peasants and only one was female. The gang was led by Chen XX, Au-Yang XX, Li XX, and Pak XX. Some of them had previous criminal records and had been recently released from prison. In another two robbery cases in 1997, Au-Yang and Pak killed two of their victims with knives at the victims' residences. In 1995, Chen led his gang of four to rob several businesses and stole 360,000 yuan. In March 1996, Chen's gang began using handguns and stole 238,000-yuan worth of motorcycles. In 1996, the gang committed 17 more robberies, targeting businesses in Guangzhou. In early 1997, the gang changed its targets, from robbing businesses to burglary. In January 1998, the gang committed seven armed robberies. Their last crime occurred on 6 February 1998, and soon afterwards they were arrested and tried by the Intermediate People's Court in Guangzhou. Among the 16 defendants, 11 were convicted and were given the death penalty. The other five received from 5–15 years' imprisonment.[8]

Another serious case involved a gang of 10 male and 6 female robbers (all in their twenties) who committed a series of highway robberies between 1993–94. The gang was led by Chang Shao-pang. The female members would pose as prostitutes and tempt taxi drivers on their way to and from the airport in Shenzhen. The girls led the drivers to their apartments where they would be murdered. The gang used this method in seven cases. The gangsters sometimes wore PSB uniforms and ordered the drivers to go to a designated place. As soon as the drivers arrived, the gangsters would kill them and their bodies would be dumped in the countryside. Their vehicles were sold afterwards. The gang members were eventually arrested and either executed or imprisoned.[9]

Cross Border Crime

One important factor in the Guangdong crime scene is that some criminal acts have been planned on the Mainland and carried out in

Hong Kong. This is because Guangdong is still in the early stages of economic development, whereas Hong Kong has been well-developed economically for some time. Evidence shows that Hong Kong and Mainland Chinese criminals have co-operated to commit crimes in Hong Kong. After committing the offences, they retreat back to Guangdong and try to avoid detection from both the PSB and Hong Kong police. Serious cross-border criminal offences have included armed robbery, kidnapping, smuggling and the production of counterfeit CDs, credit cards, etc. Since the economic reform process began, the number of lorries travelling between Hong Kong and Guangdong has increased rapidly. Unfortunately, criminals have made use of these opportunities to engage in cross border criminal activities. These criminal activities can be classified into the following categories:[10]

(a) Armed robbery in Hong Kong: in the early 1990s gangsters armed with automatic hand guns, machine guns and grenades, robbed jewellery shops and banks in Hong Kong nearly every week. Most of these robberies were successful. The Hong Kong police later learned that the robbers committing these crimes had been recruited by local organized crime syndicates from China. They were smuggled into Hong Kong with their weapons and then slipped back to the Mainland after the robbery. They would receive a sizable sum of money for their work but gave the jewellery to local criminal syndicates in Hong Kong. As long as they did not commit any offences on the Mainland, they would not be detected by the PSB or Hong Kong police. By the end of 1992, the Hong Kong police had increased surveillance along the border in the northwestern part of the New Territories where the gangsters had crossed and had arrested many of them. In addition, the Hong Kong police stepped up co-operation with the Guangdong police who arrested many of these robbers in China. As a result, the number of armed robberies in Hong Kong fell sharply in 1993 and 1994.

(b) Smuggling of electrical appliances, automobiles and trucks from Hong Kong into China: With the living standard of Mainlanders having risen over the past decade, their demands for consumer electrical appliances, such as air-conditioners, television sets, and video-recorders, have also increased. However, as the government has put high tariffs on these imported foreign electrical products (mainly those produced in Japan), its citizens have shown a preference for those on the black market, which sell at a much lower price. Demand for luxury automobiles has also increased in China. More recently, the theft of trucks from Hong Kong has increased. As long as the demand for certain products exists, the smuggling will continue.

(c) The smuggling of dangerous drugs, antiques, cigarettes and counterfeit CDs from China to Hong Kong. As the abuse of heroin and other psychotropic substances continues to rise in Hong Kong, the demand for drugs increases. The main place for growing opium is the so-called Golden Triangle which links Burma, Thailand and southwest China. The refined heroin is then smuggled from the southwest provinces of China, and then through Guangdong province and into Hong Kong. In addition, valuable antiques, which are stolen in China, are smuggled into Hong Kong and then sold to collectors, both from Hong Kong and abroad. After the Hong Kong government sharply increased taxes on cigarettes in 1993, foreign cigarettes have been smuggled into Hong Kong in large quantities and sold on the black market at much lower prices. Counterfeit CDs have been made in large quantities in China and then smuggled into Hong Kong and sold there.

In the early 1990s, the almost weekly occurrence of armed robberies of jewellery shops and banks in Hong Kong by criminals from Guangdong shocked the general public. Although these types of robberies begun to subside after 1992, several high profile criminal cases have occurred since then. The most notorious involved a criminal gang led by Cheung Tse-keung and Yip Kai-foon. Yip was born in China and came to Hong Kong in 1978. He robbed a jewellery shop in 1979 but was arrested. In 1984, he led a group of armed robbers and robbed several goldsmith shops and exchanged fire with the Hong Kong police. He was arrested and imprisoned but escaped from the prison hospital four years later. In 1991–92, his gang robbed five goldsmith shops in Kwun Tong, Kowloon, in June 1991 stole HK$5 million dollars worth of jewellery. In March 1992, Yip's gang robbed two goldsmith shops in Kowloon, and escaped with HK$7 million dollars' worth of jewellery. Yip became the most wanted criminal by the Hong Kong police. Yip's gang planned to kidnap two tycoons in Hong Kong on 13 May 1996 but ten days before the kidnap was due to take place, Yip was shot by the Hong Kong police and paralyzed. He was tried and sentenced to 41 years in prison in 1997. However, Yip still received HK$75 million from the kidnapping because he had participated in the planning. He gave a large amount of money to his brothers and sister in China who were arrested by the Guangdong PSB in July 1998.[11] On 18 April 1996, Yip's partner in crime, Cheung Tse-Keung (nicknamed "Big Spender") unsuccessfully tried to rescue him from Stanley Prison.

On 23 May 1996, Cheung's gang kidnapped Victor Li, the son of Hong Kong tycoon Li Ka-shing. Li paid Cheung's gang HK$1.07 billion for the safe return of his son. On 29 September 1997, the gang kidnapped real estate tycoon P.S. Kwok, and received the HK$600 million ransom they had demanded. However, neither Li nor Kwok reported their cases to the Hong Kong police. Instead, Li Ka-shing reported the case to the Chinese authorities in Beijing. As a result, the PSB in Guangdong were ordered to put an end to Cheung's criminal activities in September 1997. Cheung was finally arrested by the PSB in Jiangmen, Guangdong, on 25 January 1998. Cheung and four gang members were tried and found guilty. They were executed in Panyu on 5 December 1998.[12]

Another example of cross border crime took place on 21 July 1998 when three women and two young girls were poisoned with cyanide and found dead at Telford Gardens, in Kowloon. The murderer, Li Yuhui, was a 46 year-old native of Shantou, Guangdong province. Li moved to Hong Kong in June 1998 and worked as a fortune-teller. His three victims, Mrs. Lam, Choi and Tsui, all in their forties, were wealthy but had unhappy marriages. They had an intense interest in fung shui and fortune telling. The three women hoped to live beyond 100 years old and offered HK$1.3 million to Li to perform a fung shui ritual increase their mortality and solve their marriage problems. Li told the women that they could buy an extra year's life for every HK$10,000 they paid to him. The rite was held at Mrs. Tsui's flat in Telford Gardens. Li asked the three women to write down details of their unhappy family affairs on a piece of paper which was to be offered in the rite. This paper later led the Hong Kong police into believing that the killing was a suicide pact. Li asked Mrs. Tsui to give two cups of "holy water" (which actually contained cyanide) to her daughters, who were told to stay in their bedrooms so that they would not disturb the ritual. He later gave each of the women a cup of poisoned water. After the five victims were dead, Li rearranged the premises to make it look as though the women had committed suicide, and took the HK$1.3 million. He returned to Shantou that night, and exchanged about HK$600,000 for RMB on the black market and deposited the money in various bank accounts belonging to his relatives.

Two days later, Li learned from the news that the killings had been made public and he was wanted in connection to the crime by the Hong Kong police. He left Shantou and went to Hubei province. The Hong Kong police sought assistance from the PSB in Guangdong province and went to Shantou to conduct investigations. A cross province manhunt launched, and the Hubei police arrested Li on 15 September 1998 in Wuhan. Li confessed to the killings and was handed over to the Shantou police on 19 September. On 9 October 1998, Hou Tougfen, Taskforce Deputy Director of the Guangdong PSB, stated that the police had recovered HK$600,000 and 700,000 RMB from the offender. According to the criminal law of the PRC, because Li was a Chinese citizen, he could be put on trial in China. However, the HK$1,300,000 was returned to Hong Kong.[13]

Table 13.2
Types of Criminal Offences Reported in Guangzhou, 1990–94

Types of Crime	1990	1991	1992	1993	1994
1) Criminal offences	63,166	60,184	47,198	55,447	60,870
Crime rate 0/000	106.3	99.9	77.1	89.0	95.6
Increase rate(%)	+5.0	-4.7	-21.6	+17.5	+9.8
2) Serious offences	21,092	23,652	22,737	30,984	36,928
% of criminal Offences	33.4	39.3	48.2	55.9	60.7
Increase rate	+12.4	+12.1	-3.9	+36.3	+19.2
3) Public Security					
Offences	36,253	47,486	54,601	74,976	47,963
Increase rate(%)	-1.7	+30.9	+14.9	-8.9	-3.6

Table 13.3
Criminal Offences Reported in Guangzhou 1990–94

Offences	1990	1991	1992	1993	1994
Murder	89	126	158	209	262
Serious wounding	138	78	107	169	167
Robbery	2,823	4,442	6,262	7,380	8,978
Muggings	2,188	3,114	2,125	3,696	6,204
Blackmail & kidnapping	A.O.E.	11	18	109	137
Armed robbery	169	104	150	119	157

Table 13.4
Criminal Cases filed by the PSB in Guangzhou

Items	1995	1996	1997
No. of cases filed	59,775	53,236	47,903
No. of cases detected	35,951	33,275	28,384
Detected rate	60.14%	62.50%	59.25%

Source: *Statistical Yearbook of Guangzhou, 1998,* (Beijing: China Statistical Press, 1998), p. 518.

From this murder case, we can see that Li came to Hong Kong and deceived the three female victims. After he had murdered the five victims, he returned to China in the hope of enjoying his fortune there. Fortunately, the Hong Kong police sought assistance from the Guangdong PSB after they suspected Li of the murder. With the co-operation of the Guangdong police, Li was finally arrested. This shows that cross border crime can only be tackled though cross border police co-operation.

The Crime Scene in Guangzhou

In order to understand the crime scene in Guangdong province, it is necessary to examine Guangzhou, which has the highest crime rate in the province. Criminal offences in Guangzhou have risen since the early 1990s, especially for serious criminal offences. In the following tables, criminal offences from 1990 to 1994 were recorded as follows:[14]

From the tables above, it can be seen that the total number of criminal cases reported to the police in Guangzhou constituted about 47% of all cases in the city. The total number of serious criminal cases also increased rapidly and constituted 60.7% of all criminal offences reported in the city in 1994. It increased by 75% between 1990 to 1994. Public security offences are minor offences, including victimless crimes, such as drug abuse, prostitution and gambling, civil and family cases. etc. which increased gradually. Table 13.3, which has a breakdown of the statistics of criminal offences in Guangzhou between 1990–94, suggests that robbery and muggings witnessed the greatest increases; about three times during those four years.

As can be seen from Table 13.4, the number of criminal cases in Guangzhou from 1995 to 1997 decreased.

The Opinions of Guangzhou Residents Towards Crime

As crime has become a serious social problem in Guangdong province, it is important to understand the concerns of ordinary people. In Guangzhou, several opinion polls have been conducted on people's opinions regarding the crime problem in the city. In Table 13.6 and 13.7, two surveys (carried out in 1992 and 1994) revealed the following opinions:[15]

The above questionnaire survey was conducted by the PSB and the Public Opinion Research Centre in Guangzhou by random sampling. It can be seen that people's evaluation of the law and order

Table 13.5

A Statistical Report of the Cases Closed by the Primary
and Intermediate Courts in Guangzhou, 1995–98 (Jan to July)

Type	1995		1996		1997		1998 (1–7)	
	Cases	Persons	Cases	Persons	Cases	Persons	Cases	Persons
Threat to National Security	1	1	1	1	2	2	0	0
Crimes against Persons	443	620	594	851	588	904	307	485
Threat to Public Security	199	247	317	424				
Crimes against Property	4,922	7,832	5,621	9,153	5,150	8,477	2,544	3,967
Disruption to the Socialist Market Economy	95	147	124	186	114	161	67	105
Disruption to the Family	12	17	16	21				
Bribery and Corruption	145	168	149	166	107	115	72	75
Disruption to the Management of Socialist State	604	856	686	954	684	993	357	458
Others	14	14	12	12	10	10		

Source: Data supplied by the Research Division, Intermediate People's Court of Guangzhou, August 1998.

Table 12.6

Opinions on the Law and Order Situation in Guangzhou (by percentage)

Year	Very Good	Better	Average	Worse	Very Bad	Total
1992	18.7	33.3	35.8	6.1	6.1	100
1993	4.4	54.5		37.1	4.0	100
1994	6.3	14.1		58.2	21.4	100

Table 13.7

The Sense of Safety when Living in Guangzhou (by percentage)

Year	Safe	Quite Safe	Not Quite Safe	Not Safe	Total
1992	19.9	47.7	26.3	6.1	100
1993	4.7	43.6	41.2	10.5	100
1994	4.0	28.8	45.2	22.0	100

situation in the city deteriorated rapidly in 1994 as 58% of the respondents believed it as "getting worse" and 21% saw it as "very bad". Another survey was conducted on the sense of safety for those living in Guangzhou. The results can be seen in Table 12.7. People's sense of safety living in Guangzhou has decreased since 1993. In 1994, the situation worsened as 45% considered it as "Not Quite

Safe" and 22% as "Not Safe". The last two items constituted about 67% of the total responses.

Reactions to Crime in Guangdong

The Public Security Bureau

Officers from the Guangdong PSB admitted to the author that the police have confronted many problems under the market economy.[16] Firstly, there have been drastic changes in the social structure under the market economy, but the provincial police have not made enough adjustments to meet the challenges posed by the new economic system. The PSB lacks the necessary equipment and specialists to tackle the rapid growth of criminal activities. Criminals are increasingly using sophisticated techniques and equipment to commit criminal offences, and then move to other places afterwards, making detection very difficult.

Secondly, the police have lagged behind in their strategy of social control. Before the mid-1980s, the police employed a static strategy of controlling the household population, as the governments could control food coupons and household registration. However, under the market economy, people are free to move anywhere they like, so consequently there is a large mobile population in Guangdong and a large number of people moving in and out of the province.

Thirdly, regarding police conduct in the province, under the adverse influence of capitalism, some police officers have treated the people unfairly and unjustly and sometimes used violence. Some police officers have not performed their duties according to the laws and regulations but at their own discretion and abused their power. Some have even taken bribes to protect vice-establishments. As a result, the police have lost the confidence and trust of the people, and this has made crime detection more difficult.

Lastly, on the public relations aspects, the two police officers admitted that the police in Guangdong have neglected to seek the support of the people. The police of many developed nations usually

Table 13.8

**The Characteristics of Inmates Confined to the Institutes of
Reform Through Education in Guangdong Province, August 1998**

Items	No. and Percentage
Total number of inmates	40,400 persons
Youths under 28 years old	82.3%
Female inmates	6%
Offences	
Number of relapsed drug addicts	13,400 persons (33.16%)
Offences against property	33.44%
Offences against persons	26.63%
Disruption of public order	5.77%
Education Level	
Illiterate	1.43%
Primary education	37.62%
Junior secondary education	51.59%
Origin of Inmate	
Inmates from outside Guangdong Province	52.86%

Source: The Provincial Bureau of Reform Through Education.

seek to maintain a good relationship with the people who will help
the police in return. Therefore, many police departments in
developed nations maintain a public relations unit. However, the
Guangdong PSB have not been encouraged to do so, and some
departments still neglect the opinions of ordinary people. In order to
improve the image of the police and the judicial branches (such as the
police, prosecutors and the courts), several well-publicized cases have
been broadcast on television since August 1998. The trial of the
"Two Pistols and One Axe" case has been broadcast on the
Guangzhou television network. Such broadcasts are intended to
show the people that "crime does not pay", as well as to highlight
the effectiveness and efficiency of the police.

The Confinement of Offenders and the Rehabilitation of Ex-offenders

The confinement of offenders in China is divided into two categories,
namely, prison and the Institute of Reform Through Education.
Guangdong uses both categories in the fight against crime. The
prisons are managed by the provincial Prison Bureau. Offenders are

arrested by the police, prosecuted, and convicted and sentenced by the court. About 40,000 inmates are serving prison sentences in the province. The second category is the Institute of Reform Through Education. A suspect-offender is arrested by the police and can be sent to an Institute of Reform Through Education without going through any legal or judicial procedures. The offender is considered to have committed a minor offence which is not serious enough to constitute a criminal offence.

The provincial Bureau of Reform Through Education has provided a statistical report on the number of inmates confined in Guangdong province as follows.[17]

The Rehabilitation of Ex-offenders

Success in the rehabilitation of offenders and ex-offenders is vitally important to maintain public security in society. Unfortunately, several research reports have indicated that among the offenders arrested by the police, a large proportion of them were ex-inmates discharged from prisons and institutions of reform through labour. This is because there are no full-time paid professional social service workers helping the ex-offenders. Instead, they are taken care of by their residential district officials, who provide help and advice on a voluntary basis. Since the district officials are fully occupied with their daily routines and are not professionally trained to deal with the problem of the ex-offenders, the ex-offenders cannot receive the adequate counselling and social services they need. In addition, as it is very difficult to find employment in China today because of the restructuring of SOEs leading to large-scale redundancies. Moreover, the surplus population in rural areas has caused a heavy economic burden to the nation. The surplus rural population has entered the more developed areas of the nation, such as some cities in Guangdong province, to look for employment. These factors make it difficult for ex-offenders to find work.

Fortunately, in some well-developed and managed communities, ex-offenders are taken good care of by their family, countrymen and officials. One of them is Lujiang village, at the southeastern edge of

Guangzhou city. The following section shows how ex-offenders have received rehabilitation treatment there.

Rehabilitation

Mr. Wu was born in 1969.[18] After finishing primary school, he helped his parents sell vegetables as their farmland was taken back by the government for development. At the end of the 1980s, he became involved in criminal activities. He was arrested by the police for breaking into a shop and stealing a dynamo worth 9,000 yuan. In 1990 the courts handed him a nine-year prison sentence. He was sent to an Institute of Reform Through Labour in 1990. Because of his good conduct at the Institute, he was released in 1995. He stated that he had suffered a great deal in prison and would never commit another crime. After his release from prison, he helped his mother selling vegetables in the market. Mr. Wu said that he did not feel discriminated against or rejected by his village. In August 1997, he was recommended to join the Village Security Patrol Team and works from 6–8 hours each day. His salary is 500 yuan a month.

Mr. Che was born in 1964 to a peasant family.[19] After finishing junior secondary school, he worked as a vegetable wholesale distributor and supplied vegetables to local restaurants. In the mid-1980s, he started gambling and this led to family disputes. By the end of 1986, he was in trouble with the police and was sent to receive Thought Reform Education in an institute for four months. After he returned home, he worked for his mother selling vegetables for six years. He later started a small business but it was not very successful. In April 1997, he was recommended by the Village Secretary and later elected by the villagers to serve as the Vice-Chairman of the Village Co-operative Association. He worked part-time and earned 500 yuan a month. He thanked the Village Secretary who had encouraged him to turn over a new leaf. However, his own determination and will power were also very important, for a person must try to help himself. He must show others that his behaviour has changed and win the trust of other people.

Crime Prevention

As Guangdong is a big province and has a large number of migrants from other provinces, it has suffered from high crime rates. At the same time, the PSB are short of funds to recruit more police and purchase advanced crime-fighting equipment. Under such conditions, the police have to rely on local districts to establish safety patrol teams themselves, for the purpose of maintaining law and order. The followings cases show how the local safety patrol teams are organized and function.

Crime prevention is a very important part in the maintenance of law and order in society. Guangdong has enjoyed the fruits of economic development since the mid-1980s, but it has been confronted with a serious crime problem. The Police Chief of the Guangdong PSB, Chan Siu-Kay, admitted in an interview that Guangdong had a serious crime problem. However, the number of criminal cases has greatly declined since 1995, especially during the period 1996–97. He put the fall in crime down to the police department's emphasis on the comprehensive management of public security. Also, local public security police units have been established. Since 1993, about 47,000 local security units have been established covering more than 60% of the districts in the province. Those districts with security teams have experienced a decline in criminal activities, much to the satisfaction of the local residents. The local government adopted a comprehensive security scheme and educated the people to look out for suspicious people or activities in their local community. However, each household has to contribute to the monthly salary of the patrol team members. Chan also stated that the police have established patrol teams in different districts to keep a close eye on the local community and to react quickly to crimes when they occur. As a result, bicycle theft and burglary cases declined 23.5 and 13.5% respectively in 1998.[20]

The operation of these crime prevention systems can be seen in practice in the case of Lujiang.[21] Before China adopted the reform policies in the early 1980s, Lujiang was a rural village. However, in the 1980s the village experienced drastic changes. Most of the farmland was taken away by the government for industrial and urban development, leading to increased pollution. As a result, the peasants could no longer engage in farming anymore and depended for their livelihood on rents collected from their former farmland for survival. With unemployment high, many former peasants could not find suitable jobs. The younger generation was not willing to work unless they could earn a high salary, i.e., more than 1000 yuan per month. Under such conditions, many former peasants and their children found themselves out of work and this caused many social problems. They spent their time eating, drinking, gambling and playing sports. In response, the village Party secretary and officials have organized sporting tournaments for the villagers of different ages. For the teenagers, about half of them have entered vocational and technical senior secondary schools and the other 30–40% entered regular senior high schools, with some eventually going to university.

The composition of the village population has also changed. As Lujiang has already been incorporated into Guangzhou city, many outsiders have moved in and urbanized village. The original residents comprise only one-fourth of the village population. Many outside residents come from other provinces and cannot speak Cantonese, the local dialect. As Lujiang has become part of a big city, the public order situation has worsened. In order to deal with these problems, the village was allowed to form its own Village Security Patrol Team to maintain law and order. There are three patrol teams and they patrol the village 24 hours a day. The team has 32 members and each member earns about 1,100 yuan per month, an average salary level in Guangzhou city. The patrol members wear uniforms and carry electric batons and gas pistols. As a result of these patrols, the villagers feel that crime is being kept under control.

Summary and Discussion
The Causes of Rising Crime in the PRC and Guangdong Province

There are four main causes leading to the rising crime rate in the PRC in general and Guangdong province in particular. The first is the widening income disparity in the PRC and Guangdong. Before China adopted the policy of economic reform and opening to the outside world in the early 1980s, income distribution among the Chinese people was fairly equal. However, during the reform era, a small proportion of people became economically better-off. This group of people included businessmen, and those in control of the means of production and distribution of resources. However, the great majority of common people still live in poverty, especially those living in the inland provinces. The second cause is the problem of unemployment. Since China embraced the market economy and reformed its industries, the central government has cut down on subsidizing loss-making SOEs. As a result, many of those industries have closed down and laid-off millions of workers. In addition, there are millions of unemployed peasants in rural areas. They have to look for jobs in the urban areas of developed provinces, and Guangdong is one of the most attractive places for them to go.

The third reason is the particularities of the high growth centre of Guangdong. During the reform era, most of the economic and industrial developments were concentrated in the coastal provinces in the southeast, such as Guangdong and Fujian. Moreover, most foreign industrial investment has been concentrated in the PRD region. As a result, millions of workers from less-developed provinces have rushed to the PRD region looking for work. Many of them cannot find employment and resort to illegal means to make ends meet. So while the developed areas, especially the PRD region, have enjoyed the fruits of prosperity, they have also suffered from the negative aspects of rapid economic development.

The fourth reason is the geographic location of Guangdong, adjacent to the advanced economy of Hong Kong, which has provided opportunities for the growth of cross-border crime.

Theoretical Implications

From the viewpoint of criminological theories, criminologists hold that income inequality and disparity in wealth can easily create a sense of deprivation among the poor, especially in urban areas where the rich and the poor live side by side. Social structure theories of crime see crime as a consequence of inequality in the distribution of material resources. Lack of economic opportunities, the social disorganization of inner-city neighbourhoods, and the unrealized expectations of affluence are hallmarks of inequality. They are the products of a social organization that puts some people at a disadvantage in the competition for scarce resources. Crime is therefore an unexceptional consequence of economic, social and political disadvantage.[22] The data currently available, which shows that most of the criminal offences in Guangdong have emerged in the well-developed cities, especially in Guangzhou and Shenzhen, tends to confirm this social structure theory of crime.

Types of Criminal Offences in Guangdong

China is a developing country, but Guangdong is the most developed province in the nation. Since the reform era began, China's primary objectives have been to improve the living standards of its people. Therefore, the Chinese people hope that their standard of living can be improved. However, a small proportion of people became wealthy very quickly. The have-nots may become envious and may resort to illegal means to make money. Therefore, most of the criminal offences in Guangdong are aimed at obtaining wealth from the victims, including violent crime against persons. Violent crimes, such as robbery and muggings, are widespread. Commercial and white-collar crime has grown in number, as there are plenty of business and financial activities being conducted in the province. Crimes involving bribery, corruption, embezzlement and deceit have risen sharply since the early 1980s. It is partly because the laws and rules regulating these commercial activities are either non-existent or lag behind the pace of commercial development.

Cross border crime between Guangdong, Hong Kong and Macau is also a negative product of the province's economic development. The smuggling of electrical appliances, motor vehicles and fuel between Guangdong and the outside world, especially Hong Kong, has flourished. In addition, criminals in Guangdong slipped into Hong Kong and robbed banks and jewellery shops nearly every week in the early 1990s. After the robberies had taken place, the criminals escaped back to Guangdong through the northwest border of the New Territories in Hong Kong. Fortunately, the Hong Kong policy increased border surveillance in 1992 and number of bank robberies carried out by Mainland Chinese subsided.

However, in the late 1990s, cross border crime seemed to be entering a new phase with the activities of the gang led by Cheung Tze Keung, who kidnapped two Hong Kong tycoons and received HK$1.8 billion in ransom money, the largest ransom ever paid in a kidnapping case in the world. But the arrest, trial and execution of Cheung and his gang in Guangdong in 1998 may have helped to reduce the potential for similar activities by other gangs.

Reactions to Crime

While the Chinese people were happy to reap the fruits of the economic reforms through improved living standards, an unexpected by-product also emerged: rising crime. The Chinese authorities were shocked by this high crime wave which swept across the nation. Unfortunately, Guangdong province has been hit hardest by criminal offences. Ordinary people are alarmed, and are frightened of becoming victims of crime.

The Public Security Bureau (PSB)

The PSB are at the forefront of efforts to tackle the crime problem in China. The police were shocked by this sudden crime wave, which was so huge in size and sophisticated in techniques. As most of the suspects come from other provinces, they can easily escape and leave the crime scene. There are huge numbers of migrants in the province, especially in Shenzhen and Guangzhou, making it difficult for the police to detect and trace these criminals. The police in the province are short of funds to recruit more policemen and to buy advanced equipment to fight against the criminals. Also, the police have to update their strategy to confront the growing crime wave.

The Rehabilitation of Offenders

When a criminal is convicted and serves a prison sentence, he carries a negative label. In prison or in the Institute for Reform Through Education, the prison authorities attempt to reform and rehabilitate the inmates so that they will not commit further criminal offences after they return to society. Unfortunately, many ex-offenders still commit offences after their release, as more than half of the criminals arrested in Guangdong province were ex-offenders. The reasons could be that they want to make an easy living without working hard or make a fortune in a short time. In addition, the ex-offenders find it difficult to obtain suitable employment as there are millions of workers being laid-off by SOEs. The ex-prisoners are also not well accepted or received by their relatives or members of their community. Ex-inmates are rejected or looked down upon by their community. Unfortunately, there are no professionally trained, full-time rehabilitation workers to help ex-offenders to live a normal life. Rather, the ex-inmates are left to government officials or volunteers of their residential district and these officials and volunteers cannot devote enough time to help them solve their problems. As a result, the ex-inmates have to solve their own problems.

Theoretical Implications

According to the criminological theory of labelling, the reactions of the authorities are vitally important and critical to the success of rehabilitation.[23] According to this theory, one of the factors determining whether deviance will be reduced, repeated, or even broadened to include a wider range of acts is the nature of the reactions of the group to the initial act. If the correctional authority wisely and discretely imposes firm sanctions on the individual and attempts to involve the individual in the acceptable ways of society, he will develop a good self-image. On the other hand, if the punishments are cruel, degrading, and public, particularly if the actor is forced to leave conventional society, the chances of further deviance may be heightened. Evidence from the experience of offenders in Guangdong province tends to confirm this theoretical position.

Crime Prevention

Crime prevention is critically important and essential to maintain security and order in society. However, as the PSB is short of funds, it has strongly urged all the local districts in the province establish security patrol teams to maintain security and order in their own district. In addition, the Chinese authorities began to broadcast important criminal case trials on the television after August 1998 in the belief that such broadcasts will have a deterrent effect on the common people, especially the criminals.

Future Prospects

What are the future prospects for the crime scene in Guangdong? The causes of crime in Guangdong have not changed much recently as large numbers of young workers from less developed provinces keep on coming to look for employment and so add to the floating population problem. The unemployed workers and bad elements may resort to illegal means to make a living or seek their fortune. They may be envious of the wealth some people have. Income inequality may lead some people to feel deprived of their opportunity to make a good living. Therefore, the crime problem in Guangdong will continue to exist. However, the PSB have gradually improved their ability to fight crime by recruiting more police officers and purchasing advanced equipment. Also, they have strongly urged all local districts to establish their own security patrol teams to help maintain security and order. Hopefully, the police can gain the upper hand in the fight against crime in the years to come. Another critical element that strongly affects the crime scene in Guangdong is the rehabilitation of ex-offenders, as about half to two-thirds of the criminals arrested in some developed cities in the province were ex-offenders. This is clear that the rehabilitation of offenders and ex-offenders has been unsuccessful. It is partly due to the shortage of suitable jobs for ex-offenders and the lack of professionally trained, full-time rehabilitation workers to help those ex-offenders to re-enter society. Until the ex-offenders can be fully rehabilitated and re-settled successfully in society, the crime problem may not be greatly improved. Having surveyed the negative and positive aspects of the crime scene in Guangdong, it is to be hoped that the Chinese authorities can quickly bring the crime problem in the province under control.

Notes

1. Wang Dai-Wei, "High Crime Waves and the Social Shock Model," *Juvenile Delinquency Studies*, Vol. 4, 1997, pp. 9–14.

2. *People's Republic of China Yearbook 1998/99* (Beijing: People's Republic of China Yearbook Press, 1999), p. 96.

3. *People's Court Daily* (Beijing) 24 March 1998

4. Dai Yi Sheng, "Some Thoughts on the Rising Crime Rate in China Today," *Juvenile Delinquency Studies*, Vol. 6–7, 1996, pp. 21–28.

5. "A Brief Introduction of the Serious Public Disorder in Guangdong and its Special Characteristics," a paper presented in a symposium entitled The Market Economy and Public Security Services in Guangdong, held in Guangzhou, China, 1996 (authors' name omitted)

6. *Ibid.*

7. Interview with two senior PSB officers, 20 August 1998.

8. Court file published by the Intermediate People's Court, Guangzhou, Guangdong, August 1998.

9. *Apple Daily*, 25 July 1995.

10. Che, Wai Kin, "Cross Border Crime between the China Mainland and Hong Kong in the 1990s and Preventive Measures," in *Cross Border Crime and Preventive Measures* (Beijing: China Social Sciences Press, 1995), pp. 95–109.

11. *Ming Pao*, 23, 30 July 1998; *Apply Daily*, 11 August 1998.

12. *Apply Daily*, 30 July 1998, *South China Morning Post*, 6 December 1998.

13. *South China Morning Post*, 10 October 1998.

14. "Pay Attention to the Sense of Security and Evaluate the Public Security Objectively," a paper presented in a symposium entitled The Market Economy and Public Security Services in Guangdong, held in Guangzhou, China, 1996 (authors' name omitted)

15. *Ibid.*

16. Interview with two senior PSB officers, Guangzhou, 20 August 1998.

17. Guangdong Provincial Bureau of Reform Through Education, August 1998.

18. Interview with an ex-offender in Lujiang village, Guangzhou, 19 August 1998.

19. *Ibid.*

20. Chao Hai-Shao, "Chang An" (Long Lasting Security), *Comprehensive Management of Public Security*, Vol. 1–2, 1998, p. 28.

21. Interview with a welfare worker in Lujiang village, 18 August 1998.

22. John E. Conklin, *Criminology* (London: Macmillan Publishing Co., 1992) pp. 206–209.

23. Lewsi Yablonsky, *Criminology* (New York: Harper & Row, 1991), p. 602.

CHAPTER 14

Towards a Sustainable Environment in the Pearl River Delta Region:
A Case Study of Water Pollution Legislation and Its Relevance to the HKSAR

LIN Feng

Introduction

Water pollution is a serious environmental problem in both the Pearl River Delta region (hereafter referred to as the PRD region) and the Hong Kong Special Administrative Region (HKSAR). The PRD region and the HKSAR have common borders. Consequently, water pollution in the PRD region may directly affect the environment in the HKSAR and vice versa. There exist many cross-border water pollution issues that often need the co-operation of both governments to resolve. For example, the Shenzhen River constitutes one section of the border between the HKSAR and the PRD region. The pollution in the Shenzhen River has a direct impact on the HKSAR. The seawater of both the PRD region and the HKSAR is adjacent and pollutants discharged by either side may affect the water quality of the other. Moreover, the drinking water in the HKSAR is primarily supplied from the Pearl River system by Guangdong province.[1] The seriousness of water pollution in the PRD region, especially in the Pearl River system, therefore has a direct impact upon the health of people in the HKSAR.

This chapter will first assess the seriousness of water pollution in the PRD region and the concerns of the HKSAR. It will then move on to examine the legislative framework of water pollution prevention and control in the PRD region. Thereafter, it will examine the potential impact of the HKSAR's Chief Executive's 1999 Policy Address on the prevention and control of water pollution both in the PRD region and the HKSAR. In conclusion, this chapter argues that the PRD region has a well-structured legal framework for the protection of its water environment, particularly the quality of its drinking water sources. If this legal framework is strictly operated and enforced, the quality of water resources in the PRD region can become sustainable. Co-operation between the HKSAR and Guangdong province will have a positive impact upon the sustainability of the water environment in the PRD region.

Water Pollution in the PRD Region

China's third main river is the Pearl River which runs through Guangdong province. However, there are also a number of other rivers in Guangdong, making the province one of the richest sources of water in China. Over the last two decades, the PRD region has made great economic progress. Thousands of enterprises have been established which have attracted large numbers of migrants from other provinces seeking work. Now the PRD region has become the most densely populated place in Guangdong province. Together with its rapid economic development and population growth, waste water discharged by industry and urban residents in the PRD region has increased dramatically. In 1996, for example, the PRD region discharged a total of 2.5 billion tonnes of wastewater, which amounts to 75% of all the waste water discharged in Guangdong province.[2] Factories in the PRD region annually released 790 million tonnes of wastewater. Residents therein discharged 1.94 billion tonnes of waste water.[3] This means about 70% of the total waste water in the PRD region is discharged by residents, and the remaining 30% by industries. Due to the discharge of large quantities of waste water into the Pearl River water system consequential to rapid industrialization and urbanization,[4] the quality of the river's water has deteriorated seriously over the years.[5] It has been reported that many people living close to the Pearl River do not have good quality drinking water.[6] As a result, many cities within the PRD region, such as Guangzhou and Shenzhen, have to get their drinking water from upstream points further away. The lack of good quality drinking water because of pollution is a worsening problem.[7]

The HKSAR's drinking water is primarily supplied by Guangdong province from the Dongjiang River (the East River) of the Pearl River system. It is natural for HKSAR residents to be concerned about the deterioration of the Dongjiang's water quality. It has been reported that the people living along the Dongjiang discharge both their living and farming waste water directly into the river without having it processed.[8] Consequentially, the percentage of nitrogen and ammonia materials in the river's water has increased rapidly, as well as the level of bacteria.[9] All those components and bacteria may directly affect the health of Hong Kong people who drink the water. In order to remove those components and kill the bacteria, more chloride compounds have to be used in the processing of water supplied from the Dongjiang.[10] The Hong Kong media has reported that the water quality in the Dongjiang has deteriorated dramatically,[11] and that investigations carried out by NGOs show that the quality of drinking water in the HKSAR has deteriorated too.[12] One report even stated that the water quality of all rivers in the PRD region is below Chinese national standards for drinking water, i.e., below level three.[13] However, both the Guangdong provincial government and the HKSAR government have rejected these reports. The Guangdong provincial authorities have argued that industrial pollution in the PRD does not affect the quality of water supplied to the HKSAR. According to information obtained from the Guangzhou municipal Environmental Protection Bureau (EPB), the water quality of Dongjiang water is at level two, which is one level above the national standard for drinking water.[14] The Chief Executive of the HKSAR, Tung Chee-hwa, claimed in his 1999

Policy Address that drinking water in the HKSAR meets international standards.[15]

Though different views exist as to whether or not the water supplied to the HKSAR is up to international drinking water standards, it is indisputable that the water quality in the PRD region has deteriorated over the years. This is acknowledged by China's official national newspaper, the *People's Daily*.[16] An official from the Guangzhou municipal EPB also confirmed this to the author.[17]

In order to stop the further deterioration of water quality in the PRD region and also to ensure that the sources of drinking water for both local and HKSAR residents are up to at least national drinking water quality standards, various measures have been taken. The Guangdong provincial people's government, as well as other local people's governments within the PRD region, have worked towards the strengthening of the legal framework for the protection of all water bodies, especially the sources of drinking water. They have also made efforts to provide sewage treatment facilities along the Dongjiang,[18] and to strengthen the enforcement of relevant water pollution prevention and control legislation, in particular enforcement actions against pollution at source.

Moreover, Guangdong province and the HKSAR government have joined forces to tackle the problem of the deteriorating quality of water supplied to the HKSAR. As pointed out in Tung's 1999 Policy Address, the intake from the Dongjiang has been moved upstream to avoid taking in the more contaminated water from its tributaries. Guangdong province also plans to construct a closed aqueduct to replace the existing open channel from the Dongjiang intake to the Shenzhen Reservoir.[19]

Legislative Framework for the Prevention and Control of Water Pollution

The primary legal source for the prevention and control of water pollution in the PRD region is obviously Chinese national legislation, including the *Environmental Protection Law of the People's*

Republic of China and the *Law of the People's Republic of China on Water Pollution Control and Prevention* (hereafter cited as the *Water Pollution Law*). The former is the primary national law for all other national environmental legislation, though it does not contain any detailed provisions on water pollution control and prevention. The latter is the main national legislation focusing directly on water pollution prevention and control. It was enacted in 1985 and amended in 1996. The main reason for its amendment was that the central government realized that water quality throughout the country had deteriorated very quickly over the last two decades and serious problems had arisen due to water pollution.[20] As a result, the original legal measures were no longer adequate to prevent further deterioration of water quality.[21] Under such circumstances, the *1996 Amendments* were adopted. Another source at national level is the 1990 *Detailed Rules for the Implementation of the Water Pollution Prevention and Control Law* (hereafter cited as the *Detailed Rules for the Implementation*). With the adoption of the *1996 Amendments* to the *Water Pollution Prevention and Control Law*, the *Detailed Rules for the Implementation* was not amended accordingly. So they will only be valid to the extent that they are consistent with the amended *Water Pollution Law*. Those provisions inconsistent with the *1996 Amendments* are no longer applicable.

At local levels, various regulations have been adopted by both provincial and municipal governments in Guangdong for the prevention and control of water pollution in the PRD region. At the provincial level, there are four regulations; namely the 1991 *Guangdong Provincial Regulations on the Protection of Water Quality of the Dongjiang System*,[22] the 1991 *Regulations on Water Quality Protection of Drinking Water Sources of the Dongjiang-Shenzhen Water Supply Project*,[23] the 1993 *Methods on Administration of Meeting Water Quality Standards at the Border of Cross-Regional Rivers in Guangdong Province*,[24] and the 1998 *Guangdong Provincial Regulations on the Protection of Water Quality in the Pearl River Delta Region*.[25] According to an official from the Guangdong provincial EPB, the Guangdong provincial people's government has been slower in the enactment of local regulations to protect water quality than other provinces in China.[26] But now the Guangdong provincial government, including both the provincial people's congress and the people's government (the executive branch), has realized the necessity of strengthening its work on water pollution prevention and control. More local legislation will be enacted in the near future, and existing legislation will be vigorously enforced.[27]

At the municipal level, the Guangzhou municipal government adopted the *Guangzhou Municipal Regulations on Pollution Prevention and Control of Drinking Water Sources* in 1987.[28] The Guangzhou municipal people's government adopted a master project plan entitled "Green Mountains, Clean Waters and Blue Sky Project Plan". Though it was issued in 1998, it was planned to cover the period 1996–2000. It laid out the objectives to be achieved within this time period. This project plan, according to an official from the Guangzhou municipal EPB,[29] only has a guiding effect and does not have any binding force. Nevertheless, it is an official master plan issued by the local people's government. Similarly, other cities within the PRD region, such as Shenzhen and Zhuhai, have also adopted local legislation on the protection of drinking water sources in their jurisdictions.

It is fair to say that in the PRD region, plenty of local legislation has been adopted for the protection of water sources, especially for surface drinking water sources. The issues which need to be discussed are whether or not these legislative measures are adequate for the protection of water sources, and whether or not their enforcement is satisfactory. As it is beyond the scope of this chapter to conduct an in-depth examination into every aspect of all the legislation mentioned above, the following sections will focus on several essential aspects of these laws.

General Legal Provisions on Water Pollution Prevention and Control

These general legal provisions on water pollution prevention and control refer to those applicable to the prevention and control of water pollutants as well as the protection of water sources, either for drinking purposes or otherwise. The 1996 *Amendments to the Water Pollution Law* incorporated several new measures, i.e., comprehensive planning, the three simultaneous steps requirement, public participation in environmental impact assessment, total quantity control of water pollutants, and the head responsibility system.

Comprehensive Planning

The 1996 *Amendments to the Water Pollution Law* require comprehensive planning for preventing and controlling water pollution. Unified plans should be made on the basis of river basins or regions. Plans for preventing and controlling water pollution of major rivers should be formulated by the State Environmental Protection Agency (SEPA) together with the department of planning, the water conservancy administration department and other departments concerned, as well as relevant provincial governments, autonomous regions and municipalities directly under the central government.[30] Such plans should be submitted to the State Council for approval.[31] Local people's governments shall, in accordance with the approved plans, work out plans for preventing and controlling water pollution for their own administrative regions and incorporate such plans in the long-term, medium-term and annual plans of their administrative regions for national economic and social development.[32] However, the Pearl River system has not yet attained such a status mainly because its water quality is not that bad in comparison with other much more seriously polluted water basins in China.[33] It is therefore the task of the Guangdong provincial people's government to protect the quality of water.

In order to implement the amended *Water Pollution Prevention and Control Law*, Guangdong province adopted the *Guangdong Provincial Regulations on the Protection of Water Quality in the Pearl River Delta Region* (henceforth cited as the *PRD Regulations*) in November 1998.[34] The *PRD Regulations* was adopted after it became clear that water pollution in the PRD region had become a serious problem.[35] The Guangdong provincial government realized that it would not be sufficient for an individual city or county to protect an individual river or a section of a specific river. In order to solve the problem of polluted drinking water in the PRD region, a comprehensive regional approach had to be taken. In so doing, it was hoped that the water resources in the PRD region could become sustainable. This objective is clearly stated in Article 1 of the *PRD Regulations*, which provides that the regulation is enacted to protect the water quality in the PRD region, to prevent and control water pollution, to ensure the safety of drinking water and to realize the sustainable use of water resources.

By the terms of the *PRD Regulations*, the Guangdong provincial government is responsible for dividing the whole PRD region into different water environmental quality function zones and setting water quality targets for all zones.[36] More specifically, all rivers, lakes, reservoirs and other surface water sources should be included in different water environmental quality function zones, and water quality standards should be set for all of them.[37] Such zones do not necessarily correspond with the geographic administrative demarcation. In such cases, the Guangdong provincial government should set the borderline, the water quality standards for those rivers crossing different administrative units and make clear which administrative unit is responsible for the water quality at the border.[38] At present, the Guangdong provincial EPB is still in the process of preparing for the division of the whole province into different water environmental quality function zones. Once that is completed, the *PRD Regulations* can come into full operation.[39] Once the comprehensive planning for water pollution prevention and control is fully implemented, the future of water quality protection looks brighter in that comprehensive planning takes the PRD region as one unit in its regional planning. More specifically, through comprehensive planning, maximum output of water pollution prevention and control can be assured within tight financial constraints. Furthermore, interaction between water bodies within different administrative units within the PRD region can be harmonized through comprehensive planning. However, the exact effect of comprehensive planning still depends on the political will of the Guangdong provincial government to implement comprehensive planning. It has been argued by the Guangdong provincial EPB that the political will is there, as the governor and Party secretary of the provincial government have clearly expressed their intention to prioritize environmental protection.[40] However, whether or not the political will is really there remains to be seen.

Licensing Mechanisms

Environmental scholars have argued for years for the adoption of a licensing system in national environmental legislation for the purpose of pollution prevention and control.[41] However, due to strong opposition from industry, licensing mechanisms have not yet been incorporated into the fundamental environmental legislation, i.e., the *Environmental Protection Law*.[42] The *Water Pollution Law* is the only legislation that has incorporated a licensing system because of the seriousness of the water pollution problem in China.[43]

Licensing mechanisms are also implemented for the discharge of water pollutants in the PRD region. Each enterprise which needs to discharge water pollutants has to register with the local EPB and inform it of the equipment which discharges water pollutants, its own prevention and control facilities, and the kinds, quantity and the density of water pollutants to be discharged when the business is under normal operation. After verification the local EPB will issue a licence for the discharge of water pollutants in accordance with the requirements for total quantity of water pollutants.[44]

In order to ensure that the licensing system will work properly, there must be proper supervision and enforcement mechanisms. For that purpose, enterprises discharging water pollutants are required to install measuring facilities at discharging points to measure the quantity of water pollutants discharged. They also have the responsibility to ensure that such facilities work properly.[45] Such data will help the local EPB to monitor the water pollutants discharged in the locality. If the enterprise discharging water pollutants causes serious water pollution, it can be ordered to rectify the situation within a certain time limit.[46] The *PRD Regulations* requires the enterprise concerned to report to the local EPB for an inspection after the problem has been rectified.[47] However, the regulations are silent on the penalties that may be imposed if the enterprise fails to rectify the situation within the specified time limit.[48] It should be noted here that the criterion for issuing such an order is that the discharge of water pollutants has caused serious water pollution. The *PRD Regulations* does not mention whether or not the discharge should be within the permitted quantity. It is not clear what the local EPB will do if the discharge of water pollutants exceeds the permitted quantity but has not caused serious water pollution. According to previous practice, it is very likely that the EPB will only impose a fine.

Total Quantity Control of Water Pollutants

In theory, in order to ensure that water quality standards can be achieved, there should be a ceiling for the total quantity of pollutants to be discharged into a specific watercourse, either a river or a lake. This is the so-called mechanism of total quantity control of discharged water pollutants, which has been widely adopted by many other countries. Chinese environmental law scholars advocated its incorporation into environmental legislation for years.[49] This mechanism was eventually introduced in the 1996 *Amendment to the Water Pollution Law*. It was hailed as an essential achievement in water pollution legislation.[50] Ironically, however, its incorporation was mainly due to the disasters which were caused by serious water pollution in various parts of China rather than the efforts of environmental law scholars.[51] Now for all water bodies that conform to the relevant water pollutants discharge standards,[52] but fail to attain the relevant national water quality standards, people's governments at or above county level may institute a system for the control of total discharge quantity of major pollutants.[53]

Following the incorporation in the *Water Pollution Law* of the requirement of total quantity control of pollutants to be discharged into a specific watercourse, the *PRD Regulations* also incorporated such a requirement. First, for each administrative unit within the

PRD region, the total discharge quantity of water pollutants will be set. Second, the total quantity of pollutants permitted to be discharged at each specific point, as well as to a specific section of river, will also be set by the local EPB.[54] Third, the pollutants to be discharged into a watercourse by all kinds of construction projects should not exceed the control target of the total quantity of water pollutants for that administrative unit or emission point or section of watercourse concerned.[55] The Guangdong provincial EPB, in consultation with other relevant provincial governmental departments, allocates the control target of the total quantity of water pollutants for each local administrative unit. Then each local EPB bears the responsibility to ensure that water pollutants discharged by enterprises and individuals into the watercourse within its jurisdiction do not exceed the control target.[56] If the total discharge quantity of water pollutants of a county or municipality exceeds the target, the EPB at the next level above can set a time limit for that county or municipality to reduce the discharge of water pollutants in order to meet the control target.[57] Usually, local EPBs allocate the control target for each of the enterprises discharging water pollutants and a time limit will be set for them to meet the target.

For those areas already exceeding the control target of total quantity of water pollutants, the local EPB cannot approve the environmental impact assessment report for any new construction projects which will discharge more pollutants.[58] Without such approval, no project can go ahead. If the project is deemed really necessary, the local EPB concerned has to cut the total discharge quantity of water pollutants first in order to ensure that the addition of new pollutants will not exceed the total target amount. Moreover, approval has to be obtained from the EPB at the next level above.[59]

The Guangdong provincial government has pledged to achieve the objective of total quantity control of water pollutants and to meet national water pollutants discharge standards by the end of 2000 throughout the province. In the case of Guangzhou, its municipal government has issued a master plan for the protection of the environment, which clearly states the adoption of total quantity control of pollutants.[60] At present, however, only one city within the PRD region has met provincial water pollution prevention and control objectives. That city is Shenzhen, where all water bodies have met the total discharge quantity of water pollutants targets as well as national and local water pollutants discharge standards.[61] It is foreseeable that the water quality in the PRD region will improve significantly if all water bodies in the region can meet both total discharge quantity target and water pollutant discharge standards. Given that the central government and the Guangdong provincial government have made a commitment to strictly enforce all water pollution prevention and control legislation, there are grounds for optimism that water quality in the PRD region will improve gradually.

The Head Responsibility System

Each local people's government, including municipalities, counties and townships, within the PRD region will be responsible for the water environmental quality within its jurisdiction.[62] The EPBs within the people's governments at different levels are the governmental organs designated to exercise supervision and administration of the protection of water quality within their jurisdictions.[63] Other relevant governmental organs will play their roles in the protection of water quality in so far as the water quality is related to its primary function. For example, the administrative department in charge of food hygiene will be responsible for the hygiene supervision of the water quality of drinking water sources and will assist in the investigation and handling of pollution accidents of drinking water sources.[64]

Since 1985, the executive branches of the governments at all levels in China have moved from a traditional collective responsibility system to a head responsibility system. This head responsibility system has also applied to all governmental departments of the executive branch, including EPBs. The *PRD Regulations* states clearly that the head responsibility system should be adopted for water pollution prevention and control in the PRD region.[65] Consequently governmental officials in charge of water environmental quality take personal responsibility for failing to achieve statutory obligations in water pollution control legislation.[66] For example, the *PRD Regulations* provides that all enterprises along the rivers relating to the Dongjiang-Shenzhen Water Supply Project, which discharge water pollutants, should find funds for the prevention and control of water pollution and fulfill their pollution control and eradication tasks on schedule.[67] Then, it is the responsibility of the local EPB, especially its head, to ensure that enterprises within its jurisdiction meet such statutory requirements. Otherwise, he or she takes personal responsibility. In theory, the adoption of the head responsibility system should contribute to strict enforcement of environmental legislation. Given that local EPBs are not independent and subject to the leadership of the local people's government, whether the new system will have any substantial contribution to water pollution prevention and control remains uncertain.

The Three Simultaneous Steps Requirement

The three simultaneous steps requirement is China's contribution to environmental management and protection. It means that for all newly built, rebuilt, and expanded projects or projects undergoing technological transformation, their facilities for the prevention of pollution or other public hazards should be designed, constructed or put into operation simultaneously with the main projects. This requirement has also been incorporated into the *Water Pollution Law* by the *1996 Amendments*. If this requirement is not met, the said project will not be permitted to go into operation.[68] If the project is already in operation, the relevant local EPB can issue an order of suspension and also impose a fine.[69] All the facilities for treating and processing water pollutants must be kept in normal operation and under constant monitoring.[70] If an enterprise deliberately fails to do so, the relevant local EPB at or above county level may impose similar penalties on the enterprise concerned.[71] If this requirement is strictly enforced, the discharge of new water pollutants can be effectively prevented and controlled. According to information from the Guangdong provincial EPB, more than 90% of enterprises in the PRD region have met this requirement.[72]

Environmental Impact Assessment and Public Participation

An owner of a construction project is required by law to prepare an Environmental Impact Assessment (EIA) report and submit it to the local EPB.[73] This is required for all projects which may discharge water pollutants. In the case of the PRD region, this requirement has been met by all enterprises in the last couple of years.

In the process of conducting environmental impact assessment for all new enterprises which may discharge water pollutants, the comments and suggestions of the units and residents in the surrounding area of the proposed construction project should be considered.[74] This is a new requirement incorporated into both national and local environmental legislation since 1998. The strict enforcement of this requirement will contribute to the democratization of the EIA process. But the views of the citizens are only one kind of consideration which needs to be taken into account in the EIA process. Those views may not necessarily affect the EIA statement or report.

Summary

The above discussion of the general provisions contained in both national and local environmental legislation targeted at water pollution prevention and control shows that a lot of measures have been incorporated into legislation. Some of them are applicable to all kinds of pollution prevention and control, and some are specifically targeted at water pollution prevention and control. The Guangdong provincial government and various local governments within the PRD region have made a commitment to strictly enforce those provisions. Given the existence of this political will, it is foreseeable that a serious deterioration of water quality in the PRD can be halted due to strict enforcement of such provisions.

Industrial Waste Water Pollution Prevention and Control

One major source of water pollution is industrial pollutants. The prevention and control of industrial pollution of water has to comply with all the aforementioned general statutory provisions. In addition, both Chinese national and local legislation have some provisions specifically for the prevention and control of industrial water pollution. For example, the amended *Water Pollution Law* forbids construction of any small enterprises, lacking measures for prevention and control of water pollution, that seriously pollute the water environment, such as chemical pulp mills, printing and dyeing mills, dyestuff mills, tanneries, electroplating factories, oil refineries and pesticides manufacturers.[75] Failure to do so can lead to the local people's government issuing a closure order.[76]

In the case of the PRD region, certain prohibitive measures have been incorporated into the *PRD Regulations* for the protection and control of industrial water pollution. First, certain kinds of small enterprises that may cause serious water pollution, such as small chemical pulp mills, tanneries, electroplating, printing and dyeing, dyestuff, oil refineries and pesticides factories, are prohibited from being constructed and operated in the PRD region.[77] This prohibition has the effect of implementing Article 23 of the amended *Water Pollution Law* in the PRD region.[78] The scope of enterprises to be prohibited is exactly the same. However, Article 18 of the *PRD Regulations* is stricter than Article 23 of the *Water Pollution Law*. Within the PRD region, the construction and operation of those enterprises as mentioned in Article 18 of the *PRD Regulations* is strictly prohibited regardless of whether or not those enterprises have installed facilities for the prevention and control of water pollution. However, outside the PRD region, but within Guangdong province as well as in most other parts of China, the establishment and operation of these enterprises is still permissible under Article 23 of the *Water Pollution Law* provided that they have installed facilities for the prevention and control of water pollution. Second, all poultry farms within the PRD region must process all their waste, including waste water, to ensure that they will be harmless for discharge into any watercourse. Waste water is only allowed to be discharged into watercourses provided that it has been processed and meets the prescribed statutory standards.[79] Third, it is prohibited to dump any solid waste into any watercourse within the PRD region. Appropriate measures should be taken for the storage, transportation as well as disposal of solid waste to ensure that it will not cause water pollution[80] Fourth, all newly built harbours have to establish facilities to collect residual oil, waste oil, waste water containing waste oil, as well as solid wastes from ships.[81] All ships are prohibited from discharging waste into watercourses.[82] The actual implementation of this provision is very important. This is because the current practice is that most ships sailing in inner rivers in the PRD region, as well as in any other parts of China, discharge their waste, especially waste water, directly into the watercourse. Fifth, the production, loading and unloading, as well as the transportation of various oils and poisonous products, have to be equipped with safety facilities to ensure that such products do not leak. It is also required that contingency measures have to be available in case of accidents.[83]

The above discussion shows that statutory provisions on the prevention and control of industrial water pollution in the PRD region are very strict. The enforcement of the relevant water pollution legislation is also very strict and effective. Guangzhou is a good example. The total economic output of Guangzhou has increased ten times over the last two decades. But the industrial water pollutants discharged by enterprises now are less in quantity than two decades ago.[84] This is mainly due to the vigorous enforcement of various water pollution prevention and control legislation, which started in Guangzhou in the 1970s. Now almost all enterprises in Guangzhou have to go through the EIA process and must comply with the three simultaneous steps mechanism.

It should be noted that in urban areas of the PRD region, enforcement of water pollution legislation has been satisfactory. In rural areas, enforcement against industrial water pollution has also been strengthened. Due to the lack of human resources, however, some entrepreneurs still intentionally ignore the requirements of water pollution legislation and discharge industrial pollutants directly into watercourses. However, so long as they are discovered, the relevant local EPB will strictly enforce relevant water pollution legislation against them.[85] It is therefore fair to say that the prevention and control of industrial water pollution in the PRD region is reasonably satisfactory.

Residential Waste Water Pollution Prevention and Control

As pointed out at the very beginning of this chapter, residential waste water constitutes a large percentage of the total quantity of waste water discharged into the watercourse in the PRD region. Guangzhou is a good example. According to its master plan, the increase rate of residential waste water is at 8% per year, and about 80% of residential waste water is discharged into the Pearl River system without any treatment.[86] Certain sections of the Pearl River within Guangzhou city have several times become dark and emitted a terrible odour, and drinking water sources have been seriously threatened.[87] This statement in the master plan is supported by information obtained from the Guangzhou municipal EPB.[88]

As for legal measures for the prevention and control of residential waste water, Chinese national legislation only contains certain general stipulations. The amended *Water Pollution Law* only provides that relevant governmental organs at all levels are required to incorporate protection of urban water sources and prevention and control of urban water pollution in their urban planning. They should also provide facilities for central treatment of urban sewage under the principle of polluter-pays.[89] Except for this, there are no other detailed provisions in national legislation.

The *PRD Regulations* also has certain provisions for the purpose of implementing the provisions of the *Water Pollution Law* in the

PRD region, and provides more detailed provisions. It requires that all cities within the PRD region construct urban waste water processing facilities. Those towns with a population of more than 10,000 should also construct such facilities.[90] However, its feasibility is highly questionable given that the construction of such facilities is very expensive. In the case of China, it is unlikely that a town with a population of only 10,000 can afford to construct such facilities. Moreover, it is also questionable whether requiring each city or town to process its own waste water is the best way to handle pollution caused by residential waste water. It may well be more cost effective if it can be collected and processed more centrally for a bigger geographical area.

The *PRD Regulations* also lays down a timetable. It stipulates that by 2005 at least 40% of urban residential waste water should be processed, and that by 2010 at least 70% of urban residential waste water should be processed.[91] Today, two waste water processing plants are under construction in Guangzhou. After their completion, it is expected that the processing rate in Guangzhou, the biggest city in the PRD region, will reach about 60%.[92] Hence, it is fair to say that such a plan is not too ambitious. However, it remains to be seen whether or not that can be achieved throughout the whole PRD region, as many small cities and towns may not be able to afford to construct their own waste water processing plants. In the meantime, it is not clear how the remaining waste water will be handled. It is very likely that current practices will be followed. That means it will be continuously discharged directly into the watercourse. Estimates need to be made whether or not the discharge of 40% of total residential waste water into the watercourse will still make it possible for the water in the PRD region to sustain its quality.

The *PRD Regulations* also requires that the water coming out of a waste water processing plant after being processed meets relevant national or local water quality standards. Otherwise, the relevant local government can issue an order setting a time limit for the plant concerned to meet the required standard, and fines may be imposed for the discharge of processed water in excess of either national or local standards.[93]

The legal issues relating to the prevention and control of residential waste water are not difficult, nor is the relevant technology. The real issues are the political will of the government and its financial resources. While there exists consensus that industrial water pollution should be tightly controlled, such consensus does not seem to exist with regard to the urgency for the prevention and control of residential waste water. Moreover, it remains a low priority for local governments within the PRD to budget money for the construction of waste water processing plants. Hence, they should be pressured to do so.

Special Measures for the Protection of Drinking Water Sources

Due to the direct impact of the quality of drinking water sources upon the health of humans, the Chinese government realized the urgency of protecting drinking water sources more than a decade ago. Various pieces of legislation have been adopted at both national and local levels for that purpose.

National Legislation

The National Environmental Protection Agency[94] adopted the *Regulations on Pollution Prevention and Control in the Protection Zone of Drinking Water Sources* early in 1989 (hereinafter referred to as the *1989 Regulations*).[95] The *1989 Regulations* has the objective of protecting both surface and underground drinking water sources. As far as surface drinking water sources is concerned, it sets three specific zones, i.e., a first-grade protection zone, a second-grade protection zone and a drinking water source protection zone. The first-grade protection zone is at the centre; the second-grade protection zone surrounds the first, while the drinking water protection zone is outside the second protection zone. Different water standards are set for different water protection zones and various restrictions are imposed on the activities which may be undertaken within different protection zones, with the most restrictive measures set for the first-grade protection zones.[96]

The *1996 Amendments to the Water Pollution Law* incorporates some special measures to protect drinking water sources in order to ensure public health. First, the *1996 Amendments* grants authority to the people's governments to delineate surface water source protection zones for domestic and drinking water according to law. The division of water resources into different zones as contained in the *1989 Regulations* was incorporated into the *1996 Amendments*. Certain water areas and land-based areas near the intakes of domestic and drinking surface water sources may be delineated as first grade protection zones. Those areas beyond the first-grade protection zones may be delineated as protection zones of other grades. All such protection zones shall be indicated by clear geographic demarcations. The first-grade protection zones have the most stringent requirements. Prohibition is imposed on various activities such as the discharge of sewage into water bodies, construction or expansion of any projects that have nothing to do with water supply facilities, and protection of water sources, travel, swimming or the undertaking of any other activities that may possibly cause pollution to the water body. The violation of these prohibitive provisions may lead to the suspension of its operation or the closing down of its business.[97] Secondly, for any sewage outlets already built in the first-grade protection zones, local people's governments shall order them to be dismantled or treated within a specific time limit.[98] Third, enterprises are required to employ clean production techniques that facilitate high utilization efficiency of raw and semi-finished materials, reduce discharge of pollutants and improve management in order to decrease the discharge of water pollutants.[99] These measures are directly applicable in the PRD region and have to be complied with by enterprises and local people's governments concerned.

Relevant Legislation in the PRD Region

Special protective measures have been taken by the Guangdong provincial people's government as well as some other local governments in the PRD region to ensure that drinking water sources for Guangdong province as well as for the HKSAR are properly protected and not unduly polluted. Several local regulations have been promulgated to protect drinking water sources.[100]

The Dongjiang Regulation

In the PRD region, the protection of drinking water sources dates back to 1981 when the *Guangdong Provincial Regulations on the Protection of Water Quality of Dongjiang System* was enacted by the Standing Committee of the Guangdong provincial people's congress.[101] That regulation was made a formal local legislation one decade later in 1991 (hereafter referred to as the *Dongjiang Regulations*). It stipulates that the protection of water quality, prevention and control of water pollution, as well as the guarantee of drinking water for the residents living along the riverside and water supply for the HKSAR is its legislative objectives.[102] It has incorporated various detailed measures for the protection of water sources. First, it has emphasized the regulatory and supervisory role of local governments. According to the *Dongjiang Regulations*, the Guangdong provincial people's government, as well as other local people's governments at all levels within the water basin of the Dongjiang River, have the obligation to set water protection targets, and governmental leaders are responsible for the realization of such targets. They are also responsible for supervising other administrative departments and enterprises to ensure that the latter fulfil their statutory obligations, i.e., to take effective measures to ensure water in the Dongjiang water system meets the prescribed water quality targets.[103] More specifically, local EPBs at all levels along the Dongjiang River are the primary supervisory and monitoring organs for the prevention and control of water pollution in the Dongjiang water system.[104] Other relevant administrative organs of the people's government will play a supplementary role when water pollution is related to their own jurisdictions.[105] Local people's governments at all levels should make reasonable planning for the location of industrial enterprises and strictly control the construction of enterprises which may cause serious water pollution.[106] They are required to incorporate the protection of drinking water sources and the prevention and control of water pollution into their urban planning and construction.[107] Any proposed enterprises within the Dongjiang water system have to conduct an EIA. They are also required to implement the three simultaneous steps mechanism.[108] It is especially provided that for enterprises which may cause serious water pollution, their EIA report, as well as relevant documents for the implementation of the three simultaneous steps mechanism, have to be submitted to the relevant EPB for examination and approval.[109] The setting up of certain enterprises which are regarded as very serious water pollution sources, such as pesticide factories, chemical paper pulp mills, enterprises using heavy metal as raw materials and so on, have to get the approval from the Guangdong provincial EPB.[110] Other enterprises need to get approval from relevant municipal EPBs.[111] According to one source, the implementation of an EIA as well as the three simultaneous steps mechanism in the PRD region is close to 100%.[112]

Second, specific requirements have been set for the purpose of reducing the impact of residential waste water upon drinking water sources. The *Dongjiang Regulations* provides that all riverside towns and cities with a population of 10,000 or more should build facilities to handle residential waste water.[113] At least this has been the requirement since 1991 for all towns and cities in Guangdong province including the PRD region. Now almost ten years later, this objective has still not been achieved. As mentioned earlier, the officially stated objective is to process only 40% by 2005 and 70% by 2010.[114] According to information provided by an official from the Guangzhou municipal EPB, at present, only about 10% of residential waste water is processed, while the remaining 90% is directly discharged into various waters in the PRD region. In Guangzhou, there is only one sewage processing plant, and the processing rate is just over 10%. In some small cities, the processing rate is less than 10% or even zero.[115] The source also revealed that at the moment, all enterprises along rivers in Guangzhou have met the requirement for waste water discharge. They have all applied for and obtained licences for waste water discharge and met the relevant standards.[116] If purely examining the pollution caused by industrial waste water, the water quality of the Pearl River can reach level two, which is one level above Chinese national drinking water standards. But the level of pollutants caused by residential waste water is much higher than level two water.[117] That is why the water quality of the Pearl River at present is at level three upstream and at level four downstream.[118] So the pollution caused by the discharge of residential waste water is the most serious polluting source of the Pearl River. However, in the near future, this situation will not improve dramatically.

Third, the *Dongjiang Regulations* prohibits the establishment of any new points to discharge water pollutants within drinking water sources protection zones.[119] But the *Dongjiang Regulations* has one exception. If it is really necessary to construct a new point to discharge waste water within the protection zone of drinking water sources, it is possible provided that two conditions are satisfied. First, approval must be obtained from the EPB at county level or above.[120] Second, effective measures must be taken to ensure that water sources within the protection zone shall not be polluted.[121] For a region which does not have a good reputation for strict enforcement of legislation, there exist good reasons to doubt that the authority to approve the construction of new points to discharge water pollutants may be abused in practice. Different requirements exist for existing ones within various drinking water sources protection zones. Within the first-grade protection zone, the *Dongjiang Regulations* provides clearly that all existing points discharging water pollutants must be either removed from the zone or shut down.[122] The restriction is less stringent within second-grade protection zones. Water pollutants discharged within the second-grade protection zone, or any other protection zones, must be within the limit to ensure that water quality within the zone will not fall below prescribed water quality standards. If water quality falls below the prescribed water quality standards because of the discharge of water pollutants, all the polluting sources shall be required to reduce the total quantity of water pollutants discharged within a specified time limit in order to reach the prescribed water quality standards. If the water quality still fails to meet the prescribed standards after the above measures, the polluting sources must be required to be either removed from the protection zone concerned or closed down.[123]

Fourth, certain highly dangerous pollutants such as mercury, cadmium, radioactive materials, and so on, are strictly prohibited from being discharged into river sources.[124] Fifth, waste dumps and disposal facilities are prohibited from being constructed within 500 metres of the riverbank. For those already in existence, effective remedial measures should be taken to ensure that no leakages occur and their existence does not endanger the safety of water sources. Otherwise, local people's governments must remove them within a specified time limit.[125] Certain other activities, such as washing of oily or poisonous containers and so on, are also prohibited either in the body of water sources themselves or within the various protection zones.[126]

Compared with the relevant provisions in the *Water Pollution Law*, these provisions in the *Dongjiang Regulations* are much more detailed. However, some of them are still very general and need to be further defined.

The Guangzhou Regulation

As far as Guangzhou is concerned, the 1987 *Guangzhou Municipal Regulations on Pollution Prevention and Control of Drinking Water Sources* (hereafter referred to as the *Guangzhou Regulations*)[127] supplements the *Dongjiang Regulations* and provides more details about the protection of drinking water sources for Guangzhou. It has the clear legislative objective of preventing and controlling the pollution of drinking water sources for Guangzhou residents.[128] The *Guangzhou Regulations* has clearly defined the drinking water sources for Guangzhou, which are the four drinking water intake zones for four water refineries as provided in Article 19. Similarly, they are also divided into three protection zones, the only difference is that the outer zone is termed the quasi-protection zone.[129]

Within the quasi-protection zone, the following statutory requirements must be met. First, all enterprises and individuals which discharge water pollutants must take pollution prevention and control measures to ensure that the pollutants discharged meet local standards set by the Guangzhou municipal people's government. Second, if the total quantity of pollutants discharged cannot maintain the water quality at the prescribed local level, then the total quantity of pollutants must be reduced in order to ensure that the prescribed water quality is met.[130] Third, neither individuals nor enterprises should destroy forests or landscape plantation and cause the destruction of the ecological balance of the water environment.[131] Fourth, the *Guangzhou Regulations* prohibits the discharge of residual oil, or oily mixtures, rubbish, manure, industrial rubbish and other waste materials into water sources.[132] Fifth, it prohibits the use of explosives and poison to catch fish, and the use of pesticides and fertilizers must meet the relevant national regulations and standards.[133]

For the second-grade protection zone, the above restrictions all apply. In addition, several extra restrictions are imposed. First, no new discharge points for industrial waste water can be constructed. For expanded and renovated projects, the total quantity of discharged pollutants must be reduced below the quantity before expansion or renovation. If water pollutants discharged by the original project do not meet relevant standards, a time limit should be set for the project to meet the standards. If the pollution is serious, the existing project has to be removed from the second-grade protection zone.[134] Second, for newly established or already established residential zones within the second-grade protection zones, centralized waste water processing plants must be established, and ensure that discharged waste water meets the relevant standards.[135] As mentioned above, the overall processing rate of residential waste water is far below the requirement in Guangzhou. It remains impossible for the strict implementation of this statutory requirement. This shows the statutory requirement only reflects the expectation of the Guangzhou municipal people's government. But that does not mean this statutory objective cannot be indirectly achieved. One possibility is to stop the construction of any new residential areas within and remove pre-existing residential areas from the second-grade protection zone. Since the second-grade protection zone is only defined as the areas within a radius of two kilometres from the intake point of drinking water for drinking water processing plants,[136] it is feasible to maintain that area free from any residents. It is really up to the local people's government to make such decisions. However, political will is lacking. Take Shenzhen for example; in the case of the Shenzhen Reservoir, as reported by the Hong Kong media, the local people's government failed to pay sufficient compensation to the residents living very near the reservoir to move to other areas for the sake of protecting the reservoir water from being polluted by residential waste water. As a result, those residents continue to live in the protection zone.[137] Third, the *Guangzhou Regulations* prohibits the establishment of any poultry farms along riverbanks, or in any islands in the middle of any rivers within the second-grade protection zone.[138] Fourth, it prohibits the establishment of any new restaurants, which may discharge water pollutants on the surface of waters within the second-grade protection zone. Those pre-existing ones discharging pollutants in excess of relevant standards have to reduce discharges to meet the prescribed standards within a specified time limit. Failure to do so will lead to the issue of an order of removal or closure.[139] According to information obtained from the Guangzhou municipal EPB, all restaurants built on surface water in Guangzhou have been closed down. So this statutory provision has been stringently applied in Guangzhou. Fifth, the *Guangzhou Regulations* prohibits the construction of any docks for the purpose of loading or unloading rubbish, manure or poisonous goods.[140]

For the first-grade protection zone, all the restrictions discussed above apply. In addition, four more restrictions are imposed. First, there will be no anchoring of ships, no swimming and no fishing.[141] Second, there will be no expansion or construction of any buildings except drinking water processing plants.[142] Third, there will be no construction of docks, toilets, waste water channels or discharge points for waste water.[143] Fourth, there will be no undertaking of certain activities such as water surface plantation and pasturing, which may pollute the water source.[144] Moreover, the *Guangzhou Regulations* contains a catch-all provision which prohibits the undertaking of any activities within first-grade protection zone that pollute drinking water sources.[145]

It is noticeable that the strictest measures have been incorporated into the *Guangzhou Regulations* to ensure that water quality within first-grade protection zones absolutely meet the national drinking water quality standards. If the above measures are still not sufficient for the protection of the quality of drinking water sources, the *Guangzhou Regulations* authorizes the Guangzhou municipal people's government to set more stringent measures for the protection of water quality in various water protection zones.[146] Certain prohibitive measures have also been incorporated in the regulations to protect underground drinking water sources for those areas that have underground drinking water sources.[147]

The information obtained from interviews with officials from both Guangdong provincial and Guangzhou municipal EPBs indicates that if the implementation of the above statutory provisions do not have much financial implication for the local government and can be achieved immediately, the municipal EPB will stringently implement and enforce the relevant legislation. If the implementation of relevant statutory provisions requires substantial financial input from local governments as well as the construction of certain facilities, such as residential waste water processing plants, then the law has not been enforced strictly against the government. In practice, the above-discussed statutory provisions cannot be enforced immediately because waste water plants cannot be established within one day and no quick solution exists. Even if a fine is imposed upon the municipal government, it remains impossible for the residential waste water to be processed immediately as the construction of processing plants takes time. Those provisions are ahead of the actual development and are unlikely to be implemented. From the perspective of drafting techniques, it is much better if those provisions had not been included in the relevant legislation.

Dongjiang-Shenzhen Water Supply Project Regulation

As far as Hong Kong people and those residents living along the Dongjiang River are concerned, the 1991 *Regulations on Water Quality Protection of Drinking Water Sources of the Dongjiang-Shenzhen Water Supply Project* (hereafter referred to as the *Dongjiang-Shenzhen Water Supply Project Regulations*) has the objective of protecting their drinking water sources. The *Dongjiang-Shenzhen Water Supply Project Regulations* is a provincial one adopted by the Guangdong provincial people's government. It is applicable to both surface and underground waters across different regions within Guangdong province, all enterprises and individuals along the Dongjiang-Shenzhen Water Supply Project as well as the water collection areas for the Dongjiang-Shenzhen Water Supply Project.[148] A special Dongjiang-Shenzhen Water Supply Project Administrative Organ has been set up under the *Dongjiang-Shenzhen Water Supply Project Regulations* to control all the rivers relating to the project as well as all the relevant facilities and to ensure that the project itself does not cause pollution to water sources.[149] The established administrative organ also has the obligation to assist all local EPBs to protect the section of water sources within their respective jurisdictions.[150] Certain specific restrictive measures have been incorporated into the *Dongjiang-Shenzhen Water Supply Project Regulations*. Similar to all the previous legislation, various water protection zones are also set for the protection of water sources for the Dongjiang-Shenzhen Water Supply Project. The biggest zone is the rain water collection zone, which is not defined in the *Dongjiang-Shenzhen Water Supply Project Regulations*. According to its literal meaning, and also the context of the regulation, it should be the zone for the collection of rain water which may eventually flow into rivers relating to the Dongjiang-Shenzhen Water Supply Project. Drinking water protection zones are situated in the rain collection zones. It covers the water source itself and the areas of two kilometres in both depth and width from the normal water level of the river involved in the Dongjiang-Shenzhen Water Supply Project.[151] The drinking water protection zone is further divided into two specific zones. Waters in those rivers together with the areas of 200 meters both in depth and width from the normal water level mark into drinking water protection zone is defined as a first-grade protection zone.[152] The remaining part of the drinking water protection zone is defined as a second-grade protection zone.[153] Thirty meters both in depth and width from the normal water level mark into drinking water protection zone is defined as a water source protection belt.[154]

For the rain water collection zone, several requirements exist. First, prohibition is imposed on new construction or expansion of enterprises that either produce or store radioactive materials, or other goods which may cause poisonous pollution or serious organic pollution.[155] Second, there will be no new construction or expansion of enterprises using heavy metals as raw materials. Any such enterprises already in existence must not increase its existing quantity of discharged water pollutants, and the discharged waste water must meet national or provincial standards.[156] Third, prohibition exists on the use of extremely poisonous as well as highly residual pesticide or other imported pesticides which have not been lawfully registered or have not specified their components.[157] Fourth, all towns with a population of more than 10,000 should have processing facilities for residential waste water and have effective administrative measures for handling rubbish. If such requirements were not met initially at the time the *Dongjiang-Shenzhen Water Supply Project Regulations* was promulgated, those towns concerned should improve various measures within five years of the implementation of the regulation.[158] It is prohibited to discharge waste water directly into the rivers relating to the Dongjiang-Shenzhen Water Supply Project.[159] Fifth, the establishment of any industrial zones within rainwater collection zone for the Dongjiang-Shenzhen Water Supply Project must undergo an EIA and obtain approval from the relevant EPB depending on the size of the industrial zone.[160]

For second-grade protection zones, the *Dongjiang-Shenzhen Water Supply Project Regulations* contains nine specific restrictive measures. First, it prohibits the construction of new enterprises or the expansion of any old enterprises that may cause pollution and the construction of any discharge points for water pollutants.[161] Second, it prohibits the establishment of warehouses or storage places for poisonous goods. Those existing warehouses containing less than five tonnes of pesticide or less than 200 tonnes of fertilizer may be allowed provided that approval is obtained from the relevant EPB.[162] Third, it prohibits the construction of dumps or processing places for rubbish or waste.[163] Fourth, it prohibits the discharge of residual oil, waste oil, or other oily materials and the washing of oil containers.[164] Fifth, facilities for the prevention of leakage must be installed for all enterprises that use petroleum-based materials as raw materials.[165] Sixth, all vehicles transporting poisonous or hazardous materials must comply with certain formalities and have installed safety facilities for leakage prevention before they are allowed on the road.[166] Seventh, all newly constructed mines for the taking of stones must have preventive measures for water and soil loss.[167] Eighth, all medical waste water must be processed before being discharged.[168] Ninth, all enterprises which discharge radioactive materials, heavy metals, or serious pollutants or organic pollutants must be closed down or transformed to produce other products so that they will no longer discharge the previously mentioned pollutants.[169] Moreover, for a residential area with a population of 1,000 within a second-grade protection zone, appropriate sewage tunnels must be constructed to collect residential waste water for central handling. It is prohibited to discharge waste water directly into the rivers relating to the Dongjiang-Shenzhen Water Supply Project.[170]

Within the first-grade water source protection zone, all above discussed restrictions apply and four additional restrictions are imposed. First, the regulation prohibits the construction of any new and expansion of any existing industrial projects. It also prohibits all existing enterprises from discharging their waste water directly into the rivers relating to the Dongjiang-Shenzhen Water Supply Project.[171] Second, it prohibits accumulation or burying of any waste materials that may pollute the water source.[172] Third, without permission from the Dongjiang-Shenzhen Water Supply Project Administrative Organ, no fishing, plantation or digging of sand is allowed within the water sources.[173] Fourth, for a residential area with a population of 500 within the first level protection zone, appropriate sewage tunnels must be constructed to collect residential waste water for central handling. It is prohibited from discharging waste water directly into the rivers relating to the Dongjiang-Shenzhen Water Supply Project.[174]

Within the water source protection belt, which is narrower than the first-grade protection zone, three more conditions are imposed. First, the regulation prohibits new construction or expansion of buildings that have nothing to do with water supply facilities and water sources protection.[175] Second, it prohibits the dumping of rubbish or the construction of toilets.[176] Third, trees and grass should be planted within the protection belt to prevent and control pollution from the areas outside the belt and to prevent and control surface pollution.[177]

In addition, there also exist some general provisions in the *Dongjiang-Shenzhen Water Supply Project Regulations*. For any enterprises which may either directly or indirectly discharge pollutants into the rivers relating to the Dongjiang-Shenzhen Water Supply Project, they must report and register their pollution discharge with and apply for pollutants discharge licences from the relevant EPB. When the total quantity of pollutants discharged cannot guarantee that water quality in various protection zones meet the prescribed standards, a local EPB concerned may reduce the total quantity of pollutants permitted to be discharged by the enterprises.[178] But the regulation does not grant authority to the relevant EPB to close down polluting enterprises.

The Guangdong provincial people's government has strengthened its implementation and enforcement of water pollution prevention and control law in the PRD region, especially along the Dongjiang, the water supply source for the HKSAR. In 1998 alone, the provincial authority discovered 58 enterprises discharging pollutants in violation of rules and regulations, and dismantled 394 small illegal pig and poultry farms.[179] Some factories, which violated water pollution prevention and control legislation, have been prosecuted and moved out of various protection zones along the

Dongjiang waterways.[180] Moreover, Guangdong province is building an aqueduct to prevent pollutants from contaminating water in the Dongjiang relating to the Dongjiang-Shenzhen Water Supply Project.[181]

However, water quality in the rivers relating to the Water Supply Project has continuously declined from the time the *Dongjiang-Shenzhen Water Supply Project Regulations* was enacted in 1991, and it is fair to say that it may not be strict enough to protect the water quality of those rivers concerned, especially the Dongjiang River.[182] Therefore it is necessary to have more stringent statutory provisions to protect the water quality of such rivers.

PRD Regulations — Further Development

In order to further tighten the prevention and control of water pollution in the PRD region, the 1999 *PRD Regulations* was adopted.[183] The regulation does not replace the *Dongjiang-Shenzhen Water Supply Project Regulations* or any other provincial regulations. Instead, it supplements the latter. An examination of the provisions on legal responsibilities for violation of various provisions of the *PRD Regulations* shows that for first-grade protection zones, relevant local people's governments have been authorized to close down or dismantle any polluting constructions therein.[184] This provision really gives teeth to various local EPBs to enforce all environmental legislation, especially the ones discussed above. If such an order is issued, the water quality can be ensured. For second-grade protection zones, the relevant people's government only has the authority to set a time limit for the control of pollution and for the dismantling of polluting facilities if they belong to the category of industrial pollution.[185] As for other violations of the *PRD Regulations*, the only penalties are an order of rectification or an imposition of fine for failure to comply with the order. Then whether or not water quality within second-grade protection zones will be effectively protected really depends on whether the fine is high enough to have a deterrent effect upon the polluting enterprises. If the fine is lower than their costs for the control or eradication or water pollution, the payment of the fine will simply be treated as production costs by those enterprises and they will have no incentive to improve their records of compliance with water pollution prevention and control legislation. Within surface drinking water source protection zones, only serious polluting enterprises will be issued with closure orders.[186] For most other polluting activities, the penalties are mainly orders of rectification, cancellation of licences, and imposition of fines, not closure.[187] Hence, the same argument can be made for the statutory measures incorporated in the *PRD Regulations* for the protection of water quality within surface drinking water source protection zones.

While acknowledging the importance of preventing and controlling water pollution in the PRD region, the Guangdong provincial people's government has also realized that its resources are limited and it should use the limited local financial resources more effectively in order to maximize the output. For example, the Master Plan, issued by Guangzhou, has clearly stated its priority targets and focus.[188] Based on this kind of attitude, it remains to be seen whether the *PRD Regulations* can actually prevent the deterioration of water quality.

The Potential Impact of the 1999 HKSAR Policy Address on Water Pollution Control in the PRD Region

The HKSAR government has expressed its firm commitment to environmental protection in the 1999 Policy Address. It stated clearly that the HKSAR shall implement the principle of sustainable development in environmental protection. According to international environmental law, the principle of sustainable development has been defined as development that "meets the needs of the present without compromising the ability of future generations to meet their own needs. The concept of sustainable development does imply limits — not absolute but limitations imposed by the present state of technology and social organization on environmental resources and by the ability of the biosphere to absorb the effects of human activities".[189] In the HKSAR, Chief Executive Tung Chee-hwa, in his 1999 Policy Address, interpreted the principle of sustainable development as:

(a) Finding ways to increase prosperity and improve the quality of life while reducing overall pollution and waste;

(b) Meeting out own needs and aspirations without doing damage to the prospects of future generations; and

(c) Reducing the environmental burden put on Hong Kong's neighbours and helping to preserve common resources.[190]

This principle is obviously applicable to the prevention and control of water pollution. Its application requires that the water quality, especially drinking water quality, in the HKSAR be sustainable and will not cause any harm to the health of future generations.

In addition to this general principle, the policy address also stated that maintenance of the quality of Dongjiang water supplied to the HKSAR is a long-term priority for both the HKSAR and Guangdong province. Tung correctly pointed out in his 1999 Policy Address that the HKSAR cannot possibly solve all of its environmental problems single-handedly. It has to work closely with the Mainland authorities, including both central and local authorities, especially for the protection of water quality in the territory.[191] The chief executive has announced co-operation with Guangdong in six areas of environmental protection. Two of them are related to water pollution prevention and control. The first is to reinforce co-operation on controlling pollution in the Dongjiang River, as well as improving its water quality. The second is to enhance the exchange of data on the water quality in the PRD region, so as to formulate a management plan to improve the water quality around the Pearl River estuary. The HKSAR government has pledged to pay close attention to the environmental impact of town planning and development, and to strengthen its co-operation and liaison in these two aspects with Guangdong province.[192] Moreover, the policy address stated that the HKSAR government and Guangdong province will co-operate to set up a joint working group on sustainable development and environmental protection.[193]

If these policy commitments are indeed carried out, at least the following objectives can be achieved. First, more accurate data about the water pollution of the Pearl River estuary in general, and the Dongjiang River in particular, will become available. That is the pre-condition for any government to take further specific water pollution prevention and control activities. Second, there will be more technical and financial support for the prevention and control of water pollution of the Dongjiang River because the HKSAR is capable of providing such support, and has provided such support so far. Third, through mutual co-operation, the HKSAR should be able to introduce and to a certain extent require, Guangdong province to comply with international water standards. Fourth, the HKSAR may also express its views about the environmental impact of town planning and development in the PRD region, especially the impact upon water quality. Fifth, the HKSAR will play a very active role in the monitoring of the water pollution situation in the PRD region and therefore contribute to water pollution prevention and control. These are the possible impacts of the 1999 Policy Address on the prevention and control of water pollution in the PRD region. The actual impact of the policy address still depends on whether or not those commitments will be carried out in practice.

Conclusion

The above discussion shows that the PRD region has a well-structured legal framework for the control of water pollution and the protection of the water environment, especially the quality of its drinking water sources. Special water quality standards have been set for various water sources, and various mechanisms have been incorporated into both national and local legislation for reaching those standards. In order to protect the quality of water sources, some legal mechanisms are mandatory regardless of the costs to the polluters. In comparison with the relevant legislation in the HKSAR for the protection of water quality, it is fair to say that the legal framework in the PRD region is better structured. If this legal framework is strictly operated and enforced, the quality of water resources in the PRD region can become sustainable.

However, it is important to note that in the PRD region, certain legislative provisions are regarded as objectives to be achieved in the near future. Various authorities, including those which promulgate the legislation, do not treat them as strictly enforceable. Such attitudes sometimes lead to lack of strict enforcement of relevant water pollution control and water sources protection legislation. Moreover, some other factors such as lack of enforcement officers, inadequate legal penalties for violation of relevant legislation, possible abuse of discretionary power in granting special approval for emitting water pollutants and so on, may all affect the quality of the implementation of relevant water pollution control and water sources protection legislation. That will eventually affect the sustainability of water environment in the PRD region.

Due to the close relationship between the PRD region and HKSAR, as well as the actual impact of water quality in the PRD region upon the health of HKSAR residents, both Guangdong province and the HKSAR have decided to co-operate with each other in environmental protection, including the protection of water environment and drinking water sources. HKSAR residents have higher expectations of the water quality in the PRD region than the local residents. They judge the effectiveness of various mechanisms for the protection of water sources in the PRD against international standards, which are often higher than Mainland China and the PRD region's local standards. Accordingly, the HKSAR's co-operation with Guangdong province will have a positive impact upon the sustainability of the water environment in the PRD region.

Notes

This chapter is based on a research project financed by a City University small-scale research grant, which made it possible for the author to visit Guangzhou and conduct interviews with officials from the relevant EPBs in Guangdong province.

1. According to *Ming Pao*, 70% of the HKSAR's drinking water is supplied from Guangdong. *Ming Pao*, 7 August 1999.

2. *Ibid.*

3. *Ibid.*

4. See Anne Stewart and Chan Yee Hon, "Congress debates new Pearl River law", *South China Morning Post* [hereafter cited as *SCMP*], 20 November 1998, p. 7.

5. One report says that the quality of all waters within the PRD is below level four. For details, see "Zhushanjiao Tiaotiao Wujiang Bunen Ying" (No river in the Pearl River Delta region can be drunk), *Ming Pao*, 18 May 1999, A17.

6. See "Shou Zhe Zhujiang Mei Shui He Zhuai Zhu Sanjiaozhou Fazhan: Shuize Baohu Huhuan Lifa", *People's Daily*, 24 November 1998, p. 1.

7. *Ibid.*

8. *Ibid.*

9. *Ibid.*

10. *Ibid.*

11. *Ming Pao*, 18 May 1999.

12. *Ibid.*

13. In China water quality is classified into six levels, from level one to level six. The higher the number, the lower the water quality. According to national standards, drinking water should be at level three or above. Water at level four or below can only be used for industrial or irrigation purposes. In my interviews with officials from the Guangdong provincial and Guangzhou municipal environmental protection bureaux, I was informed that some rivers in the PRD region are at level two. Some rivers are at level one, though that is rare. One official pointed out that the allegation made by the Hong Kong media may be based on the collection of water samples very close to the waste water discharge point. But the river has a self-purification effect. At a certain distance away from that point, the water will meet the required standards.

14. The source admitted that the water quality in the Dongjiang has deteriorated over the years. But he pointed out at the same time that the water quality of the Dongjiang is the same as that of the water supplied to the residents in Guangzhou, i.e., all at level two.

15. *Ibid.* Chief Executive Tung Chee-hwa stated in his 1999 Policy Address that the quality of drinking water in the HKSAR is up to international standards. See the

1999 Policy Address, *Quality People, Quality Home, Positioning Hong Kong for the 21st Century* (Hong Kong: Government Printer, October 1999).

16. *People's Daily*, 24 November 1998.

17. Interview with the director in charge of environmental policy and legislation in the Guangzhou municipal EPB.

18. See paragraph 108 of the 1999 Policy Address, *op. cit.*

19. *Ibid.*

20. Qin Zhongda, the Explanation of the Amendments (draft) to the *Water Pollution Prevention and Control Law of the PRC*, document 12 of the 16th meeting of the 8th Standing Committee of the National People's Congress.

21. For a detailed discussion of the background of the amendments to the *Water Pollution Prevention and Control Law* in 1996, please refer to *ibid.*

22. This was promulgated by the Standing Committee of the Guangdong provincial people's congress on 28 February 1991.

23. This was issued by the Guangdong provincial people's government in 1991.

24. This was issued by the Guangdong provincial people's government in 1993.

25. This was issued by the Standing Committee of Guangdong provincial people's congress on 22 December 1998 and came into effect on 1 January 1999.

26. Interview with an official from the Guangdong provincial EPB.

27. *Ibid.*

28. This regulation was issued by the Standing Committee of the Guangzhou municipal people's congress in 1987 and approved by the Standing Committee of the Guangdong provincial people's congress in the same year. It was later amended in 1992 with the approval of the Standing Committee of the Guangdong provincial people's congress.

29. Interview with the director in charge of environmental policy and legislation in the Guangzhou municipal EPB.

30. See Article 2 of the *Decision of the Standing Committee of the NPC on Revising the Law of the PRC on Prevention and Control of Water Pollution*.

31. *Ibid.*

32. *Ibid.*

33. They include the Yellow River Basin, the Huaihe River, the Taihu River, the Zhengchi River, the Caohu River etc. For details see *Zhongguo Huanjin Zhuangkuang Gongbao 1997 (1997 Report of Chinese Environmental Situation)*, issued by the NEPA.

34. It came into effect on 1 January 1999. This regulation applies only to the surface water within the PRD region. It does neither apply to underground water nor to coastal sea surface water. See Article 2 of the regulation.

35. *People's Daily*, 24 November 1998.

36. See Article 7 (1) of the *PRD Regulations*.

37. *Ibid.*, Article 7 (2).

38. *Ibid.*, Article 7 (3).

39. Interview with an official from the Guangdong provincial EPB, October 1999.

40. *Ibid.*

41. See Jin Ruilin, *Huan Jin Fa Xue (Environmental Law)* (Beijing: Peking University Press, 1990), pp. 129–134.

42. Another reason is that the State Environmental Protection Bureau failed to convince the Legislative Affairs Commission of the necessity to incorporate the licensing system. That to an extent shows that the SEPA has not done enough research in this aspect.

43. In some other pieces of national environmental legislation, such as the *Atmospheric Pollution Prevention and Control Law*, licensing mechanisms have not been incorporated.

44. See Article 11 of the *PRD Regulations*.

45. *Ibid.*, Article 12.

46. *Ibid.*, Article 13.

47. *Ibid.*

48. In this situation, the relevant provision in the *Water Pollution Law*, Article 52, will be applicable, which provides that "an enterprise or institution which has caused severe pollution to a water body but has failed to eliminate such pollution on expiration of the time limit shall, according to regulations of the State, pay twice or more the fee for excess discharge, and may, in the light of consequent damage and loss, also be fined or ordered to suspend operation or close down".

49. See, for example, Jin, *Zhongguo Huanjinfa*, *op. cit.*, pp. 184–189.

50. *Ibid.*

51. Qin, the Explanation of the Amendments, *op. cit.*

52. It means that all the pollutants discharged into that water body conform to the relevant national water pollutants discharge standards.

53. See Article 6 of the *Amendments to the Water Pollution Law*.

54. See Article 8 of the *PRD Regulations*.

55. *Ibid.*, Article 9.

56. *Ibid.*, Article 8.

57. *Ibid.*, Article 8 (3).

58. *Ibid.*, Article 9 (2).

59. *Ibid.*

60. See the Master Plan of Guangzhou municipal people's government.

61. In China, Xiamen has also met the two standards.

62. See Article 3 of the *PRD Regulations*.

63. *Ibid.*, Article 6 (1).

64. *Ibid.*, Article 6 (3).

65. *Ibid.*, Article 3.

66. *Ibid.*, Article 30.

67. *Ibid.*, Article 7.

68. *Ibid.*, Article 3.

69. *Ibid.*, Article 16.

70. *Ibid.*, Article 4.

71. The local EPB may order the unit to restore the normal use or to re-install and use the facilities within a time limit, and may also impose a fine. See *ibid.*, Article 17.

72. Interview with the director in charge of environmental policy and legislation in the Guangzhou municipal EPB.

73. See the *Administration Regulation on Environmental Protection of Construction Projects 1998*, Article 10.

74. *Ibid.*, Article 15.

75. See Article 12 of the 1996 *Amendments to the Water Pollution Law*, or Article 23 of the amended *Water Pollution Law*.

76. See Article 20 of the 1996 *Amendments to the Water Pollution Law*, or Article 51 of the amended *Water Pollution Law*.

77. See Article 18 of the *PRD Regulations*.

78. It provides that; "The State shall forbid construction of any small enterprises, devoid of measures for prevention and control of water pollution, that seriously pollute the water environment, such as chemical pulp mills, printing and dyeing mills, dyestuff mills, tanneries, electroplating factories, oil refineries and pesticides manufacturers".

79. See Article 20 of the *PRD Regulations*.

80. *Ibid.*, Article 23.

81. *Ibid.*, Article 21.

82. *Ibid.*, Article 19.

83. *Ibid.*, Article 22.

84. See interview notes with the director of environmental legislation division of Guangzhou municipal EPB, which are on record with the author.

85. See Stewart and Chan, "Congress debates", *op. cit.*.

86. See the Master Plan, Chapter One, para. 2.

87. *Ibid.*

88. Interview with the director in charge of environmental policy and legislation in the Guangzhou municipal EPB.

89. See Article 9 of the 1996 *Amendments to the Water Pollution Law*, or Article 19 of the amended *Water Pollution Law*.

90. See Article 14 of the *PRD Regulations*.

91. *Ibid.*

92. Interview with the director in charge of environmental policy and legislation in the Guangzhou municipal EPB.

93. See Article 17 of the *PRD Regulations*.

94. It was later changed to State Environmental Protection Agency (SEPA).

95. This Regulation was issued by the National Environmental Protection Bureau together with the Ministry of Hygiene, Ministry of Construction, Ministry of Water Irrigation, and Ministry of Mines on 10 July 1989.

96. See the *1989 Regulations*, Chapter Two.

97. See Article 18 of the *1996 Amendments to the Water Pollution Law*, or Article 49 of the amended *Water Pollution Law*.

98. This must be done pursuant to the limits of power authorized by the State Council. See Article 10 of the *1996 Amendments* or Article 20 of the *Amended Water Pollution Law*.

99. See Article 11 of the *1996 Amendments* or Article 22 of the *Amended Water Pollution Law*.

100. These regulations were originally issued by local governments at different levels in the PRD region in order to implement the national *Administrative Regulations on Pollution Prevention and Control in the Protection Zone of Drinking Water Sources*.

101. It was promulgated by the Standing Committee of the Guangdong provincial people's congress on 28 February 1991.

102. See Article 1 of the *Dongjiang Regulations*.

103. *Ibid.*, Article 5.

104. *Ibid.*, Chapter Two.

105. *Ibid.*

106. *Ibid.*, Article 9 (1).

107. *Ibid.*, Article 10.

108. *Ibid.*, Article 9 (2).

109. *Ibid.*, Article 17.

110. *Ibid.*, Article 16.

111. *Ibid.*, Article 17.

112. Interview with an official from Guangdong provincial EPB on 28 October 1999.

113. Some cities are required to set up second level water process facilities. See Article 22 of the *Dongjiang Regulations.*

114. See the Master Plan of Guangzhou municipal people's government.

115. Interview with the director of the Legal Affairs Department of Guangzhou municipal EPB on 28 October 1999.

116. *Ibid.*

117. *Ibid.* Water quality in China is divided into six levels. Water for drinking must be at level three or below.

118. Interview with the director in charge of environmental policy and legislation in the Guangzhou municipal EPB.

119. See the *Dongjiang Regulations*, Article 23 (1).

120. *Ibid.*

121. *Ibid.*

122. *Ibid.*, Article 23 (2).

123. *Ibid.*

124. *Ibid.*, Article 24.

125. *Ibid.*, Article 25.

126. *Ibid.*, Articles 26–30.

127. This regulation was issued by the Standing Committee of Guangzhou municipal people's congress in 1987 and approved by the Standing Committee of the Guangdong provincial people's congress in the same year. It was later amended in 1992 also with the approval of the Standing Committee of the Guangdong provincial people's congress. The *Guangzhou Regulations* was amended in 1996. The main amendments include the amendment to original Article 39 (1), the deletion of Article 39 (3), the amendment of Article 45, and Article 47.

128. See the *Guangzhou Regulations*, Article 1.

129. *Ibid.*, Article 19.

130. *Ibid.*, Article 20 (1).

131. *Ibid.*, Article 20 (2).

132. *Ibid.*, Article 20 (3).

133. *Ibid.*, Article 20 (4).

134. *Ibid.*, Article 21 (1).

135. *Ibid.*, Article 21 (2).

136. *Ibid.*, Article 19 (3).

137. "Zhushanjiao Tiaotiao Wujiang Bunen Ying" (No river in the Pearl River Delta region can be drunk), *Ming Pao*, 18 May 1999, A17.

138. See the *Guangzhou Regulations*, Article 21 (3).

139. *Ibid.*, Article 21 (4).

140. *Ibid.*, Article 21 (5).

141. *Ibid.*, Article 22 (1).

142. *Ibid.*, Article 22 (2).

143. *Ibid.*, Article 22 (3).

144. *Ibid.*, Article 22 (4).

145. *Ibid.*, Article 23 (1).

146. *Ibid.*, Article 23 (2).

147. *Ibid.*, Article 25. This chapter will not discuss in detail the protection of underground drinking water sources.

148. See the *Dongjiang-Shenzhen Water Supply Project Regulations*, Articles 2 and 3.

149. *Ibid.*, Article 6.

150. *Ibid.*

151. *Ibid.*, Article 9 (1).

152. *Ibid.*, Article 9 (2).

153. *Ibid.*

154. *Ibid.*, Article 10.

155. *Ibid.*, Article 12 (1).

156. *Ibid.*, Article 12 (2).

157. *Ibid.*, Article 12 (3).

158. *Ibid.*, Article 16.

159. *Ibid.*

160. *Ibid.*, Article 17.

161. *Ibid.*, Article 13 (1).

162. *Ibid.*, Article 13 (2).

163. *Ibid.*, Article 13 (3).

164. *Ibid.*, Article 13 (4).

165. *Ibid.*, Article 13 (5).

166. *Ibid.*, Article 13 (6).

167. *Ibid.*, Article 13 (7).

168. *Ibid.*, Article 13 (8).

169. *Ibid.*, Article 13 (9).

170. *Ibid.*

171. *Ibid.*, Article 14 (1).

172. *Ibid.*, Article 14 (2).

173. *Ibid.*, Article 14 (3).

174. *Ibid.*

175. *Ibid.*, Article 15 (1).

176. *Ibid.*, Article 15 (2).

177. *Ibid.*, Article 15 (3).

178. *Ibid.*, Article 18.

179. *Ibid.*

180. Stewart and Chan, "Congress debates", *op. cit.*.

181. *Ibid.*

182. It may be argued and may well be true that the water quality may become even worse without the *Water Supply Regulations*.

183. It was enacted in 1998 and came into effect on 1 January 1999.

184. See the *PRD Regulations*, Articles 29 and 33.

185. *Ibid.*, Article 28(1).

186. *Ibid.*, Articles 18, and 33(4).

187. *Ibid.*, Article 33.

188. It should be noted that the Master Plan has also stated the application of the sustainable development principle and acknowledged the importance of overall environmental protection in the PRD region especially, and Guangdong province in general.

189. See G. H. Brundtland, *Our Common Future — The Report of World Commission on Environment and Development* (Oxford University Press, Oxford, New York, 1987), pp. 8 and 43.

190. See paragraph 86 of the 1999 Policy Address by the Chief Executive of the HKSAR.

191. *Ibid.*, paragraph 120.

192. *Ibid.*, paragraph 121. The other three are: first, to complete a joint study on regional air quality by early 2001 and to formulate long-term preventive measures as soon as possible. Second, to study the feasibility of adopting common standards for diesel fuels in both Guangdong and HK, and to draw up

an implementation plan. Third, to co-operate in forestry conservation by exchanging relevant information and technical knowledge.

193. *Ibid.*

CHAPTER 15

Solid Waste Management
in Guangzhou:
The Stumbling Block to a World Class City

Carlos Wing-hung LO and CHUNG Shan-shan

Introduction

In its last city planning exercise conducted in 1995, the Guangzhou municipal government iterated an ambitious plan to transform Guangzhou into a modern international city in fifteen-year's time through the practice of sustainable development.[1] This plan poses an arduous task in the environmental domain since Guangzhou suffers from serious problems of pollution and environmental degradation following more than a decade of one-sided concern for achieving rapid economic growth.[2] Like most Third World cities striving for economic development, Guangzhou's environmental infrastructure is underdeveloped and its pollution control capacity is inadequate to align it with other developed cities throughout the world in terms of environmental standards.[3] The lack of an integrated waste management system to produce a sufficiently clean and healthy environment, which is considered as a hallmark of a modern city, is one of the many fundamental environmental inadequacies which needs to be dealt with in Guangzhou.

Guangzhou's waste management system is currently too backward to cope with the growing amount of solid waste generation resulting from burgeoning economic and population growth. The per capita municipal solid waste generation rate jumped from 0.43 kg per day in 1982 to 1.09 kg per day in 1996, representing an increase of 153%, while the increase in the absolute amount of waste that required disposal was 217%.[4] Not only is the per capita municipal waste generation of Guangzhou higher than the average in areas of southern Thailand (0.7 kg per day in 1996)[5] and some larger cities in other developing countries, such as Delhi (0.47 kg per day in 1996)[6] and Tanga (0.33 kg per day)[7], it is also higher than that of Hong Kong (1.01 kg per day in 1996)[8] and the national average of South Korea (1.01 kg per day in 1997–98)[9].

Indeed, the problems of waste management are quite profound when one considers that the city lacks an effective system to collect, transport and dispose of solid waste from domestic sources, lacks a separate and safe procedure for handling and disposing clinical waste, and lacks proper facilities to dispose of industrial hazardous waste and radioactive waste which have already accumulated in large quantities.[10] Accompanying a growing concern over the effect of pollution on the natural environment and the adverse impact on urban sanitation resulting from ineffective waste management is mounting pressure to improve the municipal waste management system under the aspiration of turning Guangzhou into a "garden city". This is especially urgent as Guangzhou is now moving towards a "throw-away" society following the rapid improvement of people's material well being.

In his October 1999 policy speech of the Hong Kong Special Administrative Region (HKSAR), Chief Executive Tung Chee-hwa announced six areas of co-operation with Guangdong province in monitoring the impact of cross border development, including water quality control, vehicle fuel standards and regional air quality monitoring.[11] In relation to solid waste management, Tung merely reiterated the well-known position on ensuring waste movement between Hong Kong and the Mainland would be in accordance with the Basel Convention.[12] This is not, however, the most important and urgent co-operation required in solid waste management.

The waste management problems confronting Guangzhou mirror some of the existing environmental concerns in Hong Kong: a shortage of waste disposal facilities, the difficulty in arresting the growth of waste generation and the perceived frustration in carrying out domestic waste recycling and waste avoidance measures. Sharing a common problem provides an opportunity for solving the problem in a collective way. Will it be more cost-effective and environmentally beneficial to make use of excessive capacity in the waste disposal facilities across the city boundary? Will the pressure for manufacturers to adopt low waste product design and manufacturing be greater if the HKSAR and Mainland authorities specify similar requirements and control? Will voluntary source separation schemes be more successful if the people in both areas are educated to use a compatible scheme so that when they are travelling or have migrated across the border the system that is used is already familiar to them? Co-operation over these issues requires an all round understanding on the other side's waste management system. This chapter should be able to make a contribution in this regard.

Within the context of sustainable development, this chapter examines solid waste management in Guangzhou to determine the inadequacies of its waste management system. It will first review the management of solid wastes in other Third World cities before presenting an analysis of municipal waste management in Guangzhou. On this basis, it will evaluate the effectiveness of Guangzhou's waste management system. It will go on to identify the institutional constraints for sustainable waste management in Guangzhou. It will conclude by discussing the problems and prospects for sustainable waste management in Guangzhou.

Solid Waste Management in Third World Cities

Researchers on solid waste management in developing countries have found that most Third World cities have performed poorly in the management of both industrial and domestic solid waste.[13] Although it is now widely accepted that proper waste management is essential to the provision of a clean and healthy living environment, few organised efforts have been made by municipal governments in Third World cities to bring local waste under control. As a result, the problems of collection, transportation and disposal of wastes have remained unresolved to different degrees. Some cities have left more than 30% of generated solid wastes uncollected. More have found it difficult to transport the collected waste to disposal sites, and an overwhelming majority has been unable to collect the waste and dispose of it in a safe and environmentally acceptable way.[14] Indeed, improper municipal waste management in Third World cities has itself become a major source of pollution. Ground water contamination by leachate from uncontrolled landfills and air pollution from the open burning of refuse are among the most commonly found adverse consequences.[15]

This lack of performance can be accounted for by the low priority accorded by municipal governments to the conduct of sound waste management. This situation has been aggravated by poor funding, the lack of regulatory policies and legislation, the absence of economic incentives, inadequate institutional capacity, backward technology and limited public participation.[16] Recently, greater efforts have been made by some local governments to reorganize their waste management systems and introduce innovative practices as municipal leaders in developing countries have expressed a greater commitment to the promotion of healthy and sustainable cities. For example, Rio de Janeiro in Brazil has employed an integrated waste handling system to improve the efficiency of waste collection and transportation; Dakar in Bangladesh has adopted a participatory approach by involving local communities in waste collection and disposal; and Manila in the Philippines has started to practice ecological waste management with the stress on reuse and recycling.[17] Despite some initial successes found in these individual cities,[18] for most other cases, progress has been slow and improvement has been limited due to the piece-meal nature of most reform programmes. Increasingly, it is recognized that effective management of municipal waste in Third World cities requires the establishment of an integrated waste management system to tackle municipal wastes in a holistic manner.[19] It must be integrated since all types and sources of solid waste will be dealt with by means of the best available options. It is holistic in the sense that different operations and components of waste management will be systematically organized and co-ordinated throughout the entire process.[20] In the era of sustainable development, there is a demand for a sustainable waste management system which means that such an integrated management system should be operated in an economically and environmentally sustainable manner.[21]

How should one conduct a systematic and in-depth study of municipal waste management in Third World cities? Since the waste management system should be both integrated and holistic, the framework for analysis should be able to address all key aspects of waste management. It is outlined as follows:[22]

(a) Policy ideology which considers the policy priorities of the municipal government and social groups in regards to sound and effective waste management and their attitudes towards the idea of pro-active control of waste;

(b) Policy content which refers to the availability of legislation and the range of policy instruments that the regulatory agencies can employ for waste management;

(c) Regulatory process which refers to the structures of key institutions and the implementation of waste policies and regulations;

(d) Public participation which considers the participation of social and non-governmental forces in municipal waste management;

(e) Policy consequences which consider the outcomes of municipal waste management.

This comprehensive analytical scheme will help to produce a sound empirical basis for determining the effectiveness of the municipal waste management of individual cities in developing countries. Taking environmental and economic sustainability as the frame of reference, the waste management system in these cities can be evaluated by five different criteria. The first criterion is coverage and capacity, which refers to its ability to deal with all sources of waste by appropriate means. The second one is environmental impact, which refers to its ability to minimize the adverse effects on the environment in the course of waste management. The third one is implementation effectiveness, which refers to its ability to provide regulatees with economic incentives for active compliance. The fourth one is cost-effectiveness, which refers not only to the financial costs of providing waste management services and facilities but also to the cost-effectiveness in relation to the affordability of the local economy. The fifth one is the adoption of the participatory approach, which refers to the ability to involve the public and local communities in the regulatory process. Although the adoption of participatory approaches is desirable in general, it is particularly indispensable in solid waste management since the implementation of the two best options to sustainable waste management, namely, source reduction and waste recycling, can only be achieved with widespread public support and co-operation.

This chapter adopts the above formulation for the study of solid waste management in Guangzhou.

Solid Waste Management in Guangzhou

In municipal Guangzhou, waste management is divided into two separate areas: municipal solid waste and specific (including clinical, industrial and hazardous) waste. The management of municipal solid waste falls under the jurisdiction of the Municipal Construction Commission (MCC). The Environmental Health Bureau (EHB) is its major administrative organ in charge of the collection, transportation and disposal of municipal waste. It takes charge of the planning and day-to-day operation of waste facilities at the municipal level, while its local environmental health offices at the district level are responsible for carrying out the duties of waste collection and street cleaning. The EHB also plays a major role in formulating waste policies. For the monitoring and control of the environmental effect of municipal waste management, the municipal Environmental Protection Bureau (EPB) is responsible.

The management of clinical, industrial and hazardous waste is far from institutionalized. While they fall within the jurisdiction of the EPB, they are neglected areas without any proper mechanism to organize their collection and disposal.

Municipal Solid Waste (MSW)

The growing affluence of Guangzhou society in the reform era has led to a huge increase in the generation rate of MSW and changed the composition of the waste. MSW in Guangzhou consists of three parts: domestic, street-cleaning and institutional waste. Domestic waste is waste generated from domestic activities. Street cleaning waste is collected every day from the streets of Guangzhou. Institutional waste refers to waste from shopping arcades, small industrial workshops in population centres, and commercial establishments and offices.[23] Between 1983 and 1990, the per capita waste generation in Guangzhou increased by 9.5% per annum and total waste generation increased by 10%. This rapid increase in the individual waste generation rate largely accounts for the growth in total waste generation. From 1990 to 1996, this trend continued but at a slower rate, with total MSW generation increasing to about 6.6% per annum while per capita waste generation rate increased to about 5%.[24] Table 15.1 summarizes the MSW daily generation rates and per capita generation rates (for disposal) in Guangzhou in 1982 and from 1990 to 1996.

As for the waste composition, most notable is a significant decline in the proportion of sand and ash in the MSW stream since 1985. This decline is due to the increase in the civilian use of electricity and gaseous fuel at the expense of solid fuel. As a result, the proportions of other waste categories have increased with the exception of metal. This coincides with the period when per capita MSW was increasing steadily. Thus, the absolute amount of

Table 15.1

Per Capita and Annual Waste Generation for Guangzhou

Year	Tonnes per day	Per capita/day (kg)
1982	1,337	0.43
1990	2,882	0.81
1991	2,943	0.82
1992	3,005	0.82
1993	3,068	0.83
1994	3,200	0.85
1995	4,054	1.05
1996	4,246	1.09

Sources: Statistical Yearbook for Guangdong 1997 (Guangzhou: Guangzhou Environmental Health Institute, 1997), *Guangzhou shi huanjing weisheng sheshi guihua fujian (The Annex to Guangzhou Environmental Health Facilities Planning: Discussion Paper)*, Environmental Health Facility Group, March, p. 2, Table 1; and pers. comm. with Lei Z. H. on 26th August, 1997. Per capita waste figures are worked out by the authors.

putrescibles and combustibles (namely, rags, paper and plastics) per waste generator is also rising. Figure 15.1 shows the changes in MSW composition in Guangzhou during the reform era.

There are two waste collection systems co-existing in Guangzhou. The older system requires residents to bring their waste to designated containers on the street level at a designated time of day. The waste is then collected by a mix of general-purpose trucks and specially designed refuse collection vehicles and taken to landfills. Under this system, a waste collection fee of 4 yuan per month per household is charged by the sanitation stations which provide the collection service. The sanitation stations are responsible for waste collection vehicles and neighbourhood cleaning. This system has been gradually replaced by a new system which offers door-to-door waste collection. Under the new system residents are asked to set out their waste in bags for collection. The bagged waste is then collected by the sanitation station staff and placed into specially designed refuse vehicles. It is then transported either to the landfills or to a refuse transfer station where the waste is further compacted to reduce the transportation costs. Under the new system, the waste collection fee has been increased to 10 yuan per month per

Figure 15.1
Changes in MSW Composition in Guangzhou During the Reform Era

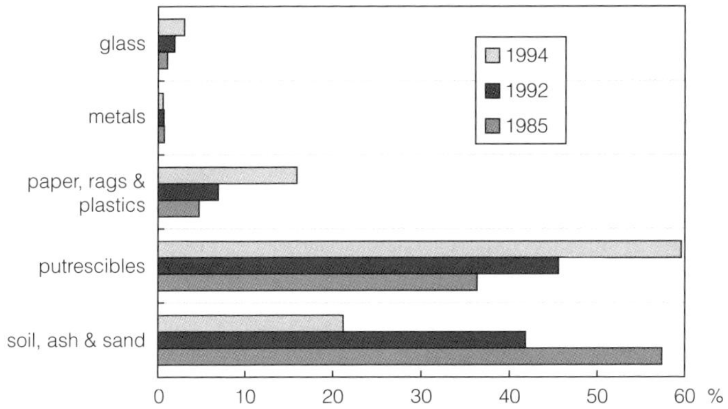

Source: S. S. Chung and C. S. Poon, "A Comparison of Waste Management in Guangzhou and Hong Kong", *Resources, Conservation and Recycling,* Vol. 22, 1998, p. 210.

household. Currently, this new collection system is serving 92% of the households that are planned to be included.[25] Disposal of waste at landfills is free in all cases. It is planned that by the year 2000, this new system will be fully implemented in the urban area of Guangzhou.

At present, MSW in Guangzhou is disposed of solely by landfilling, although there are plans to build waste-to-energy plants. There are two landfill sites in Guangzhou; the Dan Tian Shan Landfill and the Li Keng Landfill. Both are located 20–25 kilometres from the city. The operation and capital costs of landfilling were estimated at 20 yuan per tonne (at 1995 prices).[26] The Li Keng Landfill, the newer and the larger of the two, accommodates around 60% of the total waste disposed of in Guangzhou. No fee is charged for the disposal of waste collected by the EHB, but a fee of 15 yuan per tonne is charged for that privately hauled.[27] It is estimated that the capacity of these two landfills will be fully exhausted by the year 2000 and new landfills located 30–37 kilometres away from the city centre are being planned.

Clinical, Industrial and Hazardous Waste

There are three major categories of specific solid waste that need effective management. The first one is clinical waste, which has been largely left without proper regulatory control. It was estimated in 1994 that clinical waste is generated at 67 tonnes per day.[28] Currently, around 45% of the clinical waste is handled by incineration either at hospitals of large and medium size or through a contracted party. The rest (mostly produced by small-sized hospitals or clinics) is collected by the cleaning crews of district Environmental Health Offices (EHOs) and is mixed into the domestic waste stream.[29] As a result, syringes, containers of medication and patients' cleaning waste can be detected in the two MSW landfills in Guangzhou. The presence of pathogens and toxic or radioactive substances in the waste poses a major threat to the environment as well as the health and safety of the cleaning crew. Because of the adverse environmental consequences of clinical waste in the absence of proper management, a regulatory system has been planned to institute and formulate a local regulation to put it tightly under the regulatory control of the EPB.[30]

The second category is industrial solid waste, which refers to the waste generated from industrial and transport activities. The quantity of solid waste generated amounted to 3.13 million tonnes in 1995.[31] The major category of industrial waste is coal ash, representing 54% of the total quantity.[32] The rest consists of non-hazardous industrial waste, which is generally manufactured off trimmings such as different types of plastics, metals and textile waste. These materials are similar in nature to those found in domestic waste. The recycling potential and heat value for these wastes are high. It was reported that about 74% of industrial waste was recycled or reused in 1997.[33] While the recycling proportions appeared quite high, there are great variations in the environmental standards in such reuse and recycling activities, as well as the related collection and transportation procedures. In some cases, industrial waste is not reused or recycled in proper ways. For instance, some reuse processes referred to in the survey are the result of the direct use of the waste, such as animal feed and stock piling, which is a common means of industrial waste disposal.[34] In fact, little attention has been given to the disposal of industrial waste and the control of its pollution impact. Currently, there is neither an industrial waste generation registration system nor any centralized waste disposal or treatment facilities in Guangzhou. Although industrial plants are expected to reuse, recycle or dispose of the waste themselves, in most cases, they pay a negligible fee for having their industrial waste collected and disposed of at ordinary landfills. As a result, the environmental cost of industrial waste disposal and collection are very much externalized. Recently, the Solid Waste Management Centre of Guangzhou (*Guangzhou shi guti wu guanli zhongxin*) was established under the EPB to take charge of the control of industrial solid waste.[35]

The third category is hazardous waste, which has not been effectively monitored and safely disposed of. Hazardous waste has at least one of the following characteristics: flammable, explosive, toxic to human or plant lives, corrosive or radioactive. It is estimated that the industrial sector in Guangzhou generates 420,000 tonnes of hazardous waste every year.[36] Most of it is generated from industrial processes and is classified as hazardous waste in Guangzhou. This constitutes a major source of pollution. Despite its adverse environmental impact, there has been a lack of control over hazardous waste. On the one hand, the current registration system only asks industrial plants to register the category and quantity of the hazardous waste produced on a voluntary basis without proper monitoring and close supervision. The situation has been made worse in the absence of a definition of hazardous waste. On the other hand, neither the EPB nor the EHB can provide any assistance to these industrial plants in the collection and disposal of their hazardous waste. As a result, local industries have to work out their own ways of storing, transporting and disposing of hazardous waste. It is now planned to place hazardous waste under the legal regulation of a hazardous waste control centre by the year 2000.[37]

An Analysis of the Waste Management System of Guangzhou

The waste management system of Guangzhou will be analysed in terms of policy ideology, policy content, policy process, public participation and policy consequences.

Policy Ideology

Improving waste management has never been the top priority of Guangzhou's municipal authorities. In contrast with promulgated municipal regulations on protecting water sources, combating air pollution and controlling excessive noise, there is no local regulation governing waste management. Such prejudice against waste management has remained salient even in recent years as shown in the substantially greater investment in the improvement of water quality and transport network than in waste management.[38] The low priority accorded to the control of solid waste is mainly due to the lack of urgency in comparison with air, water and noise pollution that have posed greater threats to local environmental quality and have aroused popular concerns. In relative terms, the adverse effect of solid waste pollution can be delayed if enough street cleaning services and waste disposal facilities are provided.

Guangzhou has taken a progressive step by stressing the importance of waste reduction in the policy plan of *Guangzhou Agenda 21*. In this policy plan, the waste management hierarchy prioritizes sources of waste reduction, waste recycling and waste reuse.[39] This conceptual advancement acknowledges the need for "reduction, recycling and safe disposal" in the management of municipal waste. However, the prospect for a proactive approach is limited due to the lack of any clear and aggressive policy towards recycling and safe disposal.[40] This lack of explicit and systematic recognition of the waste management hierarchy by the municipal government of Guangzhou is typical of many cities in developing countries since it is more urgent to fulfill the basic needs in waste management, namely, the provision of speedy and orderly waste collection services than the higher order needs, such as resource conservation. One should notice that the adverse impacts on public health and hygiene will be immediate if the basic needs of waste collection are not taken care of, while it takes longer for any adverse consequences to become exposed in case higher order needs fail to be achieved.

With regard to public attitudes towards proactive waste management measures, the findings from several recent opinion surveys have tended to suggest a mixed sentiment. Generally speaking, most people in Guangzhou are familiar with the concepts of conserving resources and recycling, and regard them as praise-worthy behaviours. As for the commitment to proactive resource conserving actions, the findings indicated that an overwhelming majority of Guangzhou citizens have already developed the habit of recovering their own recyclables.[41] Despite the general agreement on the environmental merits of resource conservation, rapid economic development has given rise to more wasteful lifestyles among its people. Field surveys have indicated that the proportion of recyclables in the disposal waste streams in Guangzhou has increased in recent years.[42] These seemingly conflicting results indicate that while there is a measure of popular support for and public desire to attain sustainable resource and waste management (that is, higher order waste management needs), the citizens' commitment to this proactive control is still doubtful.

Policy Content

Guangzhou's waste management system lacks a solid legal basis for operation in the absence of local legislation on solid waste management. The promulgation of the national *Law on Solid Waste Pollution and its Prevention* in 1995 and the municipal *Regulations on City Appearance and Environmental Hygiene Management of Guangzhou* in 1996 were crucial steps in the creation of a legal framework for waste management in Guangzhou. However, their contributions have been limited as the former law, which sets the broad policy directions and provides an administrative scheme for waste management, is too generic for local consumption, while the latter is concerned almost exclusively with city cleaning in the definition of waste collection responsibility and the prohibition of littering. As a whole, there is no implementation rule for managing municipal solid waste, nor is there any specific local legislation to control the generation, collection and disposal of industrial and hazardous waste. The only exception is an administrative rule issued by the EPB in 1997 to totally ban the use, manufacture and sale of non-biodegradable food containers.

At the policy level, there was hardly any coherent and integrated waste management policy to deal with disposal, collection, source reduction and recycling of all different categories of solid waste until the formulation of the twenty-first century plan in 1996. Under the former remedial and reactive approach, the waste management policies were fragmented and unorganized, focusing mostly on the collection and disposal of municipal solid waste. As the drawbacks of this *ad hoc* approach of problem solving became evident, the municipal government embarked on a systematic effort to formulate sustainable waste management plans.

The first organized plan for controlling pollution emanating from solid waste in Guangzhou appeared in the *Environmental Protection Plan for Guangzhou 1996–2010* which marked the beginning of an era of integrative control of solid waste in Guangzhou. By providing a critical review of the current situation in waste management, it set the following major targets:

(a) To achieve the safe disposal of MSW in Guangzhou by 2000;

(b) To achieve a waste recycling rate of 20% by 2000, 40% by 2005 and 70% by 2010;

(c) To phase out all non-biodegradable plastic packaging material and plastic food containers before 2000;

(d) To phase out non-biodegradable agricultural film by 2010;

(e) To achieve the safe disposal or treatment of 70% of hazardous waste by 2000 and 100% by 2010.

A specific action plan for the safe disposal of solid waste was published in the *Guangzhou Agenda 21* in 1998 under the broader framework of pursuing a sustainable city. In relation to these targets, three MSW projects were formulated: the pelletised fertilizer manufacturing project, the biodegradable plastic production project and the MSW management demo project.[43]

As sustainable waste management has emerged as the new orientation, the municipal authorities have taken a number of new initiatives to improve waste management in Guangzhou. A new waste collection service offering door-to-door collection of waste has been introduced to replace the older forms of waste collection where residents had to bring their waste daily to street level collection points. The new form of collection service significantly reduces the time for waste accumulation in the street resulting in better environmental hygiene. This is accompanied by an increase in the waste collection charge from 4 yuan per household per month to 10 yuan per household per month. A government sponsored waste separation pilot programme was launched by the EHB in 1998[44] in which residents are requested to separate dry recyclables, such as paper, aluminium cans, glass, rubber, plastics and metals. At the same time, the EHB has encouraged greater involvement of the private sector in solving waste problems, particularly in waste recycling and energy recovery. For example, the municipal government has provided free infrastructure, land and raw materials to a private pyrolysis-cum-pelletised organic fertilizer plant which will chemically recycle plastic waste into industrial raw materials and turn putrescible waste into pelletised organic fertilizer. This project is expected to reduce municipal solid waste by 45,000 tonnes each year.

Currently, the management of solid waste from collection to disposal in Guangzhou is strictly a government responsibility with heavy subsidies. Part of the operation costs is recovered by charging individual households and the producers of industrial and hazardous wastes a fee for the provision of collection and disposal services. Despite the municipal authorities' plan to reduce the financial burden in waste management,[45] the market sector for waste collection and disposal is underdeveloped and the use of market instruments in solid waste management is still limited.

Regulatory Process in the Management of Waste

The regulatory process of waste management in Guangzhou is agency-dominated in a command and control manner. It features separate jurisdictions with limited co-ordination between the two regulatory agencies of the EHB and the EPB. In the management of municipal solid waste, the EHB takes up the tasks of day-to-day operation while the EPB performs the controlling and monitoring functions. Public involvement is very limited and the participation of non-governmental organizations is non-existent. Even if some sectors of society are represented, there is insufficient communication between popular bodies and the EHB or the EPB.

The limited interaction between the EHB and EPB shows only part of the picture of the problems in the separation of jurisdiction in waste management. In Guangzhou, the waste recovery sector is regulated by the Guangzhou Recyclable Management Office and the Public Security Bureau. The former is responsible for liaising and reflecting the views and forwarding requests from the recyclable collectors to the government and to issue licenses for the private waste paper collectors. The latter monitors the industry for any illegal trading of "swags" (scrap material goods obtained by illegal means) through the waste depots. There is a lack of formal communication between the EPB and these agencies. As such, the recently imposed outright ban on non-biodegradable food containers has attracted criticism from the Guangzhou Recyclable Management Office that the ban discriminates against the waste recovery sector and is not heading in the right direction.[46]

Within the environmental health system, the district EHOs are financially independent from the municipal EHBs in waste management at the local level. In operation, they are more accountable to district governments than to the EHB, leaving the latter to have great difficulty in having its policy instructions strictly followed by these district EHOs. The work of EHOs on waste collection and cleaning is fully financed by the waste charge of 10 yuan per household per month. However the billing method is a backward type of "knock on the door and collect" where no penalty is imposed on those who fail to pay. Thus about 20% of households in Guangzhou are free riders of waste collection services.[47]

In the management of clinical, industrial and hazardous waste, the EPB has been inactive and the producers of these wastes are more or less free from any regulatory control. There is a lack of institutional capacity or treatment facilities for the EPB to operate the registration system, to monitor hospitals and industrial plants, and to collect and dispose of these three different categories of waste. For most of the time, it is the waste producers which take the initiative in approaching the EPB and the municipal government for advice and assistance in the proper storage and disposal of these wastes. The inadequacies in clinical and industrial waste management have been openly acknowledged in official documents.

Public Participation

In Guangzhou, formal public participation is not a component part of the waste management system. Neither the decision-making nor the regulatory processes are open to external forces. The system is dominated by the MCC and the EPB without any formal channels for public consultation or citizen participation. All solid waste policies and regulations are undertaken by these two bureaucratic agencies in the absence of public consultation and supervision. The regulatory process is operated with a very low degree of transparency. No open consultation is conducted for people to express their opinions, nor for those affected to register their grievances even in cases where solid waste of different kinds have profound impacts on citizens. In addition, there is no public access to waste management information and statistics. The lack of genuine public scrutiny has greatly reduced the accountability of the waste management system. As a whole, public interest has been constantly neglected in favour of bureaucratic and business interests.

The municipal government has recently declared that some forms of public involvement are desirable to improve waste management.

Increasingly, opinion surveys have been conducted to collect people's views on the formulation of solid waste policies. For example, an opinion survey on domestic waste sorting was conducted by the Guangzhou Environmental Health Institute in October and November 1998 to find out the degree of popular support for the new waste sorting programmes. At the same time, citizens were encouraged to lodge their complaints against solid waste pollution and waste management services to the municipal government and its waste management agencies through the "Mayor's Hotline" and specific complaint hotlines shown in every refuse collection depot and transfer station. The improvement of people's living standards as a result of rapid economic development has made the general public more aware of the deteriorating quality of their living environment. In addition, people are now more informed of different pollution problems as the local media have indicated a growing interest in reporting local and national environmental issues. Thus people have become more vocal regarding pollution problems and the media have provided them with a channel to articulate their environmental concerns.

Policy Consequences

Policy consequences here refer to the results or outcomes of the waste management ideology, policies and legislation. Under the notion of sustainability, a waste management system should be able to give a low waste generation level, reasonably high waste recycling rates, and minimal environmental damage from waste disposal and collection. Equally important is that these objectives must be achieved at an affordable cost to the people.

Waste Collection and Disposal

Waste collection and disposal have been very backward and the pollution which has resulted from these two activities is obvious. With the introduction of the new waste collection system, there is increasing efficiency in waste collection and less adverse effects from temporary waste storage sites. However, it is still far from satisfactory as reflected in their self-evaluation. In the latest self-evaluation exercise, the adequacy of MSW collection facilities, waste collection coverage and the performance in achieving a hygienic environment during and after waste collection have been graded merely as acceptable or unacceptable.[48]

Waste Generation

The statistics over the last few years have indicated that the Guangzhou MSW system has not been able to cope with the rapid generation of waste. Table 14.1 shows that the per capita municipal solid waste generation rate has increased from 0.81 kg per day in 1990[49] to 1.09 kg per day in 1996, an increase of 34.5%. When one considers the absolute quantity of waste generated for disposal, the increment of 1,364 tonnes per day (47.3%) was even more threatening as this represents an almost 50% increase in the need to improve waste collection and disposal in this period in order to cope with the by-products of economic growth. The lack of effective waste reduction measures has accounted for this rapid increase in waste generation.

Waste Recovery Performance

Waste recovery is not a major component of Guangzhou's waste management system. It has been estimated that the overall waste recovery rate is about 40% with metals, and over 50% for waste paper and plastic scrap.[50] The relatively easy targets set for waste recovery (20% by 2000) in the *Guangzhou Environmental Protection Plan 1996–2010* indicates that waste recovery is still far from a focal area of waste management.

Currently, there is a lack of organized effort in waste recovery and the EHB's involvement has been limited to the separation of recyclables. Most recovery activities have been carried out by the private sector through an informal system. This means that most of the parties involved are not in the state sector, or waste recovery is not part of their official duties. These parties are not formally registered without being subject to any regulation. The informal nature of these waste recovery activities is best illustrated by the bottom tier of the system – the cleaning crew of the sanitation stations, the scavengers and residents. These are the frontline waste recovery parties. However, cleaning crews are prohibited by an administrative order from recovering recyclables whilst on duty.[51] Thus the waste recovery activities are carried out only when they are off duty or not checked. At the same time, scavengers and residents recover waste for reselling at recyclable depots in the neighbourhood. Although there are state-run recyclable depots, the trading volume through the state network is estimated at only one-third of the total.[52] Thus, most of the recyclables recovered are actually handled by the privately run waste depots and recyclers.

On the whole, it is difficult to evaluate the actual performance of the Guangzhou waste recovery system. Although the waste recovery rates have been officially reported and the waste recovery activities have been widely recorded, the statistics for waste recovery achievement are sparse and serial data for the waste recycling rates are not available. With the implementation of more government monitored source separation programmes, it is expected that more reliable data can be made available in the near future.

The Management of Landfills

Although the two landfills are the major venues for waste disposal in Guangzhou, both are poorly managed, falling short of international standards of sanitary landfills.[53] Pollution control measures such as impermeable lining, gas recovery and leachate treatment facilities are inadequate in safeguarding the environment from pollution. In addition, site management is poorly conducted. Waste compaction is not carried out by proper compactors but by earthmovers. There is also a lack of clear delimitation of waste loading areas and the responsibilities of the site management personnel are not clearly defined. As a result, pollution of the nearby agricultural environment has been widely recorded. It was reported that the Biochemical Oxygen Demand (BOD) and Chemical Oxygen Demand (COD)[54] concentrations of the treated leachate from both Da Tian Shan and Li Keng exceeded the city's effluent standards by more than 20 times and 10 times respectively.[55] Furthermore, the disorderly scavenging practices of the waste miners have often obstructed any timely off-loading of waste and soil covering. At the same time, it also causes injuries to the waste scavengers in the landfill proper. Thus, the presence of landfills is considered unacceptable in Guangzhou because of their pollution consequences. Opposition from the affected community on the siting and operation of waste facilities, including landfills, is common.[56]

The Costs and Benefits of Waste Management

The costs and benefits of waste management are hardly satisfactory in Guangzhou. Under the current command and control approach, the municipal government has to finance waste management in Guangzhou. It has to grant a budget to both the EHB and EPB for managing MSW and industrial and hazardous waste. The cost for MSW management is currently estimated at about 120 yuan per tonne with part of it covered by a collection fee paid by the users.[57] In order to attain reasonable standards of pollution control in landfill sites and safeguard adjacent fresh water resources, future landfills in Guangzhou will be better equipped with pollution control facilities. It was estimated that the cost for landfilling and waste collection would be at 200 yuan per tonne of waste, an increase of over 66% for each tonne of waste.[58] With the expected continuous increase in waste generation, total waste management expenditure for Guangzhou will increase by an even greater magnitude. This is a heavy burden on the municipal government, even taking into consideration the city's fast growing economy.

For clinical, industrial and hazardous waste, since most of them are disposed of in waste generators, information on waste treatment costs for individual aspects is not available. Due to the lack of a proper collection and disposal system, it is believed that the major costs for managing these wastes are not financial but environmental.

The benefits of waste management can be judged by the improvement of local hygiene and the reduction of pollution threats from solid wastes. Although it is reported that the EHB has achieved a 100% disposal rate of garbage from domestic sources, the majority of Guangzhou citizens consider environmental hygiene in the city to be unsatisfactory. This is supported by an opinion survey conducted by the Guangzhou Environmental Health Institute and the Guangzhou Public Opinion Research Centre in 1998 which indicated that only 13.4% of the respondents rated the sanitation conditions as "good" or "quite good".[59] The management of clinical, industrial and hazardous waste can be considered as ineffective as the official documents have made it explicit that the pollution threats from this waste has been increasingly serious due to the lack of regulatory control.

Evaluating the Effectiveness of Guangzhou's Solid Waste Management System

The effectiveness of Guangzhou's solid waste management system will be evaluated in this section using the following criteria: coverage and capacity, environmental impacts, implementation effectiveness, cost effectiveness and the effective use of participatory approach in the light of sustainability. In evaluating the effectiveness of the policy measures, the discussion will focus on the reference frame of integratability (of all types of waste) and holism (of all waste management operations).

Coverage and Capacity

In Guangzhou, the coverage of the waste management system is far from comprehensive and its capacity is quite limited. In terms of coverage, it covers mainly municipal solid waste. Hardly any adequate attention has been given to the management of clinical, industrial and hazardous waste. As a whole, the pollution resulting from the use of non-biodegradable materials (known as "white pollution" in China) has been widespread. Over 60% of the total quality of the clinical waste generated (67.48 tonnes were generated per day in 1994) has been mixed with municipal waste, the reuse of industrial solid waste has been low, and the effective monitoring and safe disposal of most hazardous waste is lacking. For example, in the 1995 industrial waste generation and disposal survey, it was discovered that 1,088 tonnes of hazardous waste were mixed into domestic waste, 3,042 tonnes were disposed of in normal landfills and 683 tonnes were openly combusted.[60] These findings have, however, only show a small part of a big picture, as these types of illegal or environmentally undesirable activities seemed to be covered up by waste generators and collectors.

The institutional capacity of Guangzhou's waste management system is limited. Most notable is its inability to deal with municipal waste in a satisfactory manner; the system has failed to control the rapid increase in the generation of solid waste in the last few years; the method of municipal waste collection is backward which has given rise to many environmental sanitation problems; there is a shortage of waste disposal facilities; and the system has not been able to dispose of the waste in an environmentally acceptable manner. In addition, most of the effort has been limited to the collection, transportation and disposal of MSW, while little has been done about source reduction, reuse and recycling. As for industrial and hazardous wastes, the EPB has left the disposal and transportation to the waste generators without performing any effective monitoring or control. Baseline studies of industrial waste arising and disposed of have not been carried in a continuous manner which indicates a lack of monitoring of these wastes. Although improper disposal of industrial waste is defined as an offence under the 1995 *Solid Waste Law*, it often still occurs due to the lack of enforcement and the absence of local regulations and adequate manpower.

Environmental Impacts

The waste management system in Guangzhou has created considerable adverse environmental impacts in the course of solid waste management and has itself become a source of environmental pollution. The use of garbage tanks in open areas as the major means of waste collection has generated strong odours and resulted in poor hygiene. The poor quality of the collection service has polluted the environment and generated excessive noise in the course of solid waste collection and transportation. The lack of proper pollution control facilities in the landfills has ruled out any clean and safe disposal of solid waste and this has already led to the contamination of water sources, air and soil as a result of pollution from leachate and landfill gas diffusion. As for the clinical, industrial and hazardous wastes, since the control and management is only at a rudimentary stage, little is known on the extent and magnitude of the adverse environmental impacts caused by the substandard collection, storage, disposal and reuse of these wastes. One may expect that the damaging effects should be even more serious as their control and management have been quite loose.

Implementation Effectiveness

The lack of effective implementation of waste policies and related regulations accounts for the poor performance in the prevention of environmental impairment from solid waste generation. Because of limited enforcement, those legally prohibited behaviours and activities such as littering, fly tipping, evading the payment of waste collection fees and selling and using non-degradable food containers can be commonly found. Although the collection rate of MSW is said to be 100%, the city is still plagued by solid waste pollution. Less conscious efforts have been made to ensure the transportation, storage and disposal of MSW in a safe and clean manner.

The outright ban on non-biodegradable foam plastic food containers to encourage the use of biodegradable ones is an outstanding example of implementation failure. The requirement for the use of a different container does not in itself provide an incentive for the public to reduce littering. The bio-degradable requirement is also inadequate in having a significant effect in alleviating the ecological problems caused by non-biodegradable plastics. In fact, owing to the higher cost of degradable Expanded Polystyrene (EPS) containers, non-biodegradable EPS containers are still commonly found in the marketplace more than a year after the ban was implemented.[62] In short, the ban has neither been able to achieve the environmental merits that the law-makers originally intended it to achieve, nor has it been able solve the environmental problems found in the waste management of Guangzhou.

Problems are even more explicit in the case of industrial and hazardous wastes. Currently, there is neither a registration system for the generation of industrial waste nor a central industrial waste disposal or treatment facility in Guangzhou. Effective control and regulation is almost non-existent as industries are expected to reuse, recycle or dispose of the waste themselves. Although the recycling proportions have appeared quite high, these reutilization processes may not be environmentally desirable. For instance, the direct use of waste as animal feed has been employed as a reuse process and stock piling is a common means in the disposal of industrial and hazardous wastes. Finally the monitoring of waste management has not been properly and rigorously conducted which has undermined its implementation effectiveness. As a whole, the effectiveness in the cleaning up of the urban city and the reduction of environmental impacts from solid waste has been quite limited.

Cost Effectiveness

The cost effectiveness in solid waste management is far from satisfactory in Guangzhou. This condition can be illustrated in comparison with the cost performance of the Hong Kong waste management system. Table 15.2 compares the relative cost of waste management of these two cities expressed as percentages of the monthly per capita GDP. It shows that the relative cost for landfilling, domestic waste collection and capital investment for landfills in Guangzhou are higher than those of Hong Kong. This simply means that people in Guangzhou are paying more for the waste management services than their counterparts in Hong Kong. The cost performance would be even worse if one takes into consideration the poor management of MSW in Guangzhou.

The cost performance in the management of industrial and hazardous waste is even more disappointing as the municipal government has to finance most of the operation costs. Although the

Table 15.2

Comparison of Financial Costs in Waste Management

Relative cost of	Hong Kong (HK$ per capita GDP per month)	Guangzhou (yuan per capita GDP per month)
Landfilling each tonne of waste[#]	0.65%	0.96%
Capital costs of landfill construction	0.26%	0.97%
Collecting each tonne of domestic waste[*]	3.3%	3.6%

[*] Includes basic collection cost and the cost of refuse transfer;
[#] excludes the land cost

Source: Data for Hong Kong derived from EPD, 1998 and 1999[63]; data for Guangzhou derived from Guangzhou Construction Committee and Guangzhou Environmental Health Bureau, *Environmental Hygiene Planning and Design for the city of Guangzhou.*

EPB is authorized to charge industries for the collection and disposal costs, the charging system cannot be implemented in the absence of a clear definition of industrial and hazardous waste. As a result, the charge for the collection and disposal of industrial and hazardous wastes at ordinary landfills is a nominal sum in Guangzhou, leaving the municipal government to bear the financial burden.

The Adoption of a Participatory Approach

There is a growing tendency for a wider adoption of a participatory approach in the management of solid waste. Recently a number of initiatives have been taken to augment public involvement and to identify popular demands and preferences. First of all, a series of pilot studies has been undertaken on source separation of domestic waste where the householders' co-operation is actively sought. Secondly, opinion surveys have been conducted to collect popular views on waste separation. Thirdly, the people in Guangzhou are now provided with complaint channels to redress their grievances against improper solid waste management. However, under a top-down mode of public participation, the effectiveness of these participatory arrangements is still doubtful. For example, public opinion surveys are mostly used for justifying the municipal government's waste policies as they were conducted after the policy decision was made. The use of complaint channels is even more limited as the past figures have shown that people in Guangzhou have not been vocal in waste management issues. According to the EPB, complaints on solid waste pollution received ranged from a low of seven cases to a high of 33 cases in the period between 1987 and 1997.[64] However, this lack of complaints does not mean that people are satisfied with agencies' performance in solid waste management, as most local citizens have expressed the need for an improvement in environmental hygiene in Guangzhou.[65] On the whole, public participation in waste management is hardly adequate and effective when one considers that public consultation is still not a regular feature in the formulation of waste management policies and measures, information on service performance is not accessible, and policy making transparency is low.

Institutional Constraints for Sustainable Waste Management in Guangzhou

From the above analysis, it appears that the solid waste management system in Guangzhou is not only unsustainable, but is also struggling hard to satisfy some of the basic needs in waste management. This section considers the institutional constraints for the waste management agencies to practice sustainable waste management in Guangzhou.

The Politics of Funding

The lower priority accorded to the control of solid waste in Guangzhou has constantly put both the EHB and EPB in less advantageous positions in the competition for additional resources from the municipal government to improve solid waste management. Such a trend remained salient in the formulation of *Guangzhou's Agenda 21*. Although MSW was identified in this document as one of the key aspects in the pursuit of sustainable development, only 1% of the total expenditure on priority programmes were given to MSW projects. In comparison, the planned resource allocated for improving fresh water quality and the transportation network were 25% and 63% of the total expenditure respectively.[66] The current order of priority indicates that there is a lack of active support from the municipal government to grant the waste management agencies large funds in resource allocation exercises to clean up the city.

The Lack of Economic Incentives

There is a lack of economic incentives for the EHB and its personnel to control the increase of solid waste under existing input-oriented funding arrangements. On the one hand, the size of the EHB's budget is linked with the quantity of solid waste that needs to be handled. On the other hand, the wages of individual workers in the collection and transportation of waste are decided by their workload, which means that they will receive higher remuneration for heavier workloads if more waste is generated. Thus the EHB has not been keen to promote source reduction, even though the generation of excessive solid waste goes against the official position of pursuing sustainable waste management. A performance-based budget is more preferable than one based on workload in order to internalize the incentive for the EHB and its local agencies to actively control waste generation.

The existing charging systems for municipal waste and specific waste have also failed to internalize incentive structures for seeking active co-operation from domestic households and individual business enterprises for waste reduction and recycling. For MSW, the flat rate charge for household waste collection cannot offer adequate incentives for waste control. For hazardous waste, the fees currently charged simply reflect the private costs in waste collection.

Backward Public Consciousness
on Sustainable Waste Management

The public conception of waste management in Guangzhou is mostly restricted to keeping the environment free of litter and odour. Visual cleanliness and sanitation are the public's primary concerns in MSW management. Their understanding on the issue of sustainability is limited. As indicated by a recent study on the acceptance of the New Environmental Paradigm (NEP) by Guangzhou citizens, it was found that the NEP scores of local people was a low 2.93, in comparison with that of 3.03 for American citizens in 1978 and for Hong Kong people in 1998. What is more significant is that about 5% of the respondents were unfamiliar with most of the NEP issues or statements.[67] Despite the presence of general support for waste recycling, there is apparently a lack of understanding on the importance of reducing waste at source or stopping the abuse of environmental resources as judged by the NEP score. In short, the public is not ready for a sustainable mode of waste management in Guangzhou.

Government Officials Lack of Knowledge of Sustainable Waste Management

Government officials in Guangzhou are also not prepared for the practice of sustainable waste management. The dominant paradigm of waste management remains a conventional one which focuses almost exclusively on fulfilling the basic needs in waste management with the employment of a command and control approach. In addition, the waste agencies have been struggling to improve their performance in the collection, transportation and disposal of waste. The recent plans on diversifying waste management options by introducing source separation of waste and launching safe disposal projects serves mainly the traditional objectives of waste. Measures for higher order needs in waste management such as source reduction/waste avoidance and the reuse of sources in immediate forms are not on the announced environmental protection plans for the twenty-first century. This seems to indicate that these advanced concepts are still out of the two waste agencies' frame of reference.

Lack of Channels for Public Participation

The communist political system of the Guangzhou municipal government is not amenable to open its waste management to the public. The system has been under the strict bureaucratic control of the EHB and EPB, with limited channels for citizen participation. The current command and control approach of regulation has further reinforced this authoritarian trend. There are neither formal forums for public consultation in the policy process nor institutional avenues for popular supervision in waste management. Most of the existing channels for soliciting public inputs are merely designed for the public to communicate their complaints on waste control and disposal. As a whole, the responsiveness and accountability of the waste management system to the public is limited.

The Limited Use of Economic Instruments

The use of economic instruments is limited in Guangzhou's waste management system. Despite a wide range of options which include variable rate waste disposal or collection charges, material charges, product tax, deposit refund and recycling credits that can be used for waste control, the only noted use of market instruments is the waste collection charge. Yet, the current waste collection charge adopted in Guangzhou is more for sourcing additional revenue for the EHB than promoting waste reduction. In fact, neither the EHB nor EPB have explored the full potential of economic instruments to attain more effective waste management. The EPB's failure in the use of a total ban to get rid of non-biodegradable food containers has underlined the limits of the command and control approach in waste management on the one hand, and reflected the agencies' lack of consideration given to economic options such as product tax on the other hand.

Limited Administrative Capacity

The administrative capacity of both the EHB and EPB are limited due to the lack of local waste control legislation and the absence of a well-structured management system to control and monitor solid waste generation, collection and disposal in a holistic and integrated manner.

In the management of MSW, the limited capacity of the EHB is most explicit in its inability to promote waste recycling and source reduction. Recycling activities are currently regulated by the Public Security Bureau and the Municipal Administration for Industry and Commerce. Indeed source reduction/waste avoidance is most effective if it is promoted together with green labelling, consumer education and environmentally friendly product design. However, all these are currently outside the jurisdiction of the EHB. Nor has the EHB had the capacity to co-ordinate the activities of different agencies to achieve effective waste management. A lack of a common target in waste control among these authorities constitutes a big hurdle for the formulation of a sustainable strategy and action plans for waste management in Guangzhou.

As for the management of clinical, industrial and hazardous waste, the administrative capacity of the EPB is even more restricted. Without local legislation, the authority and jurisdiction of the EPB and its division of work with the provincial environmental agency in this area remains unclear. The absence of a clear definition of hazardous waste, the non-existence of a waste generation system, and the lack of monitoring the collection and recycling of clinical, industrial and hazardous wastes as well as the lack of proper facilities for their disposal have seriously handicapped the EPB in the control and reduction of the environmental hazards generated by these three categories of waste. Although the national *Sold Waste Law* stipulates the need for proper control of these solid wastes through a registration system which requires industrial plants to report to the EPB about the quantity, storage, collection and disposal of the industrial and hazardous waste generated, the EPB simply lacks the institutional structures, resources and a set of local rules for conducting any effective control.

Conclusion

Solid waste management in Guangzhou has been underdeveloped even though the city has experienced more than a decade of rapid economic growth. There has been no systematic effort to put all solid waste under proper management and effective control. The municipal government has never accorded solid waste management as a top priority in its environmental governance as reflected in its funding formula. The solid waste management system has basically limited its scope to the collection and disposal of MSW. A set of local rules and regulations for solid waste management is not available for the EHB and EPB to exercise effective control. Facilities for the disposal of solid waste in an environmentally acceptable way are non-existent. Co-ordination and co-operation between the two waste agencies in the regulatory process has been limited. The command and control approach has kept the public from active involvement in the solid waste management system. As a result, the development of waste management in Guangzhou has been quite disappointing: the collection and disposal of solid wastes has not been properly conducted and has itself become a source of pollution; the quantity of waste generation has been out of control under a "throw-away" culture; the waste recovery rate has been consistently low; the management of the landfills has been well below sanitary standards with pollution threatening consequences; and the costs of waste management have not been rationalised in a polluter-pay arrangement while the benefits are limited to a 100% disposal of MSW.

As the solid waste management system in Guangzhou is far from institutionalized, its effectiveness in the control of solid waste is limited. The coverage of the Guangzhou system is narrow, leaving all specific wastes out of regulatory control, while its capacity is restricted as it lacks the organized strength to conduct source reduction, reuse and recycle. The adverse environmental impact arising from solid waste management is very visible throughout the process of collection, storage, transportation, disposal and reuse of solid waste. The implementation effectiveness of the Guangzhou system is limited under a control and command approach due to its inability to provide any economic incentive for inducing active compliance from the regulatees in source reduction, recycle and reuse. The cost performance of the system is less than satisfactory in comparison with that of Hong Kong in terms of its relative costs for landfilling and domestic waste collection as well as the capital investment for landfills. The involvement of the public in waste management is still marginal and conducted in a top-down manner short of any effective popular consultation and public supervision.

The prospects for rapid improvements in the Guangzhou system are far from bright when one considers the institutional constraints for the practice of sustainable solid waste management. The lower policy priority accorded to solid waste management has ruled out any greater financial commitment from the municipal government to improve the institutional strength of the management system. The economic incentive for the regulators to conduct vigorous control is not provided for under current funding arrangements. Nor is there any incentive provided for the regulatees to take active co-operation under the existing charging systems. The environmental awareness of the citizens is not developed enough to further waste reduction, recycle and reuse. The knowledge of government officials on sustainable waste management is also too limited to formulate adequate policies. There is a lack of regular channels for citizens to participate in the solid waste management system, which has reduced its accountability. Economic instruments are rarely considered in the regulatory control of solid waste control, which has kept the municipal government's financial burden heavy while this has discounted the effectiveness of the regulatory system. The administrative capacity of both the EHB and EPB is restricted in the absence of a legal basis for the exercise of effective control.

One may conclude that the Guangzhou system is neither structured in an integrated fashion nor is it able to conduct solid waste management in a holistic manner. In addition, existing institutional constraints have limited the ability of the two waste agencies to pursue sustainable waste management. In short, there is a huge gap to fill in the city's solid waste management in order to support the municipal government's aspiration of transforming Guangzhou into a world-class city. Despite all these odds, the government's recent planning effort has failed to formulate an adequate synopsis for instituting a sustainable waste management system to produce and maintain a clean and healthy living environment.

Notes

This article was prepared under the project "Countering White Pollution in China: the Case of Guangzhou" (S983) funded by a departmental research grant of the Department of Management, the Hong Kong Polytechnic University.

1. See Guangzhou shi renmin zhengfu (The Municipal Government of Guangzhou), *Guangzhou shi huanjing baohu guihua* (1996–2010) [*The Environmental Protection Plan of Guangzhou (1996–2001)*] (Guangzhou: Guangzhou shi renmin zhengfu, 1996), pp. 1–5. For a detailed discussion on Guangzhou's quest for sustainable development, see C. W. H. Lo and K. C. Cheung, "Sustainable Development in the Pearl River Delta Region: The Case of Guangzhou", in Joseph Y. S. Cheng (ed.), *The Guangdong Development Model and Its Challenge* (Hong Kong: City University Press, 1998), pp. 379–404.

2. See C. W. H. Lo, "Environmental Management by Law in China: The Guangzhou Experience", *The Journal of Contemporary China*, No. 6, Summer 1994, pp. 39–58; C. W. H. Lo and S. Y. Tang, "Institutional Contexts of Environmental Management: Water Pollution Control in Guangzhou", *Public Administration and Development*, Vol. 14, No. 1, 1994, pp. 53–64; C. W. H. Lo, S. Y. Tang and S. K. Chan, "The Political Economy of Environmental Impact Assessment in China: The Case of Guangzhou", *Environmental Impact Assessment Review*, Vol. 17, No. 5, September 1997, pp. 371–382; S. Y. Tang, C. W. H. Lo, K. C. Cheung and J. M. K. Lo, "Institutional Constraints on Environmental Governance in Urban China: The Cases of Guangzhou and Shanghai", *The China Quarterly*, No. 152, December 1997, pp. 863–874; Hon S. Chan, *et al.*, "The Implementation Gap in Environmental Management in China: The Case of Guangzhou, Chengzhou, and Nanjing", *Public Administration Review*, Vol. 55, No. 4, July/August 1995, pp. 333–340.; and Lo and Cheung, "Sustainable Development", *op. cit.*, pp. 335–378.

3. See Guangzhou shi renmin zhengfu, *Guangzhou shi huanjing baohu guihua*, *op. cit.*, p. 13.

4. S. S. Chung and C. S. Poon, "A Comparison of Waste Management in Guangzhou and Hong Kong", *Resources, Conservation and Recycling*, Vol. 22, 1998, p. 203.

5. S. Danteravanich and C. Siriwong, "Solid Waste Management in Southern Thailand", *Journal of Solid Waste Technology and Management*, Vol. 25, No. 1, 1998, pp. 21–26.

6. S. Gupta and A. Kansol, "Solid Waste Management in Indian Cities: An Analysis of Success Stories", *WARMER Bulletin*, No. 60, May 1998, p. 4.

7. R.R.A.M. Mato, "Environmental Implications Involving the Establishment of Sanitary Landfills in Five Municipalities in Tanzania: The Case of Tanga Municipality", *Resources, Conservation and Recycling*, Vol. 25, 1999, pp. 1–16.

8. Chung and Poon, "A Comparison of Waste Management", *op. cit.*, p. 204.

9. Ministry of Environment, *Waste Management*, South Korea. 1998 (http://www.moenv.go.kr/enbranch/).

10. See Guangzhou shi renmin zhengfu, *Guangzhou shi huanjing baohu guihua*, *op. cit.*, p. 13.

11. See Tung Chee-hwa's October 1999 Policy Address, "Quality People, Quality Home: Positioning Hong Kong for the 21st Century", The Hong Kong Special Administrative Region of the People's Republic of China.

12. The Basel Convention is an international agreement to control the transboundary movement of hazardous waste. The PRC is a signatory to the Basel Convention.

13. The World Bank, *World Development Report 1992: Development and the Environment* (New York: Oxford University Press, 1992); J. E. Hardoy, D. Mitlin and D. Satterthwaite, *Environmental Problems in Third World Cities* (London: Earthscan Publications Ltd., 1992); J. R. Holms (ed.), Managing *Solid Wastes in Developing Countries* (New York: John Wiley & Sons, 1984); J. C. Agunwamba, O.K. Ukpai and I. C. Onyebuenyi, "Solid Waste Management in Onitsha, Nigeria", *Waste Management & Research*, Vol. 16, No. 1, 1998, pp. 23–31; J. C. Agunwamba, "Solid Waste Management in Nigeria: Problems and Issues", *Environmental Management*, Vol. 22, No. 6, 1998, pp. 849–856; G.E. Blight and C .M. Mbande, "Some Problems of Waste Management in Developing Countries", *Journal of Solid Waste Technology and Management*, Vol. 23, No. 1, February 1996, pp. 19–27; Shuchi Gupta, K. Nohan, R. Prasad, Sujata Gupta and A. Kansal, "Solid Waste Management in India: Options and Opportunities", *Resources, Conservation and Recycling*, Vol. 24, 1998, pp. 137–154; and Damteravanich and Siriwong, "Solid Waste Management", op. cit., pp. 21–26.

14. The World Bank, *World Development Report 1992*, *op. cit.*, pp. 53–55.

15. *Ibid.*. Also Gupta *et al.*, "Solid Waste Management in Indian Cities", *op. cit.*, and Damteravanich and Siriwong, "Solid Waste management in Southern Thailand", *op. cit.*

16. *Ibid.*

17. R. Gilbert, D. Stevenson, H. Giardet and R. Stren, *Making Cities Work: The Role of Local Authorities in the Urban Environment* (London: Earthscan Publications Ltd., 1996), pp. 47–49.

18. *Ibid.*

19. Agunwamba, *et al.*, "Solid Waste Management in Onitsha, Nigeria", *op. cit.*

20. P. R. White, M. Franke and P. Hindle, *Integrated Solid Waste Management: A Lifecycle Inventory* (London: Blackie Academic and Professional, 1995); and F. Kreith, *Handbook of Solid Waste Management* (New York: McGraw-Hill, Inc. 1994), pp. 1.1–2.15.

21. *Ibid.*, p. 14.

22. This framework is formulated on the basis Hoberg's ideas presented in G. Hoberg, "Technology, Political Structure, and Social Regulation: A Cross National Analysis", *Comparative Politics*, April 1986, pp. 357–376.

23. S. S. Chung and C.S. Poon, "A Comparison of Waste Management in Guangzhou and Hong Kong", *Resources, Conservation and Recycling*, Vol. 22, 1998, p. 207–209.

24. *Ibid.*

25. Guangzhou Construction Committee & Guangzhou Environmental Health Bureau, *Guangzhou shi huanjing weisheng zhong ti gui hua (Environmental Hygiene Planning & Design for the city of Guangzhou)*, Guangzhou, 1999.

26. *Ibid.*, p. 41.

27. Personal interview with H. Li of the Environmental Health Institute, 19 April 1999.

28. Guangzhou shi renmin zhengfu, *Guangzhou shi huanjing baohu guihua, op. cit.*, p. 76.

29. Guangzhou ershiyi shiji yicheng lingdao xiaozu (The Leading Group of Guangzhou Agenda 21), *Guangzhou ershiyi shiji yicheng (Guangzhou Agenda 21)* (Guangzhou: Guangdong keji chubanshe, 1998), 152.

30. Personal interview with Li Zhanlong of the Guangzhou Research Institute of Environmental Protection Science, 23 August 1999; see Guangzhou shi jianshe weiyuanhui (Municipal Construction Committee of Guangzhou) and Guangzhou shi shirong huanjing weisheng ju (EHB), *Guangzhou shi huanjing weisheng zongti guihua* (The Master Plan of Environmental Sanitation) (Guangzhou: Municipal Construction Committee of Guangzhou and the Environmental Health Bureau, May 1999), pp. 200–209.

31. *Ibid.*, p. 147.

32. Guangzhou shi renmin zhengfu, *Guangzhou shi huanjing baohu guihua, op. cit.*, p. 75.

33. Guangzhou ershiyi shiji yicheng lingdao xiaozu, *Guangzhou ershiyi shiji yicheng.*

34. *Ibid.*, p. 147.

35. Personal interview with Li Zhanlong of the Guangzhou Research Institute of Environmental Protection Science, 23 August 1999.

36. Guangzhou Environmental Health Institute. *Planning to Abate Pollution from Solid Waste in Guangzhou: 1995–2010* (Guangzhou: Environmental Health Institute, August 1996).

37. Guangzhou ershiyi shiji yicheng lingdao xiaozu, *Guangzhou ershiyi shiji yicheng, op. cit.*, p. 147.

38. See the section, *Plans & Targets*.

39. United Nations Conference on Environment and Development, 1992, *Agenda 21*.

40. Guangzhou ershiyi shiji yicheng lingdao xiaozu, *Guangzhou ershiyi shiji yicheng*, op. cit.

41. A survey conducted by the Guangzhou Environmental Health Institute indicated that 77% of the respondents had the habit of recovering household recyclables (Guangzhou Environmental Health Institute & Guangzhou Public Opinion Research Centre, 1998). Another survey also indicated that 85% of the population has such a habit (see S. S. Chung and C. S. Poon, "The Attitudes of Guangzhou Citizens on Waste Reduction and Environmental Issues", Resources, Conservation and Recycling, Vol. 25, 1999, pp. 35–59).

42. S. S. Chung and C. S. Poon, "Recovery systems in Guangzhou and Hong Kong", *Resources, Conservation and Recycling*, Vol. 23, 1998, pp. 29–45.

43. Guangzhou ershiyi shiji yicheng lingdao xiaozu (The Leading Group of Guangzhou Agenda 21), *Guangzhou ershiyi shiji yicheng* [*Guangzhou Agenda 21*], op. cit., Annex I, p. 176.

44. See *Nanfang Ribao* (*Southern Daily*), 7 October 1998, p. 1; and *Guangzhou Ribao* (*Guangzhou Daily*), 12 January 1999.

45. See the section on *Costs and Benefits of Waste Management*

46. Personal interview of P. Z. He and Y. H. Zhang officer-in-charge and staff member of Guangzhou Recyclable Management on 16 July 1997.

47. Personal interview with H. Li of the Environmental Health Institute on 19 April 1999.

48. See p. 29, Table 4–1 of *Environmental Hygiene Planning & Design for the City of Guangzhou*, (*Guangzhou shi huanjing weisheng zhong ti gui hua*). Waste collection coverage is an aspect that is graded as not acceptable in the self-evaluation. The other aspects mentioned are graded as acceptable.

49. Guangzhou Environmental Health Institute, *Planning to Abate Pollution*, op. cit.

50. See Guangzhou ershiyi shiji yicheng lingdao xiaozu, *Guangzhou ershiyi shiji yicheng*.

51. Direct communication with the cleaning crew, 12 January 1999.

52. Chung and Poon, "Recovery Systems in Guangzhou", op. cit., pp. 29–45.

53. See Guangzhou shi renmin zhengfu, *Guangzhou shi huanjing baohu guihua*, op. cit., p. 74.

54. BOD and COD are parameters used for measuring water pollutant loading. The higher the BOD or COD loading, the worse the pollution.

55. C. Y. Lu, "An Investigation on the Municipal Waste Pollution Measures", *Huanjing yu weisheng* [*Environmental and Hygiene*], No. 2, pp. 28–33.

56. Direct communication with the staff of the Environmental Health Institute of Guangzhou, 12 May 1999.

57. See *Guangzhou shi huanjing weisheng zhongti guihua*, p. 41, Table 5–1.

58. *Ibid.*, p. 42.

59. Guangzhou Environmental Health Institute and Guangzhou Public Opinion Research Centre, *Shenghuo laji fenli shouji minyi diaocha baogao (A Report on the Public Opinion Survey on Municipal Solid Waste Separation)*, November 1998, Guangzhou, p. 2.

60. See Guangzhou Environmental Health Institute, *Planning to Abate Pollution*, *op. cit.*

61. See Guangzhou shi renmin zhengfu, *Guangzhou shi huanjing baohu guihua*, *op. cit.*, pp. 73–73.

62. See Y. Q. Zhao, "Baise wuran, nineng nata zhenyang?" (White Pollution, How Can You Tackle It?), *Yangcheng Wanbao (Yang Cheng Evening News)*, 15 August 1998, p. A7.

63. Environmental Protection Department, *Hong Kong 1997: A Review of 1996* (Hong Kong: The Government Printer, 1996); Personal communication with the Waste Facilities Business Unit of Environmental Protection Department, Hong Kong, 10 March 1999.

64. Data supplied by the staff of Guangzhou Research Institute of Environmental Protection.

65. See Guangzhou Environmental Health Institute and Guangzhou Public Opinion Research Centre, *Shenghuo laji fenli shouji minyi diaocha baogao*, p. 2.

66. Figures derived from the budget data given in Guangzhou ershiyi shiji yicheng lingdao xiaozu, *Guangzhou ershiyi shiji yicheng*, Annex I.

67. Chung and Poon, "The Attitudes of Guangzhou Citizens", *op. cit.*, pp. 35–59, 1999; and S. S. Chung and C. S. Poon, "A Comparison of Waste Reduction Practices and New Environmental Paradigm in Four Southern Chinese Areas", *Environmental Management*, forthcoming.

CHAPTER 16

Conclusion

Whither Guangdong?

Joseph Y. S. CHENG

Introduction

In March 1998, Jiang Zemin met the Guangdong delegation to the Ninth National People's Congress (NPC) and appealed to Guangdong to "enhance and create new advantages, and move further up the ladder of development". In response, the Guangdong provincial Party committee and provincial government, in the second quarter of the year, decided on ten major research topics which reflected the Guangdong leadership's priorities for the province's next stage of economic development. They were: (a) the new situation and its challenges; (b) the acceleration and development of advanced and new technology industries; (c) the further opening up of Guangdong to the outside world; (d) the improvement and upgrading of the provinces industrial structure; (e) deepening reforms and establishing the advantages of new systems; (f) the industrialization of agriculture and agricultural modernization in the Pearl River Delta; (g) the cultivation and development of new economic growth points; (h) building a pool of talents; (i) insisting on the co-ordinated development of materialistic civilization and spiritual civilization; and (j) the promotion of sustainable development.[1]

439

As revealed in the author's interviews with Guangdong cadres in the second half of 1999, they acknowledged that the following problems exist in the province's economic development. In the first place, Guangdong is entering into a peak period for the repayment of foreign loans. As a result, non-bank financial institutions and some enterprises may have problems in their capital circulation and may even encounter a debt crisis. Secondly, the economic performance and economic efficiency of many enterprises is still unsatisfactory; inadequate domestic demand has led to the idling of production capacities, and this in turn has resulted in the decline of enterprise performance. Thirdly, in the first half of 1998, some agricultural products began to suffer from sluggishness in sales, resulting in falling prices, especially among animal, poultry and aquatic products. Fourthly, the unemployment situation is still severe; some state-owned enterprises (SOEs) are in serious difficulties, and they have to cut back employment and are unable to provide for their workers who have stepped down from their work posts (*xiagang*). Finally, the law and order situation and environmental pollution remain significant public concerns.

Development Strategies

In the summer of 1999, Guangdong leaders revealed their plans to revive the economy and promote long-term development. In July, the provincial governor, Lu Ruihua, indicated in an enlarged plenary meeting of the provincial government that emphasis would be placed on four areas to promote economic growth. In the first place, market development would be considered a key link, and strident efforts would be made to develop the domestic market and expand exports. Secondly, efforts would be made to improve effective demand by increasing the incomes of the urban population, including workers' wages and retirees' pensions. Thirdly, the government would attempt to reduce the financial burden of the rural population so as to enhance its disposable income; one of the measures to be introduced would be to reduce the electricity charges in rural areas. Finally, the provincial authorities would treat education as an industry and promote spending on education.[2]

Lu would like to change the people's concept of consumption; he realizes that the establishment of a satisfactory social security system will remove people's worries and encourage them to spend. In recent years, people in China have been very concerned by possible sharp increases in expenditure on housing, medical care and education in the future, and have been reluctant to spend money. This high propensity to save has been reinforced by the changing consumption pattern as the middle and upper-middle income groups in the urban areas have mostly purchased their sets of electrical household appliances, but cannot yet afford major items such as new apartments and new cars. Lu took pride in the fact that Guangdong began to tackle the issue of market expansion as early as 1997; and considered that the province, compared with other provincial units in China, enjoyed better contacts with the outside world, could respond more promptly to changing conditions, and had developed better market mechanisms.

Lu's short-term measures were followed by more long-term strategies. In a forum on economic reforms and opening up to the outside world in August 1999, provincial Party secretary, Li Changchun, proposed a strategy to realize modernization first in Guangdong's Special Economic Zones (SEZs) and the Pearl River Delta, to promote Guangdong's economic growth through science and education, and to establish a high-tech software zone around Shenzhen and Guangzhou. Li's modernization programme aims to transform Guangdong's SEZs and the Pearl River Delta into an important base for China's high-tech industries by 2010, to strengthen co-operation with Hong Kong and Macau, to establish the SEZs and the Pearl River Delta as an export base well integrated with the global economy, and to develop the province as a pioneer in China's socialist market economic structure and a model for China's sustainable development.[3]

The International Consultative Conference in November 1999 (see Introduction) was a logical development subsequent to the important announcements mentioned above. Guangdong leaders had been aware that the province lacked high-power think-tanks like those in Beijing and Shanghai, and gathering 20 international advisors to meet its leading officials and the 21 city mayors would, at least from a publicity's point of view, help to demonstrate Guangdong's efforts to overcome its weaknesses. The list of international advisors was impressive, and included Marubeni chairman Iwao Toriumi, Lucent Technologies Optical Group president Gerald Butters, Merrill Lynch International chairman Winthrop Smith and ING Asset Management chairman Alexander Rinnooy Kan. Besides publicity and advice, Guangdong leaders certainly had the issue of foreign direct investment (FDI) in mind. Attracting major international firms to invest in Guangdong assumes increasing significance in upgrading the province's industries, and so far success has been limited. The international advisors are expected to contribute in this important area too.[4]

In the next five years, Guangdong's industrial restructuring will focus on electronic information, electrical machinery and petro-chemicals as pillar industries, and their development will much depend on technological innovations with major foreign inputs. FDI from leading multinational corporations is seen as the most impor-tant source of such foreign inputs. Guangdong leaders and the business community have been very encouraged by China's entry into the World Trade Organization (WTO). They consider that the province has been well prepared for the opportunities offered because it has been promoting an open-door policy. Relative to other provincial units, Guangdong is in the best position to enhance exports through China's WTO membership.

There was another aspect of publicity which was also a serious concern for the Guangdong leadership. During the conference, Gov-ernor Lu Ruihua, in his meetings with the international media, worked hard to dispel the notion that Guangdong had suffered a severe setback with the collapse of its leading window company, the Guangdong International Trust and Investment Corporation (GITIC), which was declared bankrupt in January 1999 with debts of 38.77 billion yuan (see Chapter 1). Lu observed that there was some "misunderstanding" about GITIC's collapse and "some newspaper reports turned this business matter into a political question". Nevertheless, Lu admitted that there were lessons to be drawn from GITIC's failure: "Business and investment institutions should really operate within the market rules of the game, and the government should not and will not guarantee their performance." Lu further acknowledged that GITIC's management was poor, including some irresponsible senior executives, and even corruption.[5]

Lu Ruihua described those reports on tensions between the central government and the provincial leadership as fabricated too; and he singled out some Hong Kong reports as particularly irresponsible.

Tackling Problems

On 10 March 1999, Premier Zhu Rongji met the Guangdong delegation to the NPC and emphasized the need to regulate the economic order according to law, and combat economic crime.[6] The prevalence of economic crime, smuggling and corruption were obvious weaknesses of Guangdong in the eyes of the central leadership. On 25 March 1999, the Guangdong leadership decided at a conference that Party, government and legislative organs above county level were to terminate their business activities by the end of the year. This followed the central government's pledge to stop the practice of the Party, the military, the State Council and the judiciary engaging in business activities. Chinese leaders hoped that the prohibition of such business involvement would strengthen Party unity, help combat corruption and smuggling activities, and further separate government functions from those of enterprises.[7] Guangdong's response was unusually prompt, and this probably reflected pressure from Beijing and the eagerness of Guangdong leaders to demonstrate their loyalty to the central leadership. Large enterprises would be taken over by the personnel and organization department of the provincial government, while the assets of other enterprises would be managed by the finance departments of the local governments concerned. Those losing money would be shut down. In the conference, a well-defined timetable was also established; investigations were expected to be completed by early July, detailed measures to terminate the business ties would be worked out before 10 August and the companies ran by Party, government and legislative organs above county level would be required to be handed over between 15 October and 20 November 1999.

In line with the central government's organizational-streamlining schedule, the Guangdong provincial government planned to reduce its organs from 57 to 40, and the civil service establishment by half. According to the Guangdong leadership's plan, organizational reforms of the provincial government were expected to be completed by September 1999, while those of the city governments would be in effect by the end of the year. At the county level and town level, government organizational reforms were to start in early 2000![8]

These measures naturally generated much resentment from cadres at various levels. Li Changchun, the provincial Party secretary, and Wang Qishan, the executive deputy governor, were widely perceived as central government appointees whose job was to exert pressure on local cadres, and the latter felt that their past achievements had not been duly recognized. There was a general perception among Guangdong cadres that corruption was an unavoidable side effect of economic development. Since corruption in Guangdong largely belonged to the type in which all parties concerned were satisfied, in contrast to the extortionary type in poor rural areas in China, cadres in Guangdong did not have much sense of guilt regarding corruption. They pointed to the economic development in the province to justify their performance, and they tended to treat anti-corruption campaigns as routine exercises largely for propaganda purposes. When the campaigns reached them or their close associates, they would explain that political struggles were the main cause. At the same time, too much emphasis on pragmatism also weakened efforts to cultivate a strong sense of the rule of law.

At the end of 1999, despite the exposure of a number of major financial and corruption scandals over the past two or three years, smuggling and corruption in Guangdong still attracted considerable attention. In a national anti-smuggling conference in Beijing in November, it was revealed that in the first nine months of the year, there were 82 major cases of recorded smuggling involving a total value of 132 million yuan in the Pearl River Delta. This was a relatively small figure, but the *Economic Daily* in Beijing named the Pearl River Delta as a "hotbed of smuggling activities". Products favoured by the smugglers included contraband fuel and cigarettes, both easily transportable and difficult to trace.[9] It is commonly held belief in China that smuggling activities usually involve local officials, customs officers and even the People's Liberation Army. A "hotbed of smuggling activities" undeniably is also a hotbed of corruption among cadres.

The cracks appearing in the tunnels of Guangzhou's 13-billion-yuan metro line, which opened in 1999, were not only a problem of negligence on the part of project managers and their contractors, but also a symbol of corruption in Guangdong. It was generally believed that one of the major causes of such shoddy work was kickbacks demanded by the various authorities involved. The problems of the Guangzhou Metro attracted not only the attention of *Renmin Ribao*, but also that of the international media.[10]

There is a general awareness among Guangdong's intelligentsia that a new type of leadership is required to lead the province's second economic take-off. Guangdong's top leaders today have ample experience in local government work; they were pioneers in Guangdong's economic reforms over the past two decades; and they were much appreciated for their enthusiasm for innovations, pragmatism, hard work and "can do" attitude. However, they are now handicapped by their inadequate formal educational qualifications, their lack of vision, and their insufficient respect for the rule of law. These are serious weaknesses in attracting FDI from major multinational corporations to support Guangdong's further economic development. In the eyes of foreign investors, overcoming such weaknesses in the new leaders of Guangdong becomes an important aspect of improving Guangdong's investment environment.

This is partly why Governor Lu Ruihua is not expected to be promoted to the position of provincial Party secretary. The other

important factor is his association with various local factions which
have been tarnished by corruption and their disrespect for the central
government's policy directives. While many local leaders of the older
generation in the province are unhappy with the central leadership's
policies, such as organizational streamlining and how it has treated
them, an increasing segment of local leaders, especially the younger
generation, are eager to win back the central leadership's trust and
confidence. They consider the latter an important factor determining
the success of the province's new development strategies. Li
Changchun and Wang Qishan are counting on the support of these
cadres in implementing their policy programmes.

Co-operation with Hong Kong

Guangdong leaders perceive China's entry into the World Trade
Organization (WTO) and the potential for co-operation with Hong
Kong as two important assets in the province's second economic
take-off. On 22 February 1999, the Guangdong provincial government released a policy document entitled *Several Opinions on Further Stepping-up of the Opening Up to the Outside World*, which
emphasized economic co-operation among Guangdong, Hong Kong
and Macau. The document sets-out the following objectives: full
exploitation of the functions of the Hong Kong–Guangdong Co-
operation Joint Conference; and the co-ordination of high-tech
industries, cross-boundary major infrastructure facilities, information networks, tourism, environmental protection and various customs and boundary issues. The focus would be on co-operation
between Hong Kong and Shenzhen: strengthening co-operation
between the two cities on the development of high-tech industries,
raising the capacities of the customs authorities on both sides of the
boundary, extending the working hours of the four check-points
along the land boundary between Hong Kong and Shenzhen, and, by
stages, allowing lorries crossing the boundary to choose their preferred check-points.[11]

At present, a number of communication and co-operation
channels have already been established between Guangdong and

Hong Kong. They include the Hong Kong–Guangdong Boundary Liaison System, the Hong Kong-Mainland Cross-boundary Major Infrastructure Co-ordinating Committee and the Hong Kong–Guangdong Co-operation Joint Conference. The latter mainly aims to promote economic co-operation, and it has been represented by the Chief Secretary for Administration, Anson Chan, on the Hong Kong side and Wang Qishan on the Guangdong side. In the third policy speech of Hong Kong's Chief Executive, Tung Chee-hwa, released on 6 October 1999, it was announced that Hong Kong and Guangdong would co-operate in six areas of environmental protection, and the two parties would set up a Joint Working Group on Sustainable Development and Environmental Protection under the Hong Kong-Guangdong Co-operation Joint Conference to co-ordinate their efforts in these areas.[12]

In general, co-operation between Guangdong and Hong Kong has not suffered from a lack of channels. However, progress has been limited and Guangdong has been dissatisfied with the limited progress. So far two important factors have been inhibiting such co-operation. The central government in Beijing has been eager to deter any interference in Hong Kong, and it has been very cautious regarding Guangdong's approach towards Hong Kong for co-operation. It is said that Jiang Zemin has issued the following warning: on Hong Kong matters, if a grey area exists, i.e., when no clear-cut guideline is available, then the official who acts will have to assume responsibility. If his action is found inappropriate, he has to resign. Thus Guangdong cadres believe that "concerning Hong Kong issues, there are no small matters".[13] The Hong Kong and Macau Affairs Office of the State Council has been given the authority to approve visits to Hong Kong by all cadres; and many cadres in Guangdong complain that it is more difficult to visit the United States than Hong Kong, and it is now even more difficult to visit Hong Kong under Chinese sovereignty than when it was a British colony. The central government's position has contributed much to the image that Hong Kong has suffered from no interference from Beijing, but it certainly has not facilitated dialogue and co-operation between Guangdong and Hong Kong.

At the same time, Guangdong leaders consider that the Hong Kong Special Administrative Region (HKSAR) government has not been enthusiastic regarding co-operation with the province. Naturally, at least in the initial years of the HKSAR, Hong Kong officials have been very concerned with preserving the territory's high degree of autonomy, and there is an inclination to maintain a distance from local governments in China. Moreover, the HKSAR government has not yet decided whether it wants a special relationship with Guangdong, or whether it should continue to treat all provincial units in China on an equal basis. On the part of Guangdong leaders, they hope that the HKSAR government will take the initiative in various joint ventures or co-operative schemes, as the central leadership is more receptive to proposals from Hong Kong and has greater trust in the HKSAR. They anticipate more difficulties if the initiative is seen to have originated from Guangdong.

Unavoidably there are some negative aspects regarding the economic integration of Hong Kong and the Pearl River Delta. There is a concern that when Hong Kong people go shopping or spend their holidays in Shenzhen and other parts of Guangdong, the retail trade, the restaurant business, etc. in Hong Kong will suffer. There are also social problems such as Hong Kong people having "second wives" in Guangdong and the spread of venereal diseases through prostitution in the province. Easy access to Shenzhen will make the acquisition of real estate there a more attractive proposition for Hong Kong people, and may result in falling property prices in the New Territories where major real estate companies still have difficulty clearing their stock. The HKSAR government therefore believes it should move slowly. Moreover, most Hong Kong officials do not know China too well.

The HKSAR government's conservatism has attracted criticism not only from Guangdong, but also from the pro-Beijing circles in Hong Kong. The former has mainly been criticized for lack of vision, and for being reluctant to study the Guangdong situation. The Shenzhen authorities had high expectations on co-operation with Hong Kong, especially in high-tech industries; and they seem to be more disappointed with the cool response from the HKSAR government. Its mayor, Li Zibin, was particularly critical of the HKSAR government's announcement of its Cyberport scheme in March 1999, as this would imply the shelving of the proposal for a joint venture high-tech science park between the two cities.[14] Moreover, Li was unhappy with the delay in implementing twenty-four-hours operation of the boundary checkpoints between Hong Kong and Shenzhen, as well as the proposal for a boundary tax on Hong Kong people going to Shenzhen. Regarding the latter, Shenzhen has threatened to impose an entry tax in retaliation.

Tung Chee-hwa's initiative on co-operation with Guangdong announced in his third policy speech will go some way towards correcting the perception that Hong Kong has been neglecting Guangdong. While the obstacles discussed above remain substantial, there has been a growing awareness in Hong Kong that the territory needs China more than the other way round.

Conclusion

It is obvious that Guangdong leaders have a good understanding of the province's problems, and they have mapped out their strategies to achieve a second economic take-off. Such strategies are well researched and represent a consensus among policy-makers at various levels. However, there are also significant areas of concern which, understandably, cannot be spelled out in blueprints for public consumption.

In the first place, Guangdong leaders have to win back the trust and confidence of the central leadership. At this stage, it means support for and co-operation with Beijing's appointees, Li Changchun and Wang Qishan, and the abandoning of the "find a bypass route to proceed when the red light is on" attitude. Without the full backing of the central leadership, Guangdong will lose not only its policy privileges, it will not be able to maintain its significant position in China's future development strategy. It can ill afford that preferences will go to its competitors.

Demonstration of a new vigour to establish the rule of law and to crackdown on corruption is essential for the improvement of

Guangdong's investment environment. Pragmatism and the "can do" attitude are no longer adequate to secure the confidence of leading multinational corporations considering major projects involving transfers of advanced technology. Crackdowns on corruption and smuggling will alter the perception of Guangdong on the part of the central leadership too. Today the provincial Party and government bureaucracy is in a position to offer reasonable remuneration and therefore should be able to crackdown on corruption. Enhancing the rule of law involves a change of attitude on the part of the cadres as well as the strengthening of legal education among them and the general public.

The cultivation of a new generation of cadres is indispensable for the successful implementation of the development strategies for the second economic take-off. In view of the age profile of the leaders at various levels of the Party and government bureaucracy in Guangdong, the turn of the century offers an excellent opportunity to retire the older generation of leaders who have presided over the spectacular economic growth of the past two decades with a new generation of leaders who are better educated, have a good understanding of advanced technology and the impact of globalization, as well as a stronger appreciation of the significance of the rule of law.

Guangdong has been a pioneer and model for China's economic reforms, and it has the ambition and the opportunity to lead in political reforms too.

Notes

1. "Guangdongsheng Lingdao Jiguan" (Leadership Organs of Guangdong) in Guangdong Yearbook Editorial Board (ed.), *Guangdong Nianjian 1999* (*Guangdong Yearbook 1999*) (Guangzhou: Guangdong Nianjianshe, August, 1999), p. 160.

2. *Ming Pao*, 27 July 1999.

3. *Ibid.*, 30 August 1999.

4. For details of the conference, see *South China Morning Post*, 15 November 1999.

5. *Ibid.*

6. *Wen Wei Po*, 11 March 1999.

7. *Ming Pao*, 26 March 1999; and *South China Morning Post*, 27 March 1999.

8. *Ming Pao*, 7 March 1999.

9. *Sunday Morning Post*, 7 November 1999.

10. *South China Morning Post*, 12 November 1999.

11. *Hong Kong Economic Journal*, 23 February 1999.

12. For the text of the policy speech, see all major newspapers in Hong Kong on 7 October 1999.

13. Based on the author's interviews with leading cadres in Guangdong in 1999.

14. *Hong Kong Economic Journal*, 12 March 1999 and 9 November 1999.

Contributors

Che Wai-kin is Associate Professor of Sociology at Lingnan University, Hong Kong. His research interests include crime and delinquency, drug abuse and rehabilitation. He is the founder and president of the Hong Kong Juvenile Delinquency Research Society and vice president of the China Juvenile Delinquency Research Society. His publications include *The Problems of Juvenile Delinquency in Hong Kong*, and several articles on drug abuse in Hong Kong.

Joseph Yu-shek Cheng is Chair Professor of Political Science at the City University of Hong Kong. He is the founding editor of the *Hong Kong Journal of Social Sciences*. His research interests include political development in China and Hong Kong, Chinese foreign policy and local government in southern China. His recent publications include *The Outlook for US-China Relations Following the 1997-1998 Summits* (co-edited with Peter Koehn, 1999), *The Other Hong Kong Report 1997*, *China in the Post-Deng Era* (1997) and *China Review 1998*.

Chung Shan-shan has been involved in waste and environmental management in Hong Kong for ten years and began research on the waste management and recycling systems of Guangdong province in 1997. She is currently working on a government commissioned study for a Material Recycling/Recovery Facility in Hong Kong. As well as conducting academic research for the Hong Kong Polytechnic University, she is also a director of Hong Kong's longest established environmental NGO, the Conservancy Association. Her recent works have appeared in *Journal of Environmental Management*, *Resources*, *Conservation and Recycling* and *Environmental Management*.

Gu Minkang is Assistant Professor in the School of Law, City University of Hong Kong. He specializes in criminal law, Chinese commercial law and Chinese company law. He has had articles published in the United States, Hong Kong and the PRC.

Alex Y. H. Kwan is Professor in the Department of Applied Social Studies, City University of Hong Kong. He has written numerous articles in Chinese on elderly care and his books include *Counselling and the Elderly* (1995) and *Gerontological Social Work Practice* (1996). In addition, he has edited *Sex and the Older Person* (1996), *Capitalist Welfare Development in Communist China: The Experiences of Southern China* (1996), *Album of Integrative Social Services — Experience and Prospects* (1997), *A Reader on Medical and Nursing Practice with the Elderly*

(1997), *A Practice Manual for Family Crisis* (1999) and *A Reader on Older Volunteer Services* (2000).

Priscilla Lau Pui King is Associate Professor and Associate Head in the Department of Business Studies, the Hong Kong Polytechnic University. She is the Co-ordinator for the MSc/PhD. programme in China Business Studies. She is one of the 36 Hong Kong SAR representatives to the National People's Congress of the PRC. Priscilla's research interests are the institutional changes and economic development of Mainland China, especially land use and property development, foreign invested firms, administrative and economic reforms and regional studies. Her recent publications include *Economic Trends of the PRC* (1994–1997), *The Fifth Dragon-The Emergence of the Pearl River Delta* (1996) and *Economic and Investment Profile of Guangdong* (1996).

Grace O. M. Lee is Assistant Professor in the Department of Public and Social Administration, the City University of Hong Kong. She is the co-author of *The Civil Service in Hong Kong* (1998) and co-editor of *Civil Service Reform in Hong Kong* (1999). She has published articles on public administration, management and labour relations in a number of journals including *International Review of Administrative Sciences*, *International Journal of Employment Studies*, *International Journal of Manpower*, *Asian and Pacific Migration Journal*, *Hong Kong Public Administration*, *Politics, Administration and Change*, *Teaching Public Administration*, *Public Policy and Administration*, and *The Australian Journal of Public Administration*.

K. K. Leung is Associate Professor in the Department of Applied Social Studies, the City University of Hong Kong. He is also President of the Foundation of China Studies and the Director of the Centre of China Studies. His research interests include political sociology in Mainland China, Taiwan, Hong Kong and Macau.

Lin Feng is Assistant Professor and Associate Director of the Centre for Chinese and Comparative Law, School of Law, the City University of Hong Kong. He specializes in comparative environmental law, labour law, constitutional and administrative law.

Carlos Wing-Hung Lo is Associate Professor in the Department of Management at the Hong Kong Polytechnic University. His main fields of research are the Chinese legal system, environmental protection and alternative delivery systems of public services. He is author of *China's Legal Awakening: Legal Theory and Criminal Justice in Deng's Era* (1995). His recent works have appeared in *The American Asian Review*, *Environmental Impact Assessment Review*, *The China Quarterly*, *Columbia Journal of Asian Law* and *Journal of Environmental Planning and Management*.

Nixon K. H. Mok is the convenor for the Comparative Education Policy Research Unit of the Department of Public and Social Administration, City University of Hong Kong. He has published papers on comparative education policy particularly in East Asia in various international journals including *Comparative Education Review*, *Comparative Education*, *Higher Education*, *The International Journal of Educational Development* and *International Review of Education*.

Ngok King-lun is a Demonstrator in the Department of Public and Social Administration, the City University of Hong Kong. His major research interests include labour policy and labour relations in China, and social policy and social problems in China and Hong Kong.

Sun Wen-bin is a Post-Doctoral Fellow at the Centre of Asian Studies, the University of Hong Kong. Her major research interests include labour relations in China, and the development of the private sector in Post-Mao China, especially family firms and Chinese entrepreneurship.

Wang Tong is a Ph.D. candidate at the City University of Hong Kong. Her research interests include corporatism, civil society and social groups in China.

K. Zeng is a Ph.D candidate in the Department of Management, the City University of Hong Kong. He is interested in international business and foreign direct investment, and has a number of academic publications in these fields.

Zhang Xian-chu is Associate Professor and Deputy Head in the Law Department, the University of Hong Kong. He is also a Co-director of the Legal Research Centre of Hong Kong University and Beijing University. His research interests include comparative law, company law, financial law and Guangdong's legal development. He co-editor and co-author of *Introduction to Chinese Law* and a contributor to *Labour Law in China*, *The Guangdong Development Model and Its Challenges*, *The New Legal Order in Hong Kong*, *China Investment Manual*, and *Financial Law of Greater China*. He has published articles in Hong Kong, Mainland China, Europe, Australia and the United States.

Zhang Xiaohe is Lecturer in the Department of Economics, the University of Newcastle, Australia and specializes in China's economic reforms and foreign economic relations and trade. In addition to many book chapters, he has contributed articles to international journals such as *China Economic Review*, *Industry and Development*, *Journal of Development Studies*, *Asian Thought and Society* and *Marketing Intelligence and Planning*.

Index